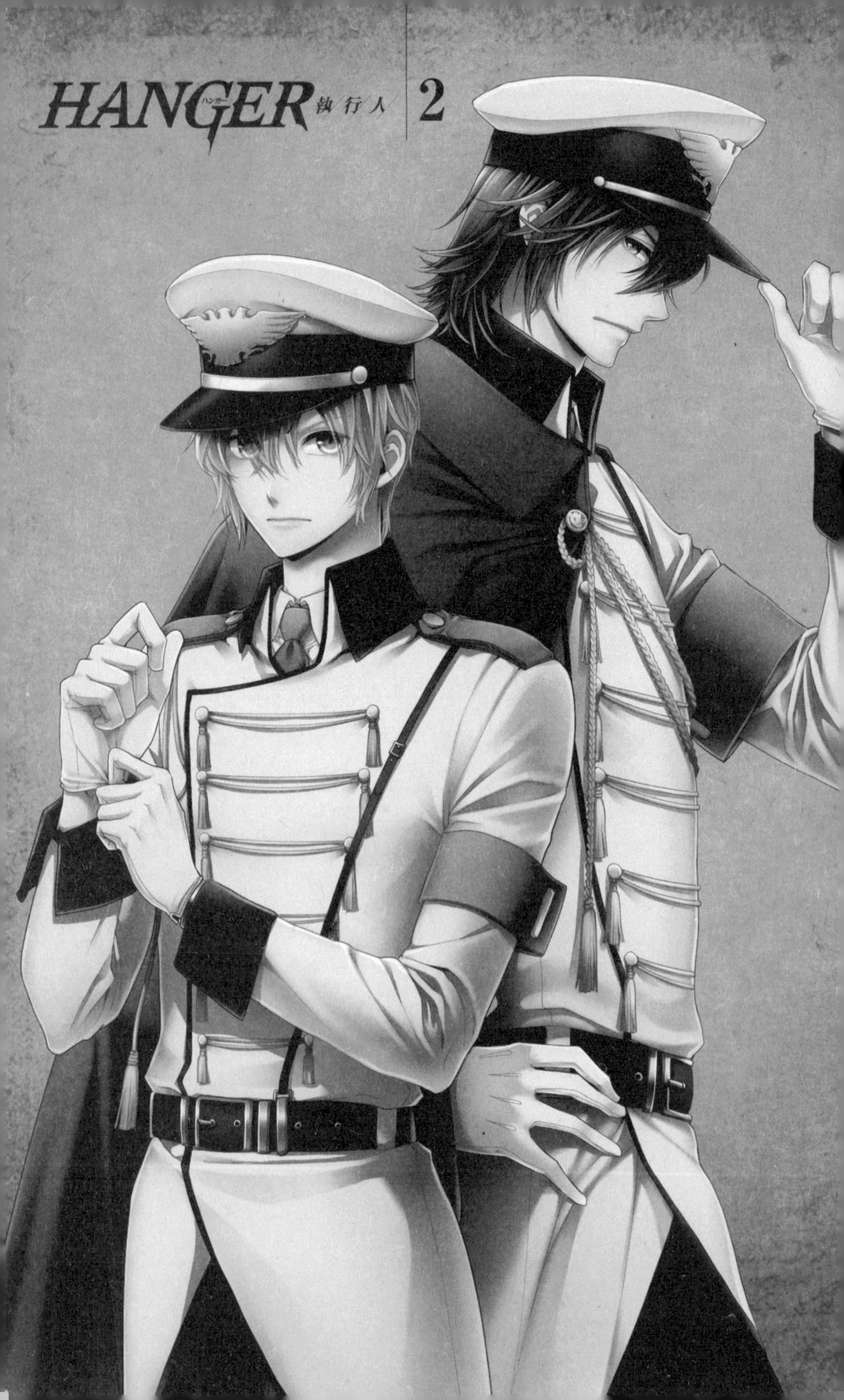
HANGER ハンガー 執行人 2

HANGER

Hirotaka Kisaragi

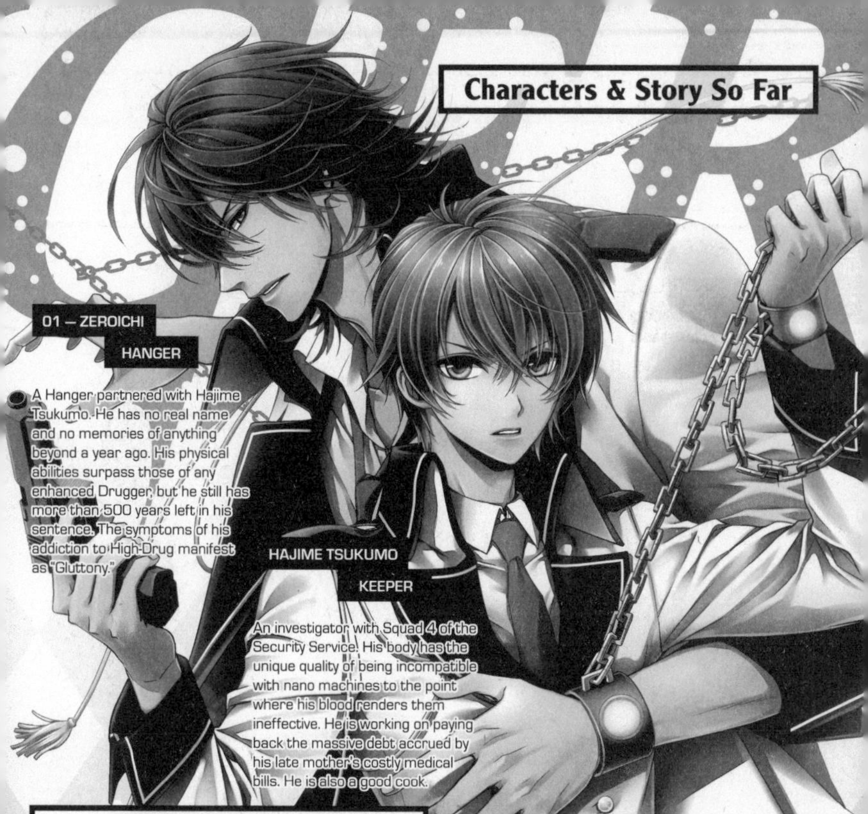

Characters & Story So Far

01 — ZEROICHI

HANGER

A Hanger partnered with Hajime Tsukumo. He has no real name and no memories of anything beyond a year ago. His physical abilities surpass those of any enhanced Drugger, but he still has more than 500 years left in his sentence. The symptoms of his addiction to High-Drug manifest as "Gluttony."

HAJIME TSUKUMO

KEEPER

An investigator with Squad 4 of the Security Service. His body has the unique quality of being incompatible with nano machines to the point where his blood renders them ineffective. He is working on paying back the massive debt accrued by his late mother's costly medical bills. He is also a good cook.

About This World

More than 100 years have passed since the end of the calendar era *anno domini* and the beginning of the new age — *anno scientia*. Following a devastating pandemic that claimed countless lives, humanity abandoned the concept of religion. The remaining population — hoping to rise above the fear that such a tragedy could strike again — embraced a new era of scientific advancement focused on strengthening the human race against illness and disease.

After years of research, scientists finally developed super-cells for physical enhancement in the form of implantable nano machines that work to fortify every function of the human body. However, an unfortunate side-effect of this advancement has also become prevalent: there are those who become obsessed with augmenting themselves endlessly, which eventually drives them to go berserk.

High-Drug, a nano machine-based narcotic that alters both body and mind, has been spreading like wildfire through the city. Users who abuse this substance, known as Druggers, run rampant as the crime rate climbs. Squad 4 of the Security Service law enforcement bureau specializes in dealing with these High-Drug-powered criminals.

Story

Upon his recent transfer to Squad 4, Hajime Tsukumo is partnered with a mysterious Hanger referred to only as 01 (Zeroichi), whose job it is to help catch criminal Druggers in exchange for a reduced jail sentence of his own. However, despite his attempts to get to know his new partner better, Hajime finds that Zeroichi only keeps pushing him further away.

When a series of terrorist attacks puts Hajime in grave danger multiple times, the true reason behind Zeroichi's coldness becomes clear: after the death of his previous Keeper, Akisato, Zeroichi is afraid of losing Hajime too.

What is a Hanger?

A convicted High-Drug abuser serving time, now tasked with hunting down active Drugger criminals in exchange for a reduced prison sentence. The term "Hanger" stems from "Hangman" — in other words, an executioner.

What is a Keeper?

A police investigator partnered with a Hanger and in charge of keeping that Hanger in check. Every Keeper has a "Lock," a device that forces their Hanger to stay within a certain perimeter and can deliver disciplinary measures when necessary.

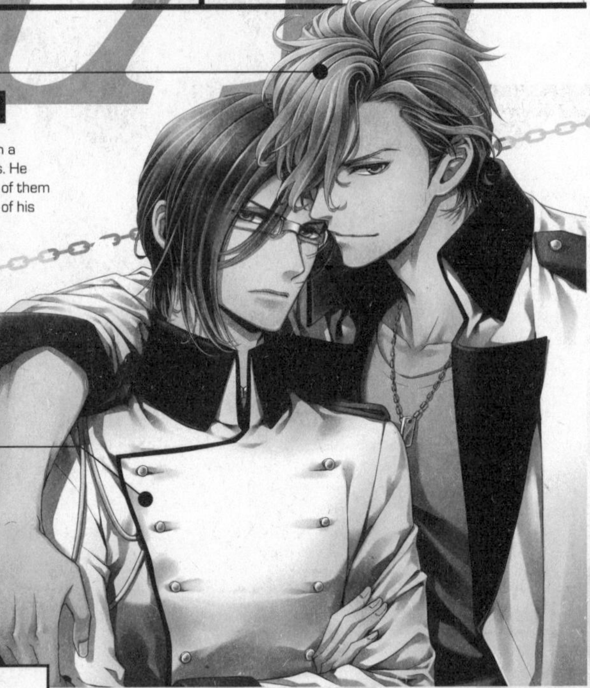

HITOTSUKI HASHIMA
HANGER

A former High-Drug dealer with a current sentence of 300 years. He has known Hibiki since the two of them were students. The symptoms of his addiction manifest as "Lust."

MASATO HIBIKI
KEEPER

Serious and hardworking almost to a fault, all he thinks about is reducing Hashima's sentence. He is the intellectual type who excels at information warfare.

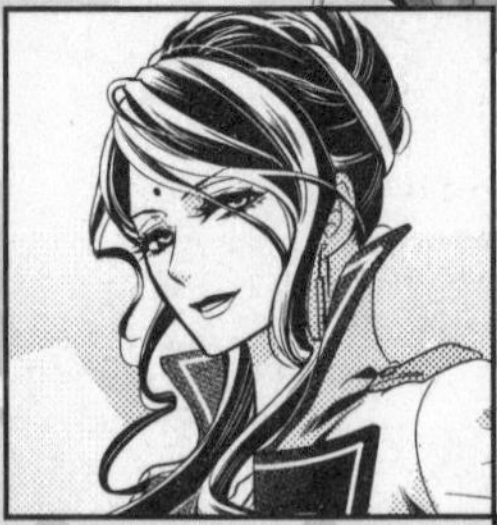

BYAKURAN
HANGER

Her ability is restoring nano machines and making them multiply rapidly in order to heal wounds. She is also capable of altering her own appearance.

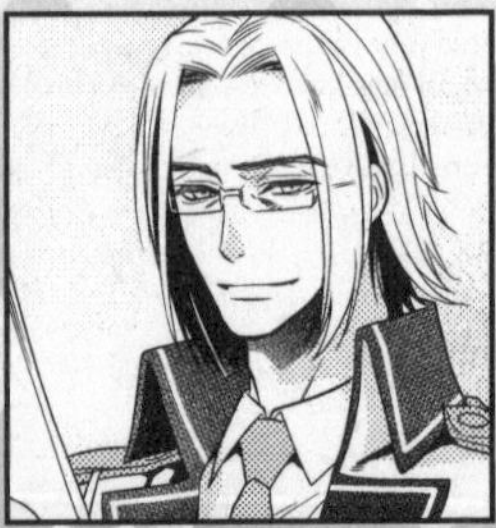

YOKO ONUKITA

Commander of Squad 4. He is Hajime and the other Keepers' superior officer. He also has a Lock that can keep all of the squad's Hangers in check if needed.

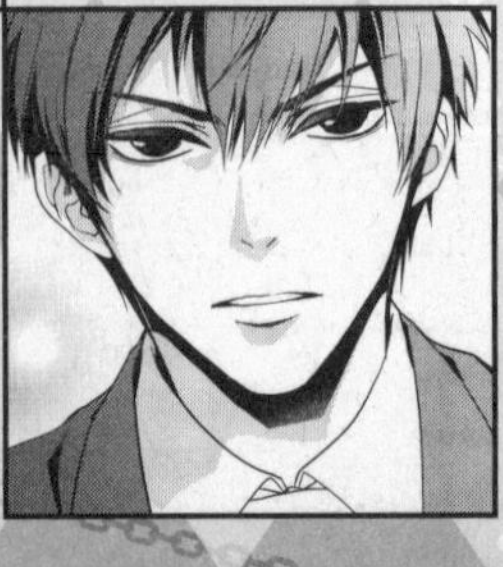

ZEMU
KEEPER

Byakuran's partner.

Table of Contents

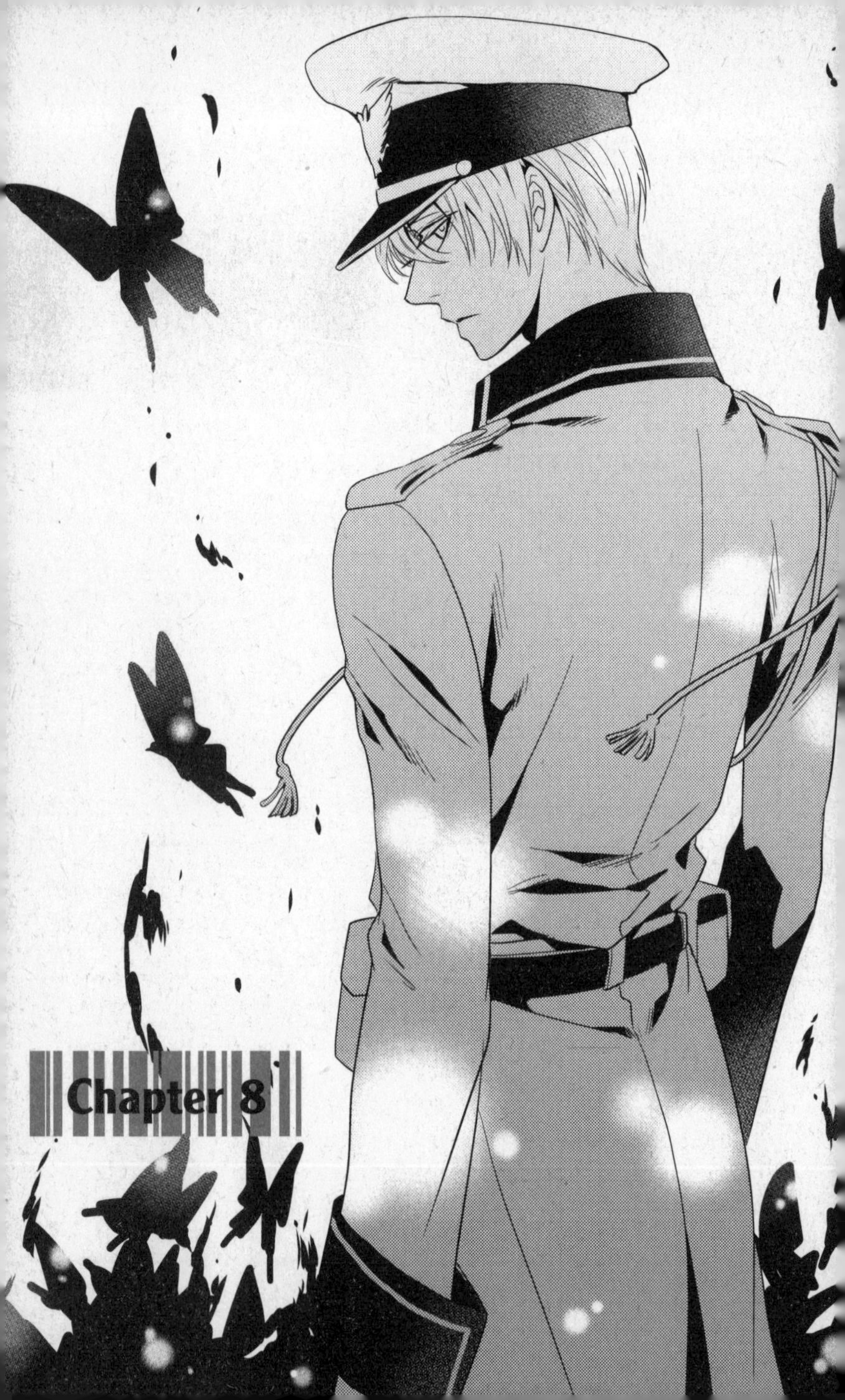
Chapter 8

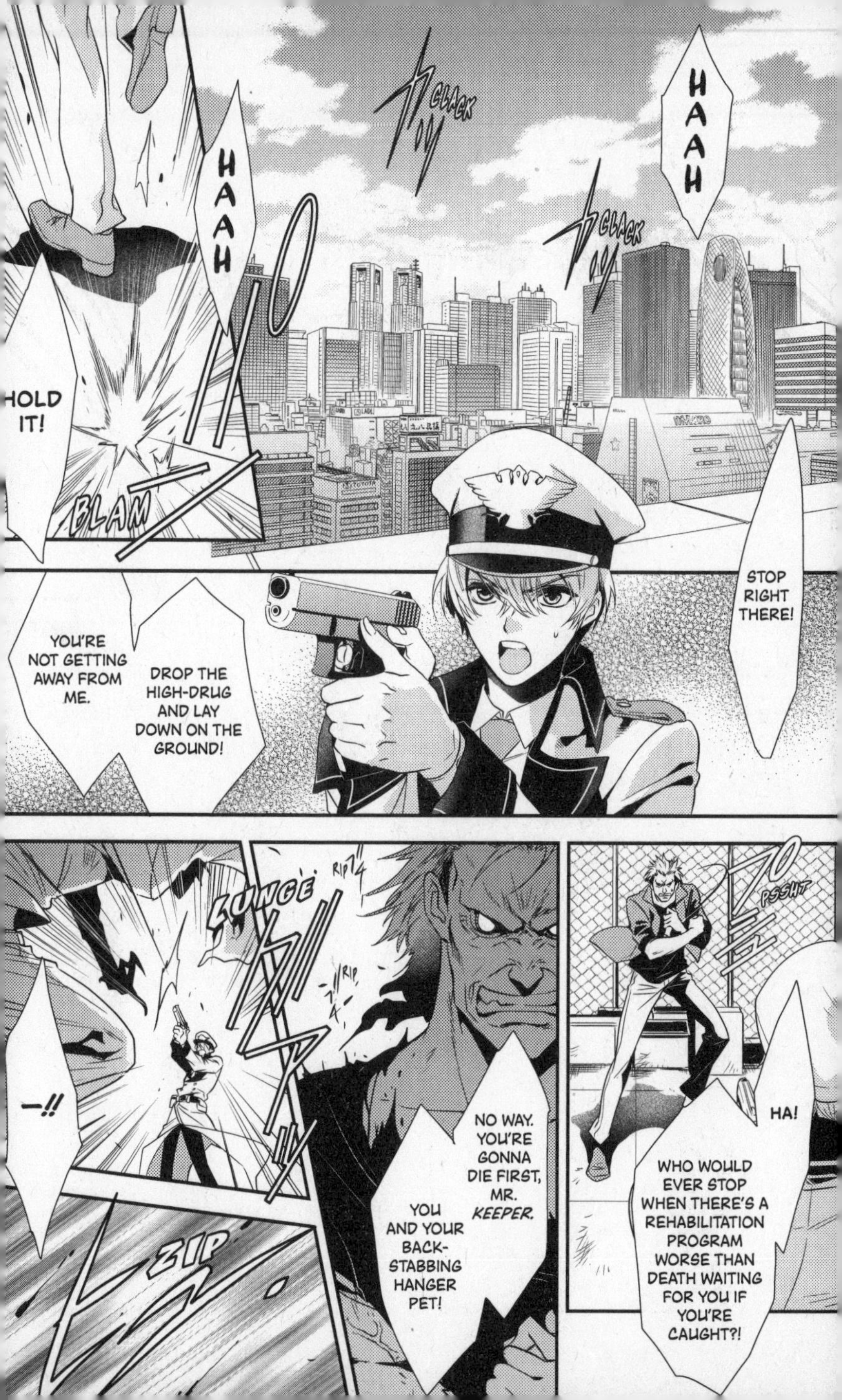
HAAAH
CLACK
CLACK
HAAAH
BLAM
HOLD IT!
STOP RIGHT THERE!
DROP THE HIGH-DRUG AND LAY DOWN ON THE GROUND!
YOU'RE NOT GETTING AWAY FROM ME.
PSSHT
HA!
WHO WOULD EVER STOP WHEN THERE'S A REHABILITATION PROGRAM WORSE THAN DEATH WAITING FOR YOU IF YOU'RE CAUGHT?!
RIP
LUNGE
RIP
NO WAY. YOU'RE GONNA DIE FIRST, MR. *KEEPER.*
YOU AND YOUR BACK-STABBING HANGER PET!
—!!
ZIP

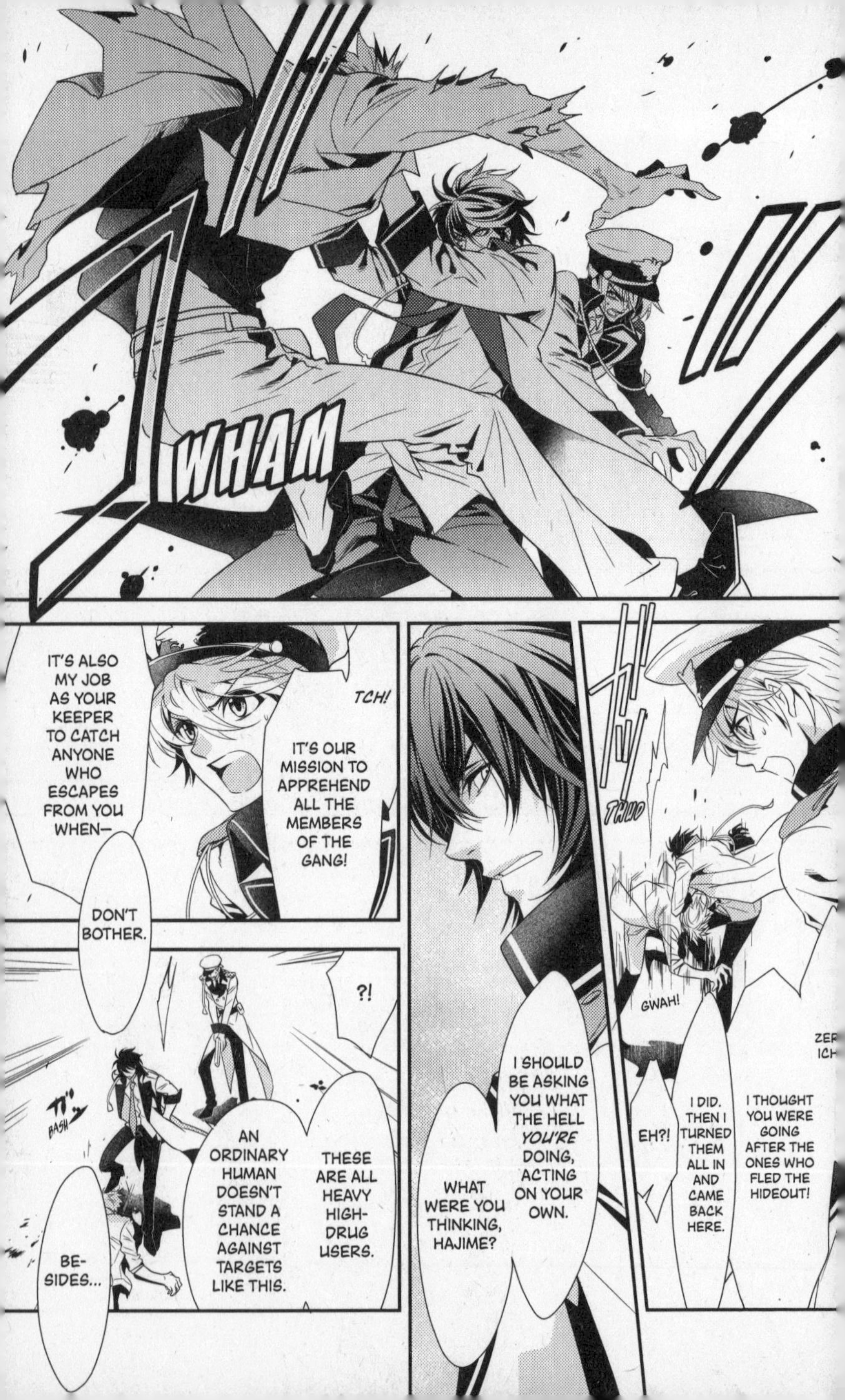

WHAM
THUD
GWAH!
I THOUGHT YOU WERE GOING AFTER THE ONES WHO FLED THE HIDEOUT!
I DID. THEN I TURNED THEM ALL IN AND CAME BACK HERE.
EH?!
I SHOULD BE ASKING YOU WHAT THE HELL *YOU'RE* DOING, ACTING ON YOUR OWN.
WHAT WERE YOU THINKING, HAJIME?
TCH!
IT'S OUR MISSION TO APPREHEND ALL THE MEMBERS OF THE GANG!
IT'S ALSO MY JOB AS YOUR KEEPER TO CATCH ANYONE WHO ESCAPES FROM YOU WHEN—
DON'T BOTHER.
?!
THESE ARE ALL HEAVY HIGH-DRUG USERS.
AN ORDINARY HUMAN DOESN'T STAND A CHANCE AGAINST TARGETS LIKE THIS.
BASH
BE-SIDES...

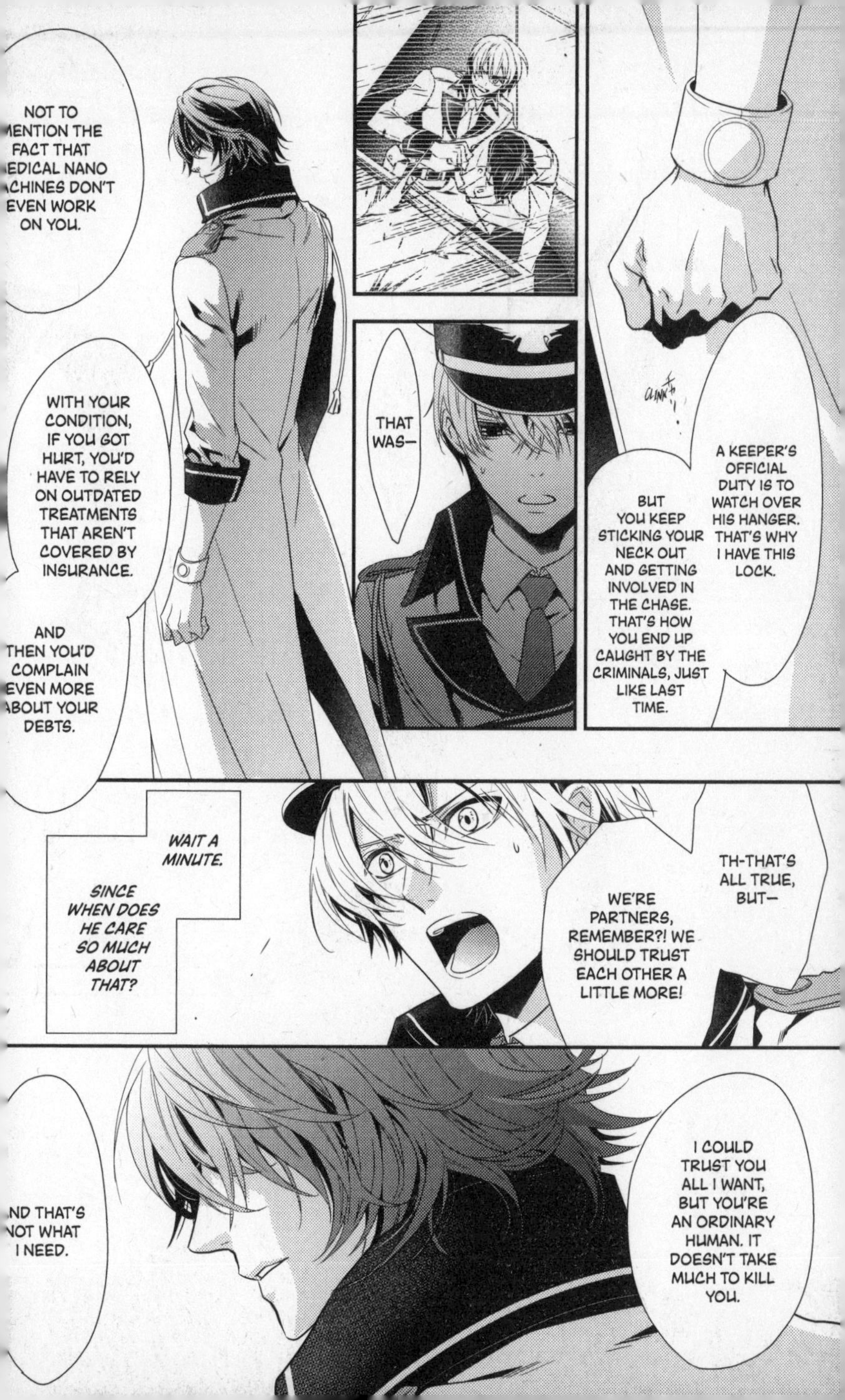

A KEEPER'S OFFICIAL DUTY IS TO WATCH OVER HIS HANGER. THAT'S WHY I HAVE THIS LOCK.
CLINK
BUT YOU KEEP STICKING YOUR NECK OUT AND GETTING INVOLVED IN THE CHASE. THAT'S HOW YOU END UP CAUGHT BY THE CRIMINALS, JUST LIKE LAST TIME.
THAT WAS—
NOT TO MENTION THE FACT THAT EDICAL NANO ACHINES DON'T EVEN WORK ON YOU.
WITH YOUR CONDITION, IF YOU GOT HURT, YOU'D HAVE TO RELY ON OUTDATED TREATMENTS THAT AREN'T COVERED BY INSURANCE.
AND THEN YOU'D COMPLAIN EVEN MORE ABOUT YOUR DEBTS.
TH-THAT'S ALL TRUE, BUT—
WE'RE PARTNERS, REMEMBER?! WE SHOULD TRUST EACH OTHER A LITTLE MORE!
WAIT A MINUTE.
SINCE WHEN DOES HE CARE SO MUCH ABOUT THAT?
I COULD TRUST YOU ALL I WANT, BUT YOU'RE AN ORDINARY HUMAN. IT DOESN'T TAKE MUCH TO KILL YOU.
ND THAT'S NOT WHAT I NEED.

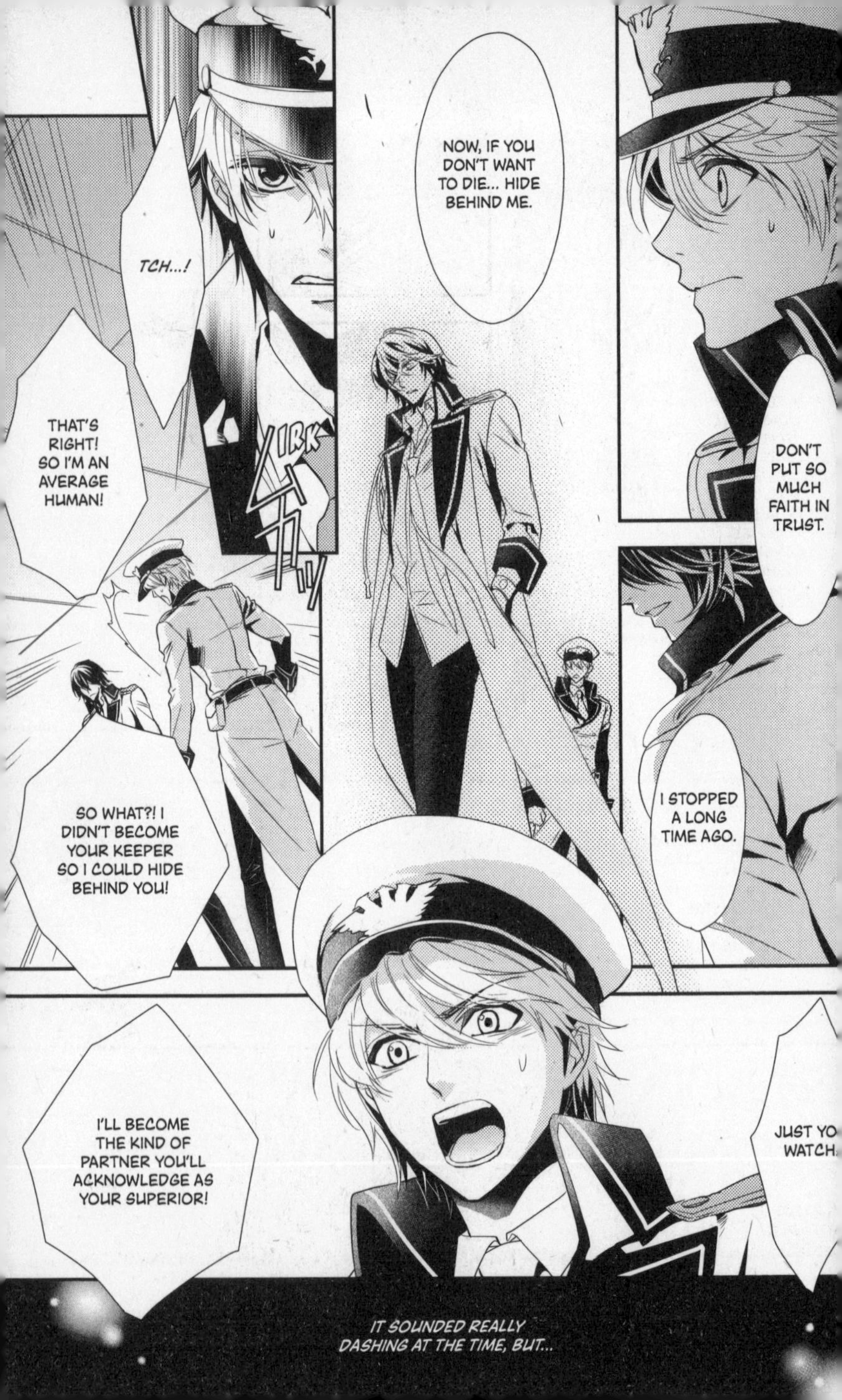
DON'T PUT SO MUCH FAITH IN TRUST.
I STOPPED A LONG TIME AGO.
NOW, IF YOU DON'T WANT TO DIE... HIDE BEHIND ME.
TCH...!
IRK
THAT'S RIGHT! SO I'M AN AVERAGE HUMAN!
SO WHAT?! I DIDN'T BECOME YOUR KEEPER SO I COULD HIDE BEHIND YOU!
JUST YO WATCH.
I'LL BECOME THE KIND OF PARTNER YOU'LL ACKNOWLEDGE AS YOUR SUPERIOR!
IT SOUNDED REALLY DASHING AT THE TIME, BUT...

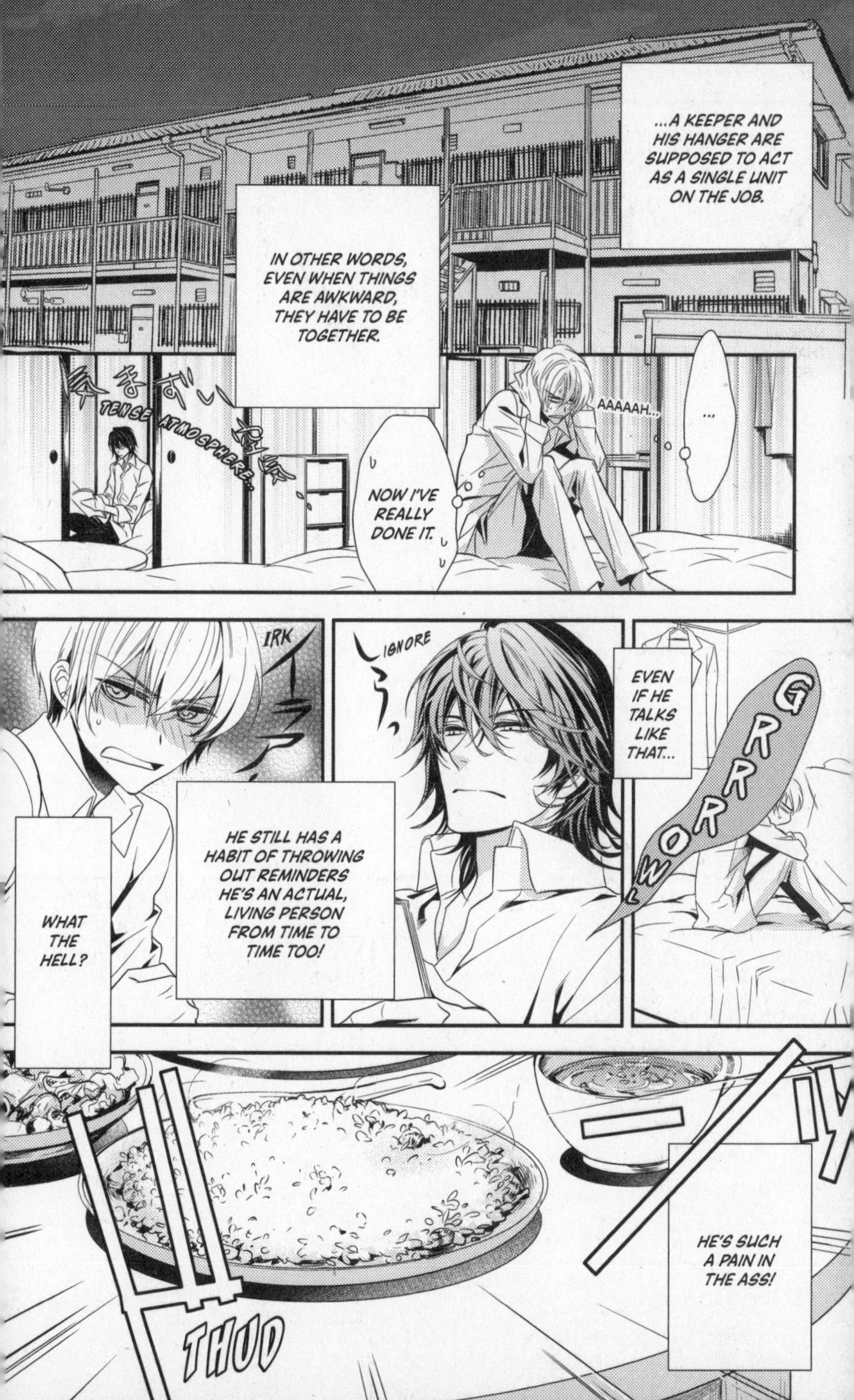
...A KEEPER AND HIS HANGER ARE SUPPOSED TO ACT AS A SINGLE UNIT ON THE JOB.
IN OTHER WORDS, EVEN WHEN THINGS ARE AWKWARD, THEY HAVE TO BE TOGETHER.
...
AAAAAH...
NOW I'VE REALLY DONE IT.
TENSE ATMOSPHERE...
EVEN IF HE TALKS LIKE THAT...
GRROWL
IGNORE
HE STILL HAS A HABIT OF THROWING OUT REMINDERS HE'S AN ACTUAL, LIVING PERSON FROM TIME TO TIME TOO!
IRK
WHAT THE HELL?
HE'S SUCH A PAIN IN THE ASS!
THUD

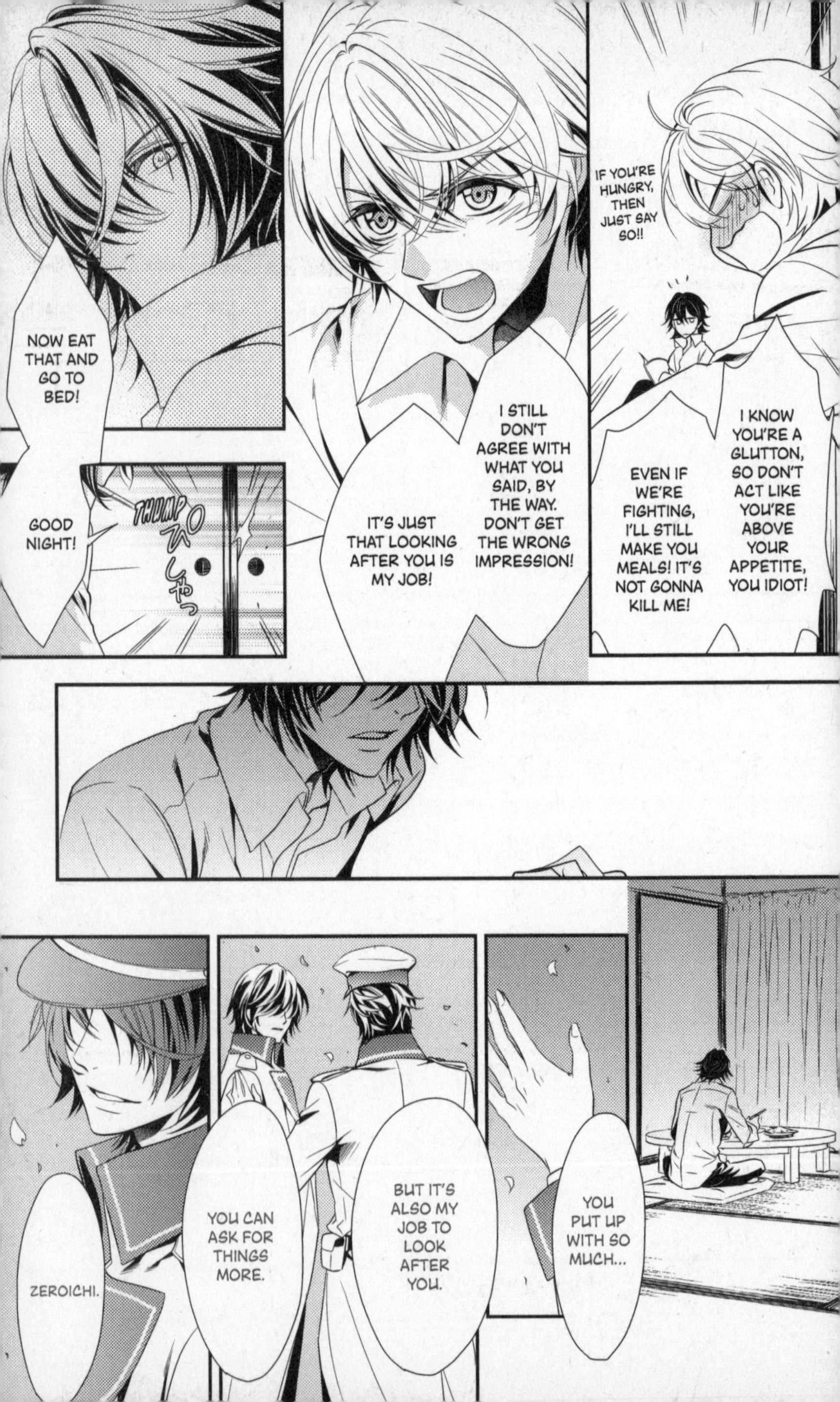
IF YOU'RE HUNGRY, THEN JUST SAY SO!!
I KNOW YOU'RE A GLUTTON, SO DON'T ACT LIKE YOU'RE ABOVE YOUR APPETITE, YOU IDIOT!
EVEN IF WE'RE FIGHTING, I'LL STILL MAKE YOU MEALS! IT'S NOT GONNA KILL ME!
I STILL DON'T AGREE WITH WHAT YOU SAID, BY THE WAY. DON'T GET THE WRONG IMPRESSION!
IT'S JUST THAT LOOKING AFTER YOU IS MY JOB!
NOW EAT THAT AND GO TO BED!
THUMP
GOOD NIGHT!
YOU PUT UP WITH SO MUCH...
BUT IT'S ALSO MY JOB TO LOOK AFTER YOU.
YOU CAN ASK FOR THINGS MORE.
ZEROICHI.

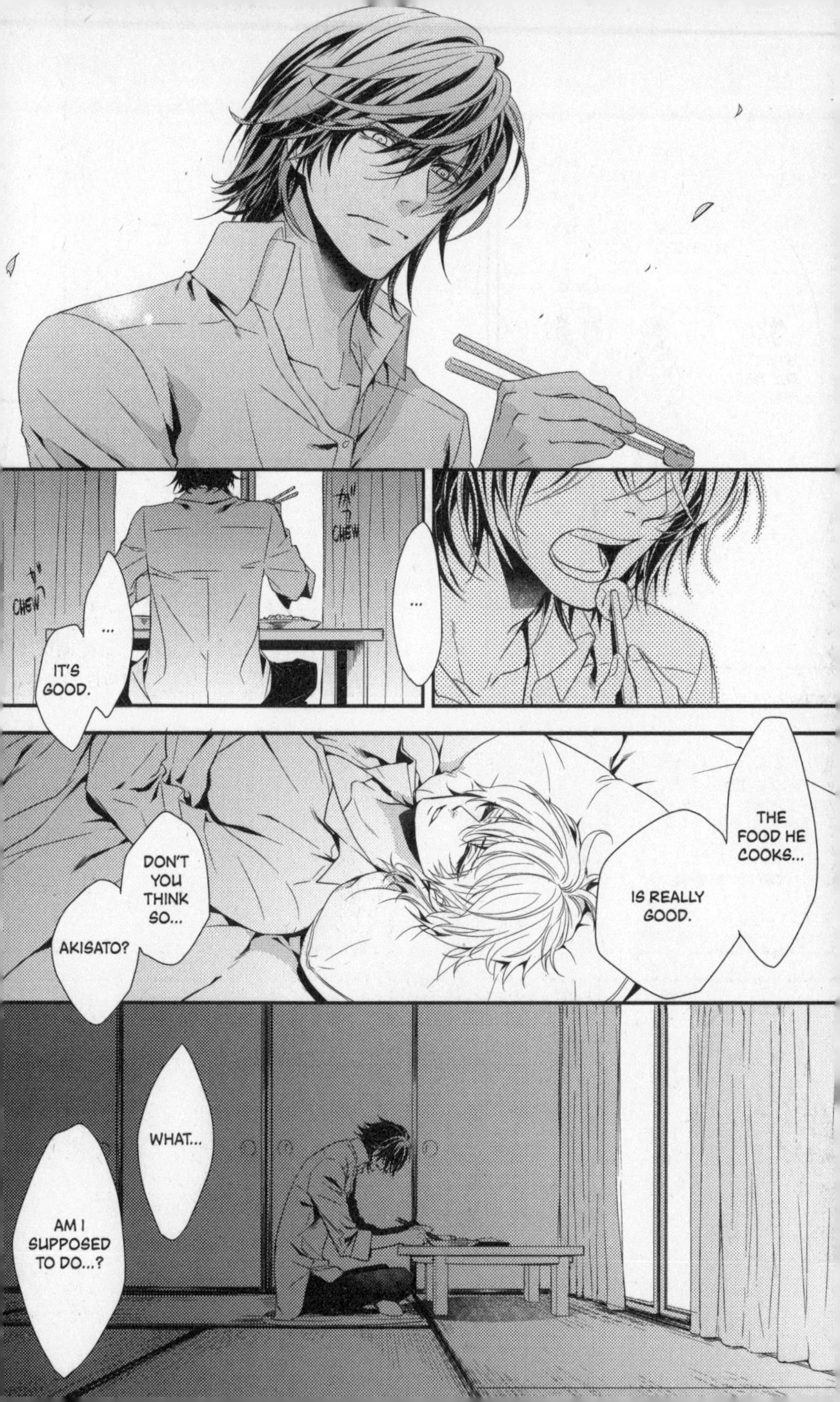
...
CHEW
CHEW
...
IT'S GOOD.
THE FOOD HE COOKS...
IS REALLY GOOD.
DON'T YOU THINK SO...
AKISATO?
WHAT...
AM I SUPPOSED TO DO...?

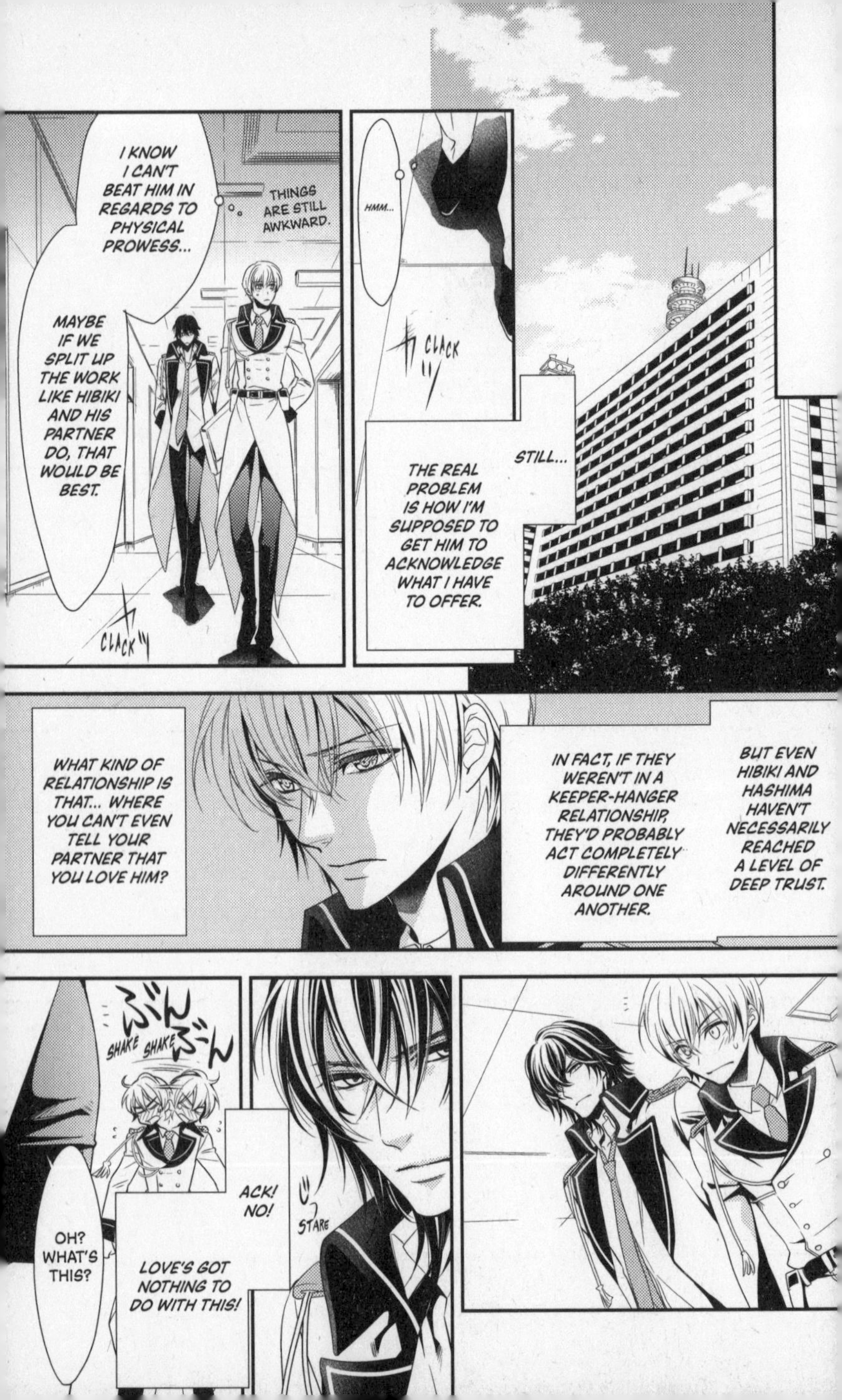
STILL...
THE REAL PROBLEM IS HOW I'M SUPPOSED TO GET HIM TO ACKNOWLEDGE WHAT I HAVE TO OFFER.
HMM...
CLACK
I KNOW I CAN'T BEAT HIM IN REGARDS TO PHYSICAL PROWESS...
THINGS ARE STILL AWKWARD.
MAYBE IF WE SPLIT UP THE WORK LIKE HIBIKI AND HIS PARTNER DO, THAT WOULD BE BEST.
CLACK
BUT EVEN HIBIKI AND HASHIMA HAVEN'T NECESSARILY REACHED A LEVEL OF DEEP TRUST.
IN FACT, IF THEY WEREN'T IN A KEEPER-HANGER RELATIONSHIP, THEY'D PROBABLY ACT COMPLETELY DIFFERENTLY AROUND ONE ANOTHER.
WHAT KIND OF RELATIONSHIP IS THAT... WHERE YOU CAN'T EVEN TELL YOUR PARTNER THAT YOU LOVE HIM?
STARE
ぶんぶん
SHAKE SHAKE
ACK! NO!
LOVE'S GOT NOTHING TO DO WITH THIS!
OH? WHAT'S THIS?

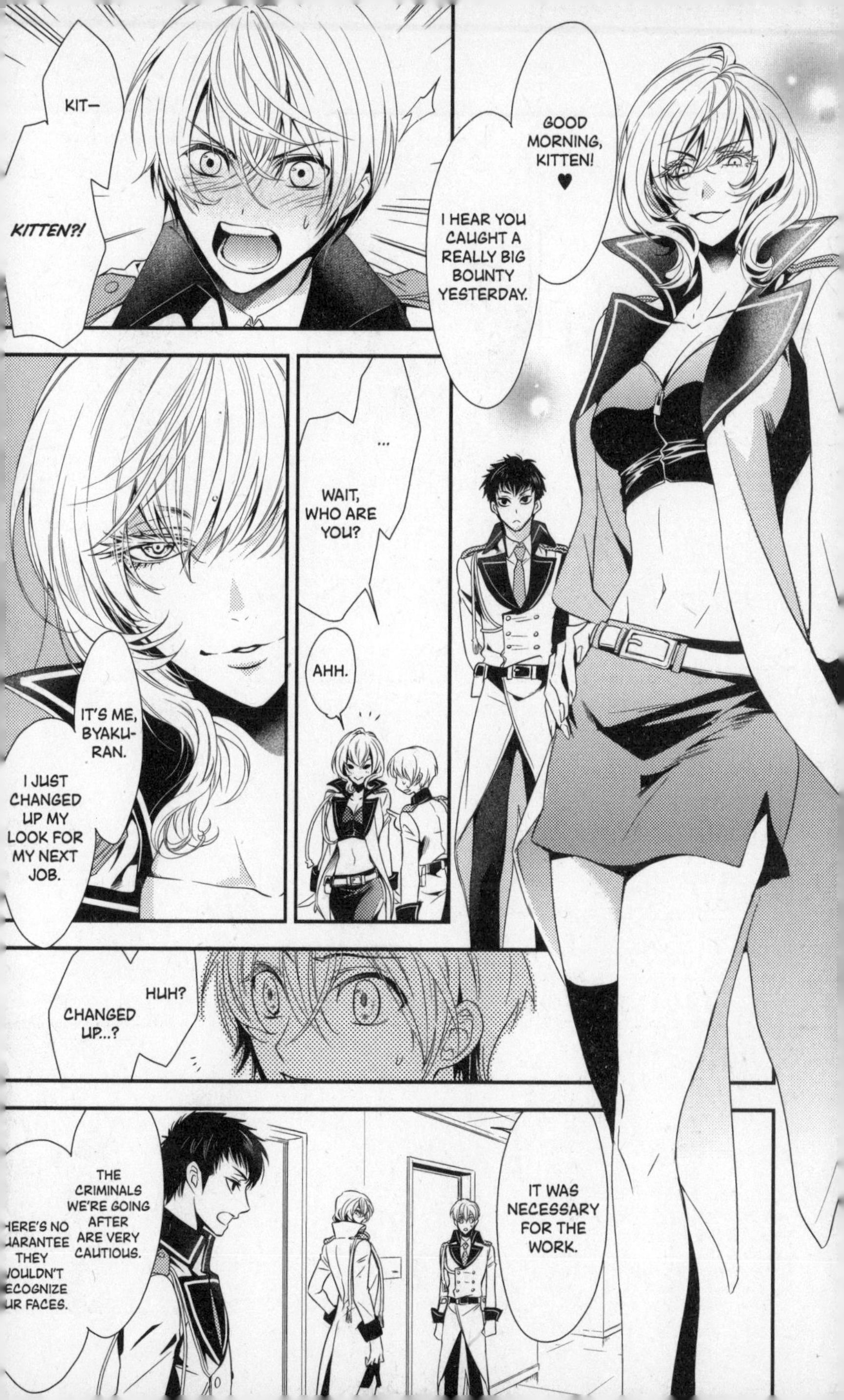
GOOD MORNING, KITTEN! ♥
I HEAR YOU CAUGHT A REALLY BIG BOUNTY YESTERDAY.
KIT—
KITTEN?!
...
WAIT, WHO ARE YOU?
AHH.
IT'S ME, BYAKURAN.
I JUST CHANGED UP MY LOOK FOR MY NEXT JOB.
HUH?
CHANGED UP...?
IT WAS NECESSARY FOR THE WORK.
THE CRIMINALS WE'RE GOING AFTER ARE VERY CAUTIOUS.
HERE'S NO UARANTEE THEY VOULDN'T ECOGNIZE UR FACES.

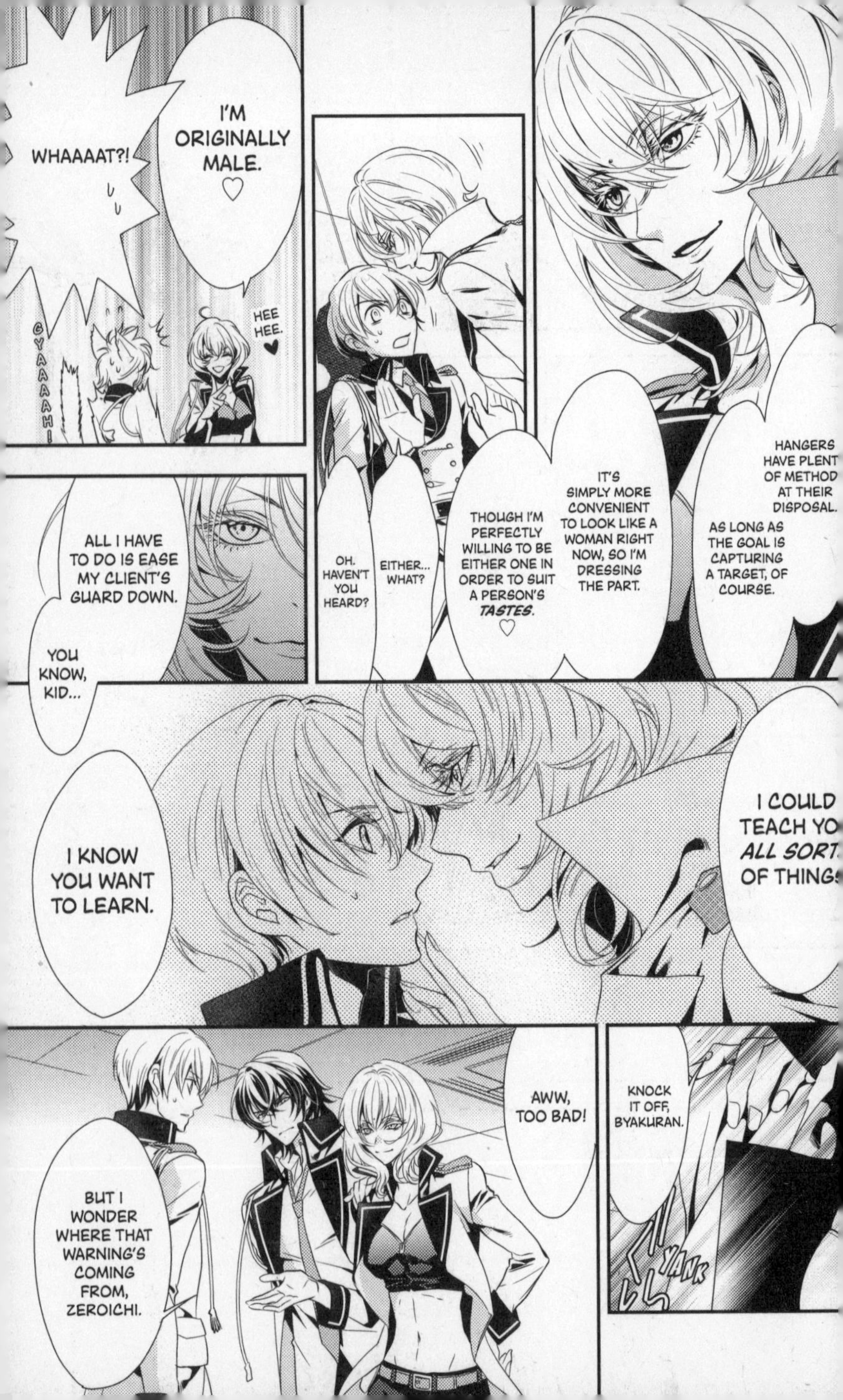
HANGERS HAVE PLENT OF METHOD AT THEIR DISPOSAL.
AS LONG AS THE GOAL IS CAPTURING A TARGET, OF COURSE.
IT'S SIMPLY MORE CONVENIENT TO LOOK LIKE A WOMAN RIGHT NOW, SO I'M DRESSING THE PART.
THOUGH I'M PERFECTLY WILLING TO BE EITHER ONE IN ORDER TO SUIT A PERSON'S *TASTES*. ♡
EITHER... WHAT?
OH. HAVEN'T YOU HEARD?
I'M ORIGINALLY MALE. ♡
HEE HEE. ♥
WHAAAAT?!
GYAAAAAH!
ALL I HAVE TO DO IS EASE MY CLIENT'S GUARD DOWN.
YOU KNOW, KID...
I COULD TEACH YO *ALL SORT* OF THING
I KNOW YOU WANT TO LEARN.
KNOCK IT OFF, BYAKURAN.
YANK
AWW, TOO BAD!
BUT I WONDER WHERE THAT WARNING'S COMING FROM, ZEROICHI.

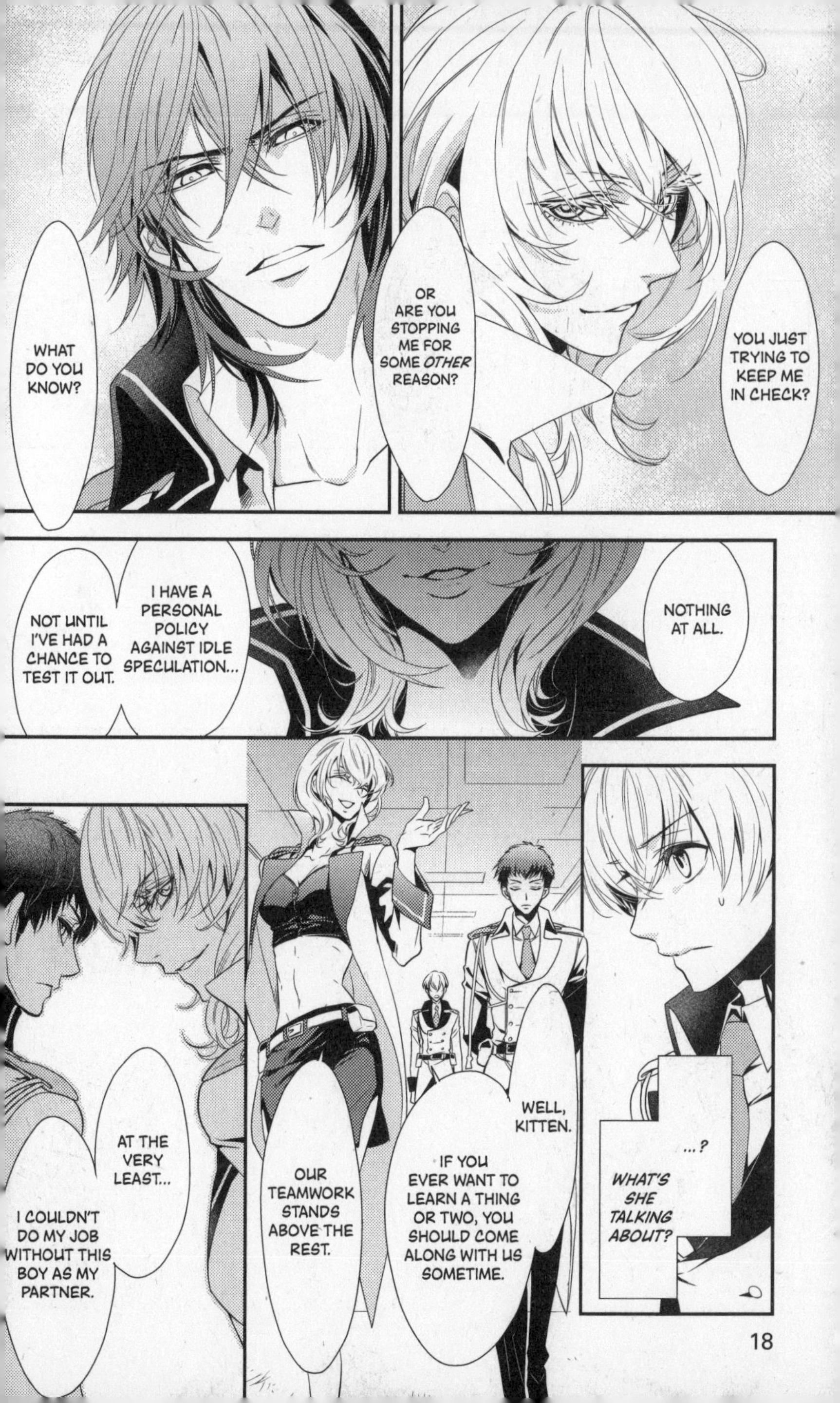
YOU JUST TRYING TO KEEP ME IN CHECK?
OR ARE YOU STOPPING ME FOR SOME *OTHER* REASON?
WHAT DO YOU KNOW?
NOTHING AT ALL.
I HAVE A PERSONAL POLICY AGAINST IDLE SPECULATION...
NOT UNTIL I'VE HAD A CHANCE TO TEST IT OUT.
...?
WHAT'S SHE TALKING ABOUT?
WELL, KITTEN.
IF YOU EVER WANT TO LEARN A THING OR TWO, YOU SHOULD COME ALONG WITH US SOMETIME.
OUR TEAMWORK STANDS ABOVE THE REST.
AT THE VERY LEAST...
I COULDN'T DO MY JOB WITHOUT THIS BOY AS MY PARTNER.

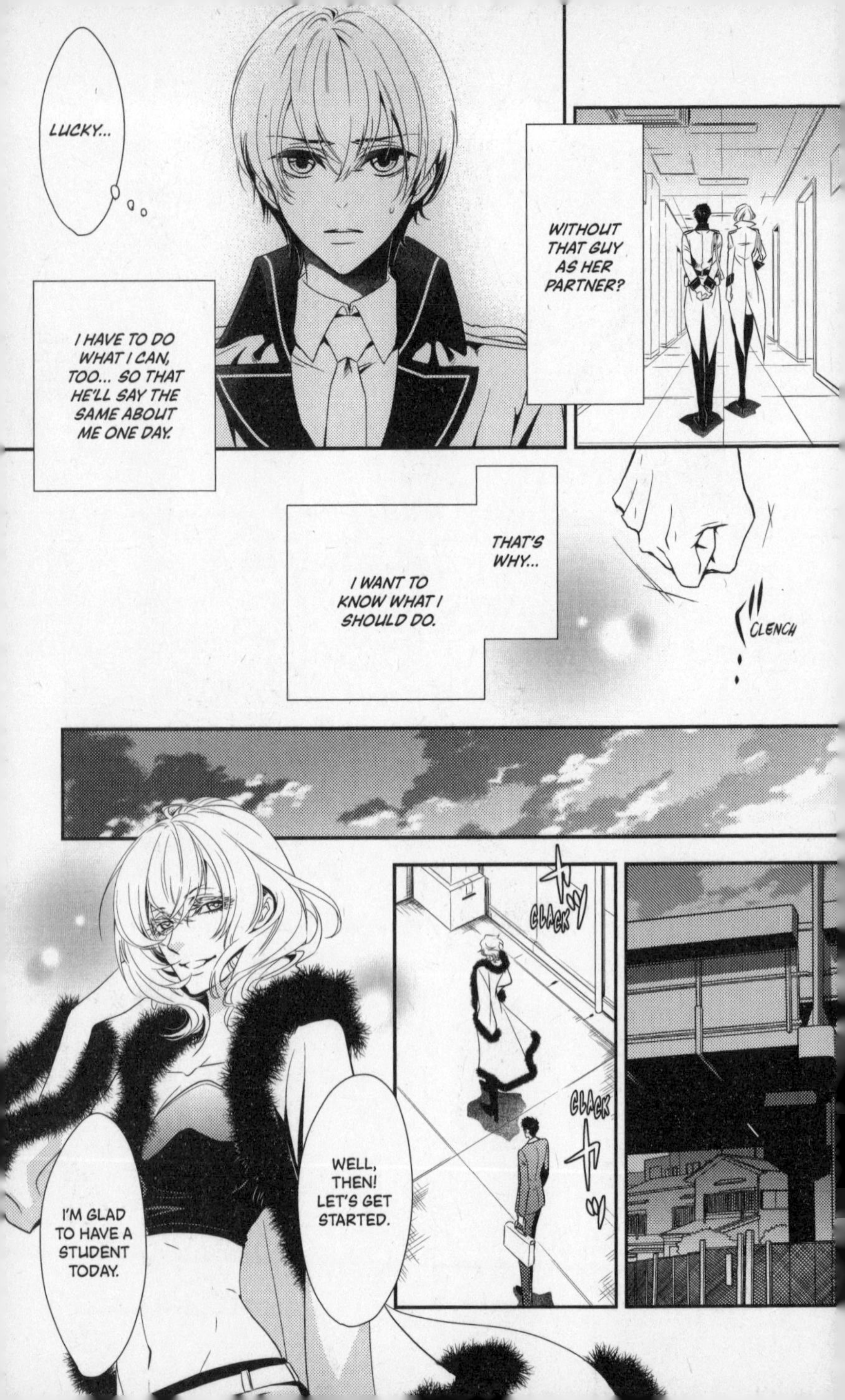
WITHOUT THAT GUY AS HER PARTNER?
LUCKY...
I HAVE TO DO WHAT I CAN, TOO... SO THAT HE'LL SAY THE SAME ABOUT ME ONE DAY.
CLENCH
THAT'S WHY...
I WANT TO KNOW WHAT I SHOULD DO.
CLACK
CLACK
WELL, THEN! LET'S GET STARTED.
I'M GLAD TO HAVE A STUDENT TODAY.

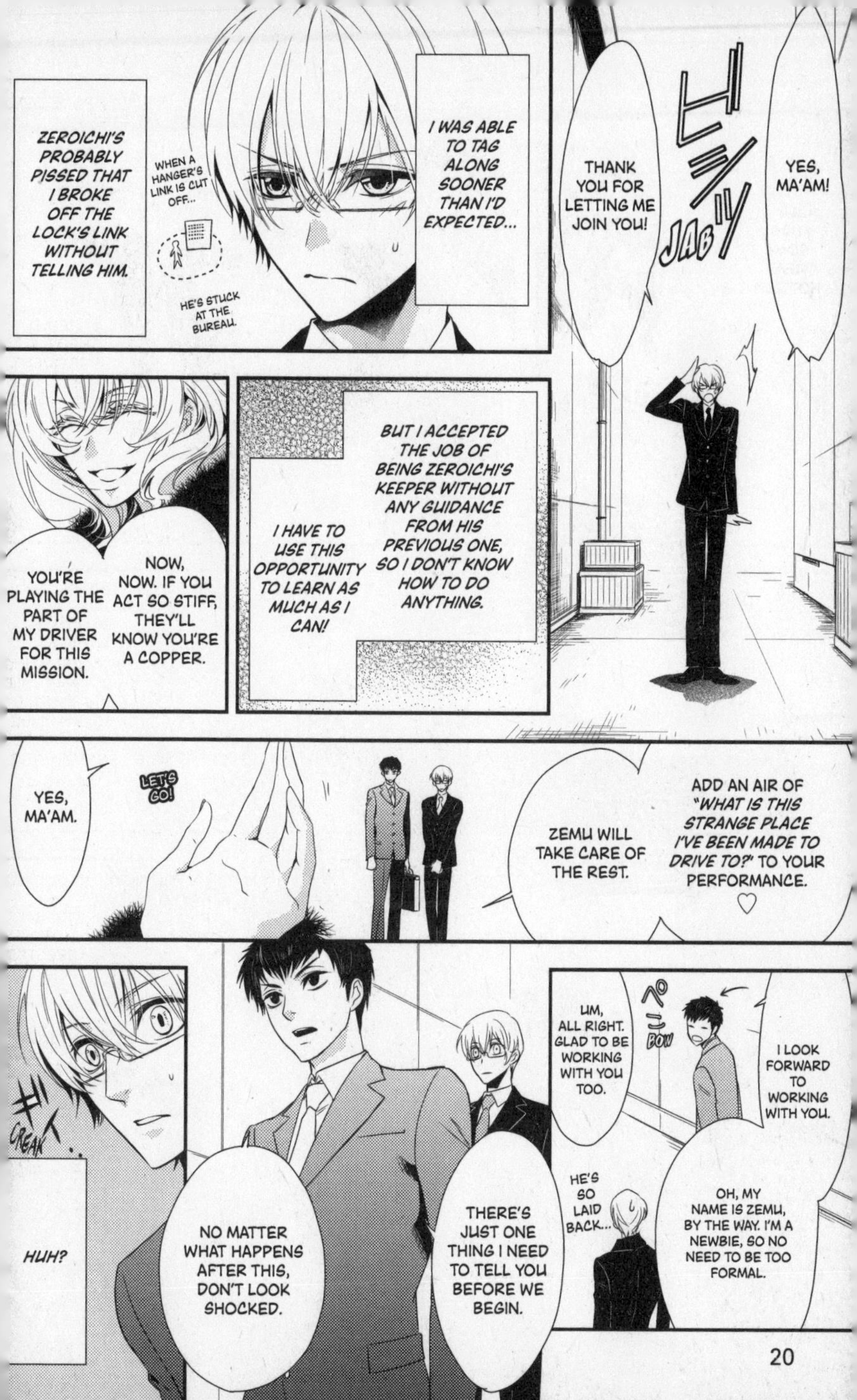
YES, MA'AM!
JAB
THANK YOU FOR LETTING ME JOIN YOU!
I WAS ABLE TO TAG ALONG SOONER THAN I'D EXPECTED...
ZEROICHI'S PROBABLY PISSED THAT I BROKE OFF THE LOCK'S LINK WITHOUT TELLING HIM.
WHEN A HANGER'S LINK IS CUT OFF...
HE'S STUCK AT THE BUREAU.
BUT I ACCEPTED THE JOB OF BEING ZEROICHI'S KEEPER WITHOUT ANY GUIDANCE FROM HIS PREVIOUS ONE, SO I DON'T KNOW HOW TO DO ANYTHING.
I HAVE TO USE THIS OPPORTUNITY TO LEARN AS MUCH AS I CAN!
NOW, NOW. IF YOU ACT SO STIFF, THEY'LL KNOW YOU'RE A COPPER.
YOU'RE PLAYING THE PART OF MY DRIVER FOR THIS MISSION.
ADD AN AIR OF "WHAT IS THIS STRANGE PLACE I'VE BEEN MADE TO DRIVE TO?" TO YOUR PERFORMANCE. ♡
ZEMU WILL TAKE CARE OF THE REST.
LET'S GO!
YES, MA'AM.
I LOOK FORWARD TO WORKING WITH YOU.
BOW
UM, ALL RIGHT. GLAD TO BE WORKING WITH YOU TOO.
OH, MY NAME IS ZEMU, BY THE WAY. I'M A NEWBIE, SO NO NEED TO BE TOO FORMAL.
HE'S SO LAID BACK...
THERE'S JUST ONE THING I NEED TO TELL YOU BEFORE WE BEGIN.
NO MATTER WHAT HAPPENS AFTER THIS, DON'T LOOK SHOCKED.
CREAK
HUH?

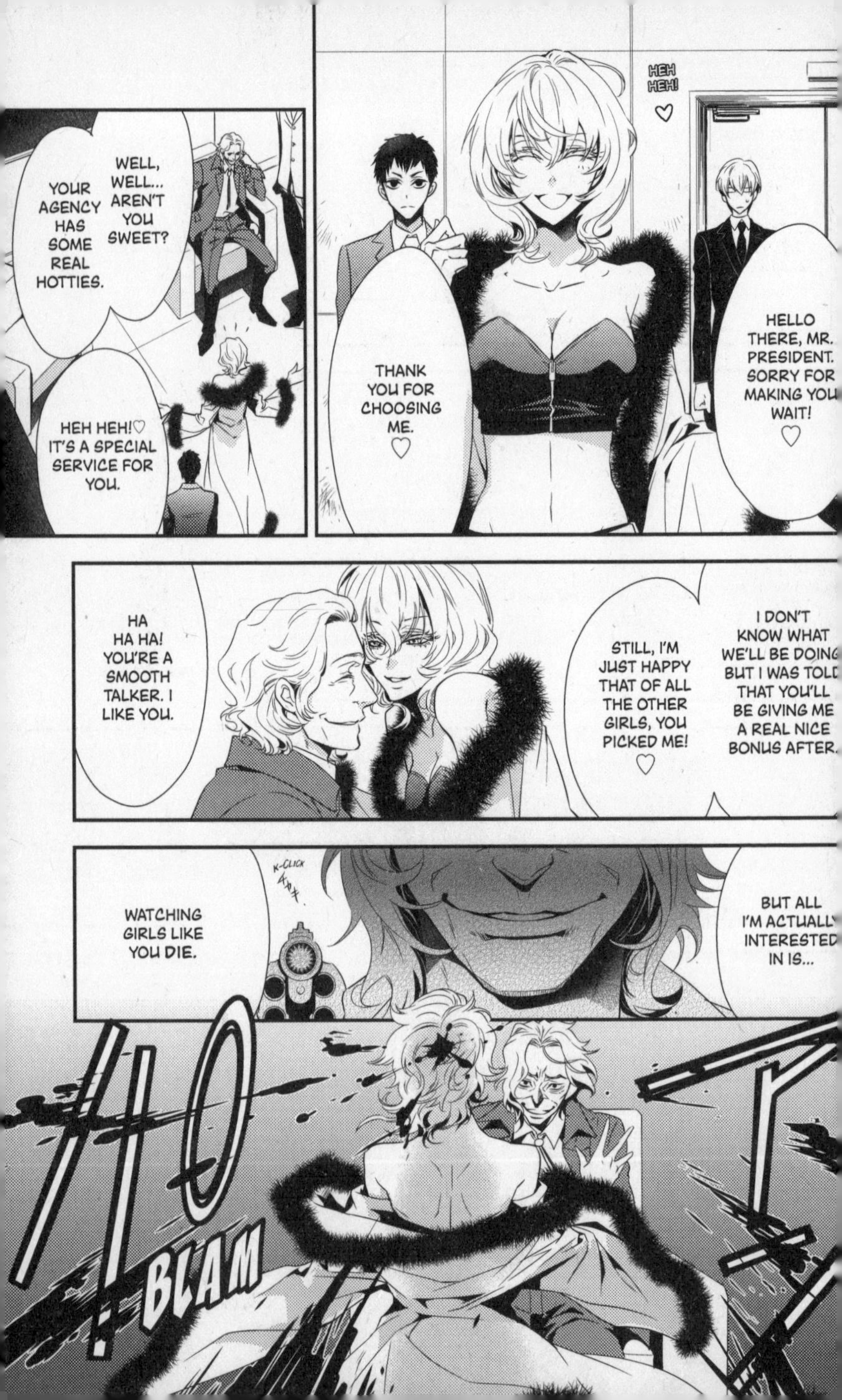
HEH HEH! ♡
HELLO THERE, MR. PRESIDENT. SORRY FOR MAKING YOU WAIT! ♡
THANK YOU FOR CHOOSING ME. ♡
WELL, WELL... AREN'T YOU SWEET?
YOUR AGENCY HAS SOME REAL HOTTIES.
HEH HEH!♡ IT'S A SPECIAL SERVICE FOR YOU.
I DON'T KNOW WHAT WE'LL BE DOING BUT I WAS TOLD THAT YOU'LL BE GIVING ME A REAL NICE BONUS AFTER.
STILL, I'M JUST HAPPY THAT OF ALL THE OTHER GIRLS, YOU PICKED ME! ♡
HA HA HA! YOU'RE A SMOOTH TALKER. I LIKE YOU.
BUT ALL I'M ACTUALLY INTERESTED IN IS...
K-CLICK
WATCHING GIRLS LIKE YOU DIE.
BLAM

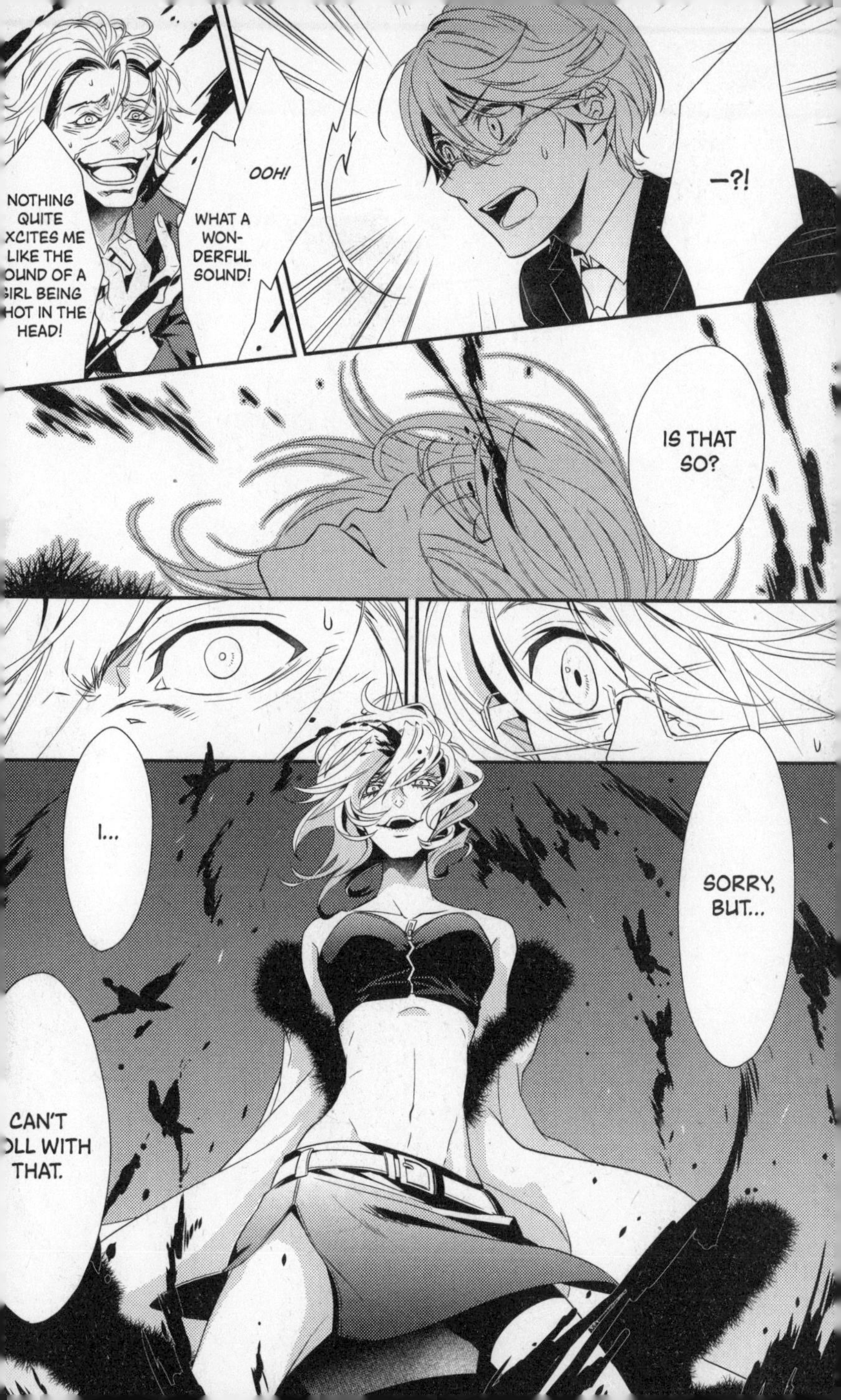
—?!
OOH!
WHAT A WON-DERFUL SOUND!
NOTHING QUITE XCITES ME LIKE THE OUND OF A IRL BEING HOT IN THE HEAD!
IS THAT SO?
SORRY, BUT...
I...
CAN'T OLL WITH THAT.

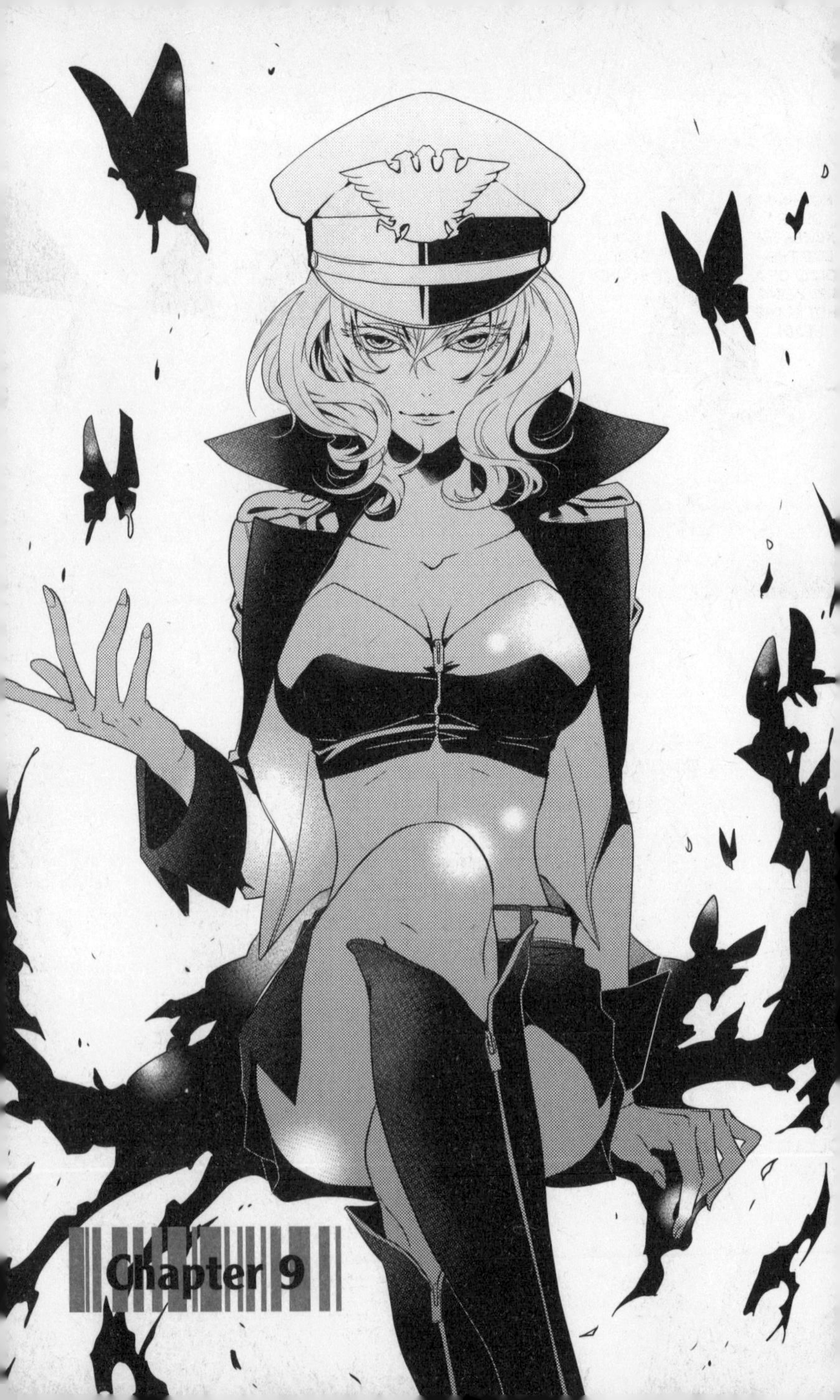
Chapter 9

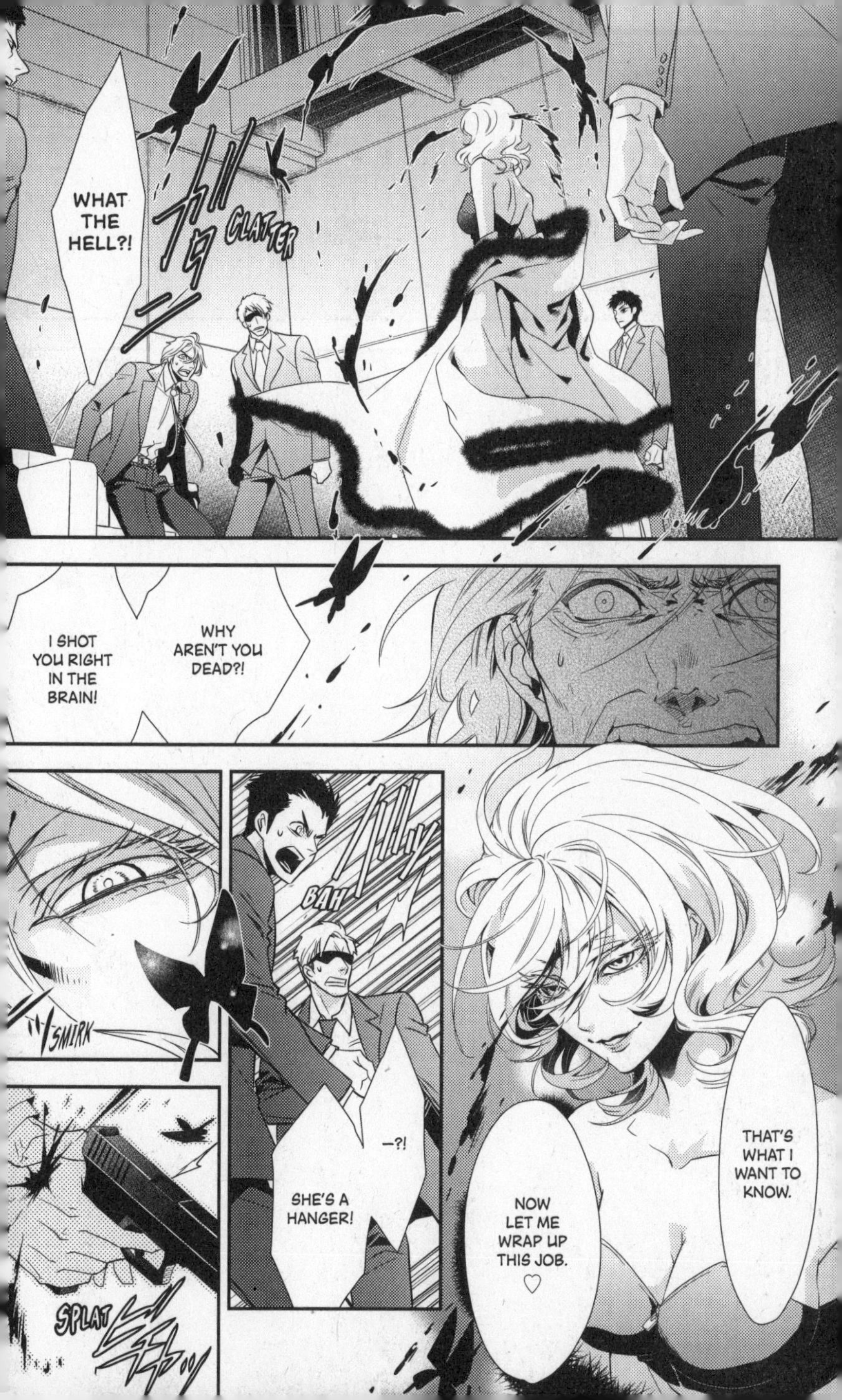
CLATTER
WHAT THE HELL?!
WHY AREN'T YOU DEAD?!
I SHOT YOU RIGHT IN THE BRAIN!
THAT'S WHAT I WANT TO KNOW.
NOW LET ME WRAP UP THIS JOB. ♡
BAH
—?!
SHE'S A HANGER!
SMIRK
SPLAT

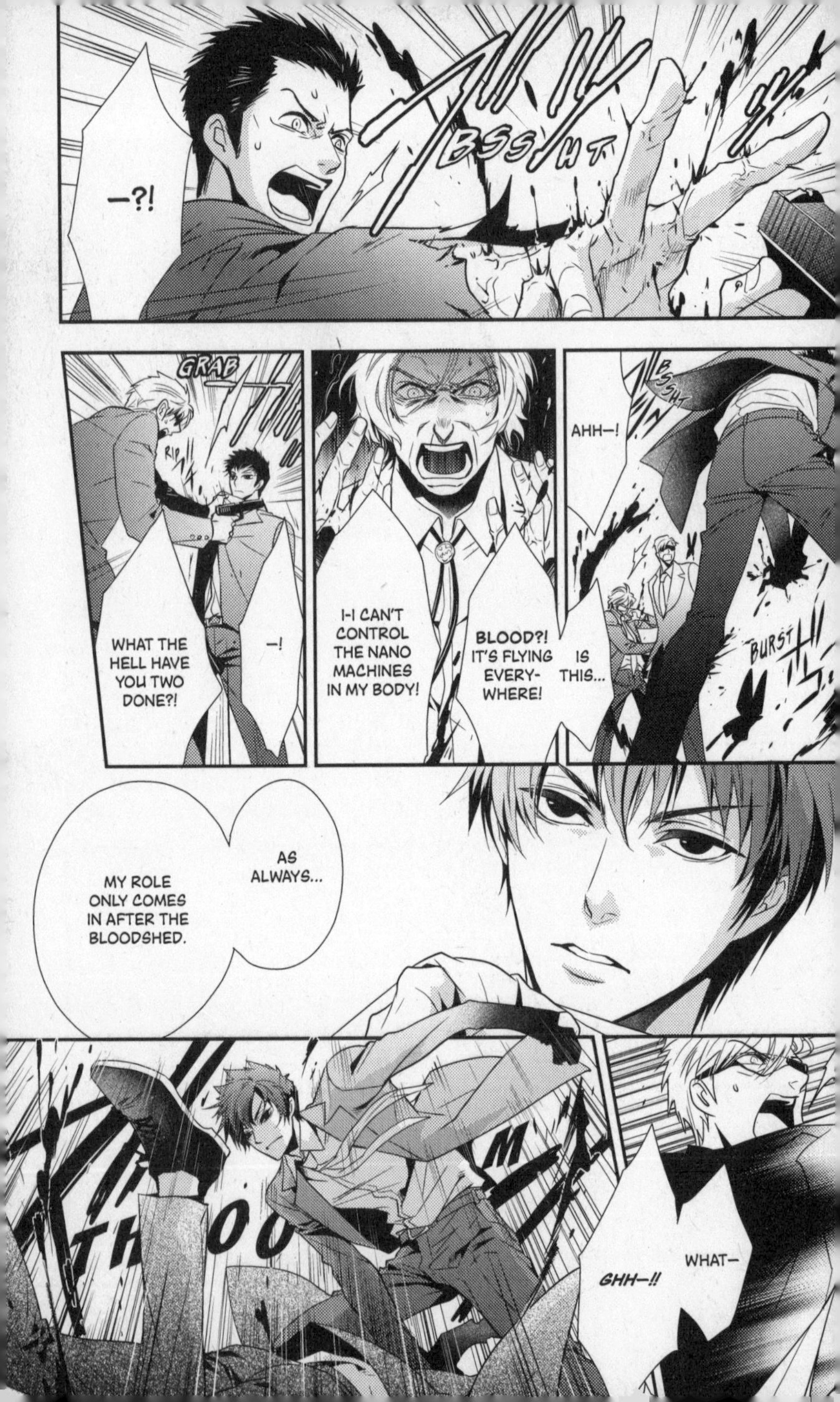
BSSHT
—?!
BSSHT
AHH—!
IS THIS...
BURST
BLOOD?! IT'S FLYING EVERY-WHERE!
I-I CAN'T CONTROL THE NANO MACHINES IN MY BODY!
GRAB
RIP
—!
WHAT THE HELL HAVE YOU TWO DONE?!
AS ALWAYS...
MY ROLE ONLY COMES IN AFTER THE BLOODSHED.
WHAT—
GHH—!!
THOOM

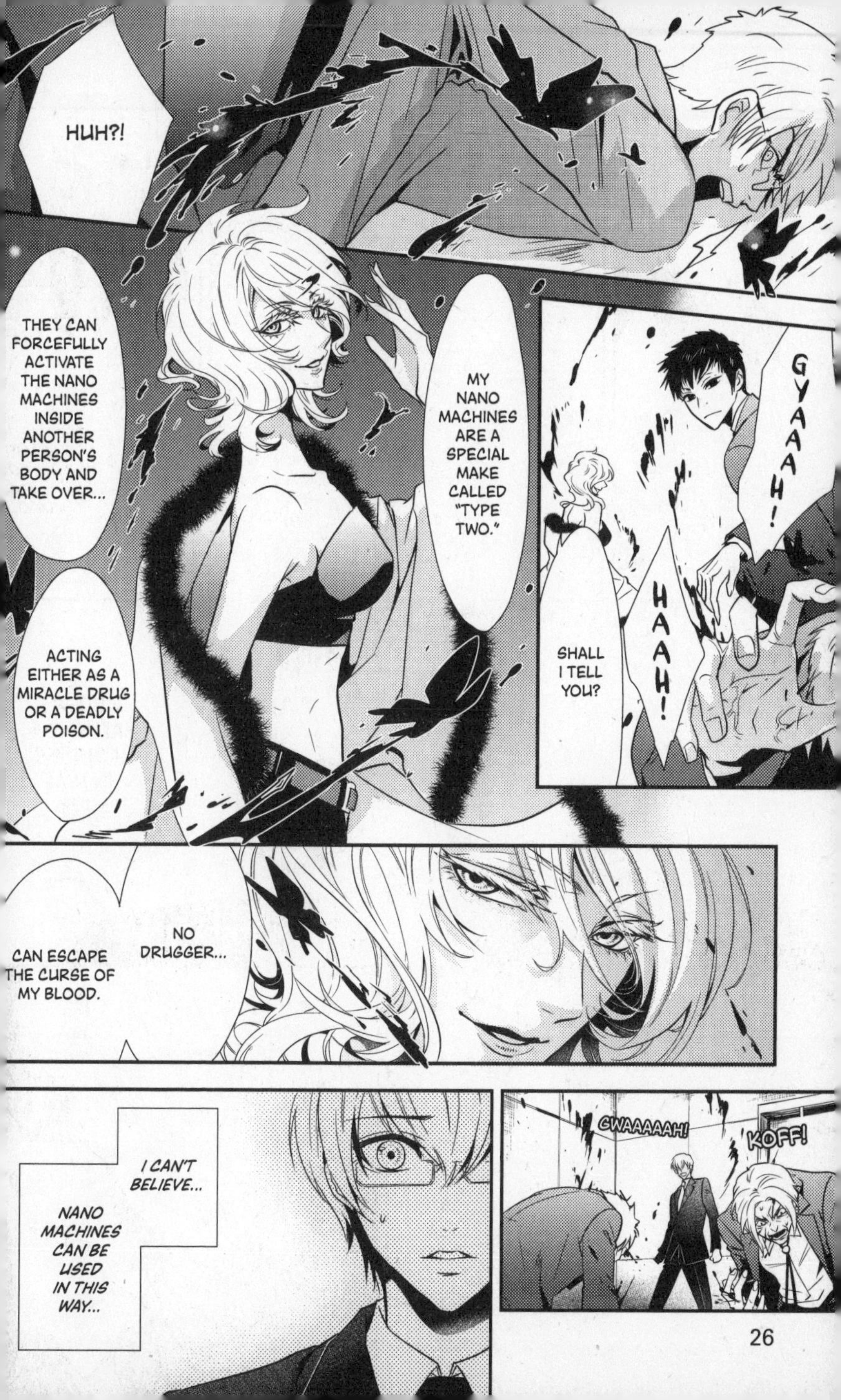
HUH?!
GYAAAH!
HAAH!
SHALL I TELL YOU?
MY NANO MACHINES ARE A SPECIAL MAKE CALLED "TYPE TWO."
THEY CAN FORCEFULLY ACTIVATE THE NANO MACHINES INSIDE ANOTHER PERSON'S BODY AND TAKE OVER...
ACTING EITHER AS A MIRACLE DRUG OR A DEADLY POISON.
NO DRUGGER...
CAN ESCAPE THE CURSE OF MY BLOOD.
KOFF!
GWAAAAAH!
I CAN'T BELIEVE...
NANO MACHINES CAN BE USED IN THIS WAY...

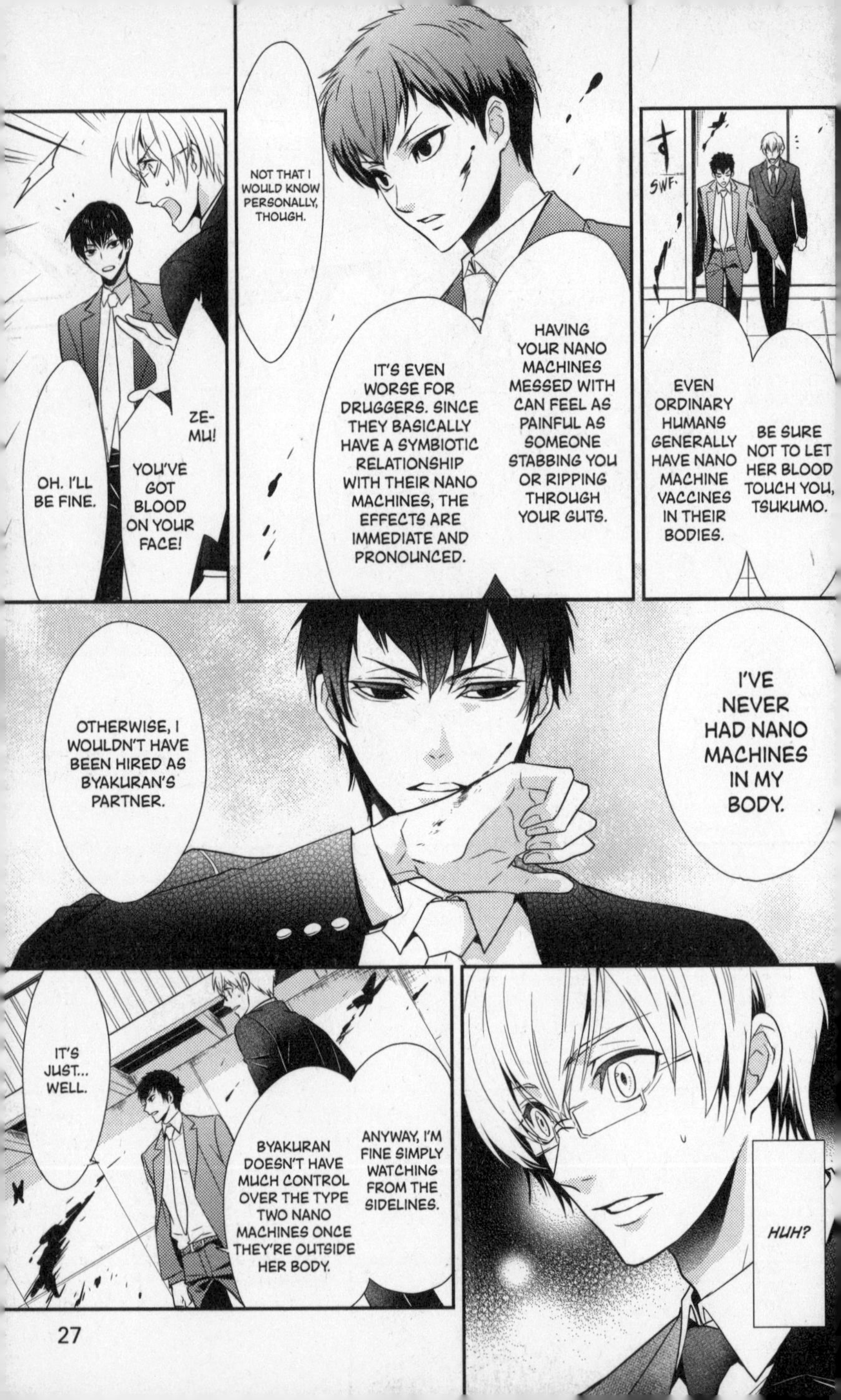
SWF.
BE SURE NOT TO LET HER BLOOD TOUCH YOU, TSUKUMO.
EVEN ORDINARY HUMANS GENERALLY HAVE NANO MACHINE VACCINES IN THEIR BODIES.
HAVING YOUR NANO MACHINES MESSED WITH CAN FEEL AS PAINFUL AS SOMEONE STABBING YOU OR RIPPING THROUGH YOUR GUTS.
IT'S EVEN WORSE FOR DRUGGERS. SINCE THEY BASICALLY HAVE A SYMBIOTIC RELATIONSHIP WITH THEIR NANO MACHINES, THE EFFECTS ARE IMMEDIATE AND PRONOUNCED.
NOT THAT I WOULD KNOW PERSONALLY, THOUGH.
ZE-MU!
YOU'VE GOT BLOOD ON YOUR FACE!
OH. I'LL BE FINE.
I'VE NEVER HAD NANO MACHINES IN MY BODY.
OTHERWISE, I WOULDN'T HAVE BEEN HIRED AS BYAKURAN'S PARTNER.
HUH?
ANYWAY, I'M FINE SIMPLY WATCHING FROM THE SIDELINES.
BYAKURAN DOESN'T HAVE MUCH CONTROL OVER THE TYPE TWO NANO MACHINES ONCE THEY'RE OUTSIDE HER BODY.
IT'S JUST... WELL.

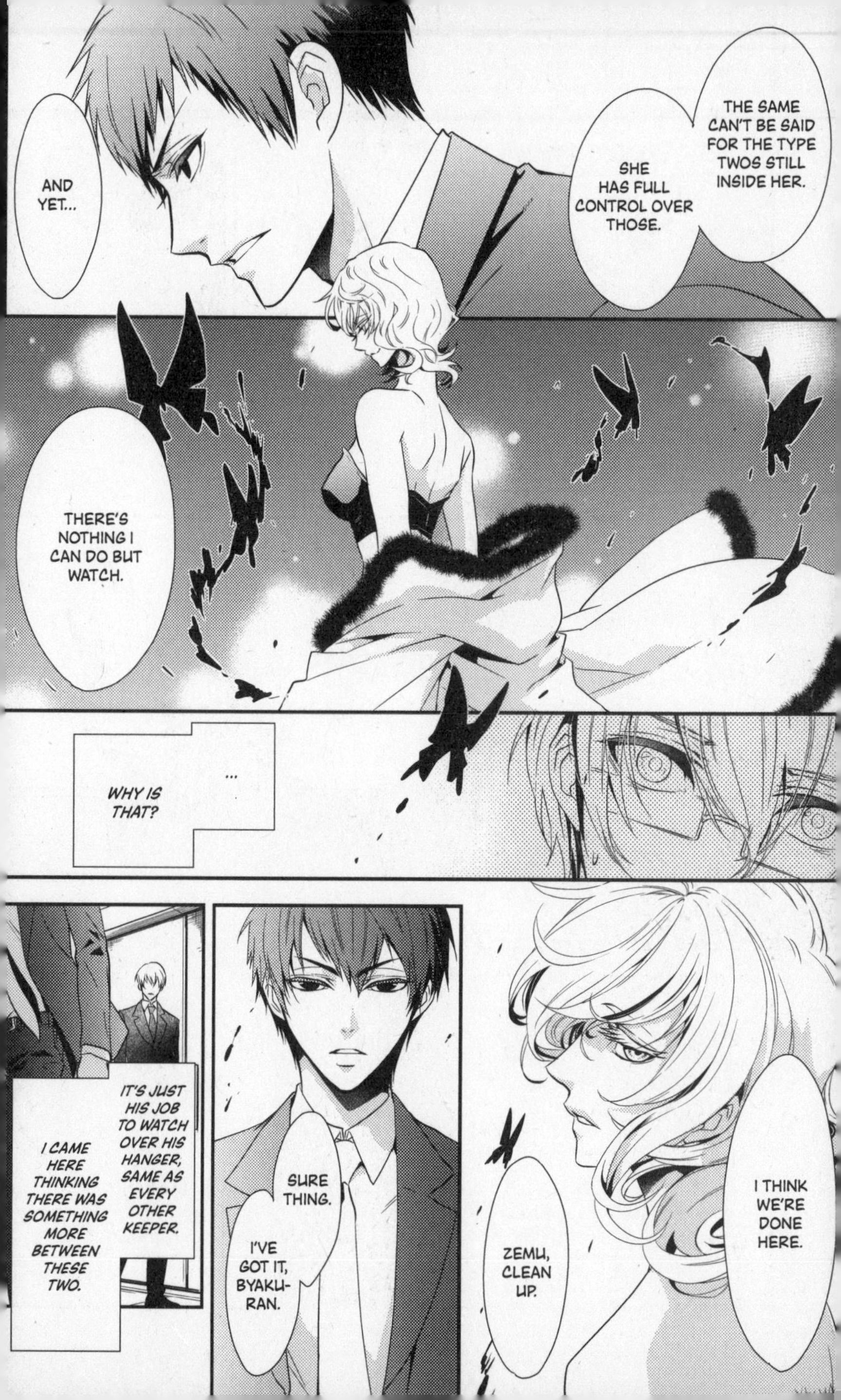
THE SAME CAN'T BE SAID FOR THE TYPE TWOS STILL INSIDE HER.
SHE HAS FULL CONTROL OVER THOSE.
AND YET...
THERE'S NOTHING I CAN DO BUT WATCH.
...
WHY IS THAT?
I THINK WE'RE DONE HERE.
ZEMU, CLEAN UP.
SURE THING.
I'VE GOT IT, BYAKU-RAN.
IT'S JUST HIS JOB TO WATCH OVER HIS HANGER, SAME AS EVERY OTHER KEEPER.
I CAME HERE THINKING THERE WAS SOMETHING MORE BETWEEN THESE TWO.

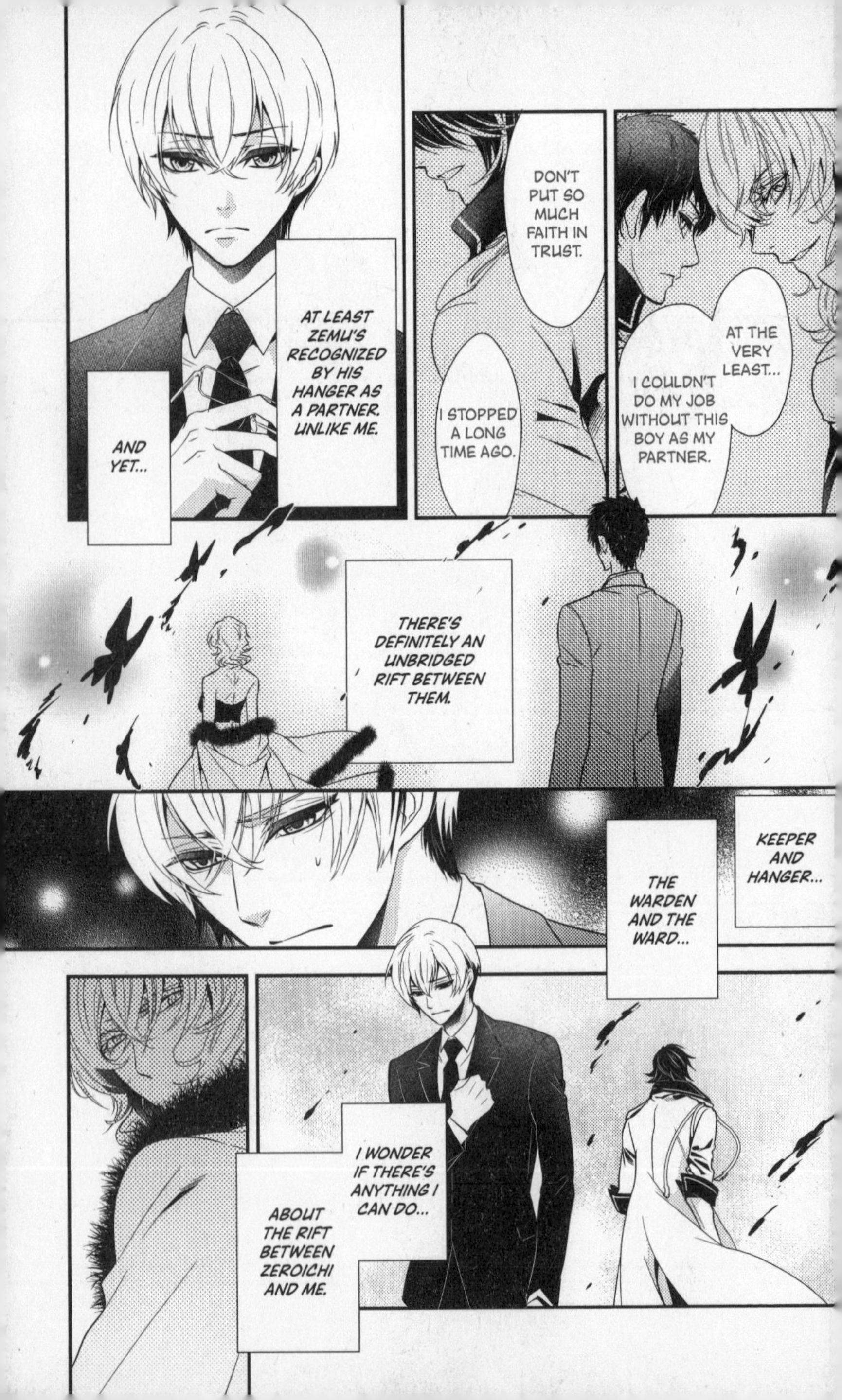
AT THE VERY LEAST...
I COULDN'T DO MY JOB WITHOUT THIS BOY AS MY PARTNER.
DON'T PUT SO MUCH FAITH IN TRUST.
I STOPPED A LONG TIME AGO.
AT LEAST ZEMU'S RECOGNIZED BY HIS HANGER AS A PARTNER. UNLIKE ME.
AND YET...
THERE'S DEFINITELY AN UNBRIDGED RIFT BETWEEN THEM.
KEEPER AND HANGER...
THE WARDEN AND THE WARD...
I WONDER IF THERE'S ANYTHING I CAN DO...
ABOUT THE RIFT BETWEEN ZEROICHI AND ME.

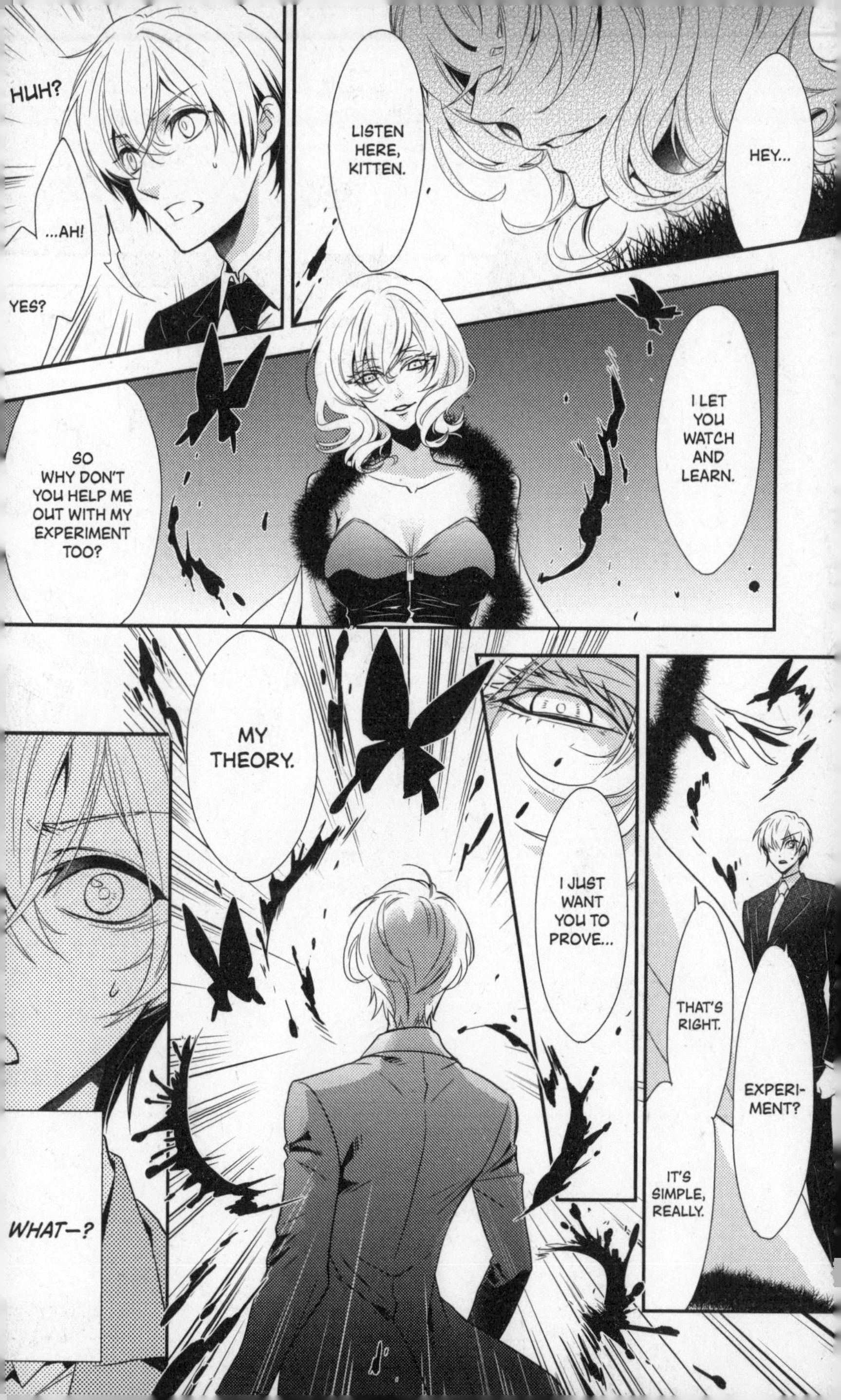
HEY...
LISTEN HERE, KITTEN.
HUH?
...AH!
YES?
I LET YOU WATCH AND LEARN.
SO WHY DON'T YOU HELP ME OUT WITH MY EXPERIMENT TOO?
EXPERI-MENT?
THAT'S RIGHT.
IT'S SIMPLE, REALLY.
I JUST WANT YOU TO PROVE...
MY THEORY.
WHAT—?

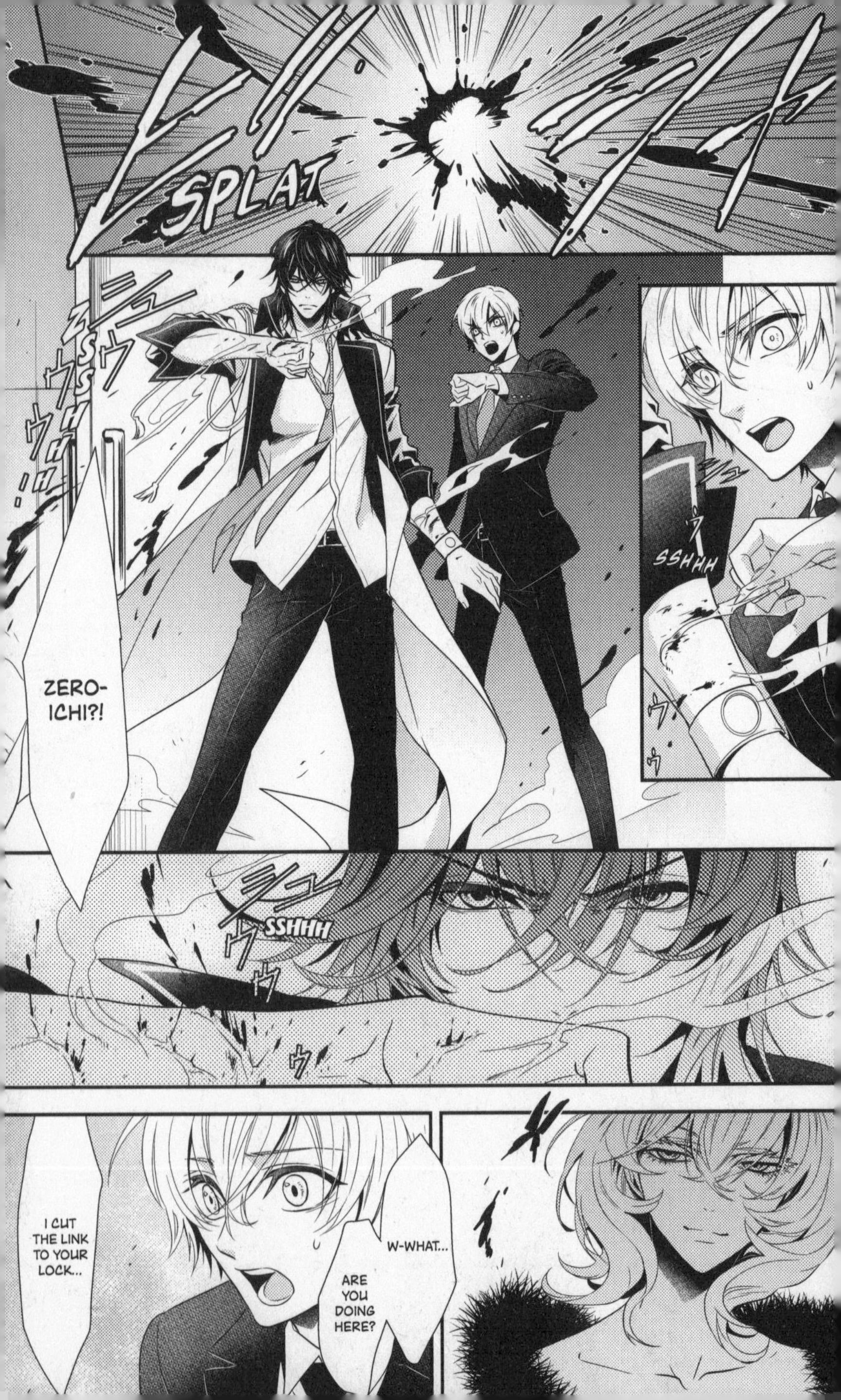
SPLAT
SSHHH
ZSSHHH
ZERO-ICHI?!
SSHHH
W-WHAT...
ARE YOU DOING HERE?
I CUT THE LINK TO YOUR LOCK...

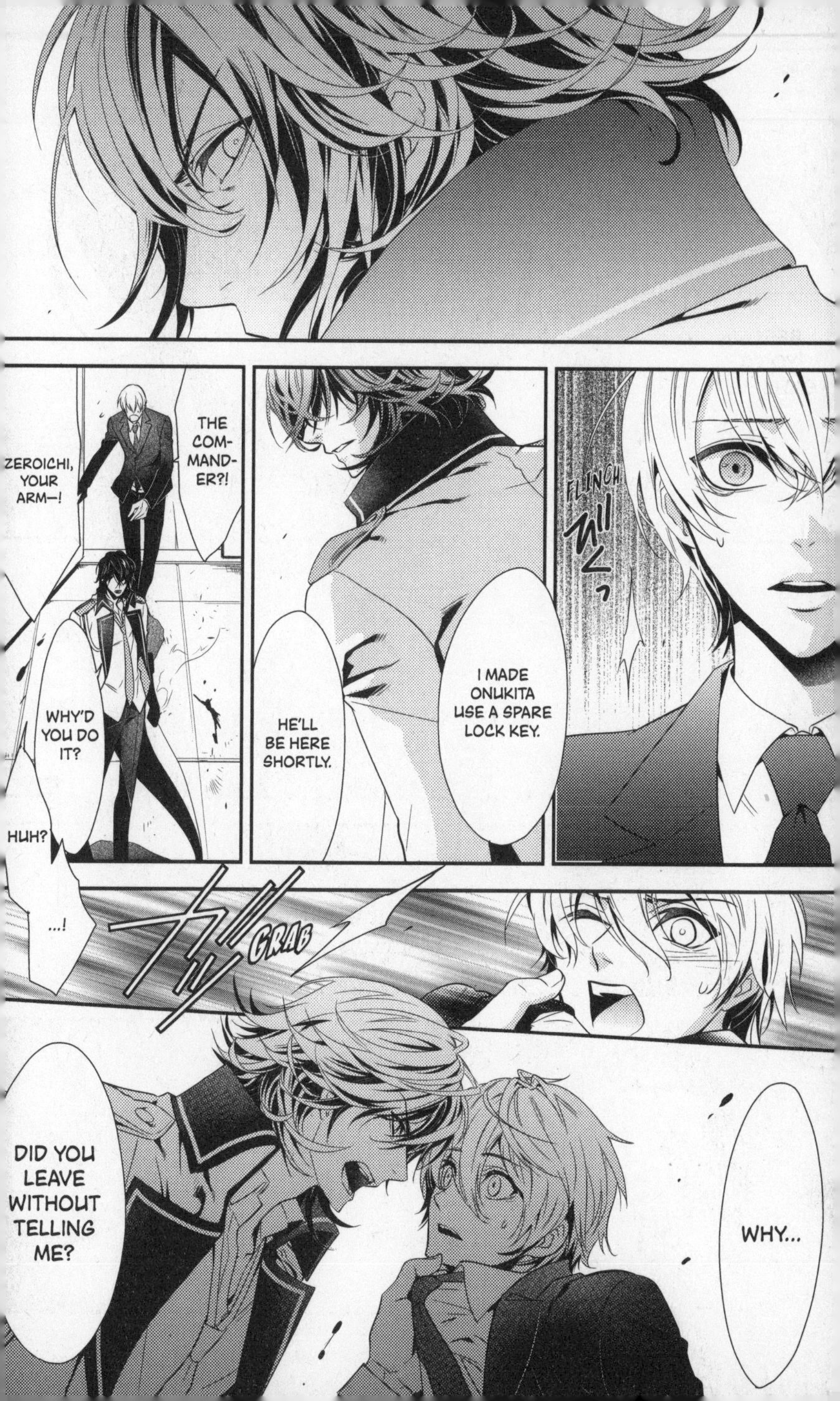
FLINCH
I MADE ONUKITA USE A SPARE LOCK KEY.
HE'LL BE HERE SHORTLY.
THE COMMANDER?!
ZEROICHI, YOUR ARM—!
WHY'D YOU DO IT?
HUH?
GRAB
...!
WHY...
DID YOU LEAVE WITHOUT TELLING ME?

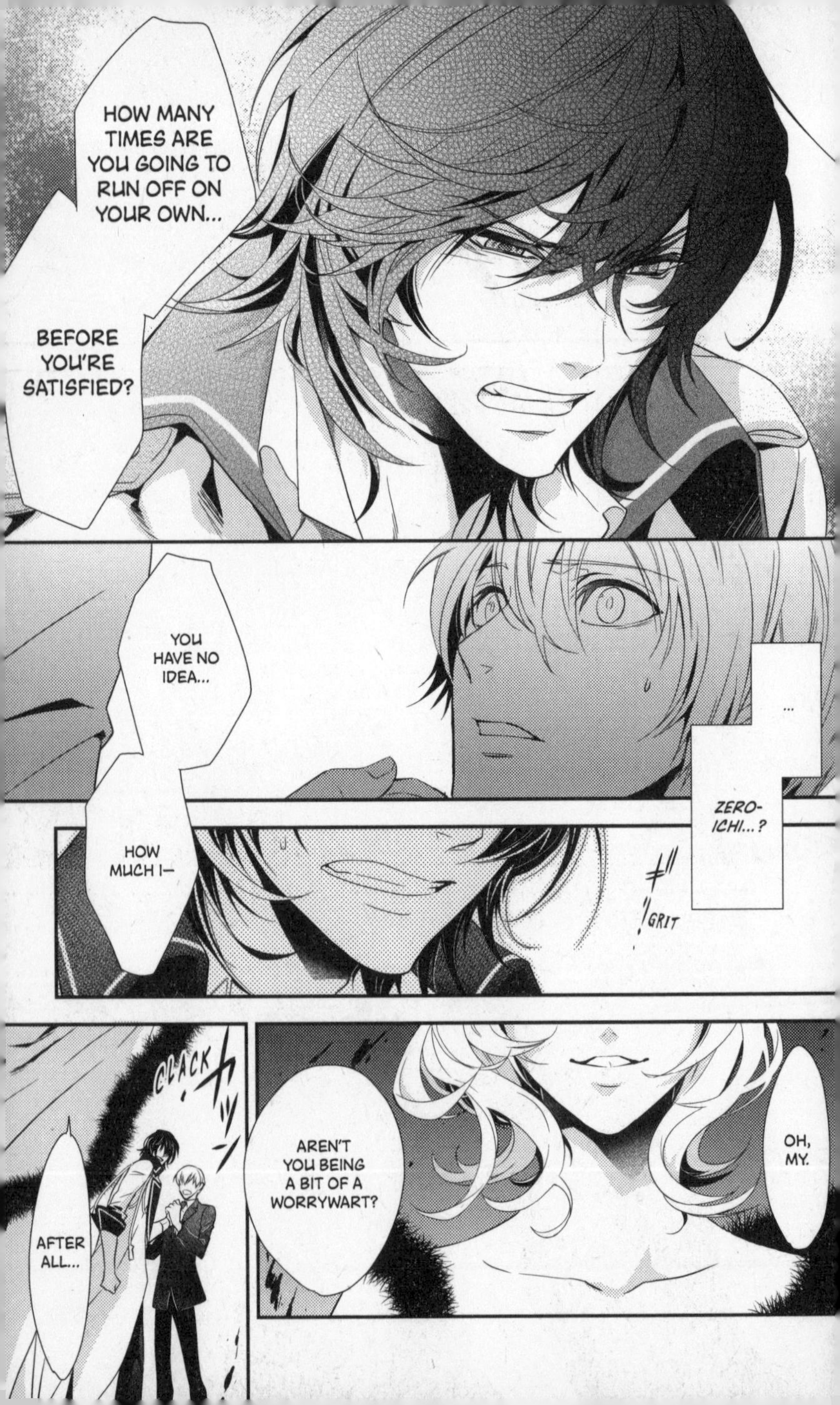
HOW MANY TIMES ARE YOU GOING TO RUN OFF ON YOUR OWN...
BEFORE YOU'RE SATISFIED?
...
ZERO-ICHI...?
YOU HAVE NO IDEA...
HOW MUCH I—
GRIT
OH, MY.
AREN'T YOU BEING A BIT OF A WORRYWART?
CLACK
AFTER ALL...

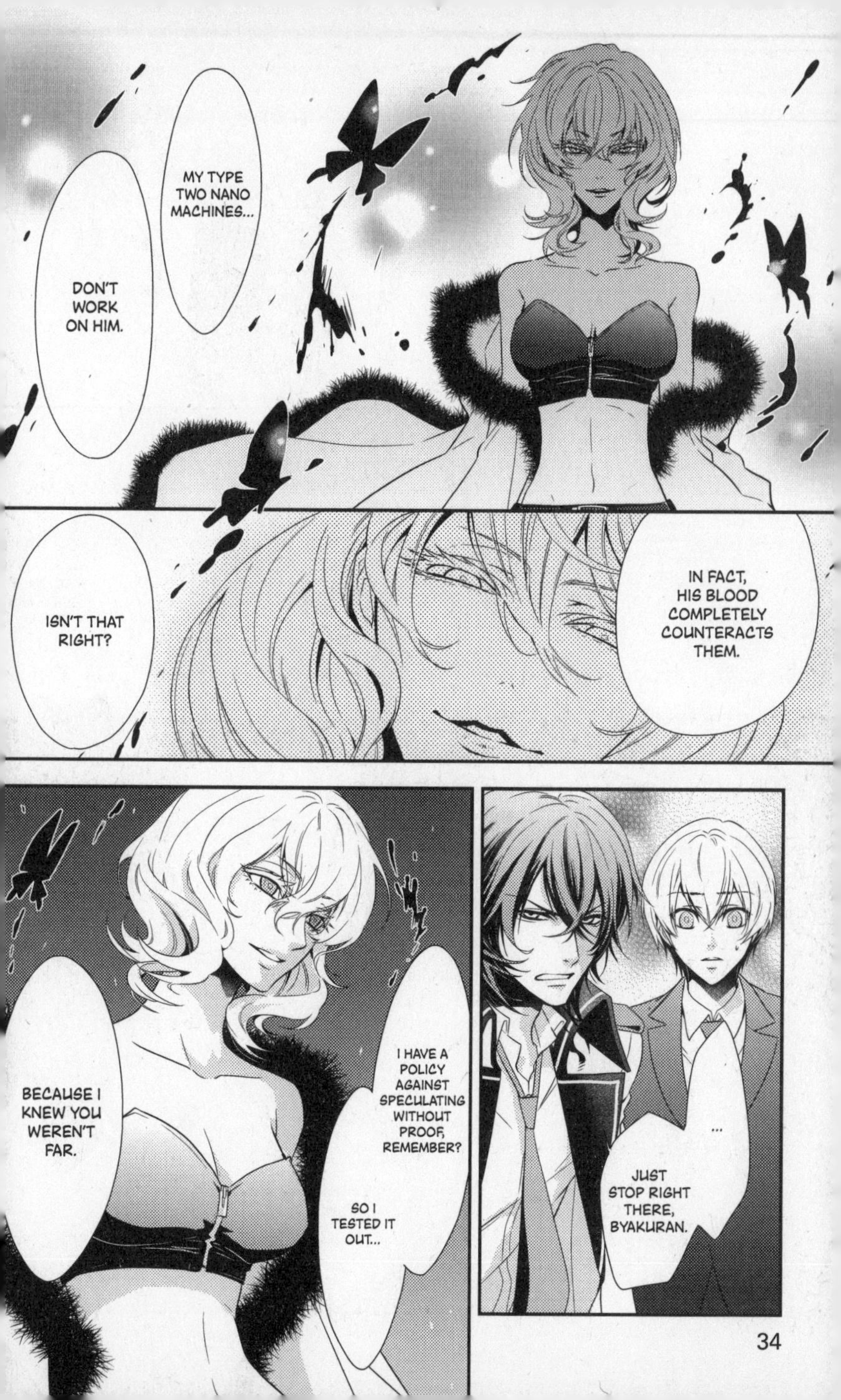

MY TYPE TWO NANO MACHINES...
DON'T WORK ON HIM.
IN FACT, HIS BLOOD COMPLETELY COUNTERACTS THEM.
ISN'T THAT RIGHT?
...
JUST STOP RIGHT THERE, BYAKURAN.
I HAVE A POLICY AGAINST SPECULATING WITHOUT PROOF, REMEMBER?
SO I TESTED IT OUT...
BECAUSE I KNEW YOU WEREN'T FAR.

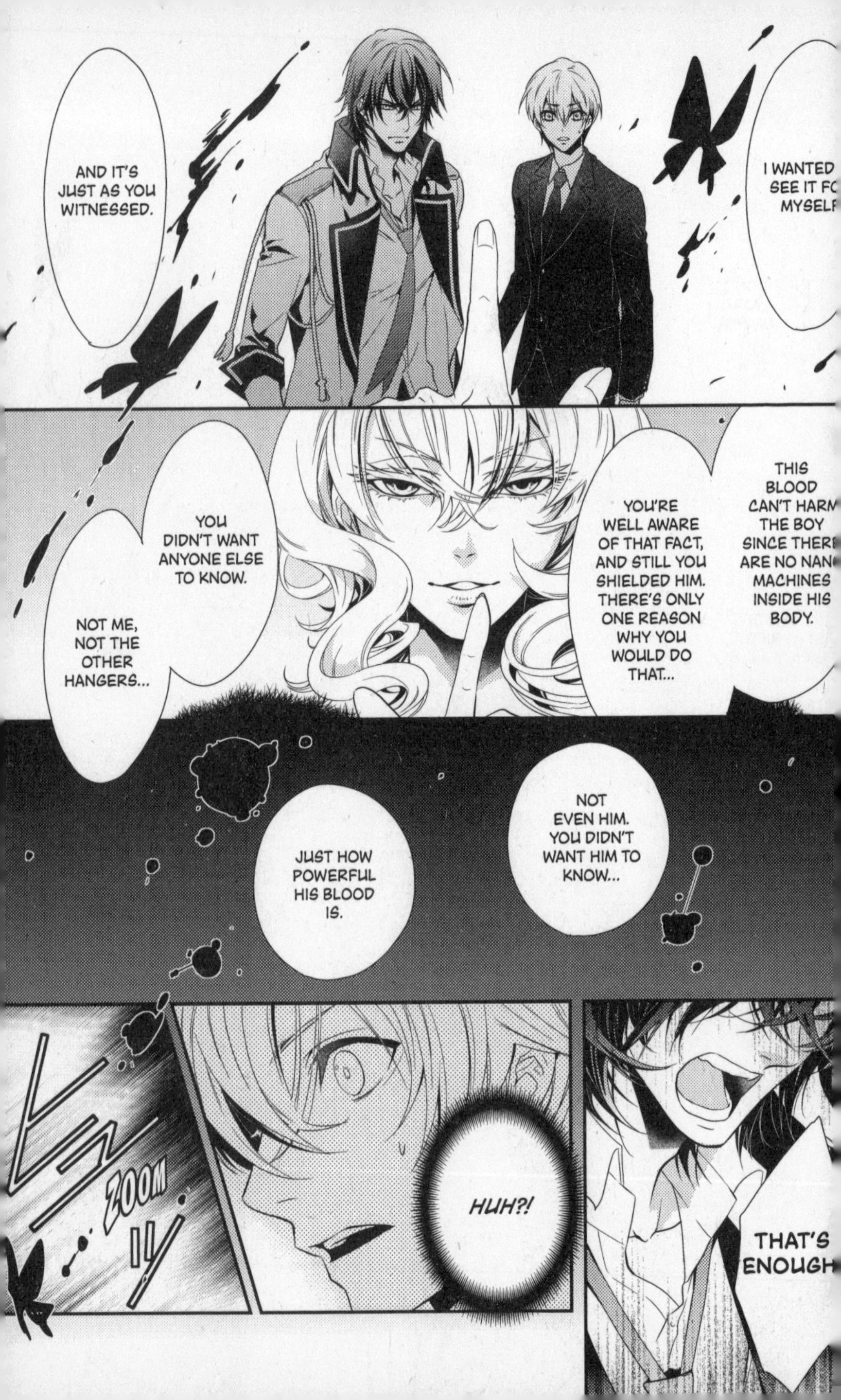
I WANTED SEE IT FO MYSELF
AND IT'S JUST AS YOU WITNESSED.
THIS BLOOD CAN'T HARM THE BOY SINCE THERE ARE NO NAN MACHINES INSIDE HIS BODY.
YOU'RE WELL AWARE OF THAT FACT, AND STILL YOU SHIELDED HIM. THERE'S ONLY ONE REASON WHY YOU WOULD DO THAT...
YOU DIDN'T WANT ANYONE ELSE TO KNOW.
NOT ME, NOT THE OTHER HANGERS...
NOT EVEN HIM. YOU DIDN'T WANT HIM TO KNOW...
JUST HOW POWERFUL HIS BLOOD IS.
THAT'S ENOUGH
HUH?!
ZOOM

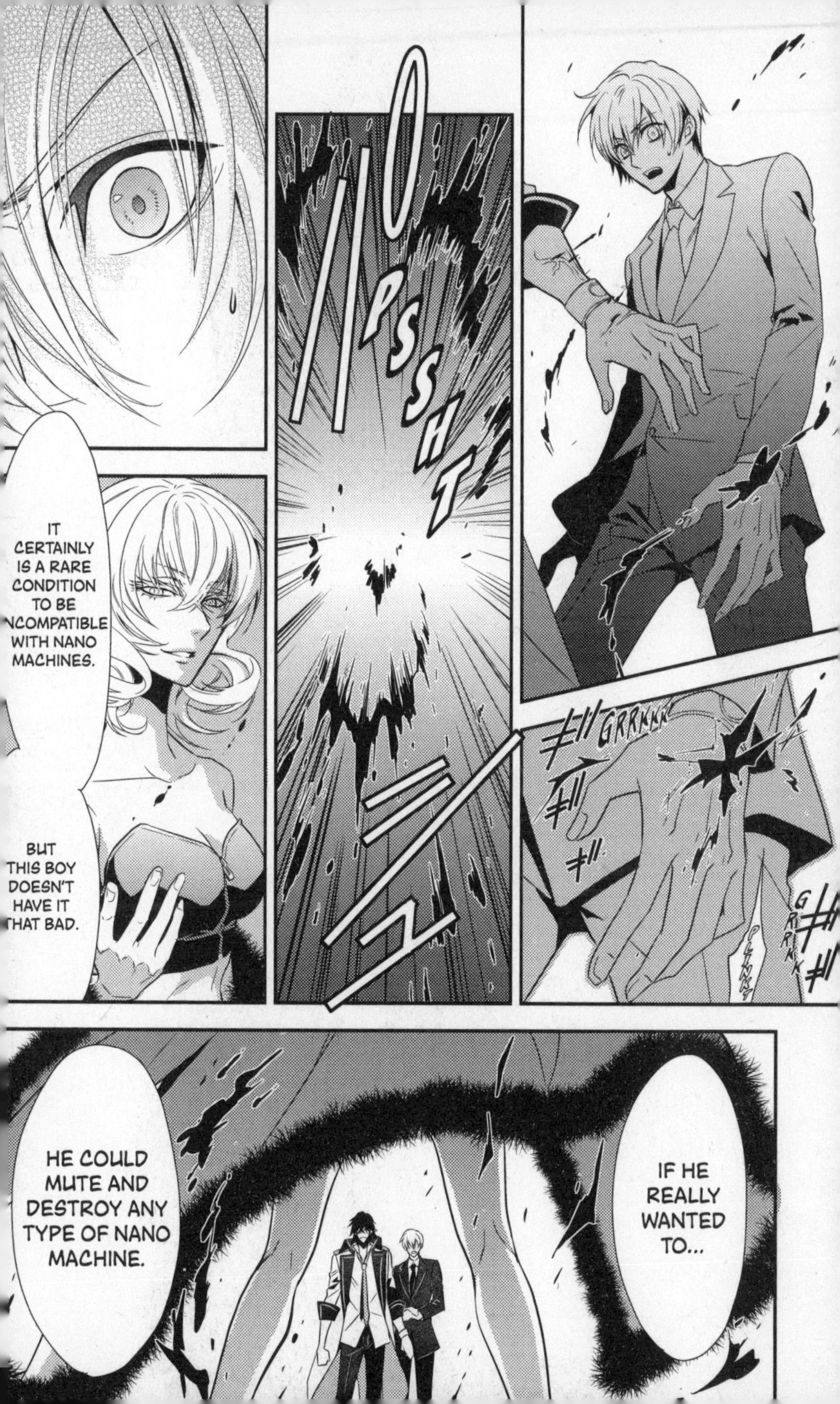
GRRKKK
GRRKK
PSSHT!
IT CERTAINLY IS A RARE CONDITION TO BE INCOMPATIBLE WITH NANO MACHINES.
BUT THIS BOY DOESN'T HAVE IT THAT BAD.
IF HE REALLY WANTED TO...
HE COULD MUTE AND DESTROY ANY TYPE OF NANO MACHINE.

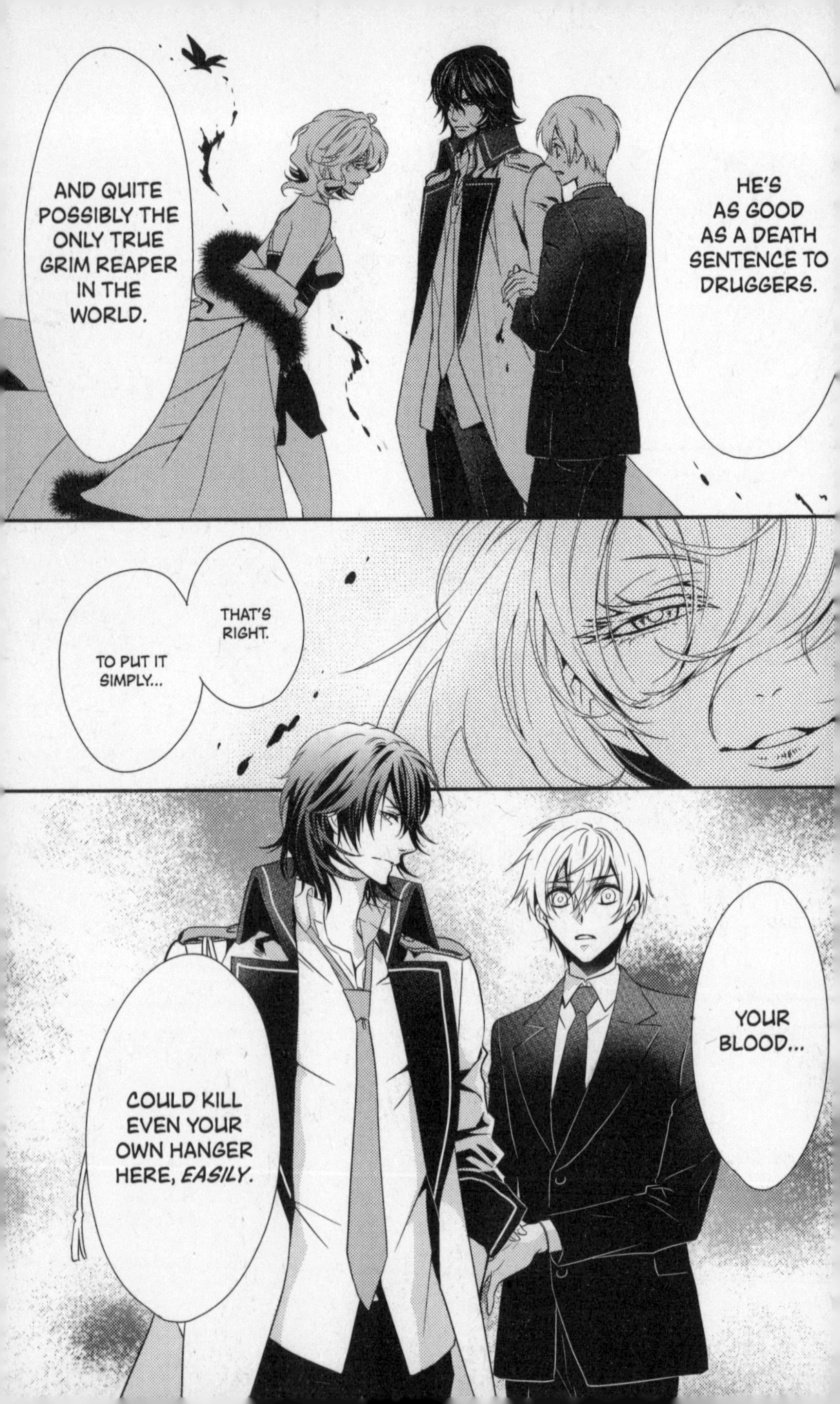
HE'S AS GOOD AS A DEATH SENTENCE TO DRUGGERS.
AND QUITE POSSIBLY THE ONLY TRUE GRIM REAPER IN THE WORLD.
THAT'S RIGHT.
TO PUT IT SIMPLY...
YOUR BLOOD...
COULD KILL EVEN YOUR OWN HANGER HERE, *EASILY*.

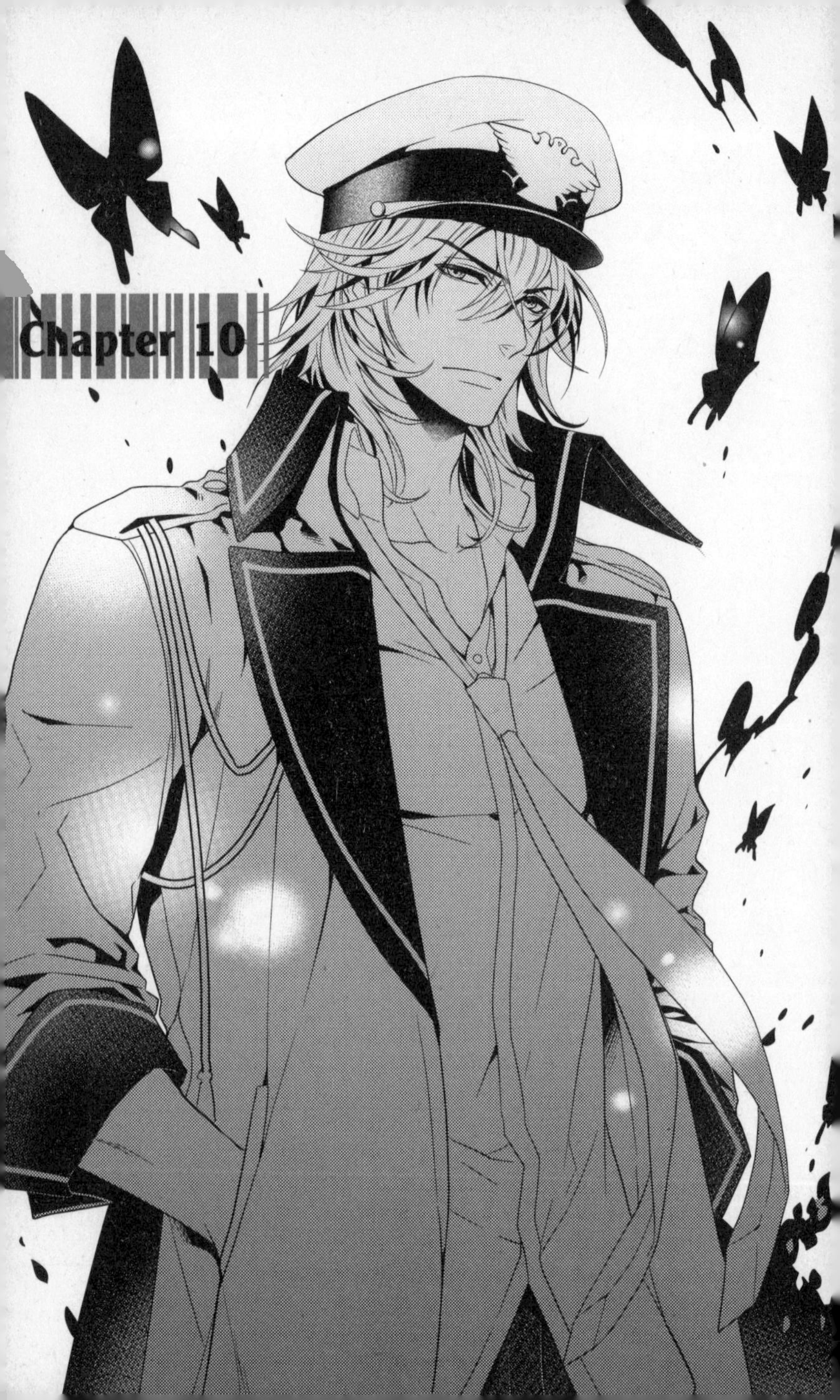
Chapter 10

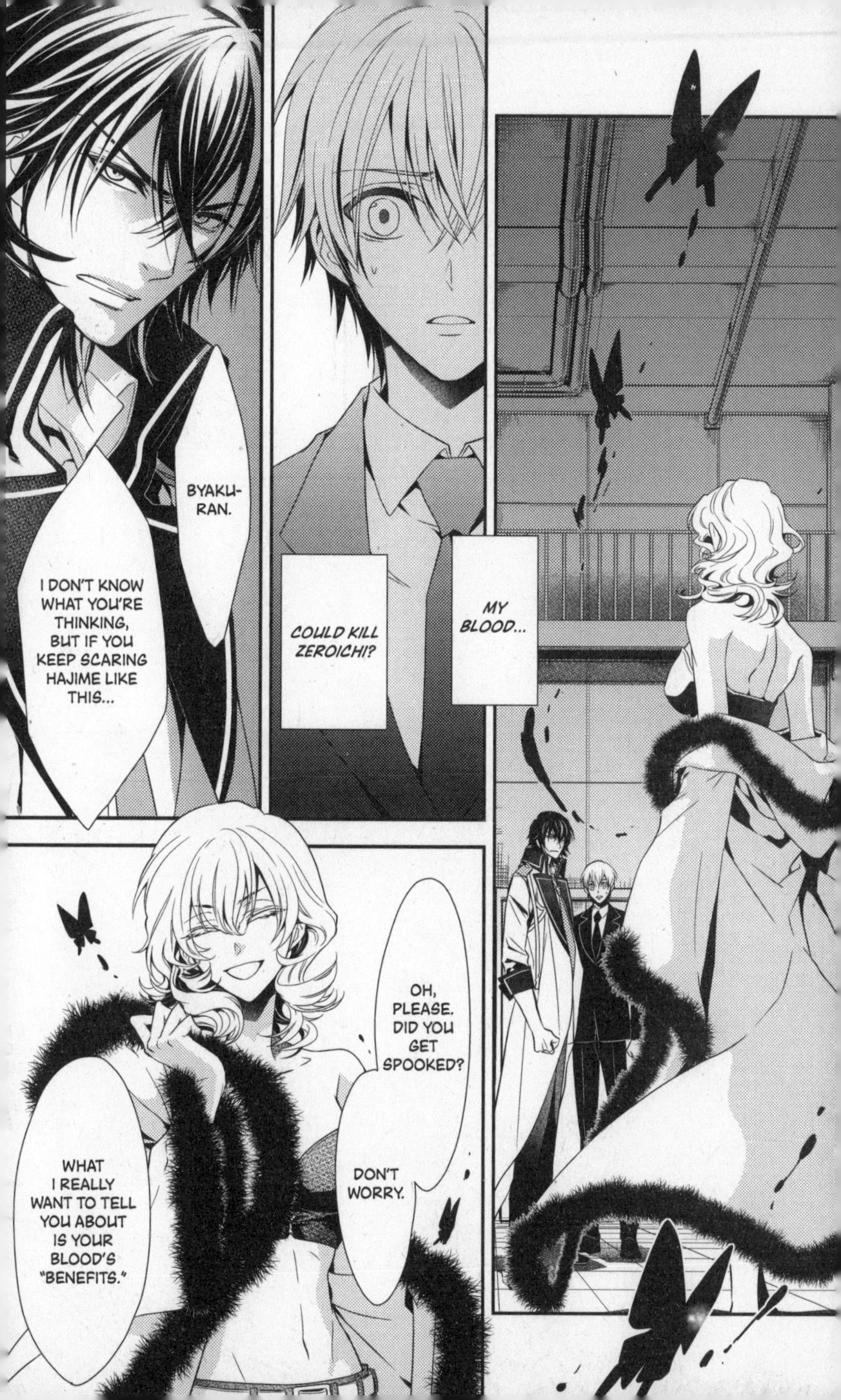
MY BLOOD...
COULD KILL ZEROICHI?
BYAKU-RAN.
I DON'T KNOW WHAT YOU'RE THINKING, BUT IF YOU KEEP SCARING HAJIME LIKE THIS...
OH, PLEASE. DID YOU GET SPOOKED?
DON'T WORRY.
WHAT I REALLY WANT TO TELL YOU ABOUT IS YOUR BLOOD'S "BENEFITS."

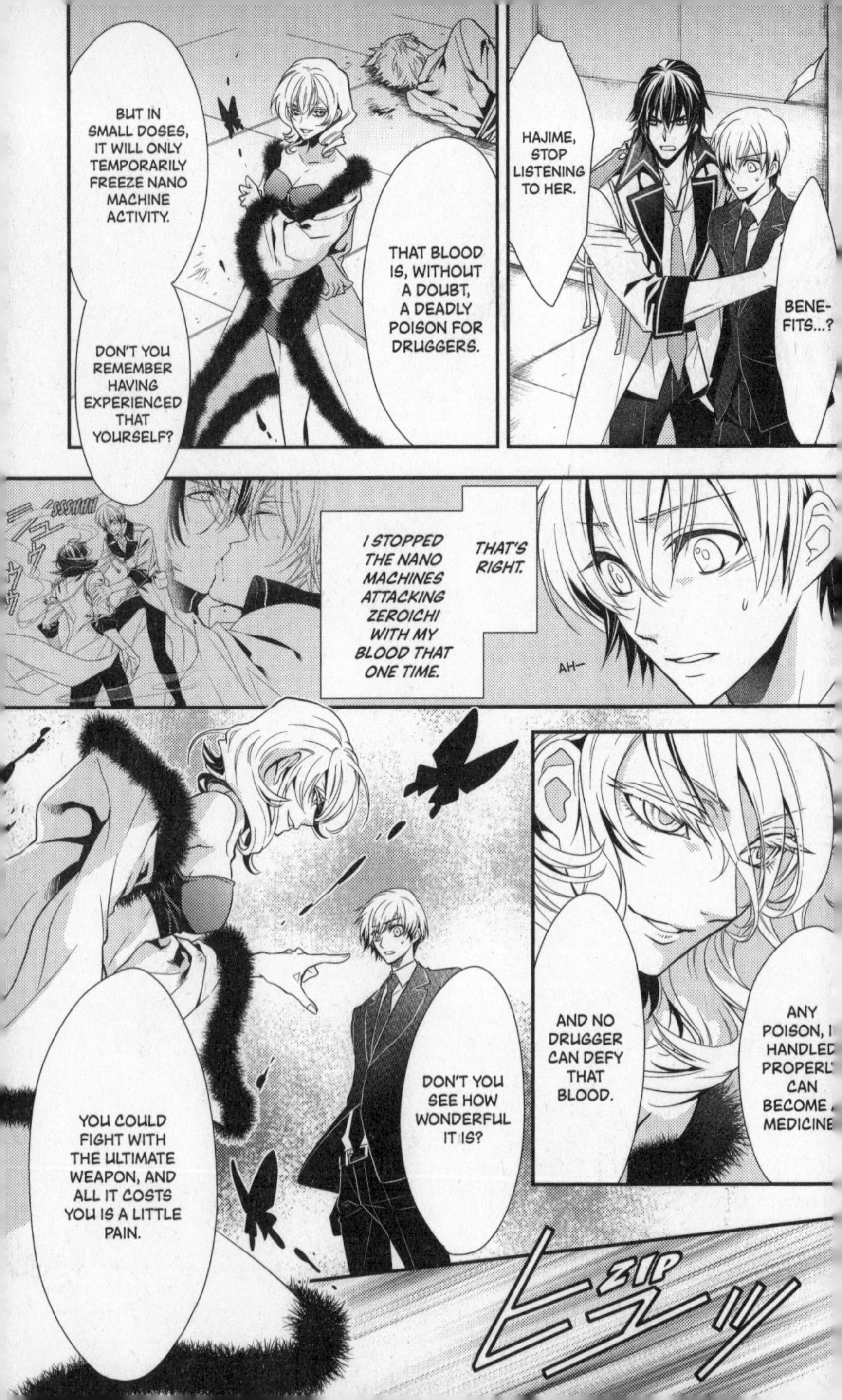
BENE-FITS...?
HAJIME, STOP LISTENING TO HER.
THAT BLOOD IS, WITHOUT A DOUBT, A DEADLY POISON FOR DRUGGERS.
BUT IN SMALL DOSES, IT WILL ONLY TEMPORARILY FREEZE NANO MACHINE ACTIVITY.
DON'T YOU REMEMBER HAVING EXPERIENCED THAT YOURSELF?
AH—
THAT'S RIGHT.
I STOPPED THE NANO MACHINES ATTACKING ZEROICHI WITH MY BLOOD THAT ONE TIME.
SSSHHH
ANY POISON, I HANDLED PROPERL CAN BECOME MEDICINE
AND NO DRUGGER CAN DEFY THAT BLOOD.
DON'T YOU SEE HOW WONDERFUL IT IS?
YOU COULD FIGHT WITH THE ULTIMATE WEAPON, AND ALL IT COSTS YOU IS A LITTLE PAIN.
ZIP

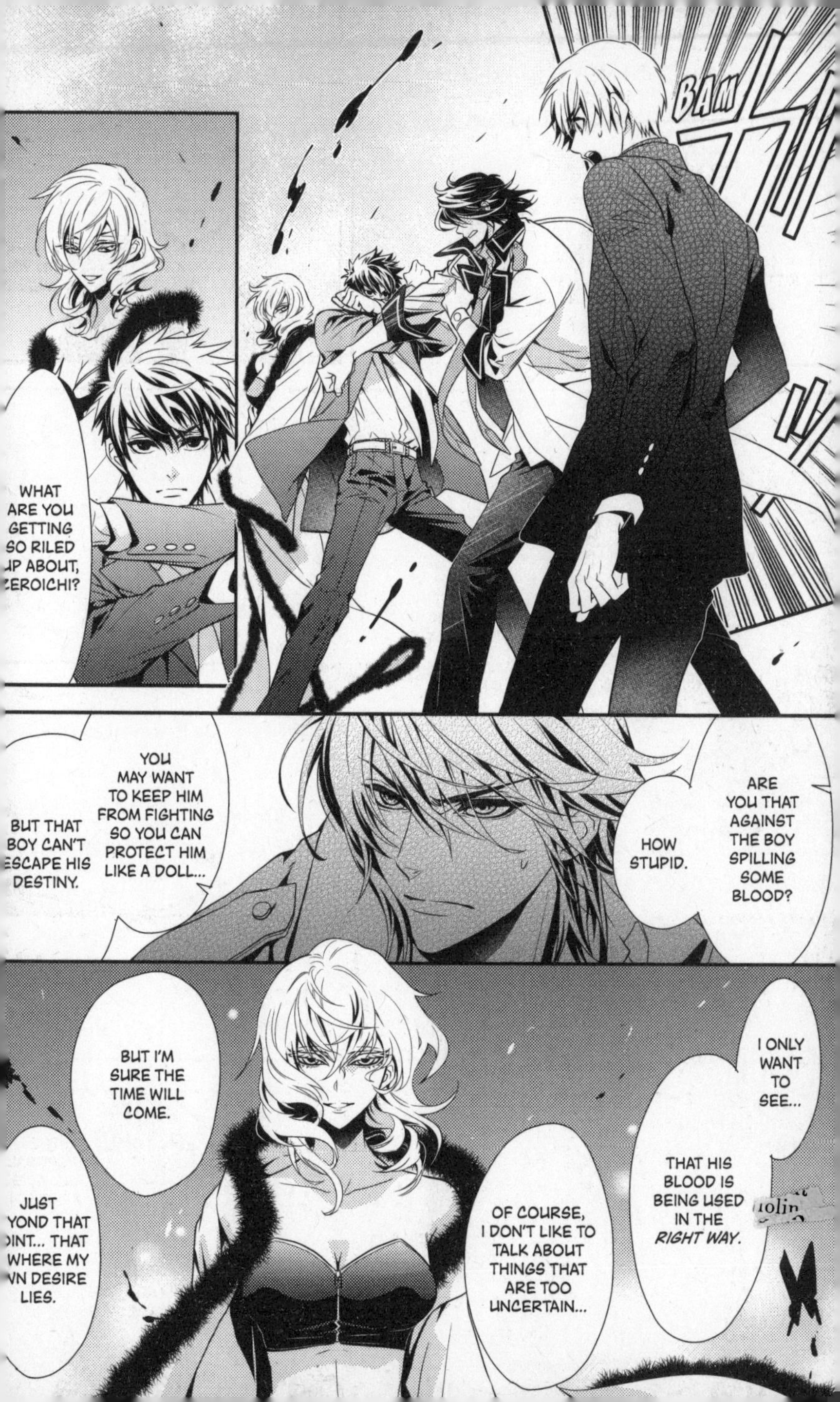
BAM
WHAT ARE YOU GETTING SO RILED UP ABOUT, ZEROICHI?
ARE YOU THAT AGAINST THE BOY SPILLING SOME BLOOD?
HOW STUPID.
YOU MAY WANT TO KEEP HIM FROM FIGHTING SO YOU CAN PROTECT HIM LIKE A DOLL...
BUT THAT BOY CAN'T ESCAPE HIS DESTINY.
I ONLY WANT TO SEE...
THAT HIS BLOOD IS BEING USED IN THE *RIGHT WAY*.
OF COURSE, I DON'T LIKE TO TALK ABOUT THINGS THAT ARE TOO UNCERTAIN...
BUT I'M SURE THE TIME WILL COME.
JUST YOND THAT OINT... THAT WHERE MY VN DESIRE LIES.

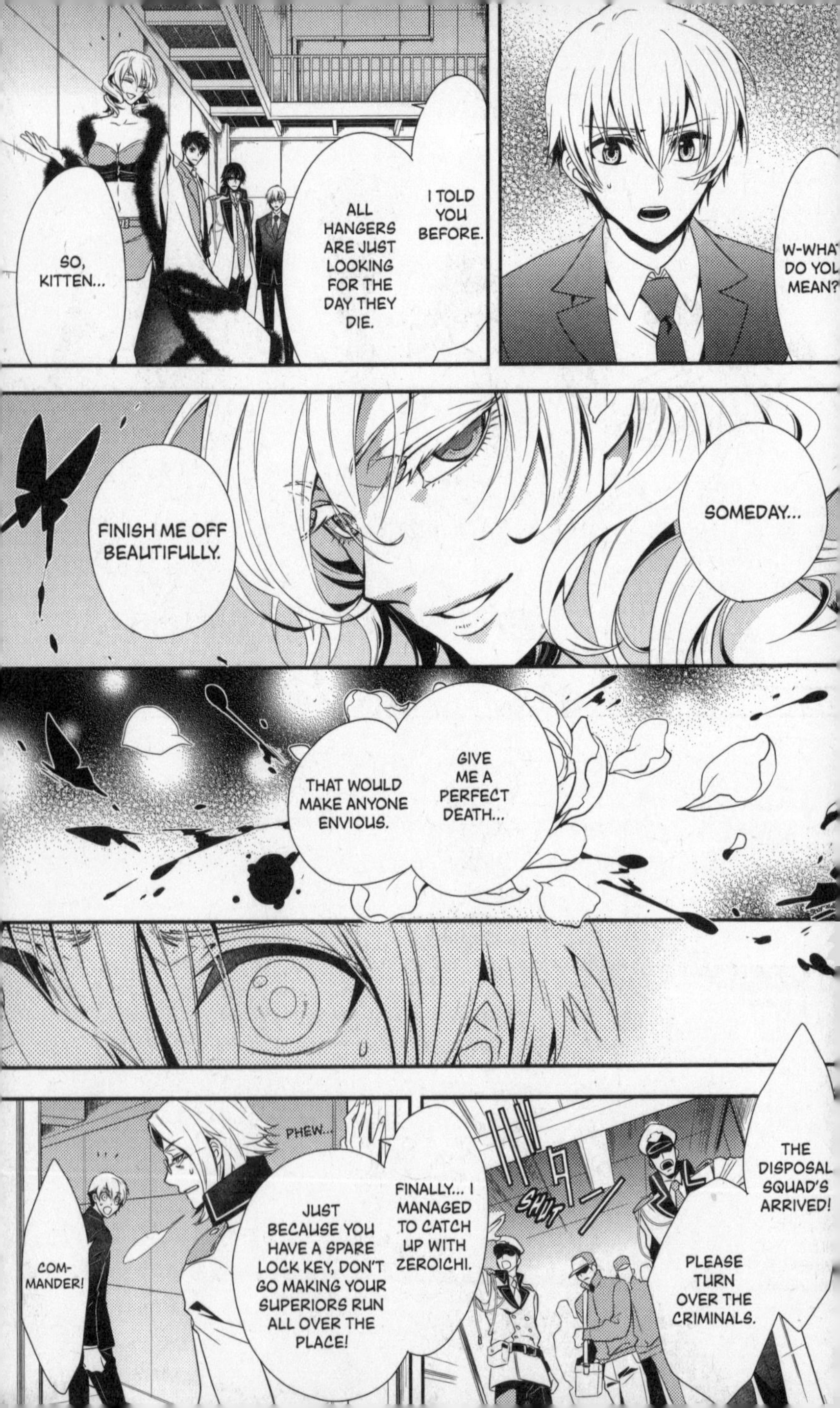
W-WHAT DO YOU MEAN?
I TOLD YOU BEFORE.
ALL HANGERS ARE JUST LOOKING FOR THE DAY THEY DIE.
SO, KITTEN...
SOMEDAY...
FINISH ME OFF BEAUTIFULLY.
GIVE ME A PERFECT DEATH...
THAT WOULD MAKE ANYONE ENVIOUS.
THE DISPOSAL SQUAD'S ARRIVED!
PLEASE TURN OVER THE CRIMINALS.
SHUT
FINALLY... I MANAGED TO CATCH UP WITH ZEROICHI.
PHEW...
JUST BECAUSE YOU HAVE A SPARE LOCK KEY, DON'T GO MAKING YOUR SUPERIORS RUN ALL OVER THE PLACE!
COM-MANDER!

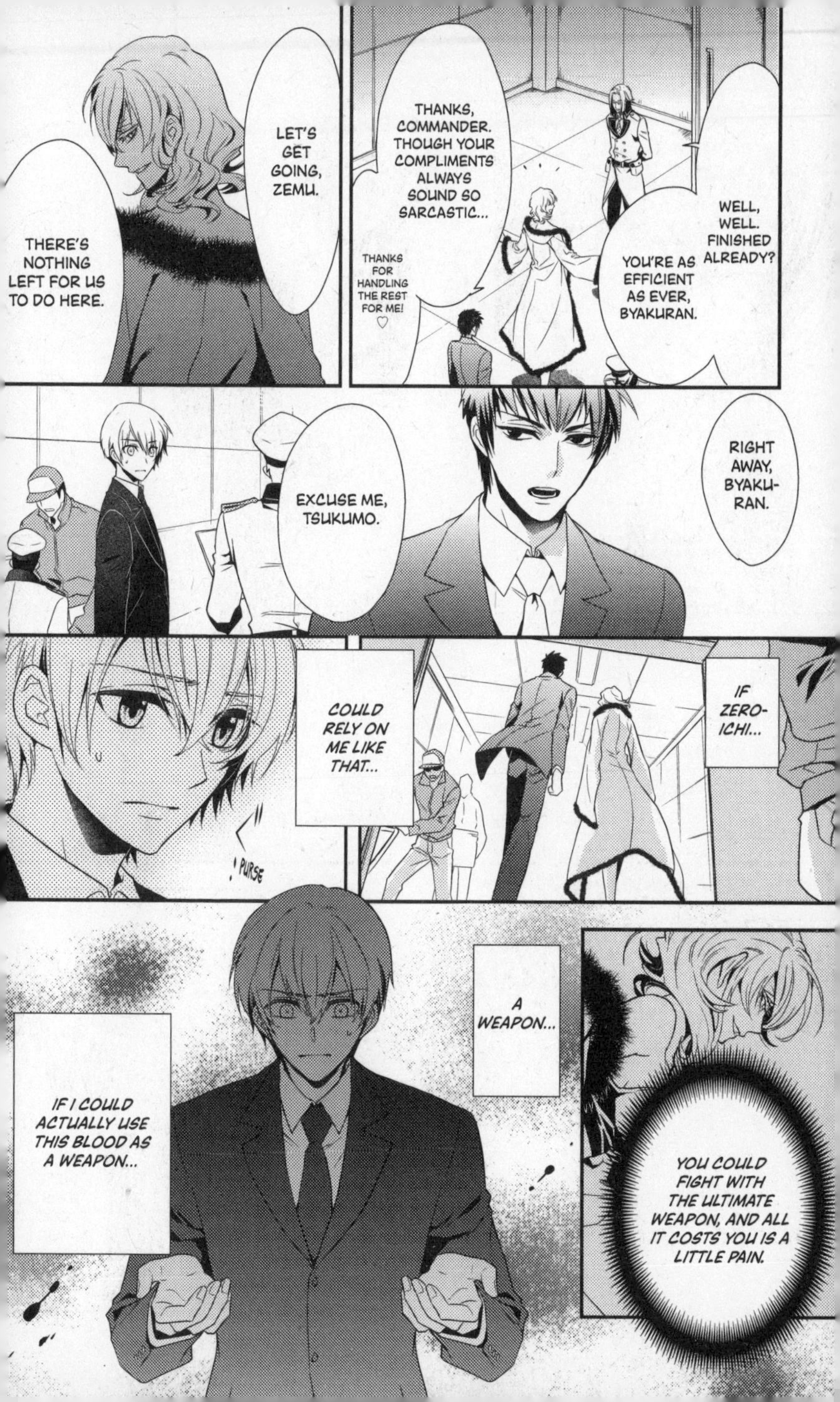
WELL, WELL. FINISHED ALREADY?
YOU'RE AS EFFICIENT AS EVER, BYAKURAN.
THANKS, COMMANDER. THOUGH YOUR COMPLIMENTS ALWAYS SOUND SO SARCASTIC...
THANKS FOR HANDLING THE REST FOR ME! ♡
LET'S GET GOING, ZEMU.
THERE'S NOTHING LEFT FOR US TO DO HERE.
RIGHT AWAY, BYAKURAN.
EXCUSE ME, TSUKUMO.
IF ZERO-ICHI...
COULD RELY ON ME LIKE THAT...
PURSE
YOU COULD FIGHT WITH THE ULTIMATE WEAPON, AND ALL IT COSTS YOU IS A LITTLE PAIN.
A WEAPON...
IF I COULD ACTUALLY USE THIS BLOOD AS A WEAPON...

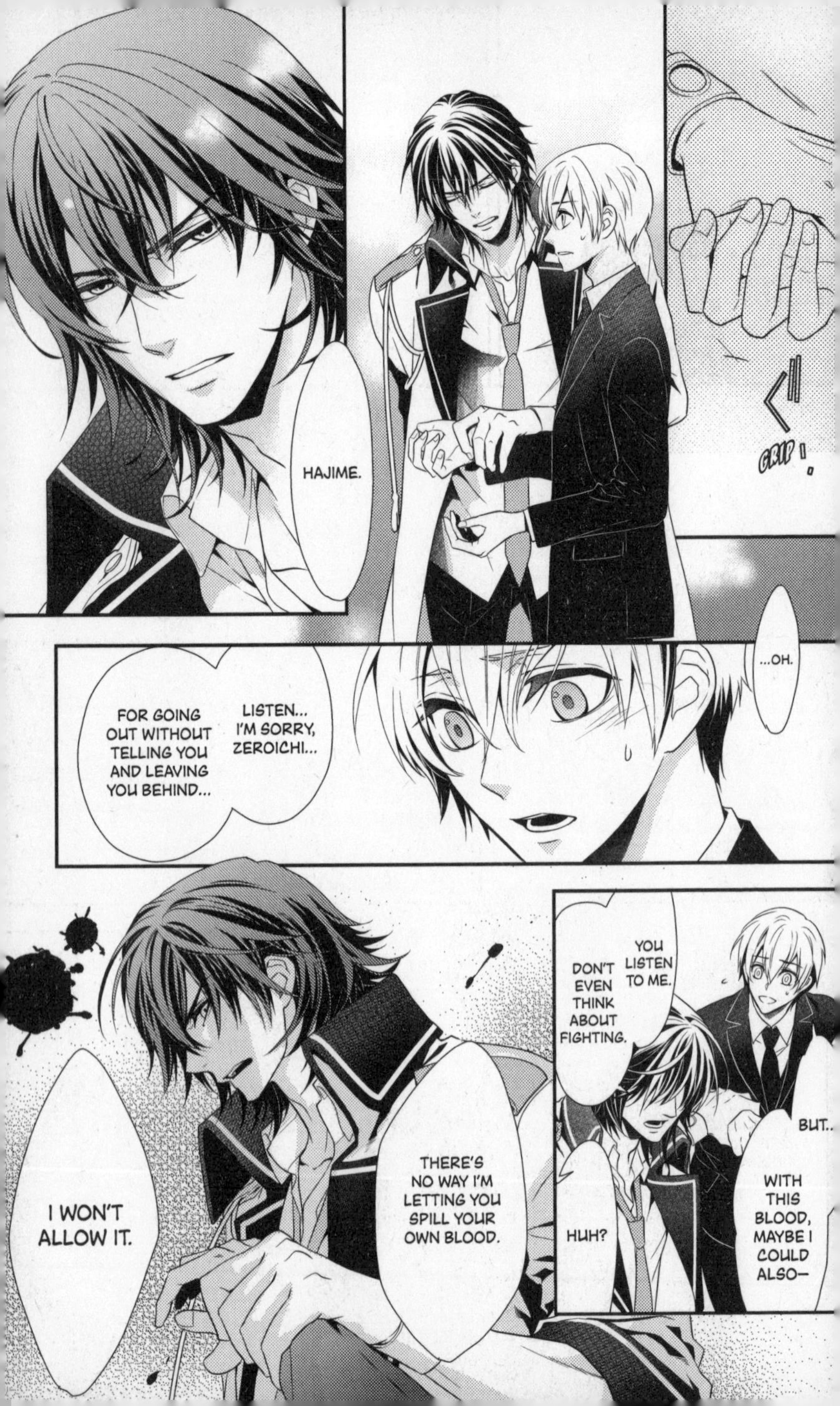
GRIP!
HAJIME.
...OH.
LISTEN... I'M SORRY, ZEROICHI...
FOR GOING OUT WITHOUT TELLING YOU AND LEAVING YOU BEHIND...
BUT..
WITH THIS BLOOD, MAYBE I COULD ALSO—
HUH?
YOU LISTEN TO ME.
DON'T EVEN THINK ABOUT FIGHTING.
THERE'S NO WAY I'M LETTING YOU SPILL YOUR OWN BLOOD.
I WON'T ALLOW IT.

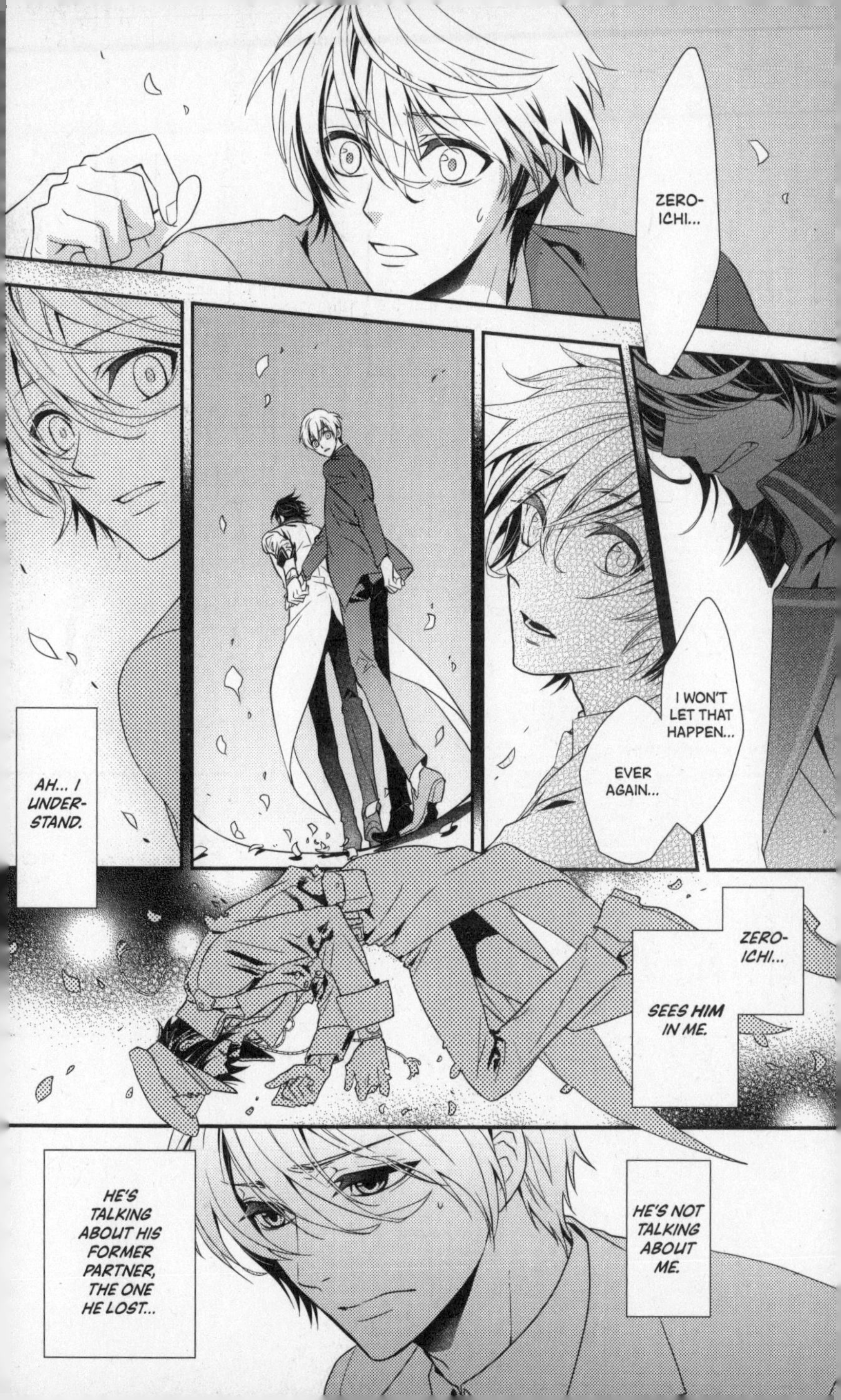
ZERO-ICHI...
I WON'T LET THAT HAPPEN...
EVER AGAIN...
AH... I UNDERSTAND.
ZERO-ICHI...
SEES HIM IN ME.
HE'S NOT TALKING ABOUT ME.
HE'S TALKING ABOUT HIS FORMER PARTNER, THE ONE HE LOST...

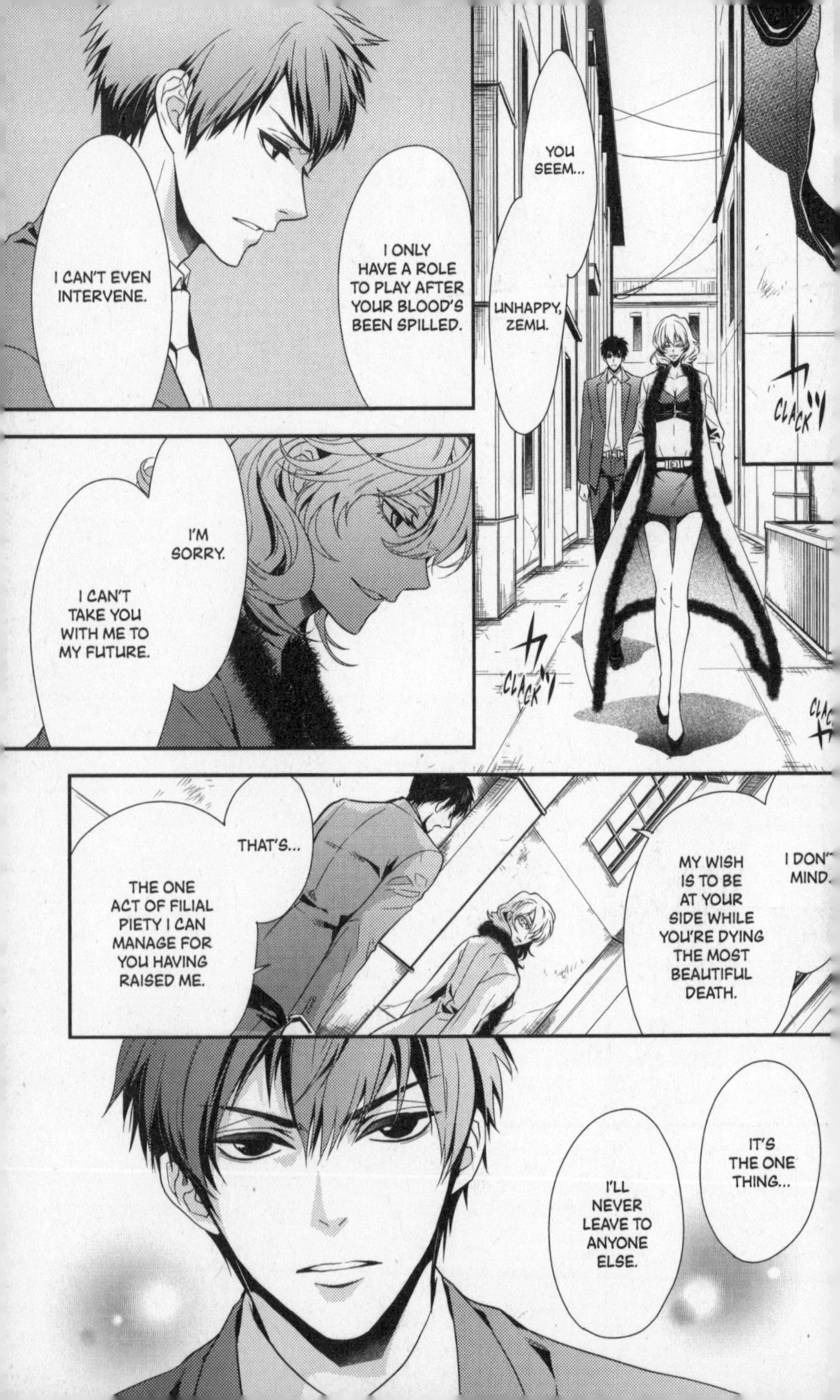

YOU SEEM...
UNHAPPY, ZEMU.
CLACK
CLACK
CLAC
I ONLY HAVE A ROLE TO PLAY AFTER YOUR BLOOD'S BEEN SPILLED.
I CAN'T EVEN INTERVENE.
I'M SORRY.
I CAN'T TAKE YOU WITH ME TO MY FUTURE.
I DON' MIND.
MY WISH IS TO BE AT YOUR SIDE WHILE YOU'RE DYING THE MOST BEAUTIFUL DEATH.
THAT'S...
THE ONE ACT OF FILIAL PIETY I CAN MANAGE FOR YOU HAVING RAISED ME.
IT'S THE ONE THING...
I'LL NEVER LEAVE TO ANYONE ELSE.

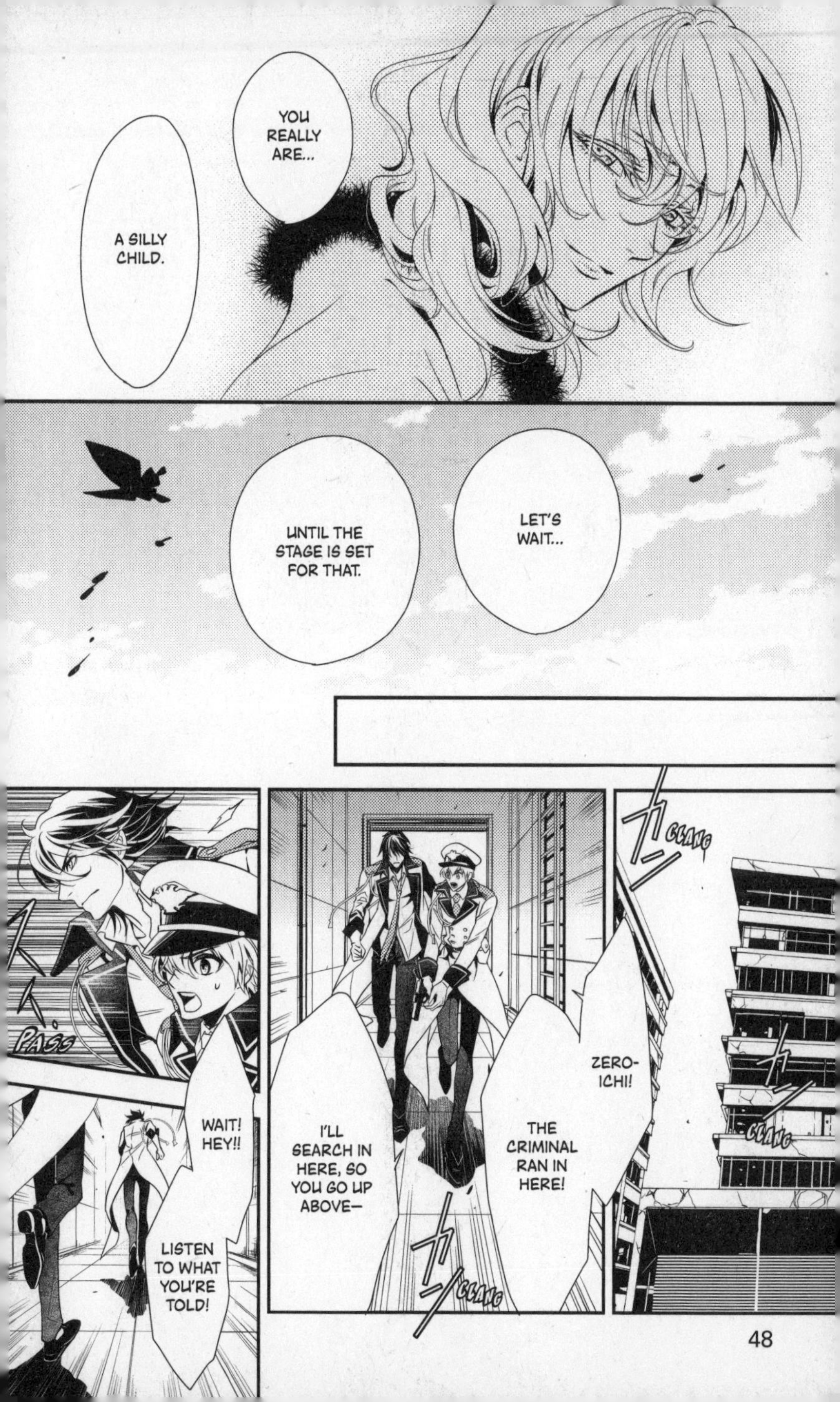
YOU REALLY ARE...
A SILLY CHILD.
LET'S WAIT...
UNTIL THE STAGE IS SET FOR THAT.
CLANG
CLANG
ZERO-ICHI!
THE CRIMINAL RAN IN HERE!
I'LL SEARCH IN HERE, SO YOU GO UP ABOVE—
CLANG
PASS
WAIT! HEY!!
LISTEN TO WHAT YOU'RE TOLD!

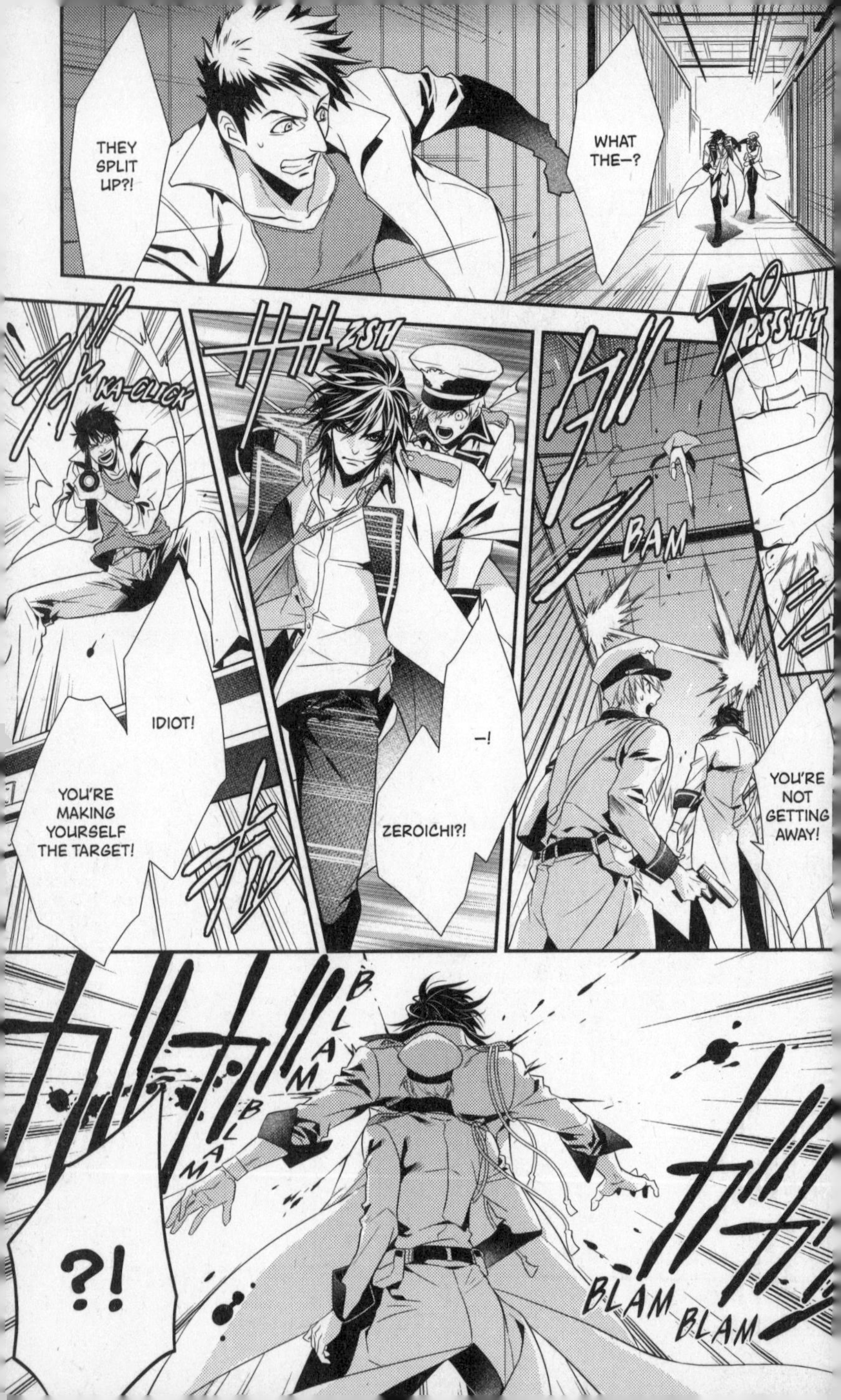
WHAT THE—?
THEY SPLIT UP?!
PSSHT
BAM
YOU'RE NOT GETTING AWAY!
ZSH
—!
ZEROICHI?!
KA-CLICK
IDIOT!
YOU'RE MAKING YOURSELF THE TARGET!
BLAM
BLAM
BLAM
BLAM
?!

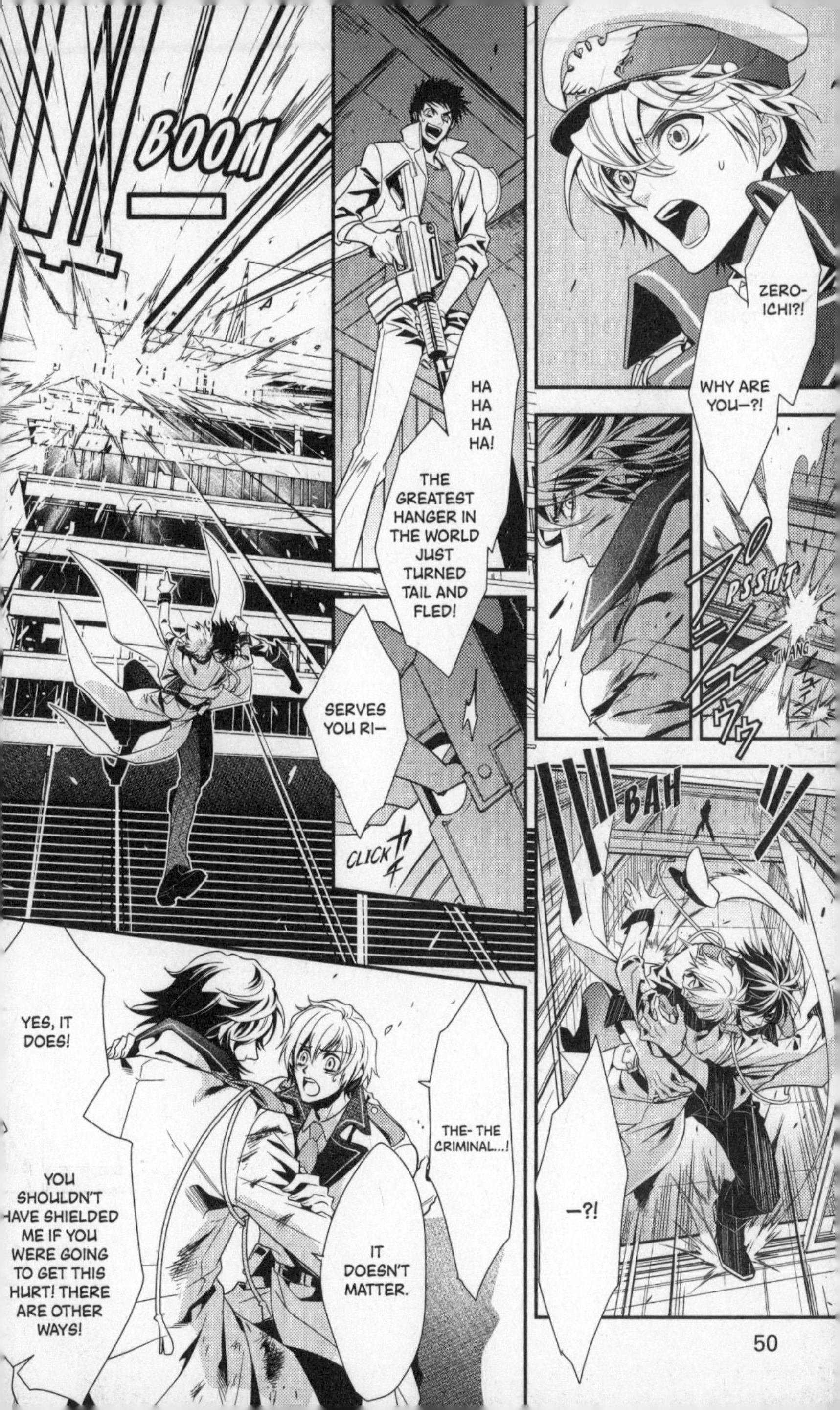
ZERO-ICHI?!
WHY ARE YOU—?!
HA HA HA HA!
THE GREATEST HANGER IN THE WORLD JUST TURNED TAIL AND FLED!
PSSHT
TWANG
SERVES YOU RI—
CLICK
BOOM
BAH
—?!
THE- THE CRIMINAL...!
IT DOESN'T MATTER.
YES, IT DOES!
YOU SHOULDN'T HAVE SHIELDED ME IF YOU WERE GOING TO GET THIS HURT! THERE ARE OTHER WAYS!

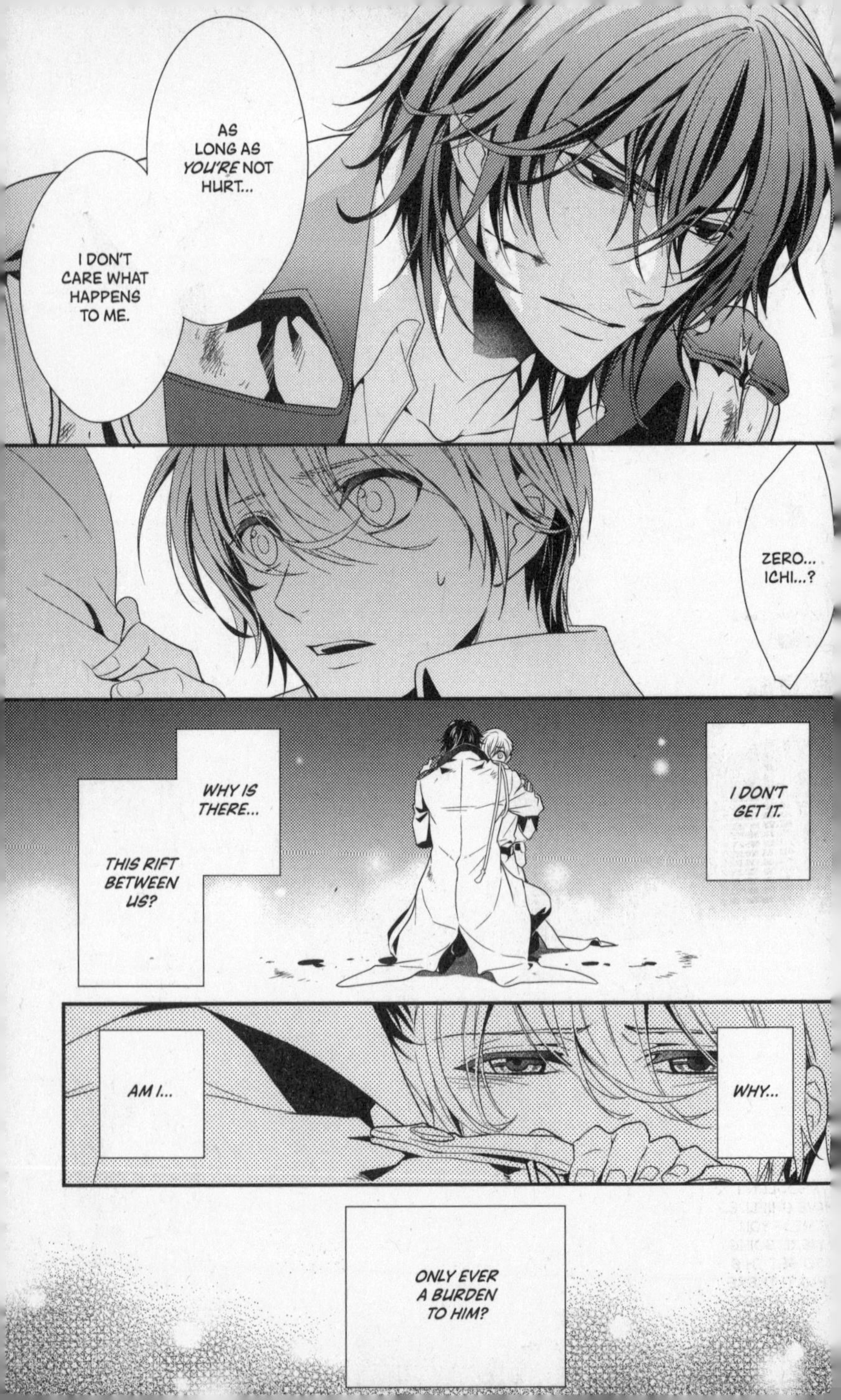
AS LONG AS YOU'RE NOT HURT...
I DON'T CARE WHAT HAPPENS TO ME.
ZERO... ICHI...?
I DON'T GET IT.
WHY IS THERE...
THIS RIFT BETWEEN US?
WHY...
AM I...
ONLY EVER A BURDEN TO HIM?

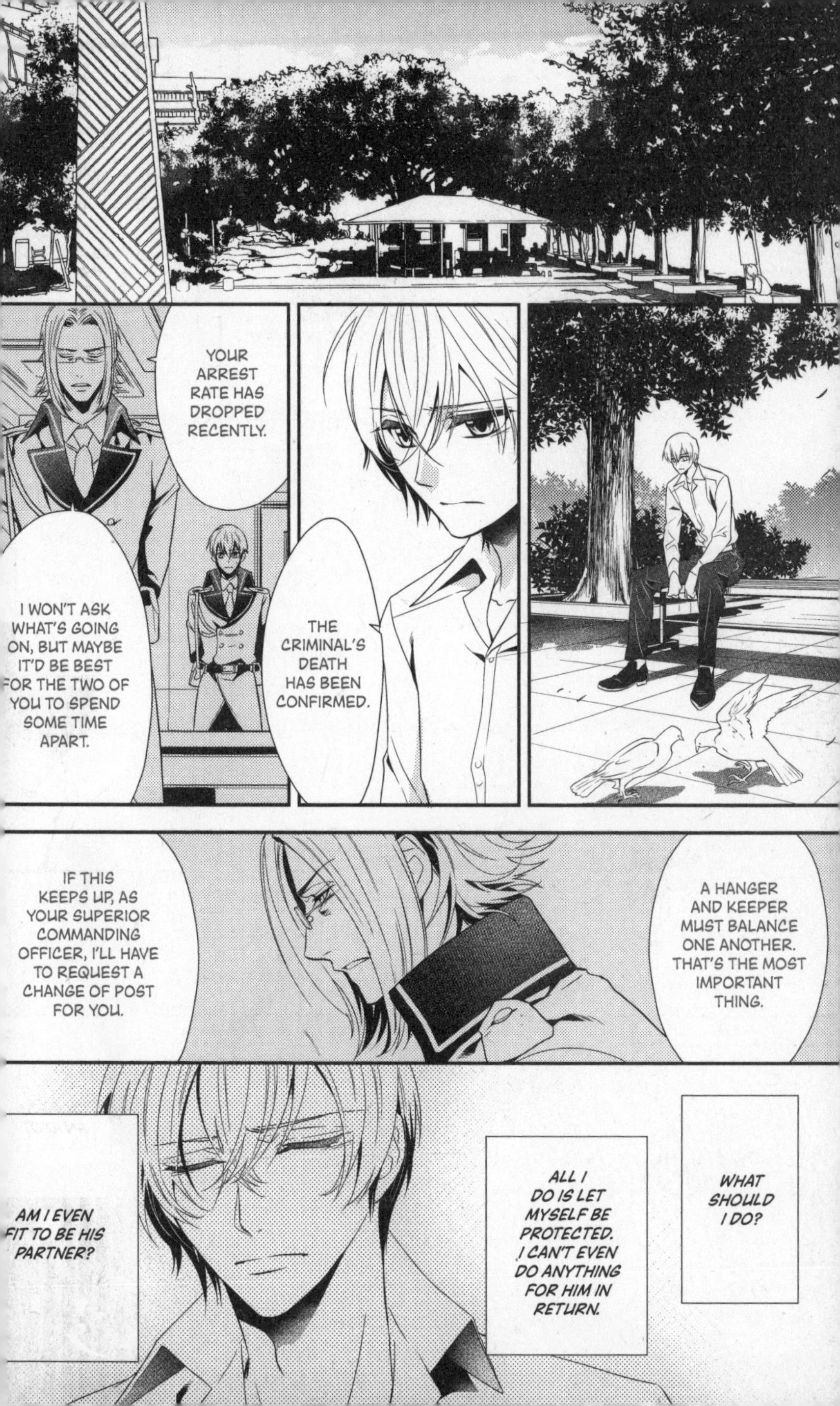
THE CRIMINAL'S DEATH HAS BEEN CONFIRMED.
YOUR ARREST RATE HAS DROPPED RECENTLY.
I WON'T ASK WHAT'S GOING ON, BUT MAYBE IT'D BE BEST FOR THE TWO OF YOU TO SPEND SOME TIME APART.
A HANGER AND KEEPER MUST BALANCE ONE ANOTHER. THAT'S THE MOST IMPORTANT THING.
IF THIS KEEPS UP, AS YOUR SUPERIOR COMMANDING OFFICER, I'LL HAVE TO REQUEST A CHANGE OF POST FOR YOU.
WHAT SHOULD I DO?
ALL I DO IS LET MYSELF BE PROTECTED. I CAN'T EVEN DO ANYTHING FOR HIM IN RETURN.
AM I EVEN FIT TO BE HIS PARTNER?

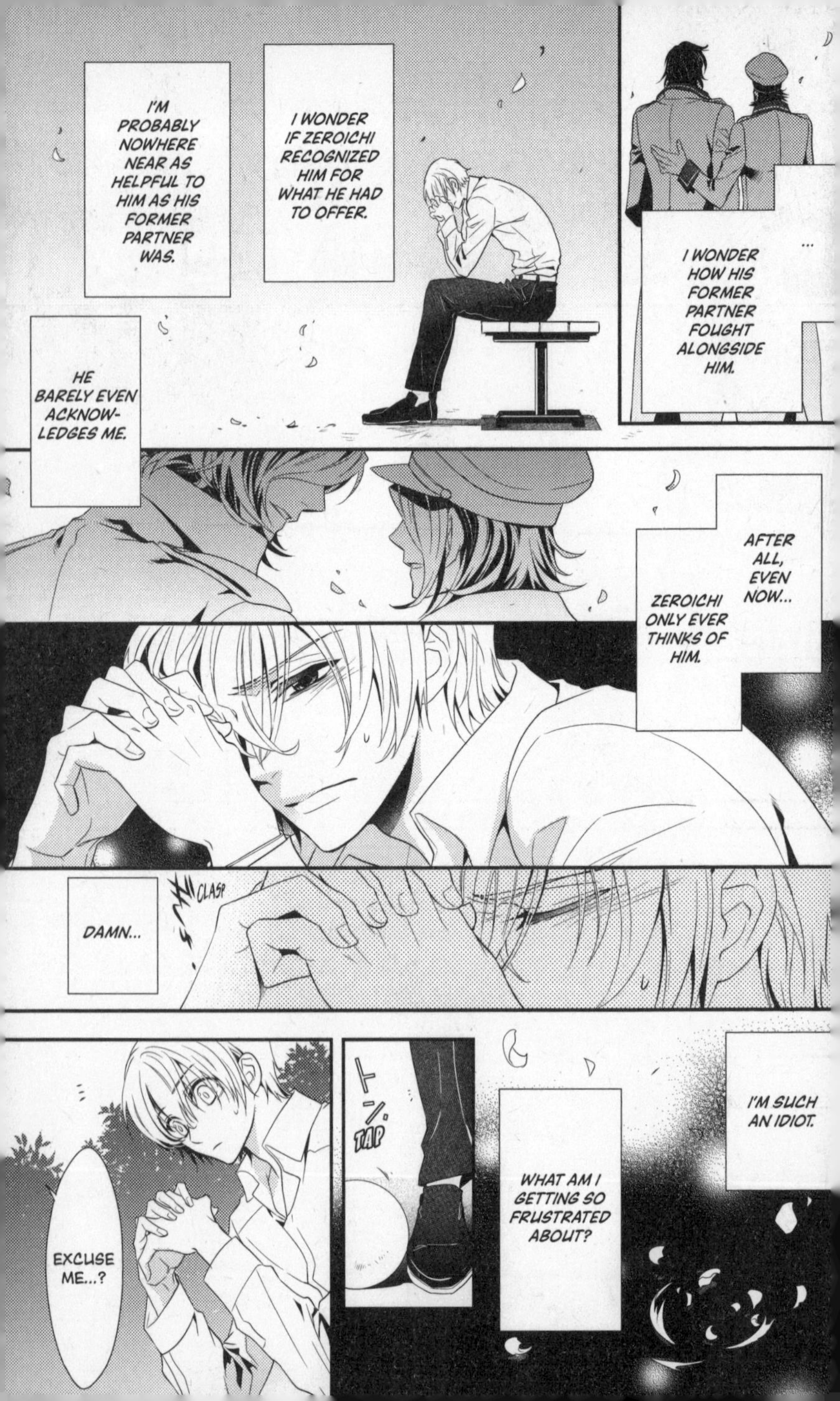
...
I WONDER HOW HIS FORMER PARTNER FOUGHT ALONGSIDE HIM.
I WONDER IF ZEROICHI RECOGNIZED HIM FOR WHAT HE HAD TO OFFER.
I'M PROBABLY NOWHERE NEAR AS HELPFUL TO HIM AS HIS FORMER PARTNER WAS.
HE BARELY EVEN ACKNOW-LEDGES ME.
AFTER ALL, EVEN NOW...
ZEROICHI ONLY EVER THINKS OF HIM.
CLASP
DAMN...
I'M SUCH AN IDIOT.
WHAT AM I GETTING SO FRUSTRATED ABOUT?
TAP
EXCUSE ME...?

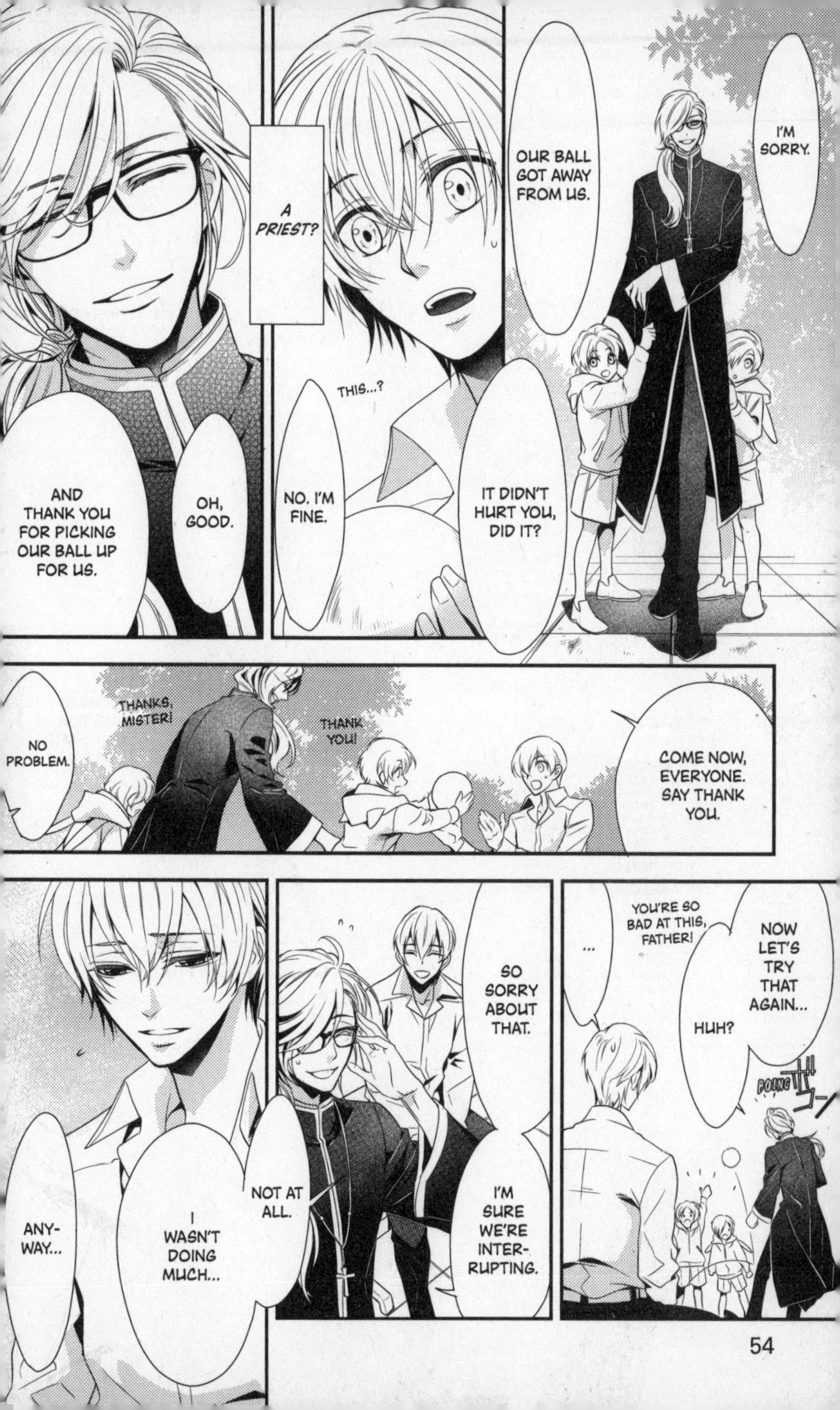
I'M SORRY.
OUR BALL GOT AWAY FROM US.
A PRIEST?
THIS...?
IT DIDN'T HURT YOU, DID IT?
NO. I'M FINE.
OH, GOOD.
AND THANK YOU FOR PICKING OUR BALL UP FOR US.
COME NOW, EVERYONE. SAY THANK YOU.
THANK YOU!
THANKS, MISTER!
NO PROBLEM.
NOW LET'S TRY THAT AGAIN...
YOU'RE SO BAD AT THIS, FATHER!
HUH?
DOING
...
SO SORRY ABOUT THAT.
I'M SURE WE'RE INTER-RUPTING.
NOT AT ALL.
I WASN'T DOING MUCH...
ANY-WAY...

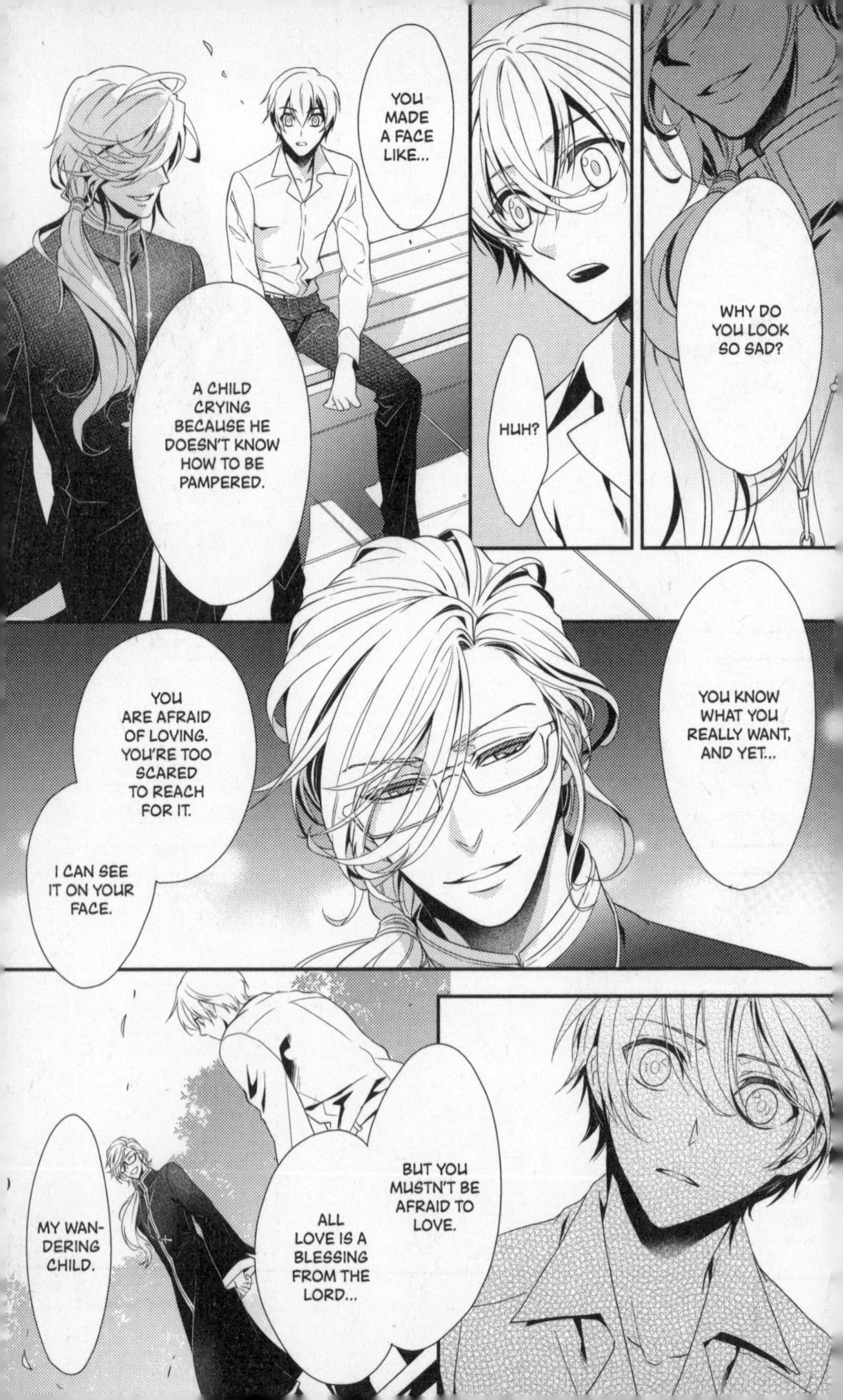
WHY DO YOU LOOK SO SAD?
HUH?
YOU MADE A FACE LIKE...
A CHILD CRYING BECAUSE HE DOESN'T KNOW HOW TO BE PAMPERED.
YOU KNOW WHAT YOU REALLY WANT, AND YET...
YOU ARE AFRAID OF LOVING. YOU'RE TOO SCARED TO REACH FOR IT.
I CAN SEE IT ON YOUR FACE.
BUT YOU MUSTN'T BE AFRAID TO LOVE.
ALL LOVE IS A BLESSING FROM THE LORD...
MY WAN-DERING CHILD.

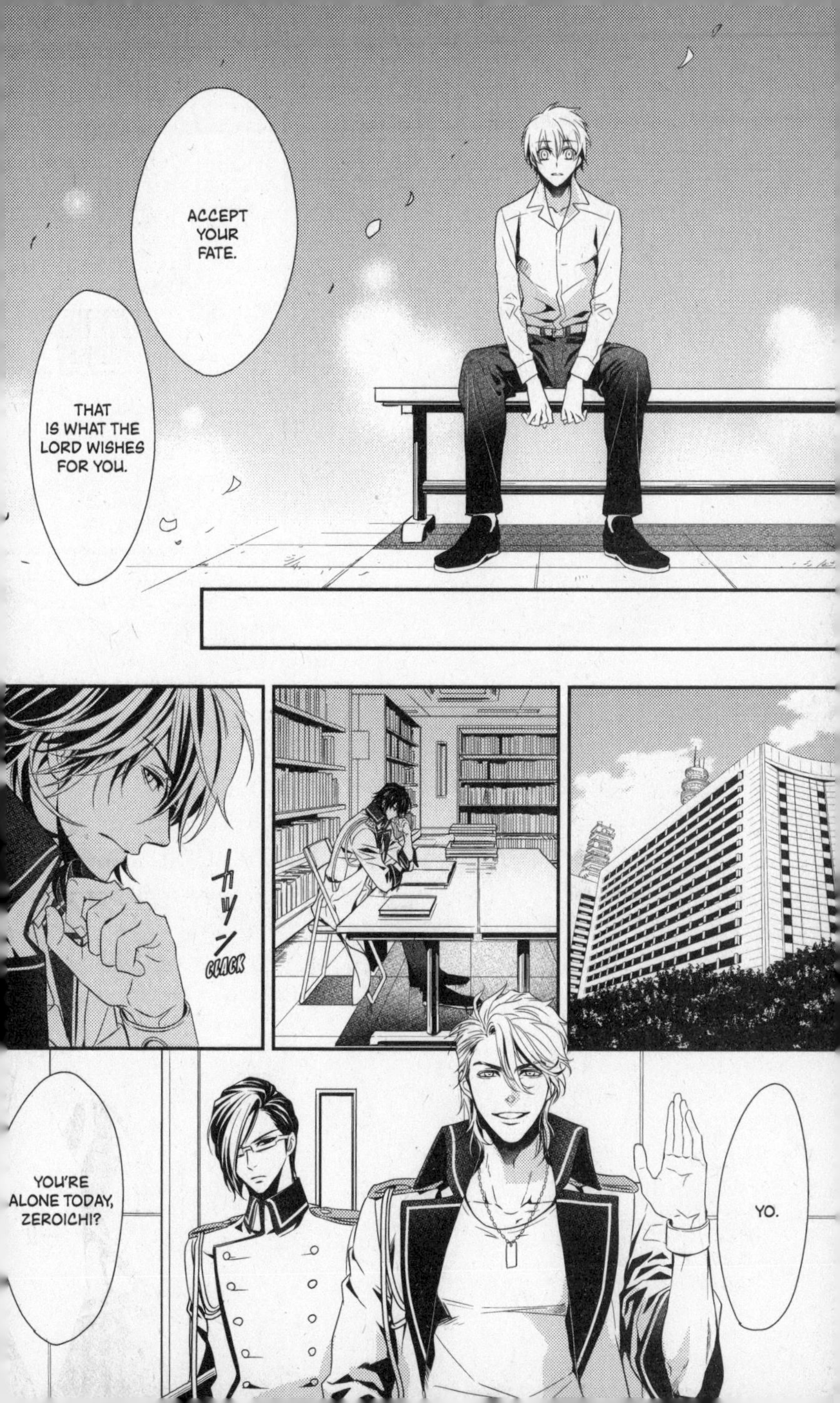
ACCEPT YOUR FATE.
THAT IS WHAT THE LORD WISHES FOR YOU.
カッン
CLACK
YO.
YOU'RE ALONE TODAY, ZEROICHI?

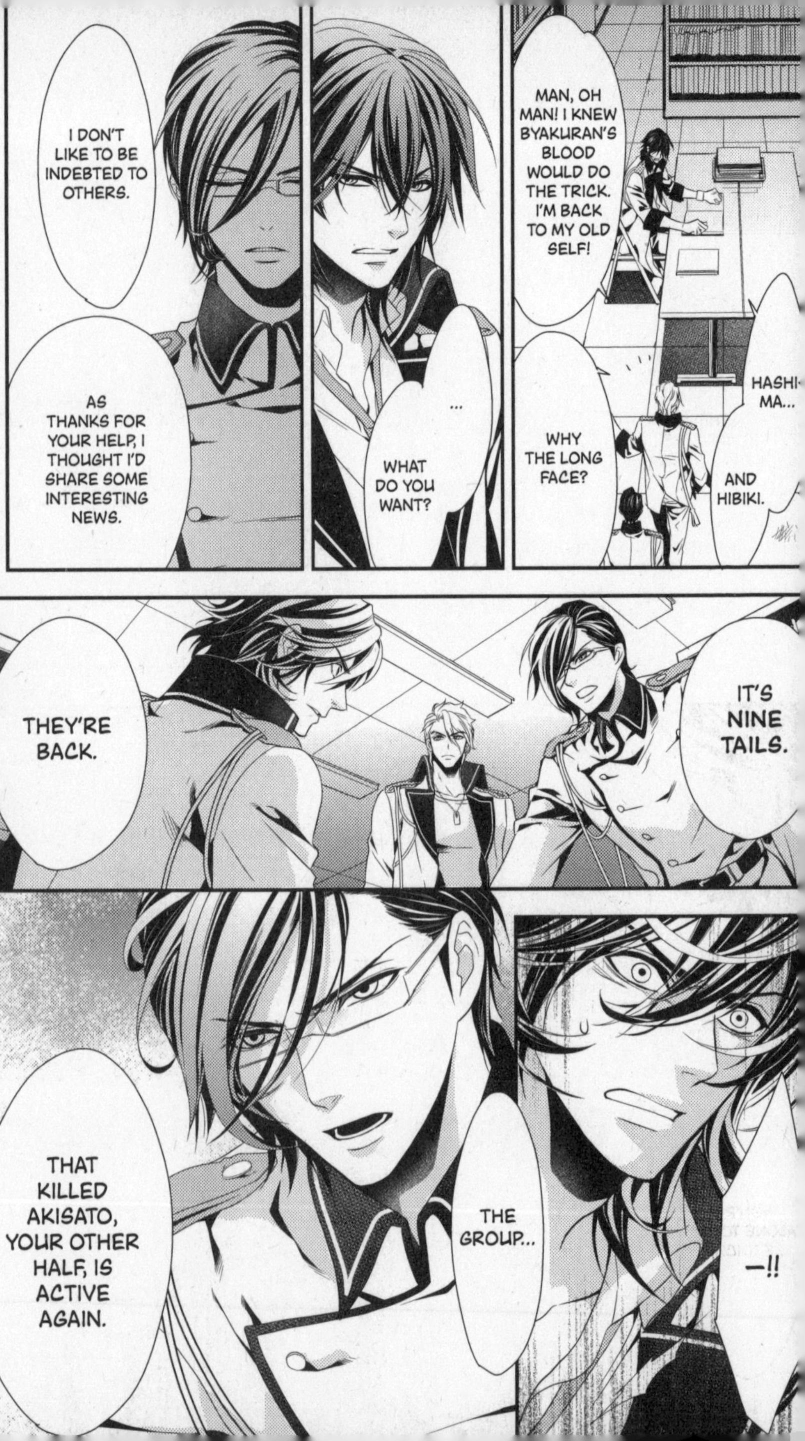
MAN, OH MAN! I KNEW BYAKURAN'S BLOOD WOULD DO THE TRICK. I'M BACK TO MY OLD SELF!
HASHI-MA...
AND HIBIKI.
WHY THE LONG FACE?
...
WHAT DO YOU WANT?
I DON'T LIKE TO BE INDEBTED TO OTHERS.
AS THANKS FOR YOUR HELP, I THOUGHT I'D SHARE SOME INTERESTING NEWS.
IT'S NINE TAILS.
THEY'RE BACK.
—!!
THE GROUP...
THAT KILLED AKISATO, YOUR OTHER HALF, IS ACTIVE AGAIN.

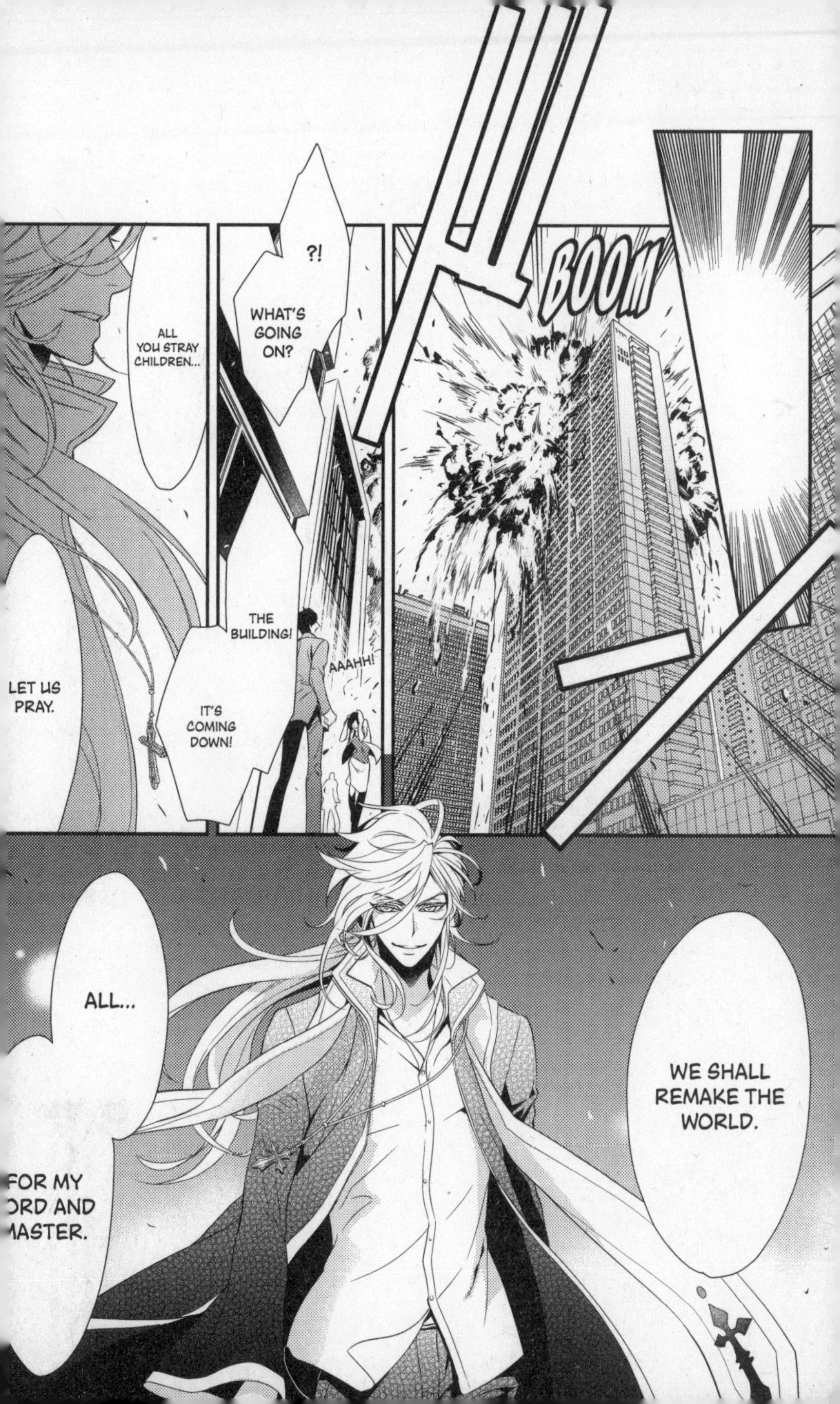
BOOM
?!
WHAT'S GOING ON?
AAAHH!
THE BUILDING!
IT'S COMING DOWN!
ALL YOU STRAY CHILDREN...
LET US PRAY.
WE SHALL REMAKE THE WORLD.
ALL...
FOR MY ORD AND MASTER.

Chapter 11

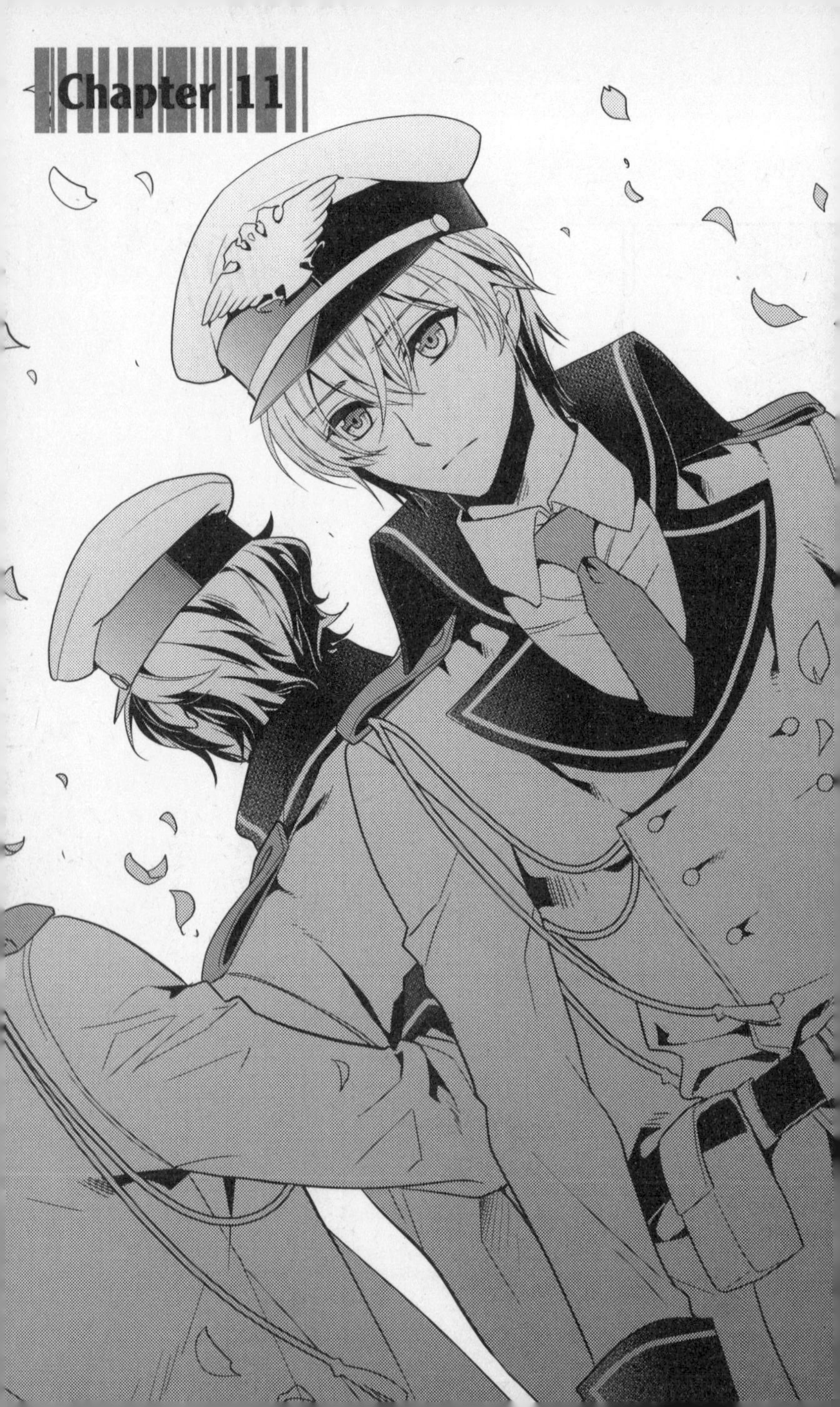

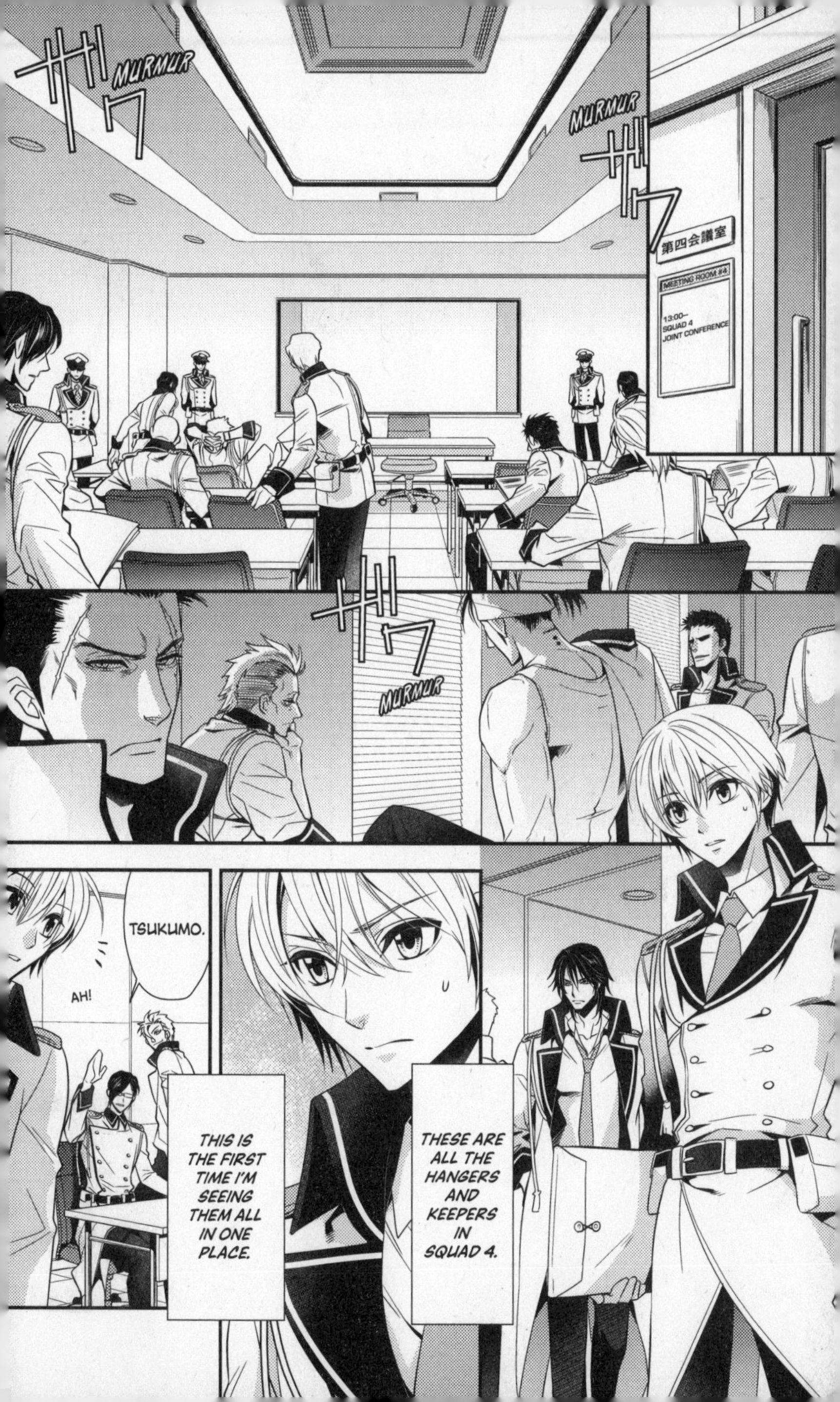
MURMUR
第四会議室
MEETING ROOM #4
13:00–
SQUAD 4
JOINT CONFERENCE
MURMUR
MURMUR
THESE ARE ALL THE HANGERS AND KEEPERS IN SQUAD 4.
THIS IS THE FIRST TIME I'M SEEING THEM ALL IN ONE PLACE.
TSUKUMO.
AH!

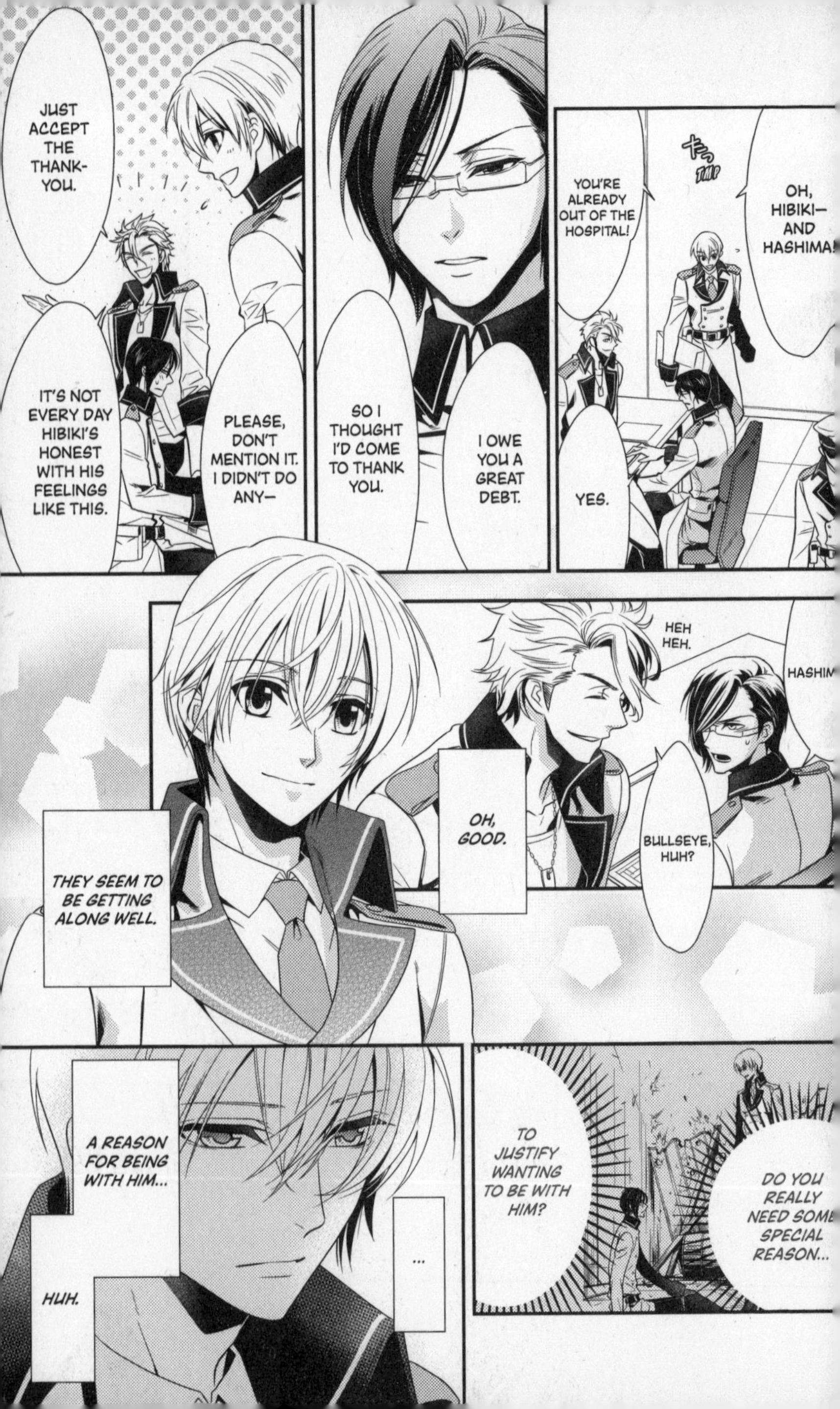
OH, HIBIKI— AND HASHIMA!
TMP
YOU'RE ALREADY OUT OF THE HOSPITAL!
YES.
I OWE YOU A GREAT DEBT.
SO I THOUGHT I'D COME TO THANK YOU.
PLEASE, DON'T MENTION IT. I DIDN'T DO ANY—
JUST ACCEPT THE THANK-YOU.
IT'S NOT EVERY DAY HIBIKI'S HONEST WITH HIS FEELINGS LIKE THIS.
HASHIM
HEH HEH.
BULLSEYE, HUH?
OH, GOOD.
THEY SEEM TO BE GETTING ALONG WELL.
DO YOU REALLY NEED SOME SPECIAL REASON...
TO JUSTIFY WANTING TO BE WITH HIM?
A REASON FOR BEING WITH HIM...
...
HUH.

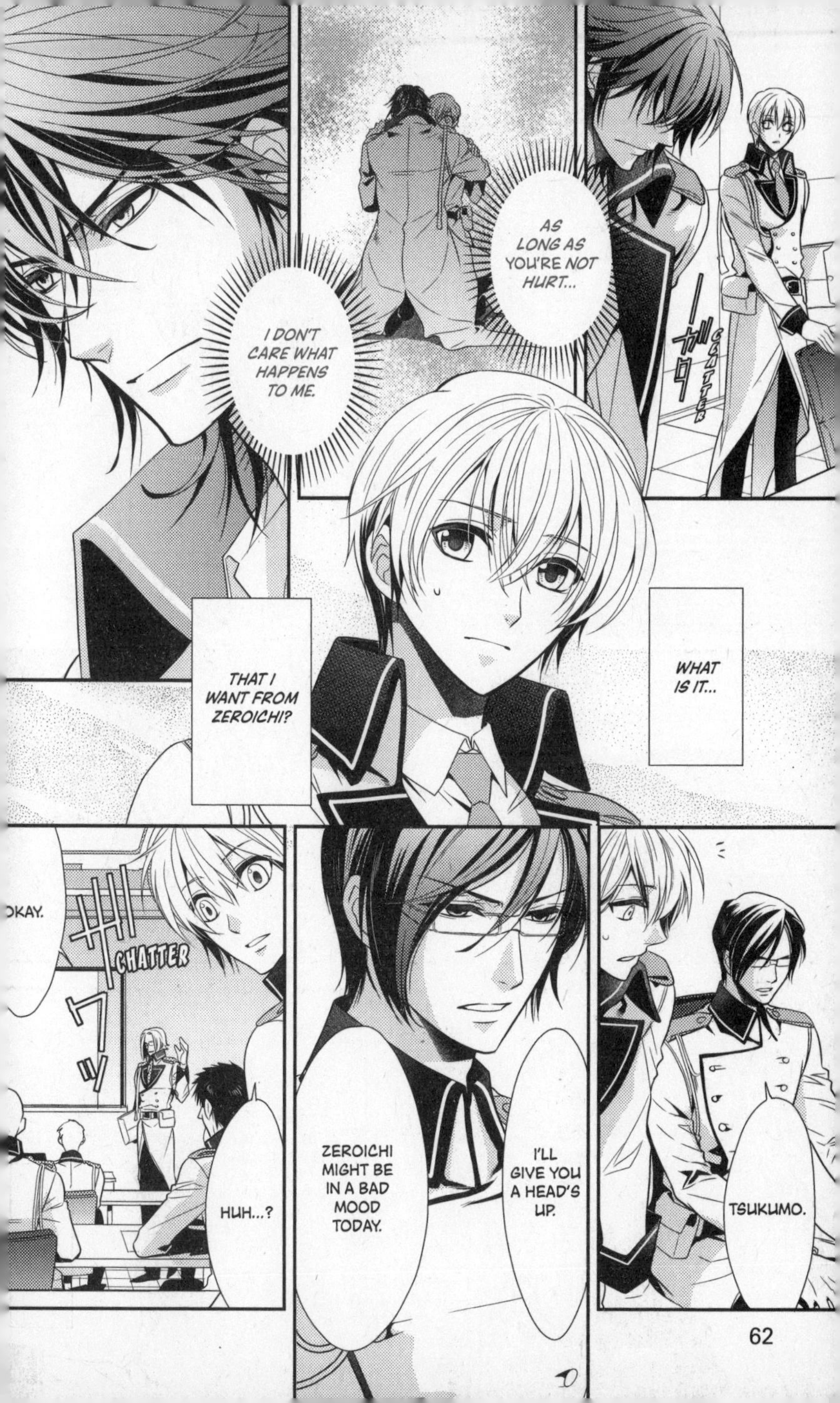
AS LONG AS YOU'RE NOT HURT...
CHATTER
I DON'T CARE WHAT HAPPENS TO ME.
WHAT IS IT...
THAT I WANT FROM ZEROICHI?
TSUKUMO.
I'LL GIVE YOU A HEAD'S UP.
ZEROICHI MIGHT BE IN A BAD MOOD TODAY.
HUH...?
OKAY.
CHATTER

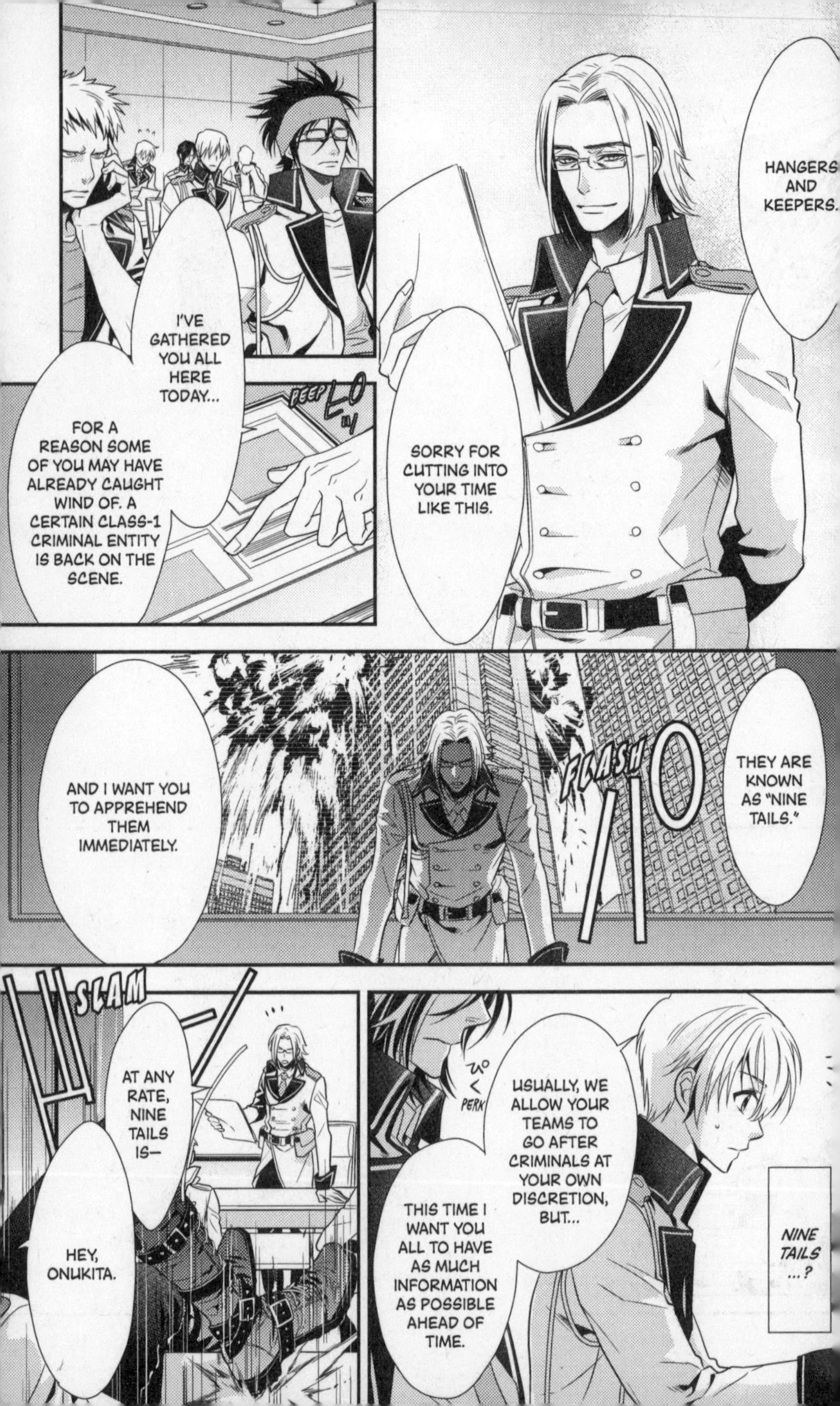
HANGERS AND KEEPERS.
SORRY FOR CUTTING INTO YOUR TIME LIKE THIS.
I'VE GATHERED YOU ALL HERE TODAY...
FOR A REASON SOME OF YOU MAY HAVE ALREADY CAUGHT WIND OF. A CERTAIN CLASS-1 CRIMINAL ENTITY IS BACK ON THE SCENE.
THEY ARE KNOWN AS "NINE TAILS."
FLASH
AND I WANT YOU TO APPREHEND THEM IMMEDIATELY.
NINE TAILS ...?
USUALLY, WE ALLOW YOUR TEAMS TO GO AFTER CRIMINALS AT YOUR OWN DISCRETION, BUT...
PERK
THIS TIME I WANT YOU ALL TO HAVE AS MUCH INFORMATION AS POSSIBLE AHEAD OF TIME.
SLAM
AT ANY RATE, NINE TAILS IS—
HEY, ONUKITA.

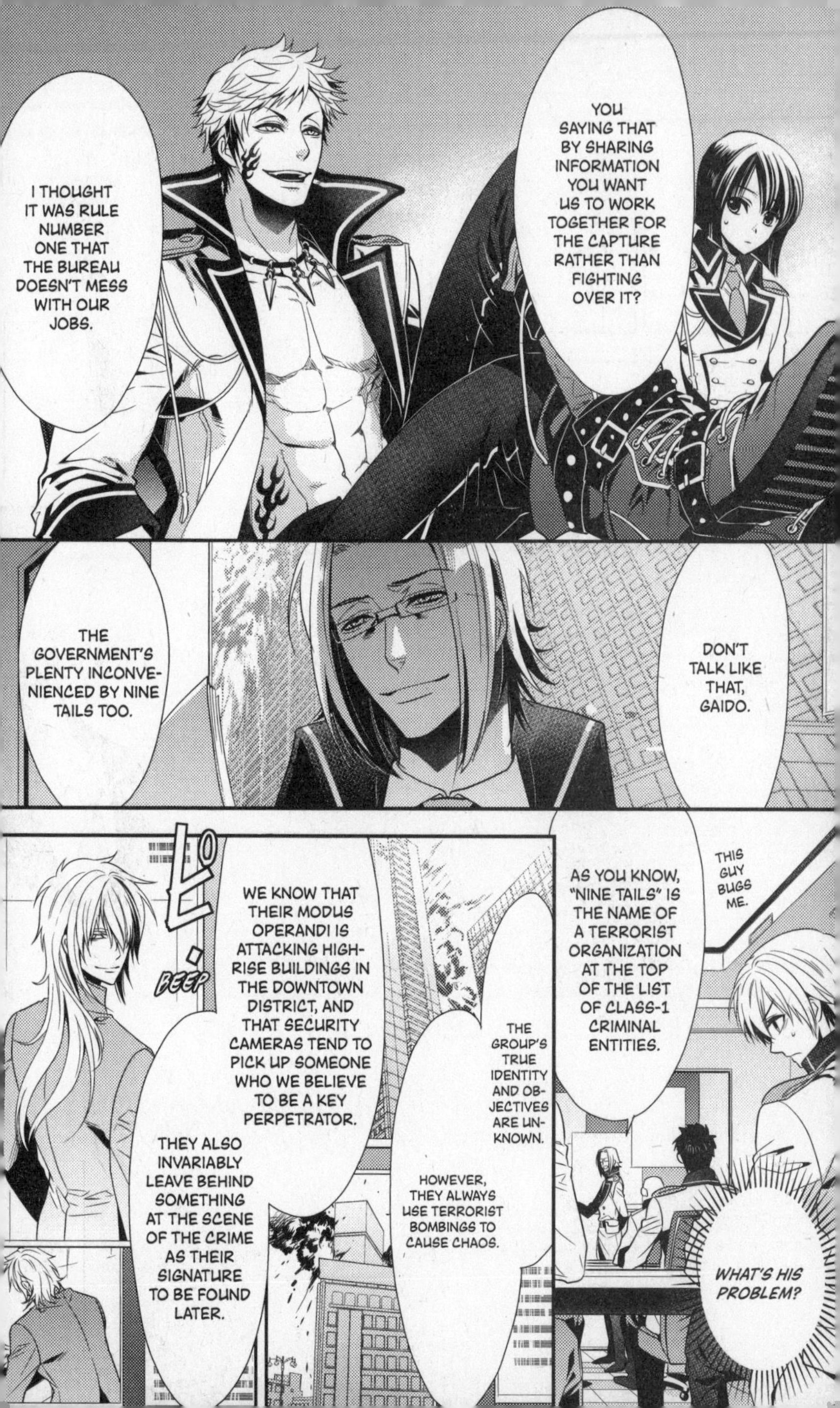

YOU SAYING THAT BY SHARING INFORMATION YOU WANT US TO WORK TOGETHER FOR THE CAPTURE RATHER THAN FIGHTING OVER IT?
I THOUGHT IT WAS RULE NUMBER ONE THAT THE BUREAU DOESN'T MESS WITH OUR JOBS.
DON'T TALK LIKE THAT, GAIDO.
THE GOVERNMENT'S PLENTY INCONVE-NIENCED BY NINE TAILS TOO.
THIS GUY BUGS ME.
AS YOU KNOW, "NINE TAILS" IS THE NAME OF A TERRORIST ORGANIZATION AT THE TOP OF THE LIST OF CLASS-1 CRIMINAL ENTITIES.
THE GROUP'S TRUE IDENTITY AND OB-JECTIVES ARE UN-KNOWN.
HOWEVER, THEY ALWAYS USE TERRORIST BOMBINGS TO CAUSE CHAOS.
WHAT'S HIS PROBLEM?
BEEP
WE KNOW THAT THEIR MODUS OPERANDI IS ATTACKING HIGH-RISE BUILDINGS IN THE DOWNTOWN DISTRICT, AND THAT SECURITY CAMERAS TEND TO PICK UP SOMEONE WHO WE BELIEVE TO BE A KEY PERPETRATOR.
THEY ALSO INVARIABLY LEAVE BEHIND SOMETHING AT THE SCENE OF THE CRIME AS THEIR SIGNATURE TO BE FOUND LATER.

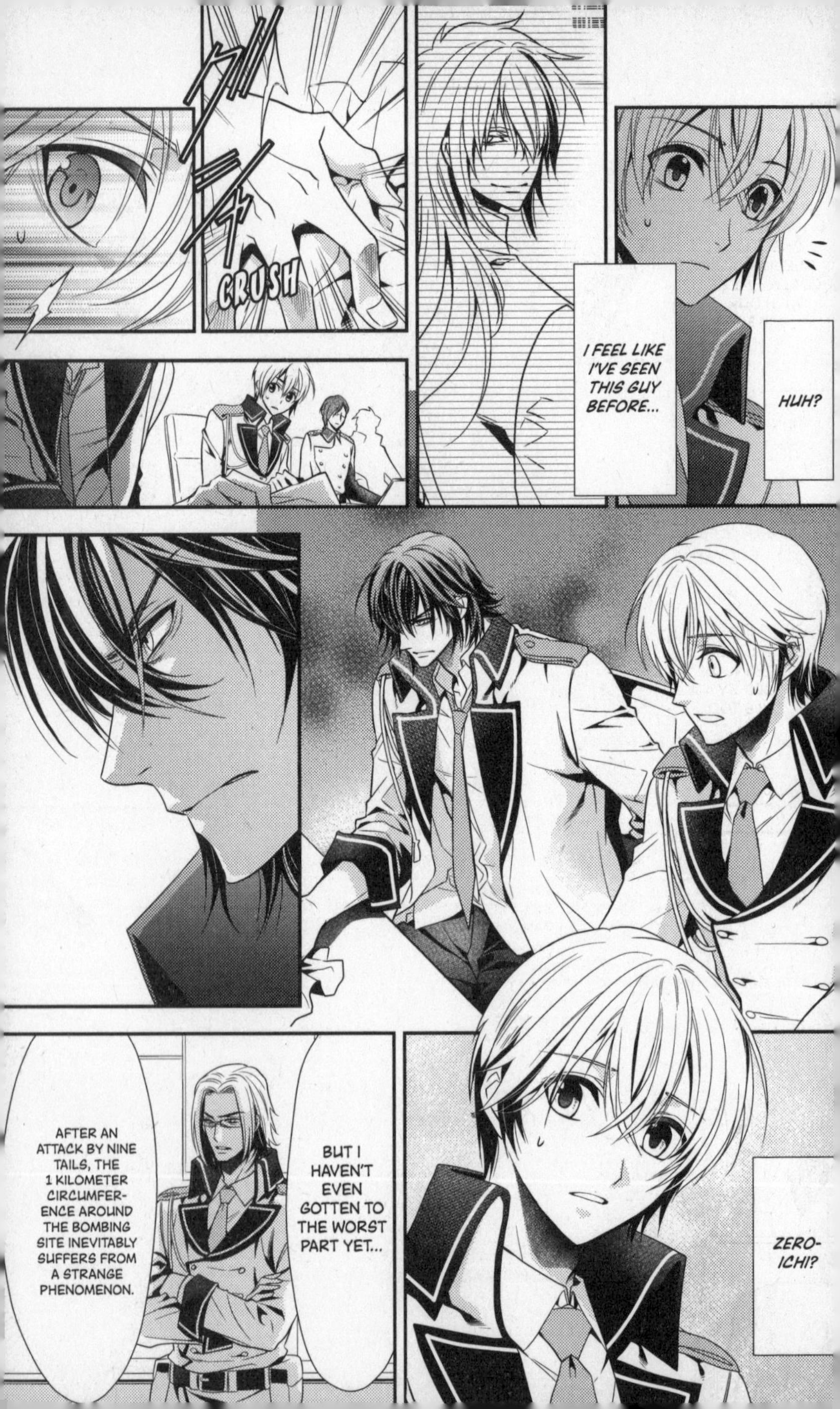
HUH?
I FEEL LIKE I'VE SEEN THIS GUY BEFORE...
CRUSH
ZERO-ICHI?
BUT I HAVEN'T EVEN GOTTEN TO THE WORST PART YET...
AFTER AN ATTACK BY NINE TAILS, THE 1 KILOMETER CIRCUMFERENCE AROUND THE BOMBING SITE INEVITABLY SUFFERS FROM A STRANGE PHENOMENON.

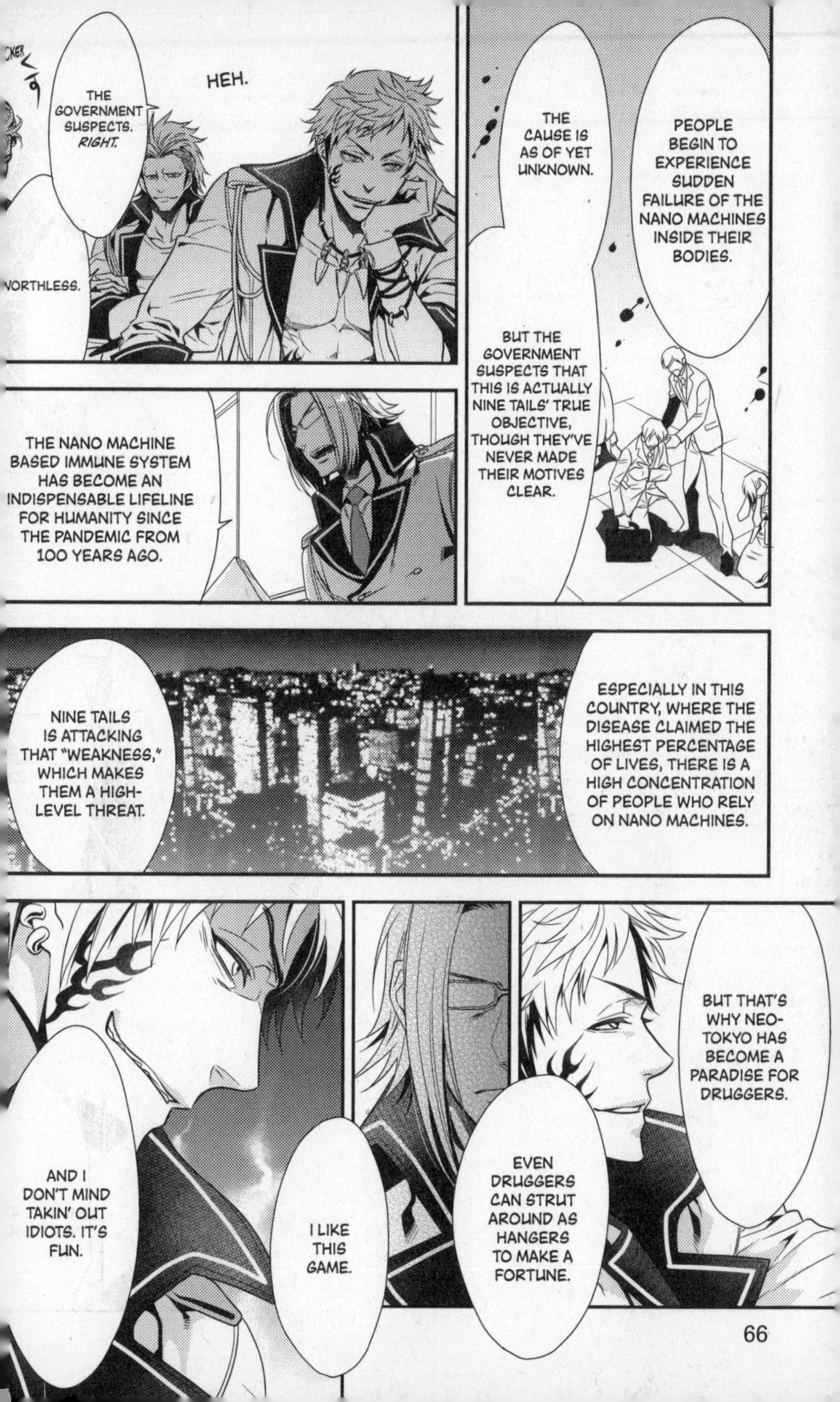
PEOPLE BEGIN TO EXPERIENCE SUDDEN FAILURE OF THE NANO MACHINES INSIDE THEIR BODIES.
THE CAUSE IS AS OF YET UNKNOWN.
BUT THE GOVERNMENT SUSPECTS THAT THIS IS ACTUALLY NINE TAILS' TRUE OBJECTIVE, THOUGH THEY'VE NEVER MADE THEIR MOTIVES CLEAR.
HEH.
THE GOVERNMENT SUSPECTS. *RIGHT.*
WORTHLESS.
THE NANO MACHINE BASED IMMUNE SYSTEM HAS BECOME AN INDISPENSABLE LIFELINE FOR HUMANITY SINCE THE PANDEMIC FROM 100 YEARS AGO.
ESPECIALLY IN THIS COUNTRY, WHERE THE DISEASE CLAIMED THE HIGHEST PERCENTAGE OF LIVES, THERE IS A HIGH CONCENTRATION OF PEOPLE WHO RELY ON NANO MACHINES.
NINE TAILS IS ATTACKING THAT "WEAKNESS," WHICH MAKES THEM A HIGH-LEVEL THREAT.
BUT THAT'S WHY NEO-TOKYO HAS BECOME A PARADISE FOR DRUGGERS.
EVEN DRUGGERS CAN STRUT AROUND AS HANGERS TO MAKE A FORTUNE.
I LIKE THIS GAME.
AND I DON'T MIND TAKIN' OUT IDIOTS. IT'S FUN.

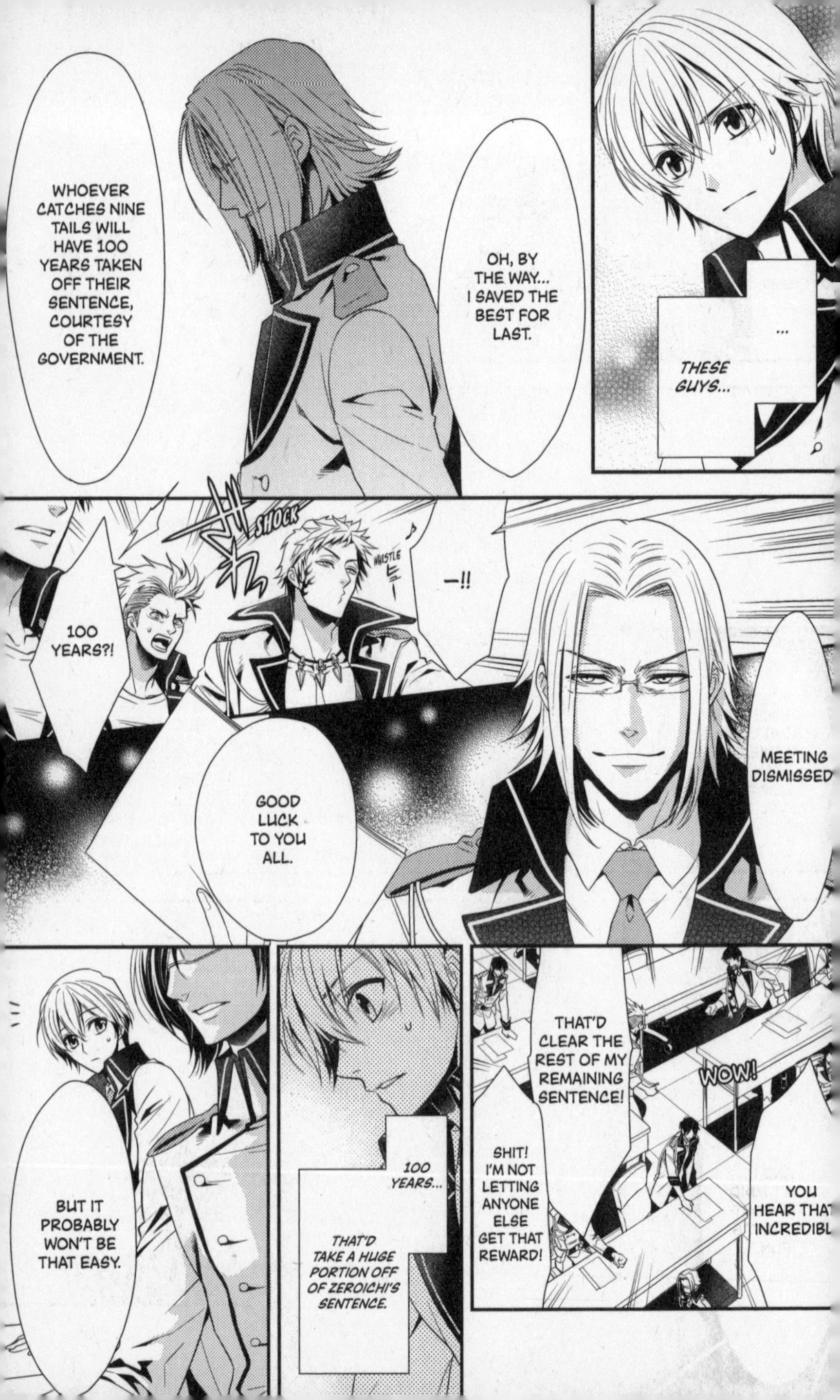
...
THESE GUYS...
OH, BY THE WAY... I SAVED THE BEST FOR LAST.
WHOEVER CATCHES NINE TAILS WILL HAVE 100 YEARS TAKEN OFF THEIR SENTENCE, COURTESY OF THE GOVERNMENT.
MEETING DISMISSED
—!!
WHISTLE
SHOCK
100 YEARS?!
GOOD LUCK TO YOU ALL.
YOU HEAR THAT INCREDIBL
WOW!
THAT'D CLEAR THE REST OF MY REMAINING SENTENCE!
SHIT! I'M NOT LETTING ANYONE ELSE GET THAT REWARD!
100 YEARS...
THAT'D TAKE A HUGE PORTION OFF OF ZEROICHI'S SENTENCE.
BUT IT PROBABLY WON'T BE THAT EASY.

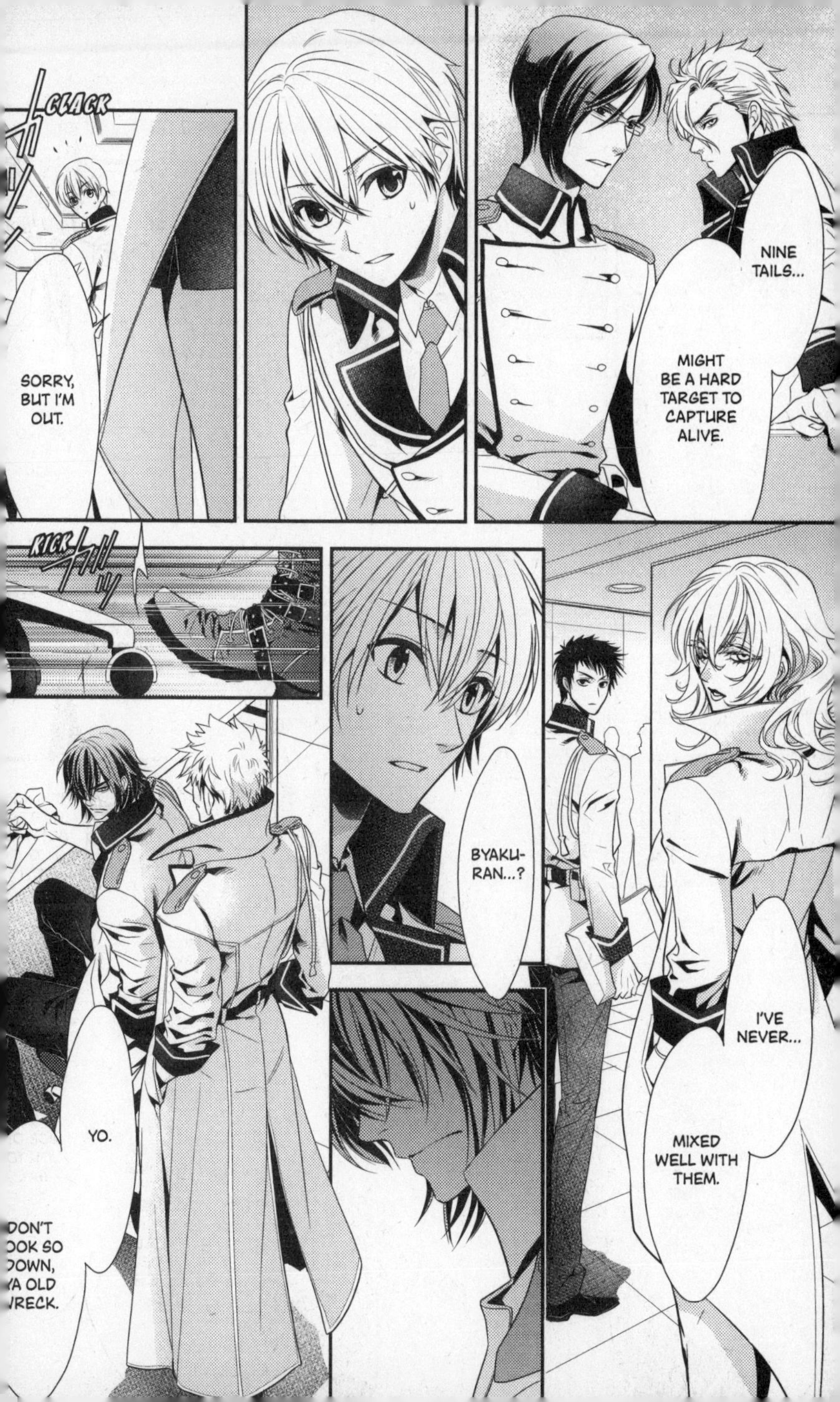
NINE TAILS...
MIGHT BE A HARD TARGET TO CAPTURE ALIVE.
CLACK
SORRY, BUT I'M OUT.
I'VE NEVER...
MIXED WELL WITH THEM.
BYAKU-RAN...?
KICK
YO.
DON'T OOK SO OWN, YA OLD WRECK.

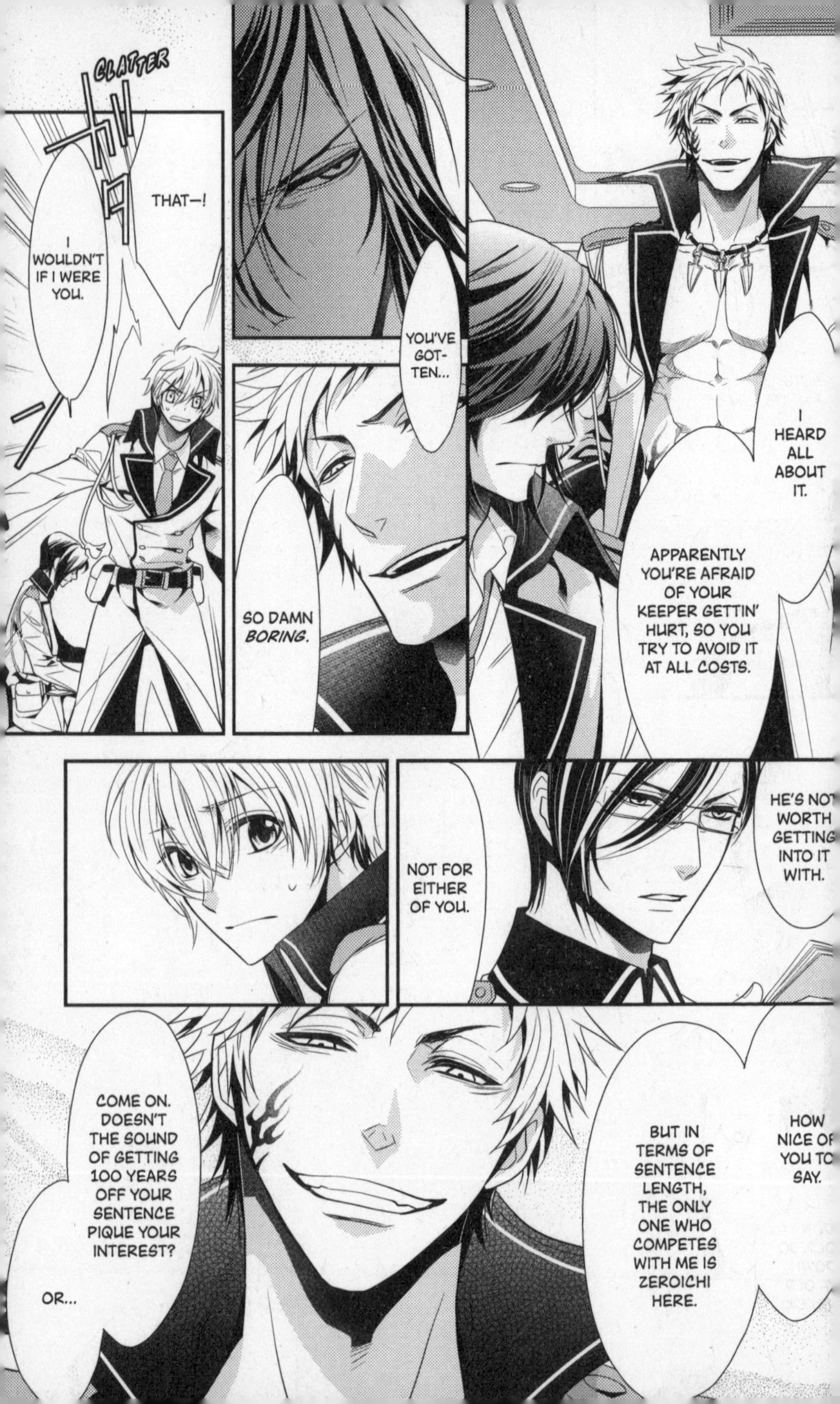

I HEARD ALL ABOUT IT.
APPARENTLY YOU'RE AFRAID OF YOUR KEEPER GETTIN' HURT, SO YOU TRY TO AVOID IT AT ALL COSTS.
YOU'VE GOT-TEN...
SO DAMN *BORING*.
CLATTER
THAT—!
I WOULDN'T IF I WERE YOU.
HE'S NOT WORTH GETTING INTO IT WITH.
NOT FOR EITHER OF YOU.
HOW NICE OF YOU TO SAY.
BUT IN TERMS OF SENTENCE LENGTH, THE ONLY ONE WHO COMPETES WITH ME IS ZEROICHI HERE.
COME ON. DOESN'T THE SOUND OF GETTING 100 YEARS OFF YOUR SENTENCE PIQUE YOUR INTEREST?
OR...

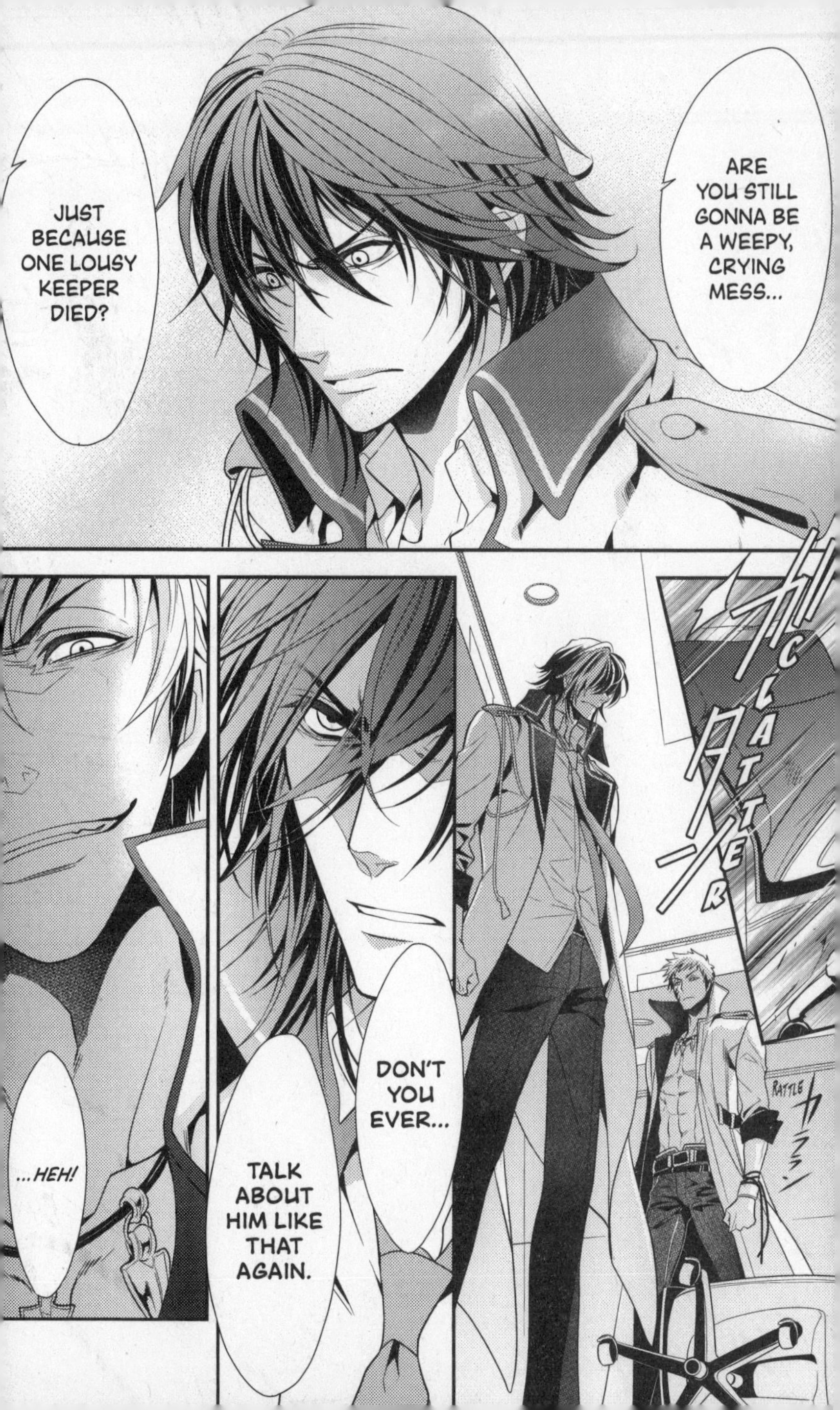
ARE YOU STILL GONNA BE A WEEPY, CRYING MESS...
JUST BECAUSE ONE LOUSY KEEPER DIED?
CLATTER
RATTLE
DON'T YOU EVER...
TALK ABOUT HIM LIKE THAT AGAIN.
...HEH!

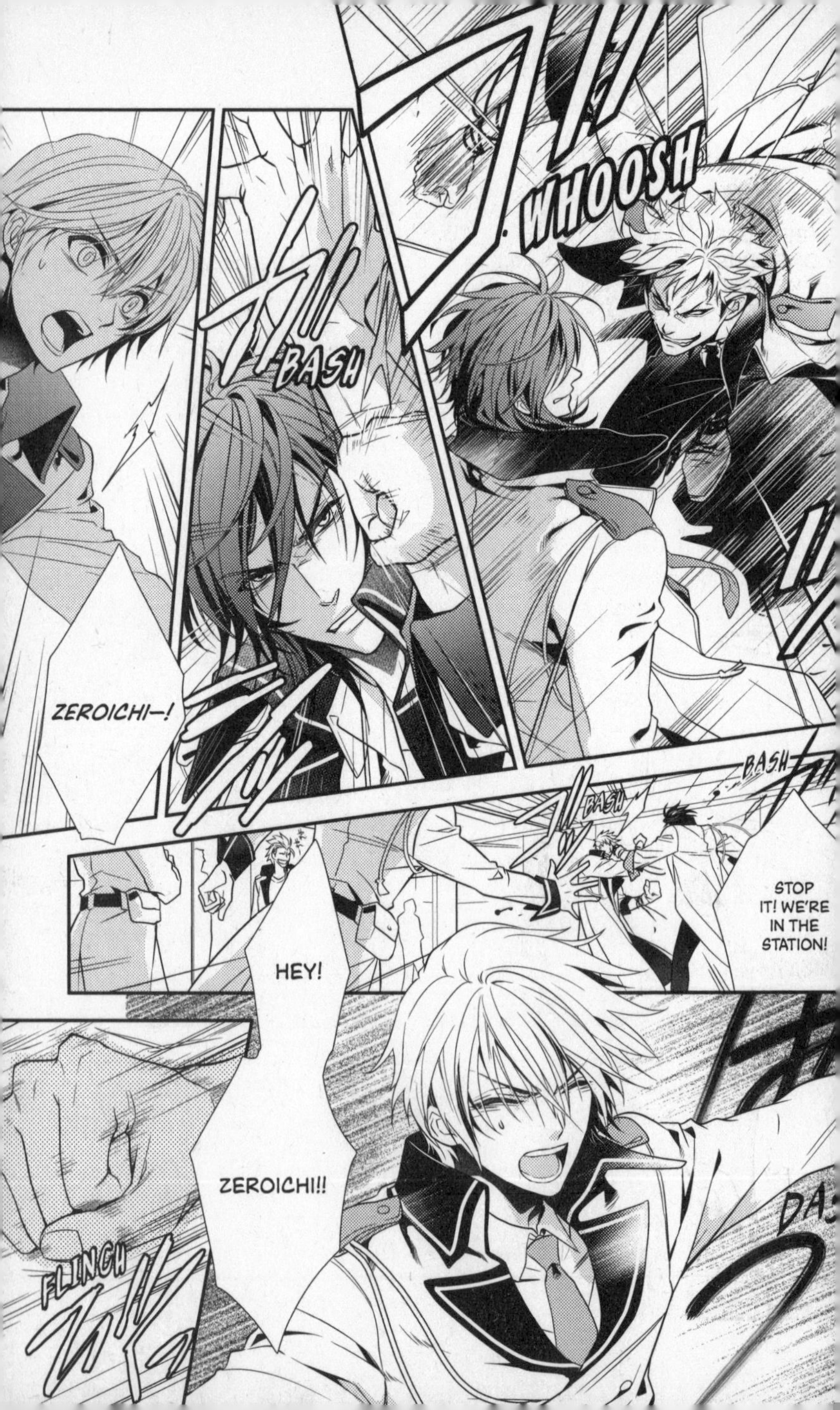
WHOOSH
BASH
ZEROICHI—!
BASH
BASH
STOP IT! WE'RE IN THE STATION!
HEY!
ZEROICHI!!
FLINCH

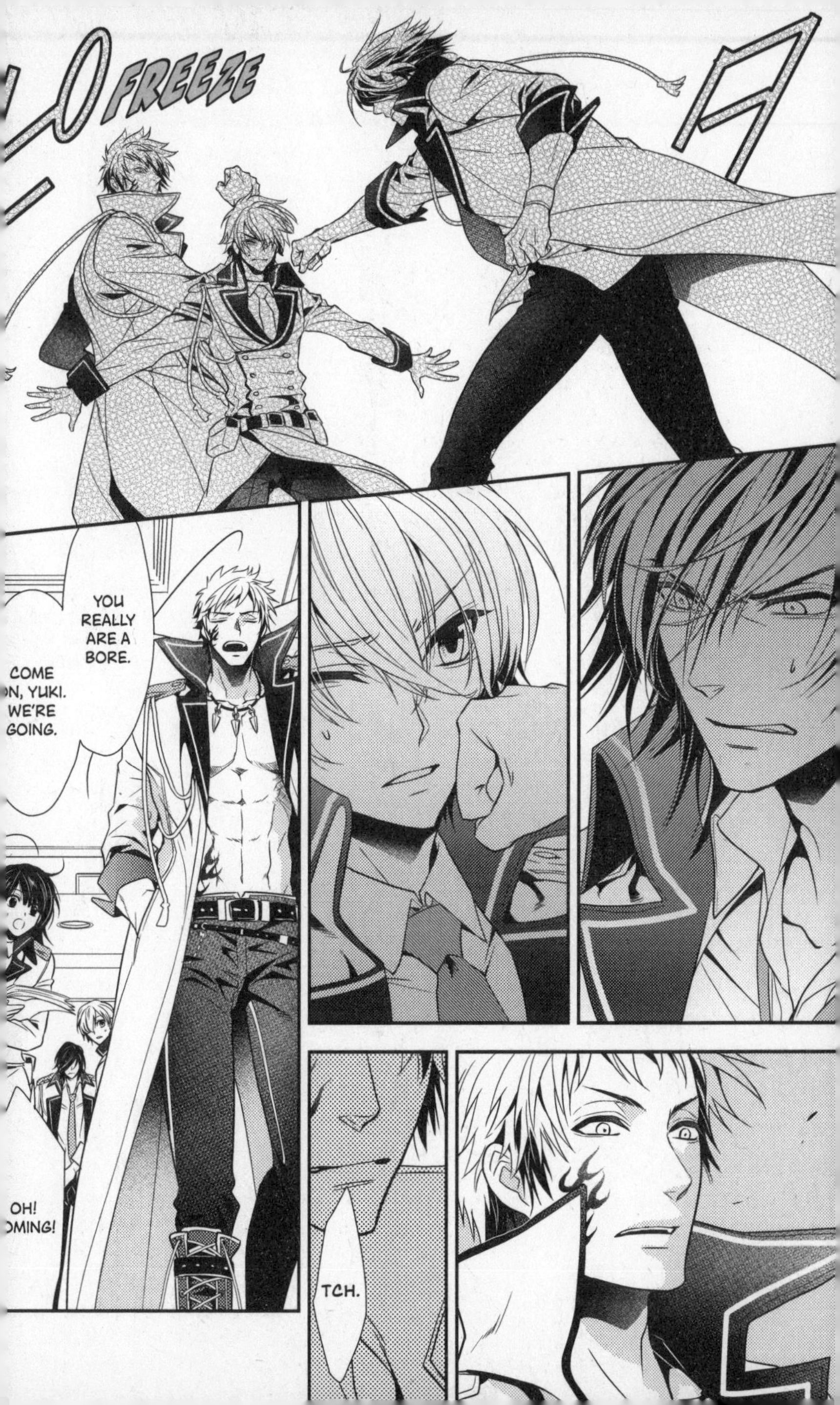
FREEZE
TCH.
YOU REALLY ARE A BORE.
COME ON, YUKI. WE'RE GOING.
OH! OMING!

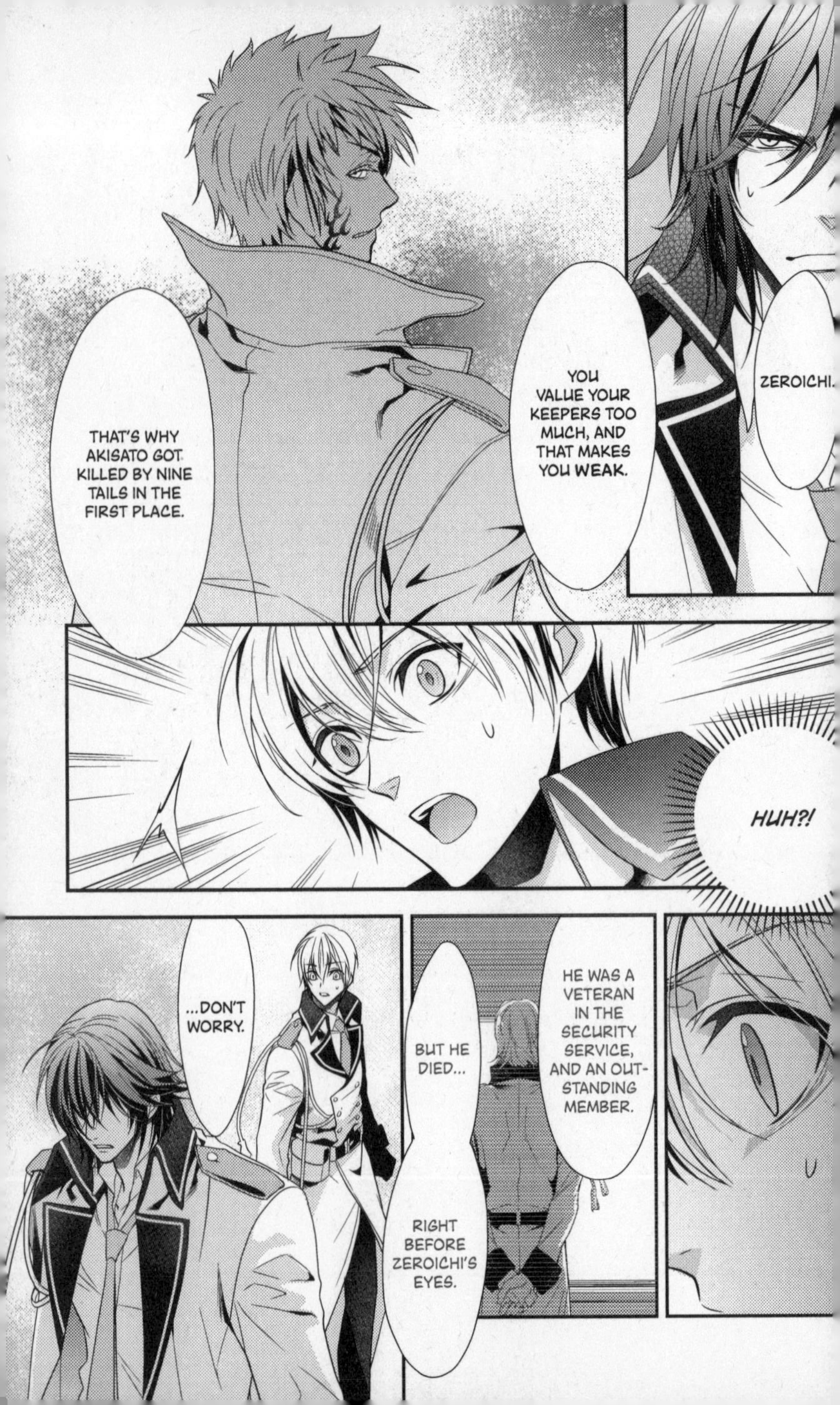
ZEROICHI.
YOU VALUE YOUR KEEPERS TOO MUCH, AND THAT MAKES YOU WEAK.
THAT'S WHY AKISATO GOT KILLED BY NINE TAILS IN THE FIRST PLACE.
HUH?!
HE WAS A VETERAN IN THE SECURITY SERVICE, AND AN OUT-STANDING MEMBER.
BUT HE DIED...
RIGHT BEFORE ZEROICHI'S EYES.
...DON'T WORRY.

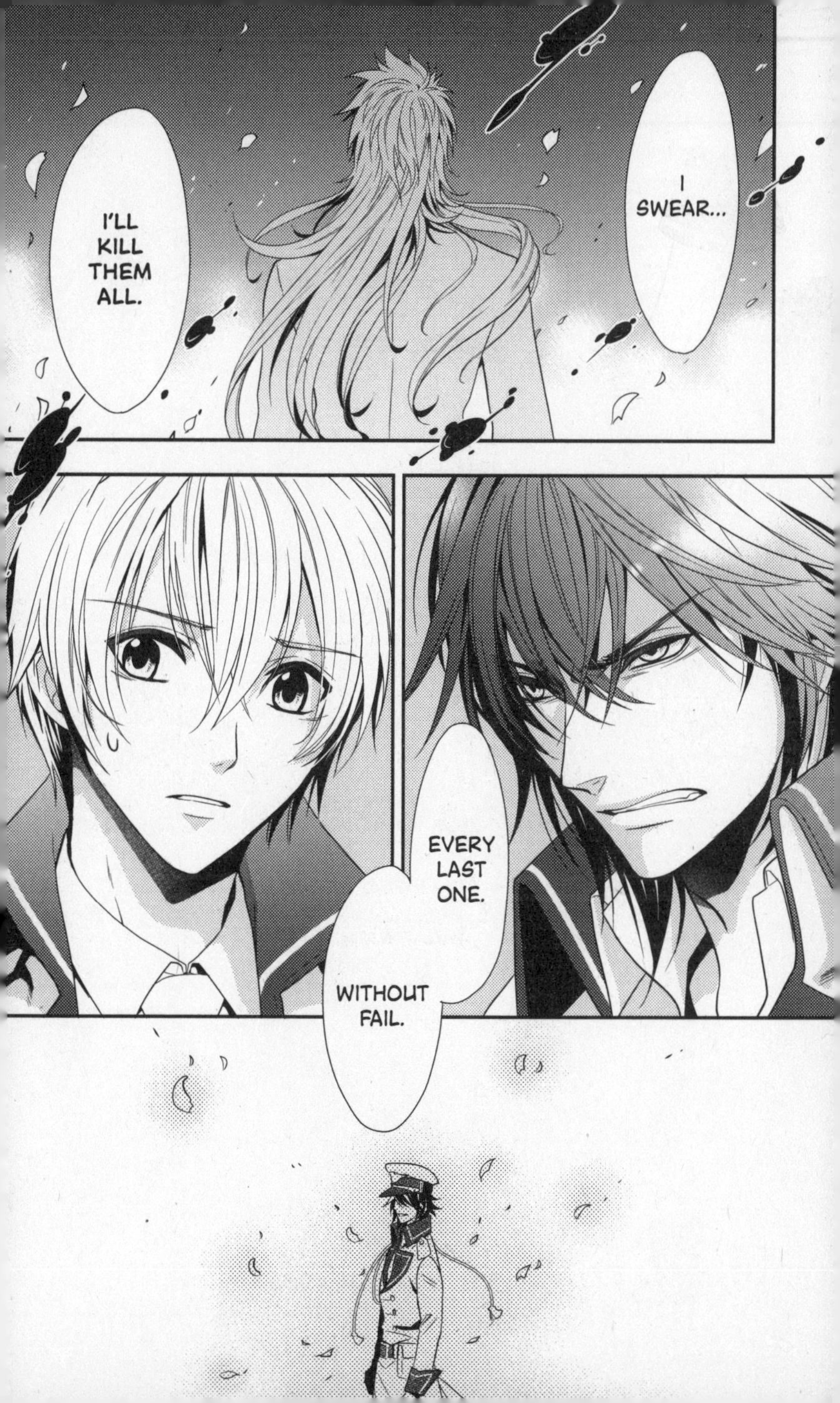
I SWEAR...
I'LL KILL THEM ALL.
EVERY LAST ONE.
WITHOUT FAIL.

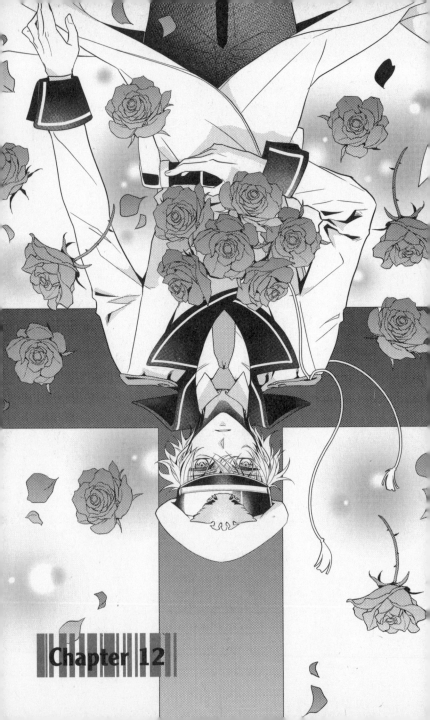

Chapter 12

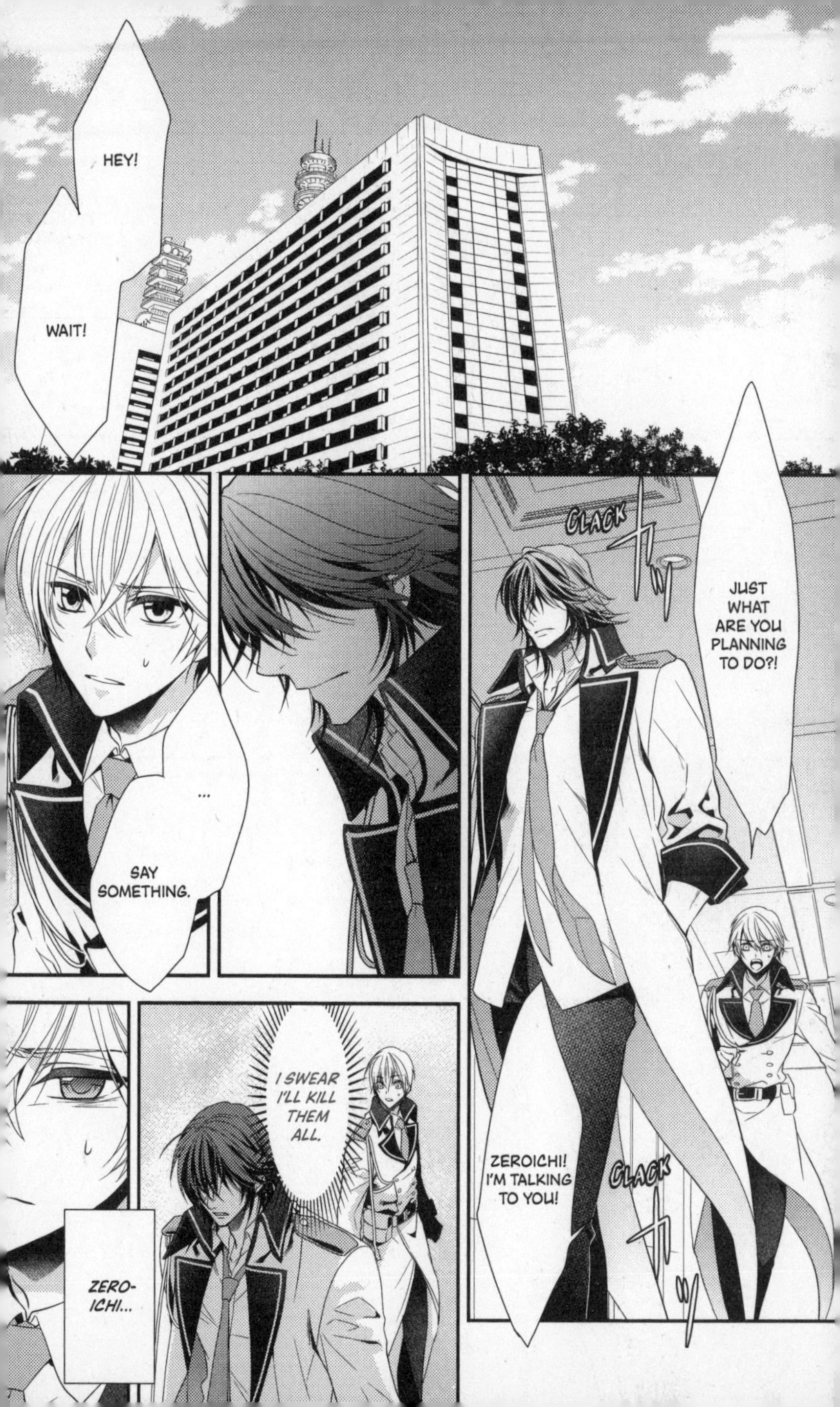
HEY!
WAIT!
CLACK
JUST WHAT ARE YOU PLANNING TO DO?!
ZEROICHI! I'M TALKING TO YOU!
CLACK
...
SAY SOMETHING.
I SWEAR I'LL KILL THEM ALL.
ZERO-ICHI...

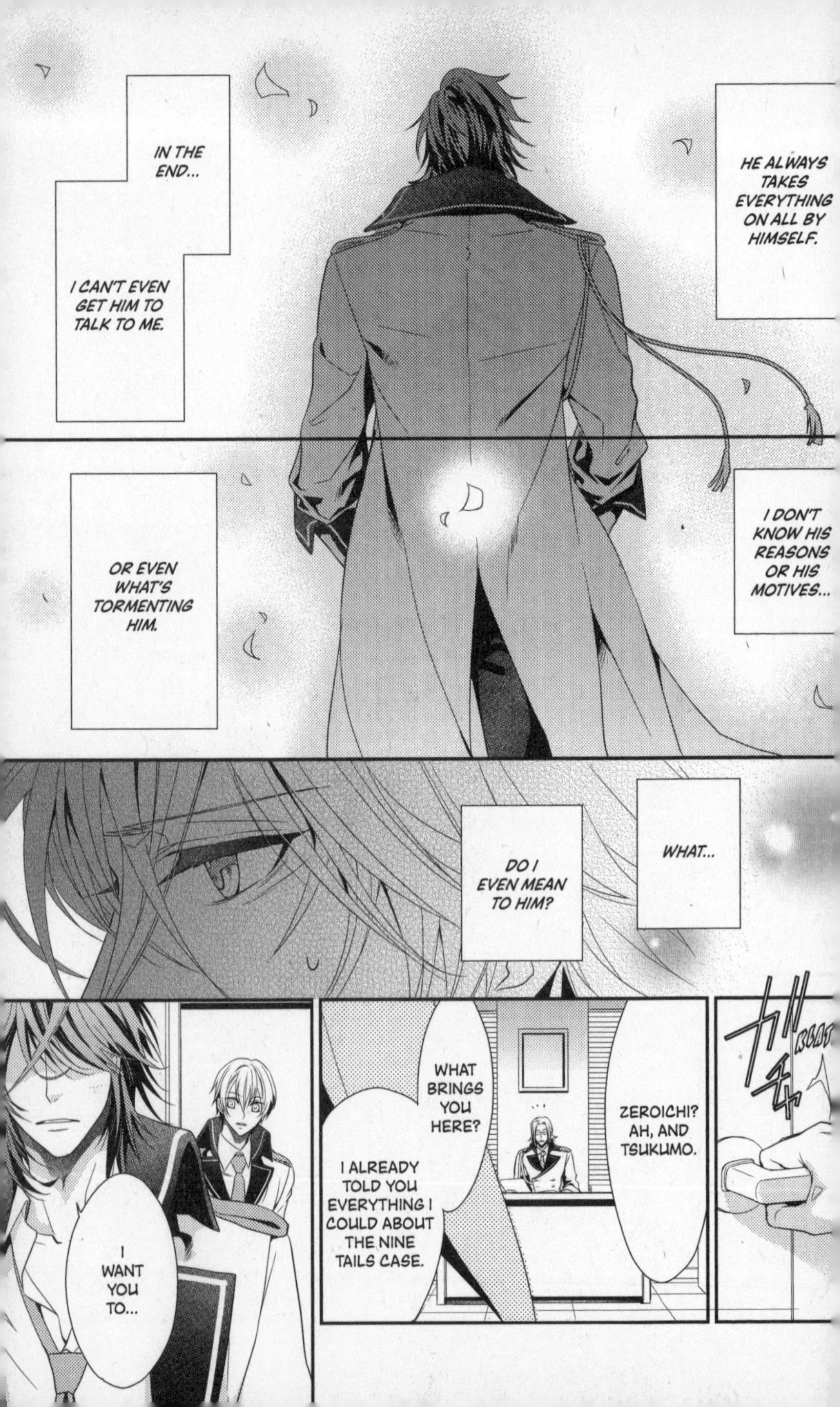
HE ALWAYS TAKES EVERYTHING ON ALL BY HIMSELF.
IN THE END...
I CAN'T EVEN GET HIM TO TALK TO ME.
I DON'T KNOW HIS REASONS OR HIS MOTIVES...
OR EVEN WHAT'S TORMENTING HIM.
WHAT...
DO I EVEN MEAN TO HIM?
KLAT
ZEROICHI? AH, AND TSUKUMO.
WHAT BRINGS YOU HERE?
I ALREADY TOLD YOU EVERYTHING I COULD ABOUT THE NINE TAILS CASE.
I WANT YOU TO...

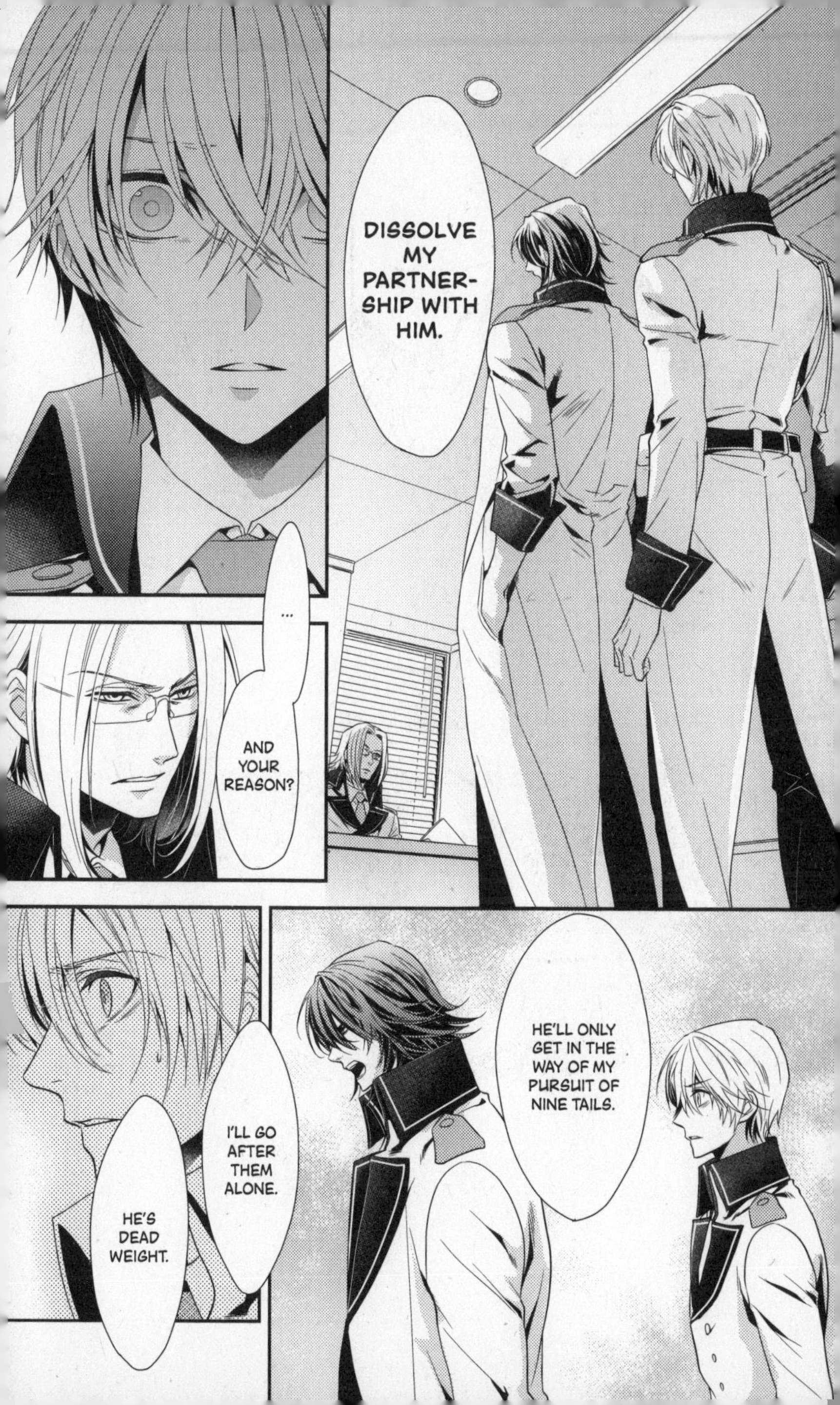
DISSOLVE MY PARTNERSHIP WITH HIM.
...
AND YOUR REASON?
HE'LL ONLY GET IN THE WAY OF MY PURSUIT OF NINE TAILS.
I'LL GO AFTER THEM ALONE.
HE'S DEAD WEIGHT.

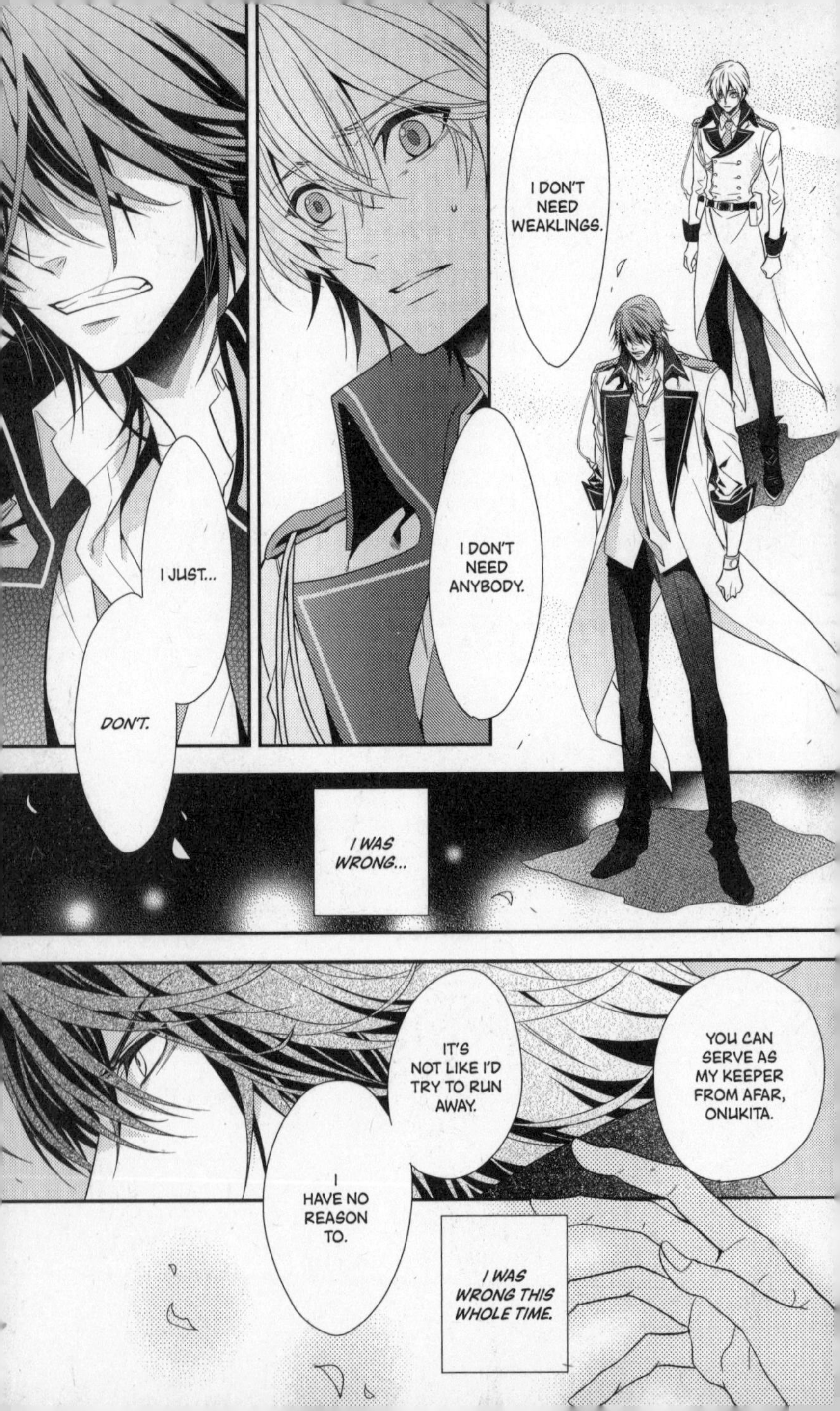
I DON'T NEED WEAKLINGS.
I DON'T NEED ANYBODY.
I JUST...
DON'T.
I WAS WRONG...
YOU CAN SERVE AS MY KEEPER FROM AFAR, ONUKITA.
IT'S NOT LIKE I'D TRY TO RUN AWAY.
I HAVE NO REASON TO.
I WAS WRONG THIS WHOLE TIME.

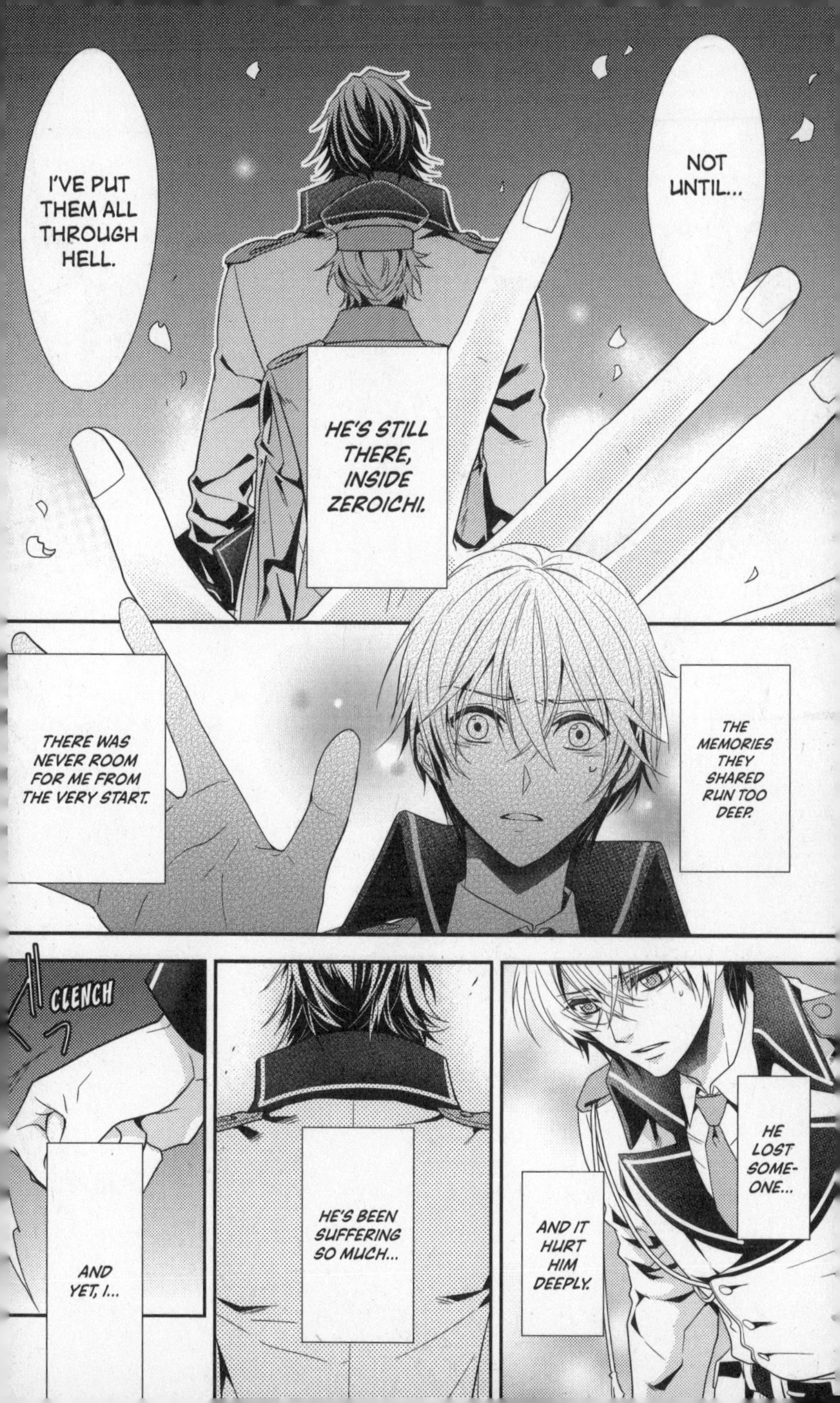
NOT UNTIL...
I'VE PUT THEM ALL THROUGH HELL.
HE'S STILL THERE, INSIDE ZEROICHI.
THE MEMORIES THEY SHARED RUN TOO DEEP.
THERE WAS NEVER ROOM FOR ME FROM THE VERY START.
HE LOST SOME-ONE...
AND IT HURT HIM DEEPLY.
HE'S BEEN SUFFERING SO MUCH...
CLENCH
AND YET, I...

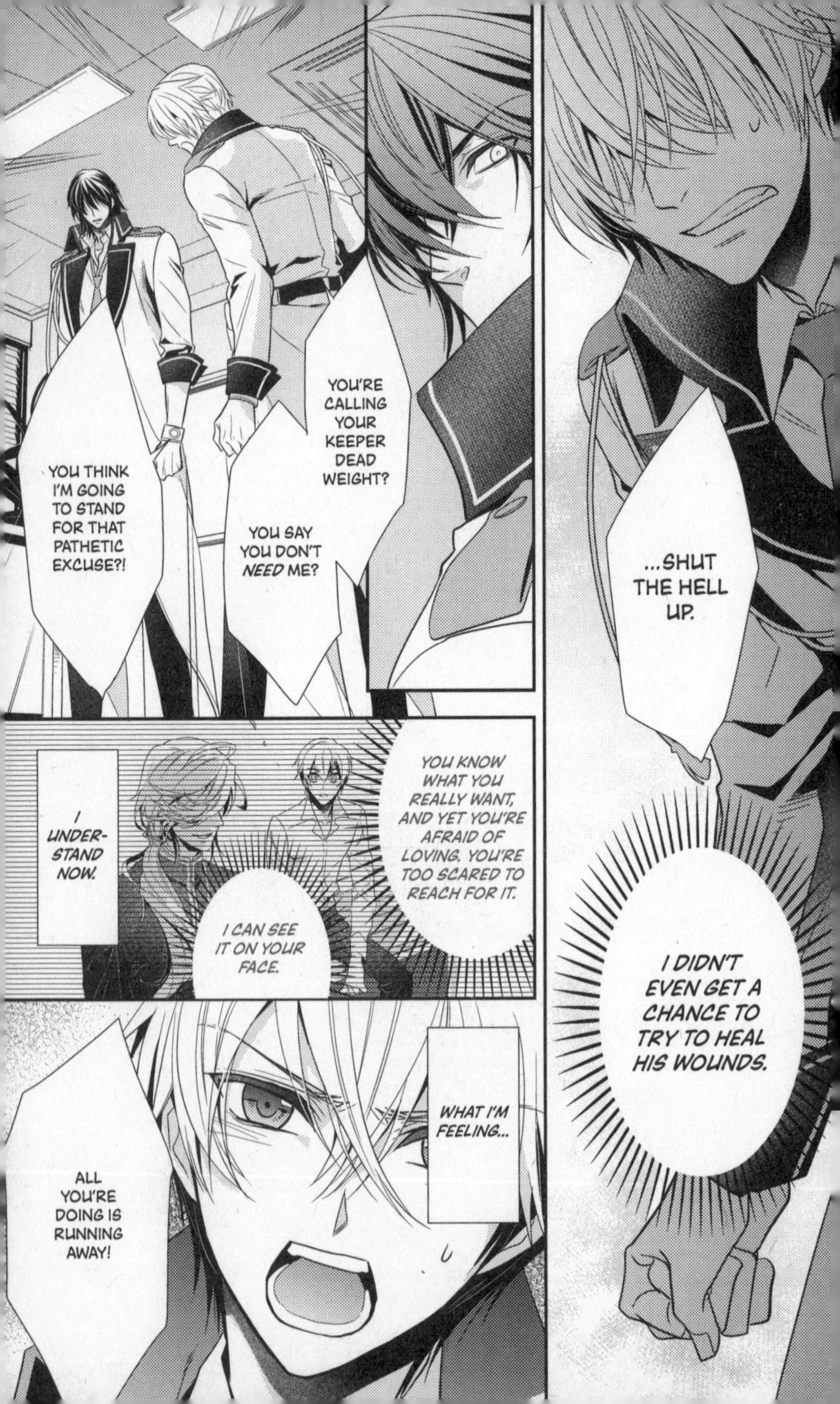
YOU'RE CALLING YOUR KEEPER DEAD WEIGHT?
YOU SAY YOU DON'T *NEED* ME?
YOU THINK I'M GOING TO STAND FOR THAT PATHETIC EXCUSE?!
YOU KNOW WHAT YOU REALLY WANT, AND YET YOU'RE AFRAID OF LOVING. YOU'RE TOO SCARED TO REACH FOR IT.
I CAN SEE IT ON YOUR FACE.
I UNDER-STAND NOW.
WHAT I'M FEELING...
ALL YOU'RE DOING IS RUNNING AWAY!
...SHUT THE HELL UP.
I DIDN'T EVEN GET A CHANCE TO TRY TO HEAL HIS WOUNDS.

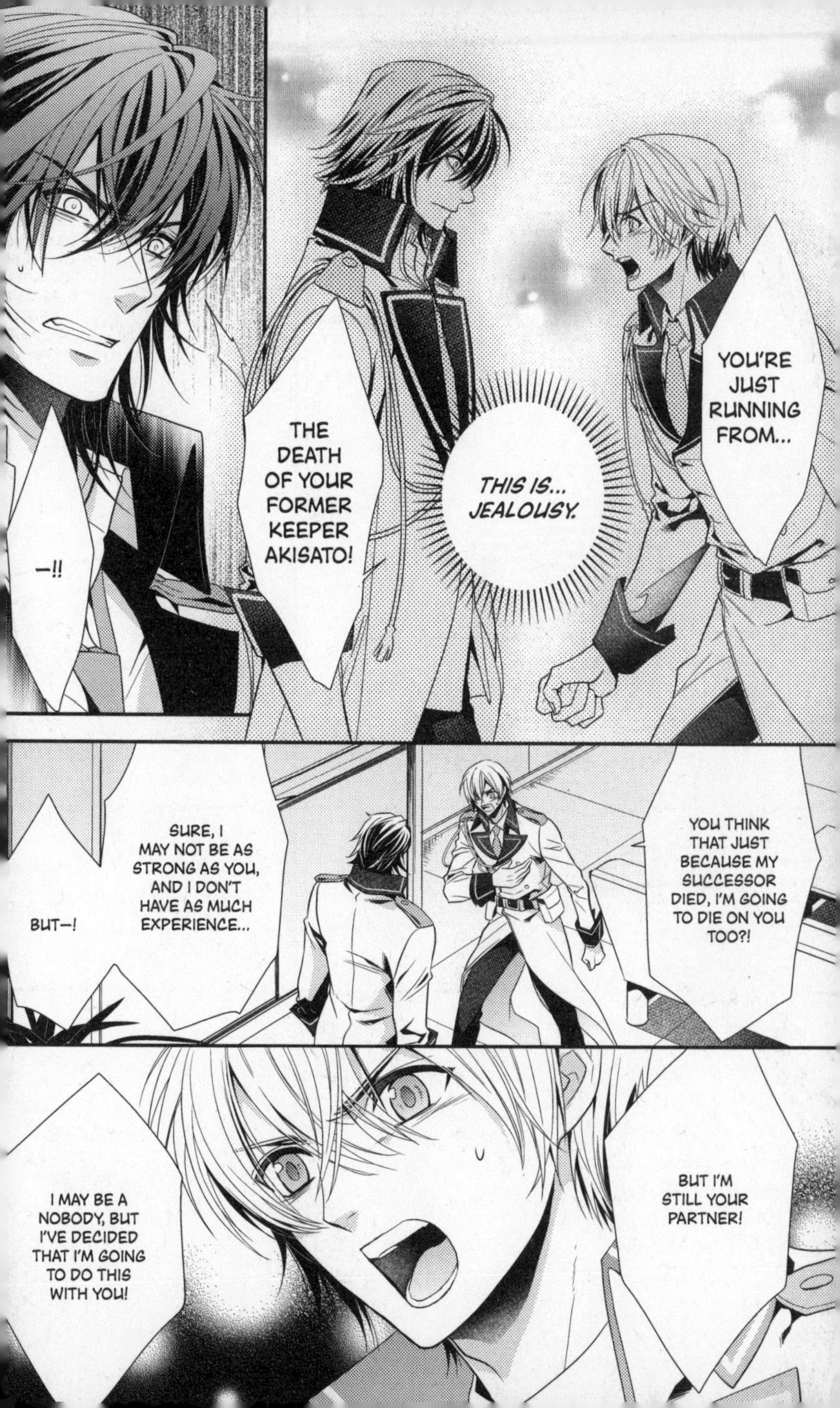
YOU'RE JUST RUNNING FROM...
THIS IS... JEALOUSY.
THE DEATH OF YOUR FORMER KEEPER AKISATO!
—!!
YOU THINK THAT JUST BECAUSE MY SUCCESSOR DIED, I'M GOING TO DIE ON YOU TOO?!
SURE, I MAY NOT BE AS STRONG AS YOU, AND I DON'T HAVE AS MUCH EXPERIENCE...
BUT—!
BUT I'M STILL YOUR PARTNER!
I MAY BE A NOBODY, BUT I'VE DECIDED THAT I'M GOING TO DO THIS WITH YOU!

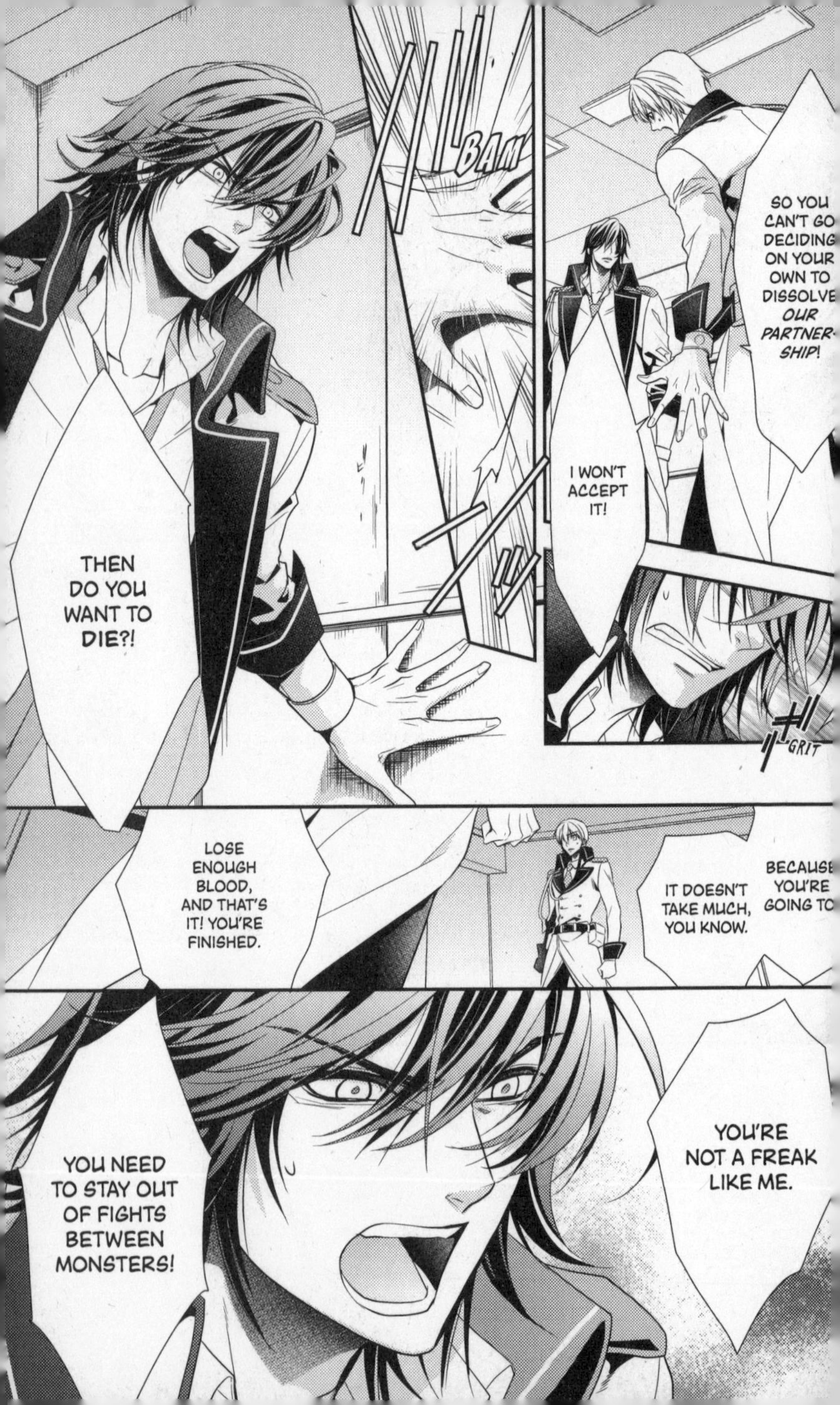
SO YOU CAN'T GO DECIDING ON YOUR OWN TO DISSOLVE *OUR PARTNERSHIP!*
I WON'T ACCEPT IT!
GRIT
BAM
THEN DO YOU WANT TO DIE?!
BECAUSE YOU'RE GOING TO
IT DOESN'T TAKE MUCH, YOU KNOW.
LOSE ENOUGH BLOOD, AND THAT'S IT! YOU'RE FINISHED.
YOU'RE NOT A FREAK LIKE ME.
YOU NEED TO STAY OUT OF FIGHTS BETWEEN MONSTERS!

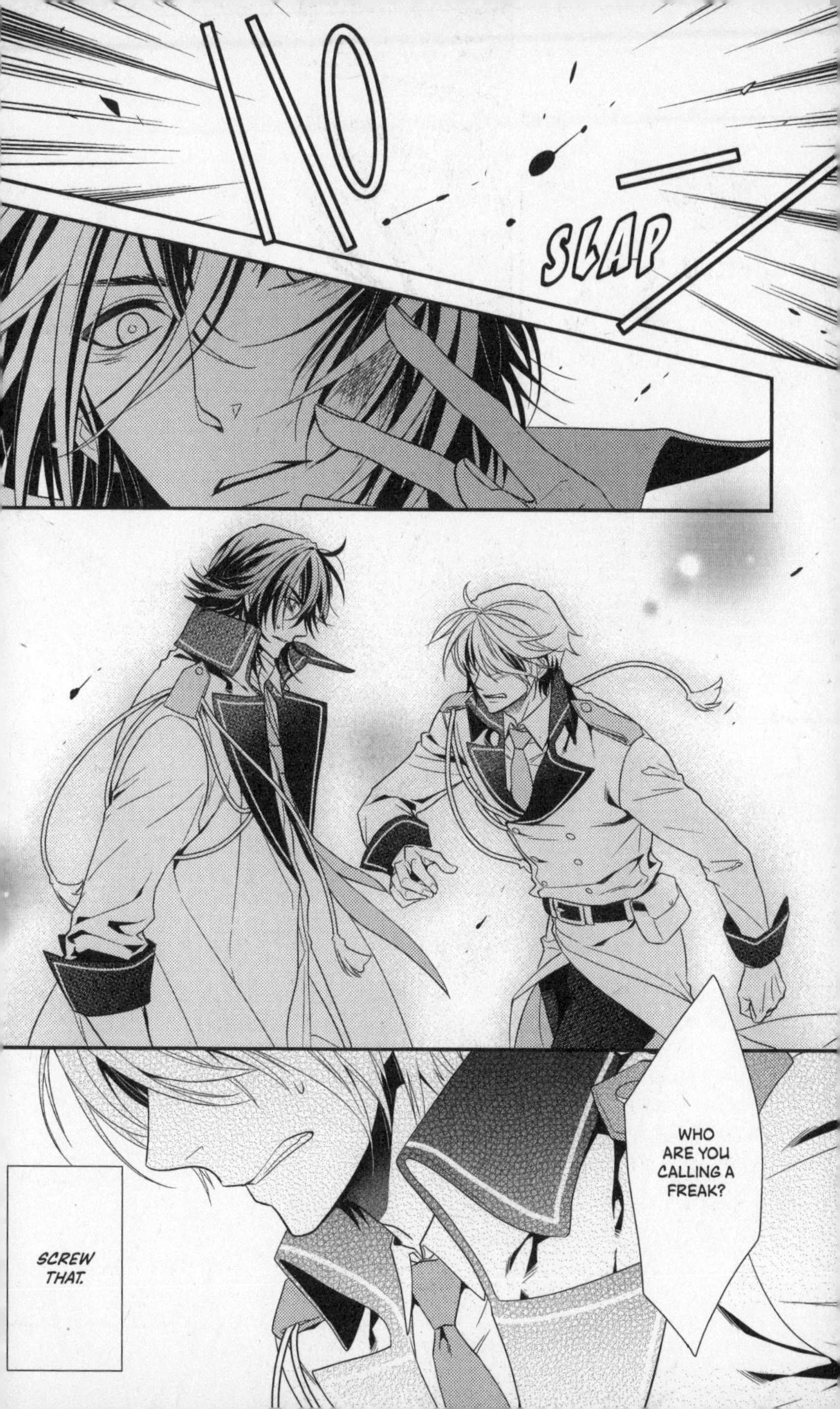
SLAP
WHO ARE YOU CALLING A FREAK?
SCREW THAT.

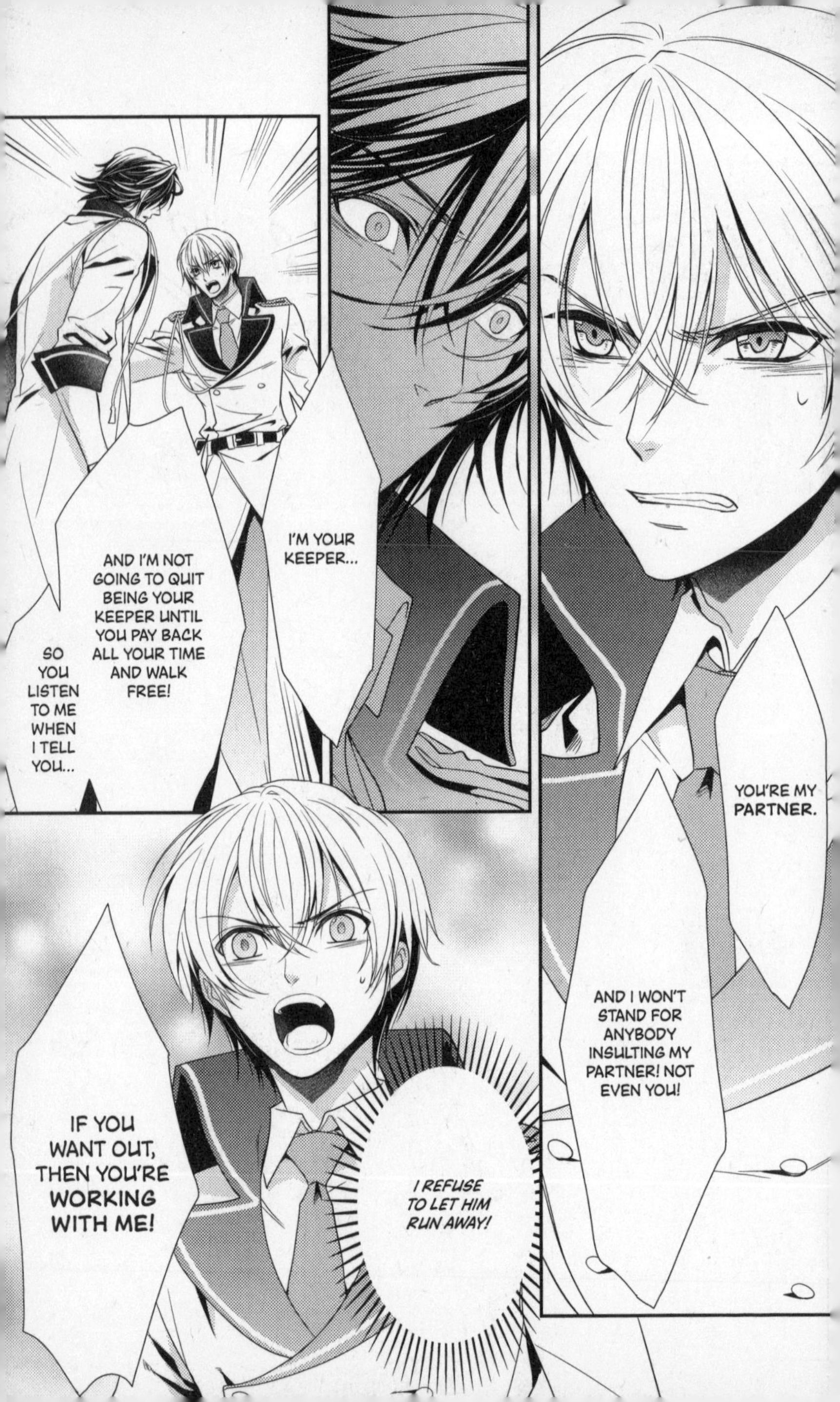
YOU'RE MY PARTNER.
AND I WON'T STAND FOR ANYBODY INSULTING MY PARTNER! NOT EVEN YOU!
I'M YOUR KEEPER...
AND I'M NOT GOING TO QUIT BEING YOUR KEEPER UNTIL YOU PAY BACK ALL YOUR TIME AND WALK FREE!
SO YOU LISTEN TO ME WHEN I TELL YOU...
I REFUSE TO LET HIM RUN AWAY!
IF YOU WANT OUT, THEN YOU'RE WORKING WITH ME!

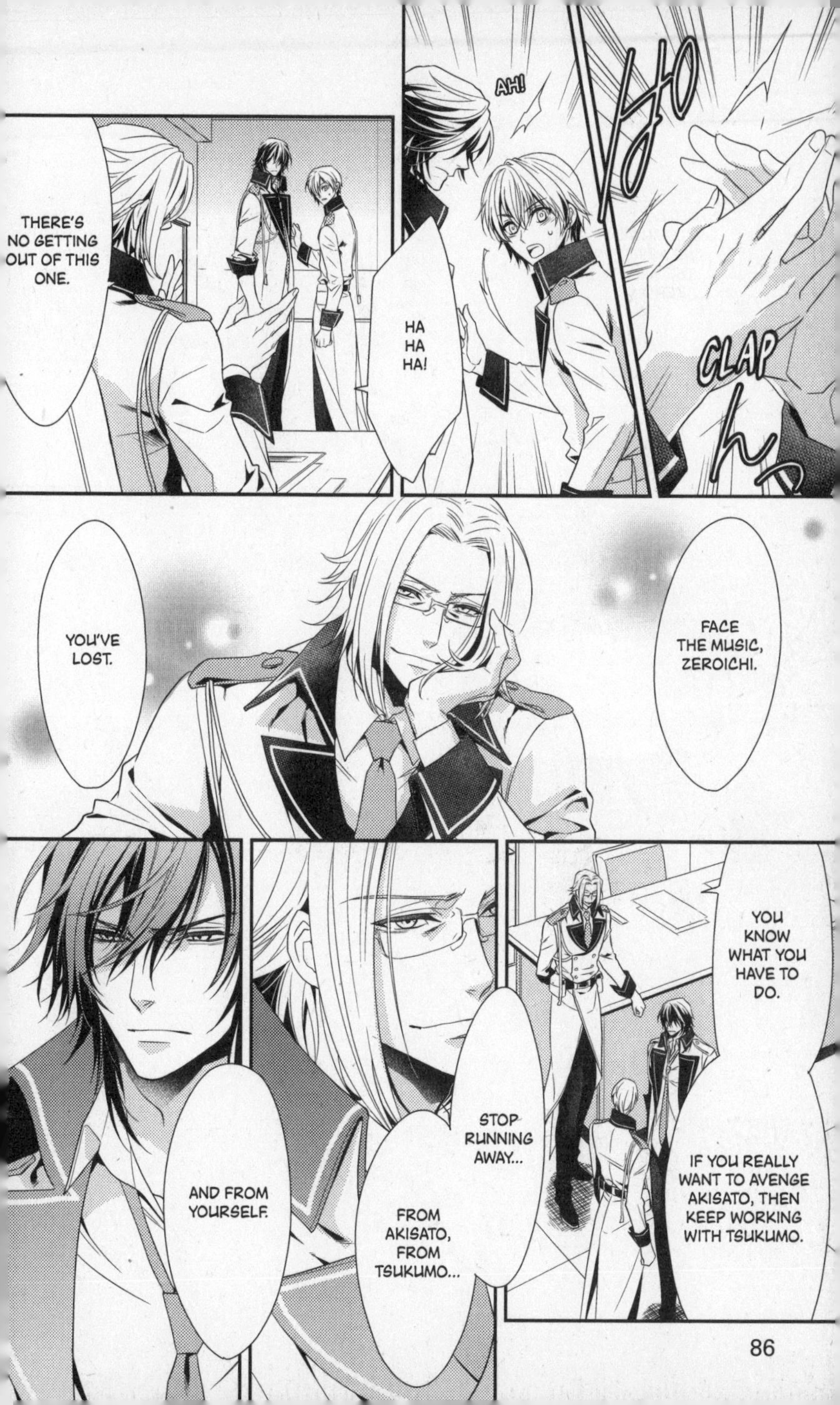
YO
AH!
CLAP
HA HA HA!
THERE'S NO GETTING OUT OF THIS ONE.
FACE THE MUSIC, ZEROICHI.
YOU'VE LOST.
YOU KNOW WHAT YOU HAVE TO DO.
IF YOU REALLY WANT TO AVENGE AKISATO, THEN KEEP WORKING WITH TSUKUMO.
STOP RUNNING AWAY...
FROM AKISATO, FROM TSUKUMO...
AND FROM YOURSELF.

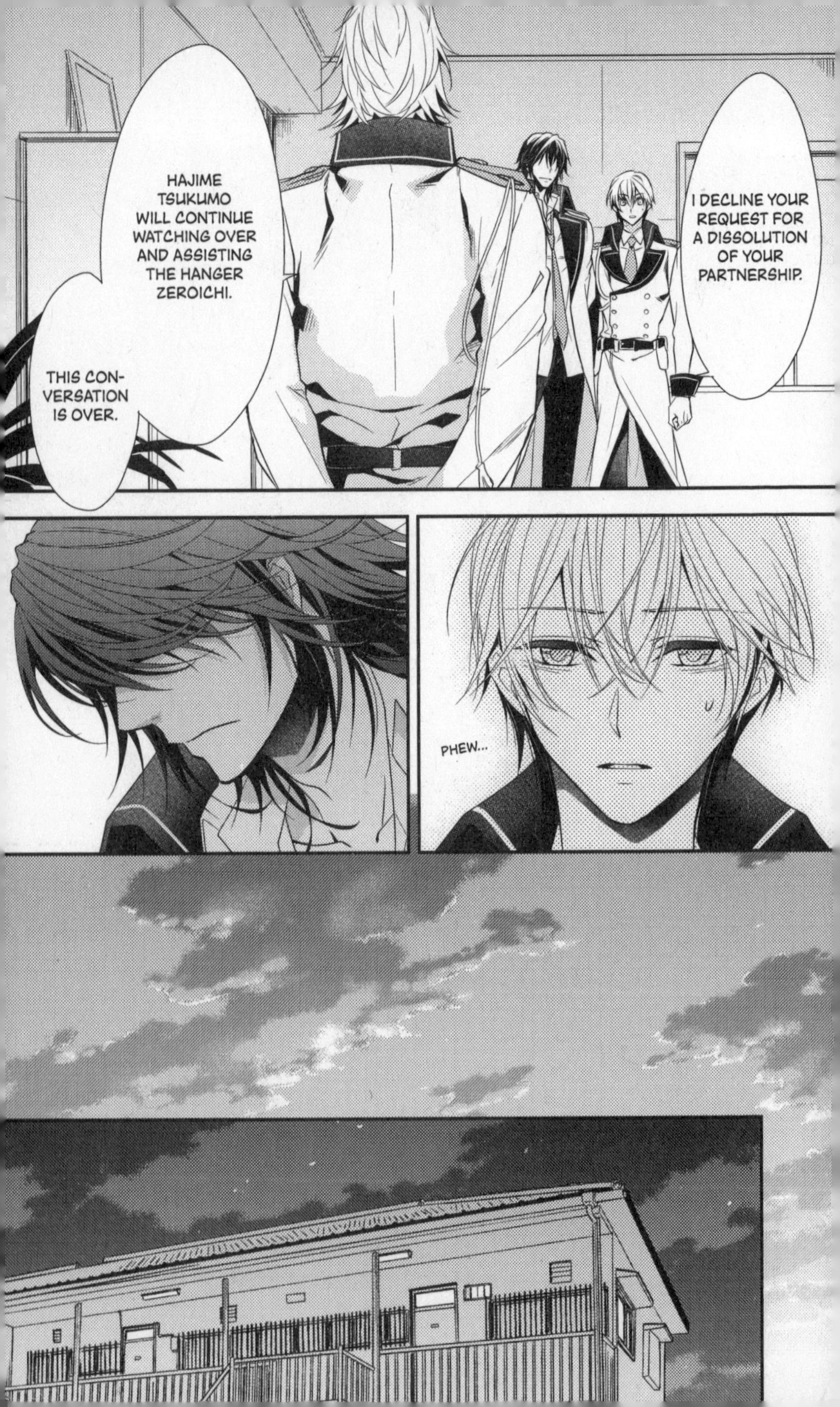
I DECLINE YOUR REQUEST FOR A DISSOLUTION OF YOUR PARTNERSHIP.
HAJIME TSUKUMO WILL CONTINUE WATCHING OVER AND ASSISTING THE HANGER ZEROICHI.
THIS CON-VERSATION IS OVER.
PHEW...

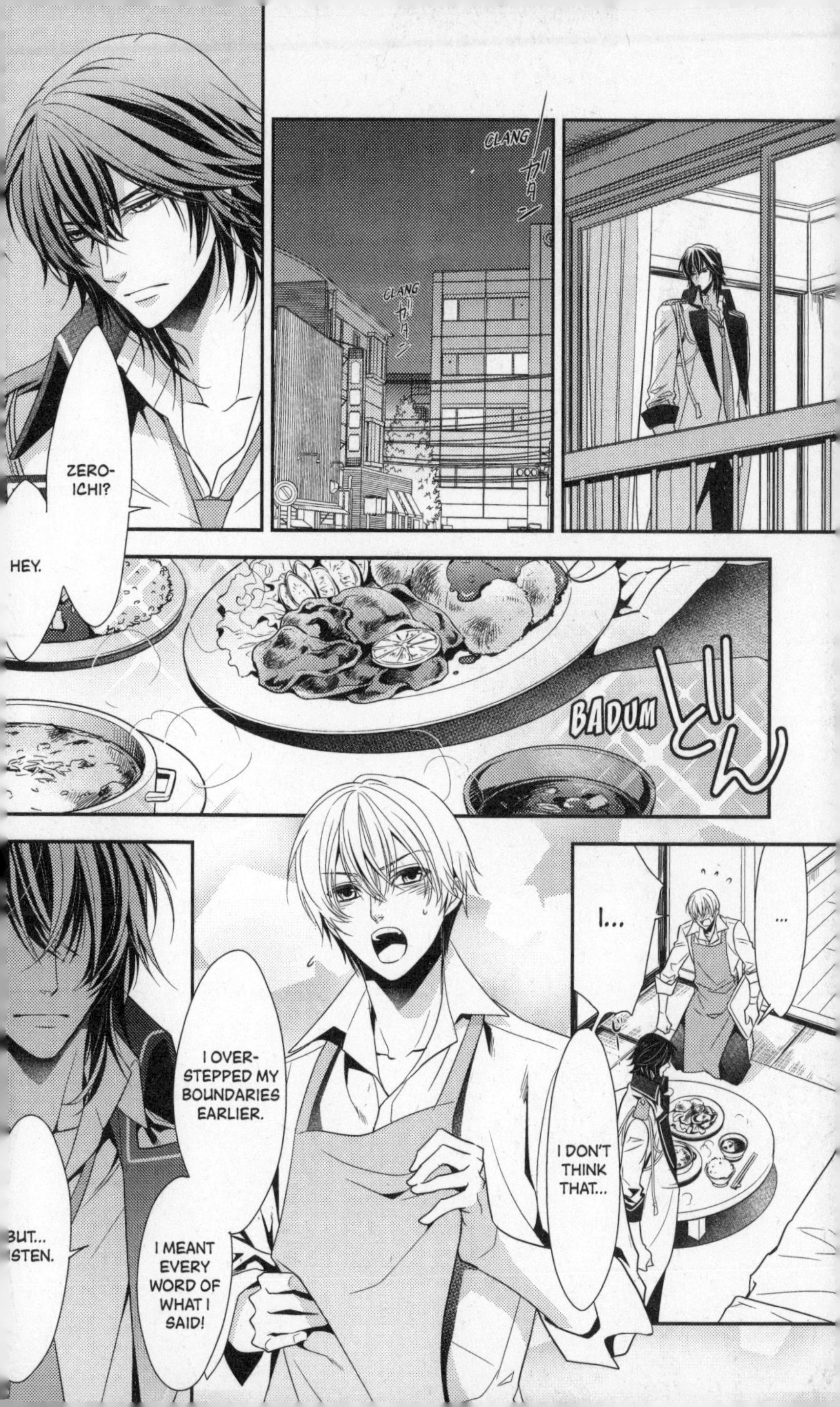
CLANG
ガタン
CLANG
ガタン
ZERO-ICHI?
HEY.
BADUM
どん
...
I...
I DON'T THINK THAT...
I OVER-STEPPED MY BOUNDARIES EARLIER.
I MEANT EVERY WORD OF WHAT I SAID!
BUT... ISTEN.

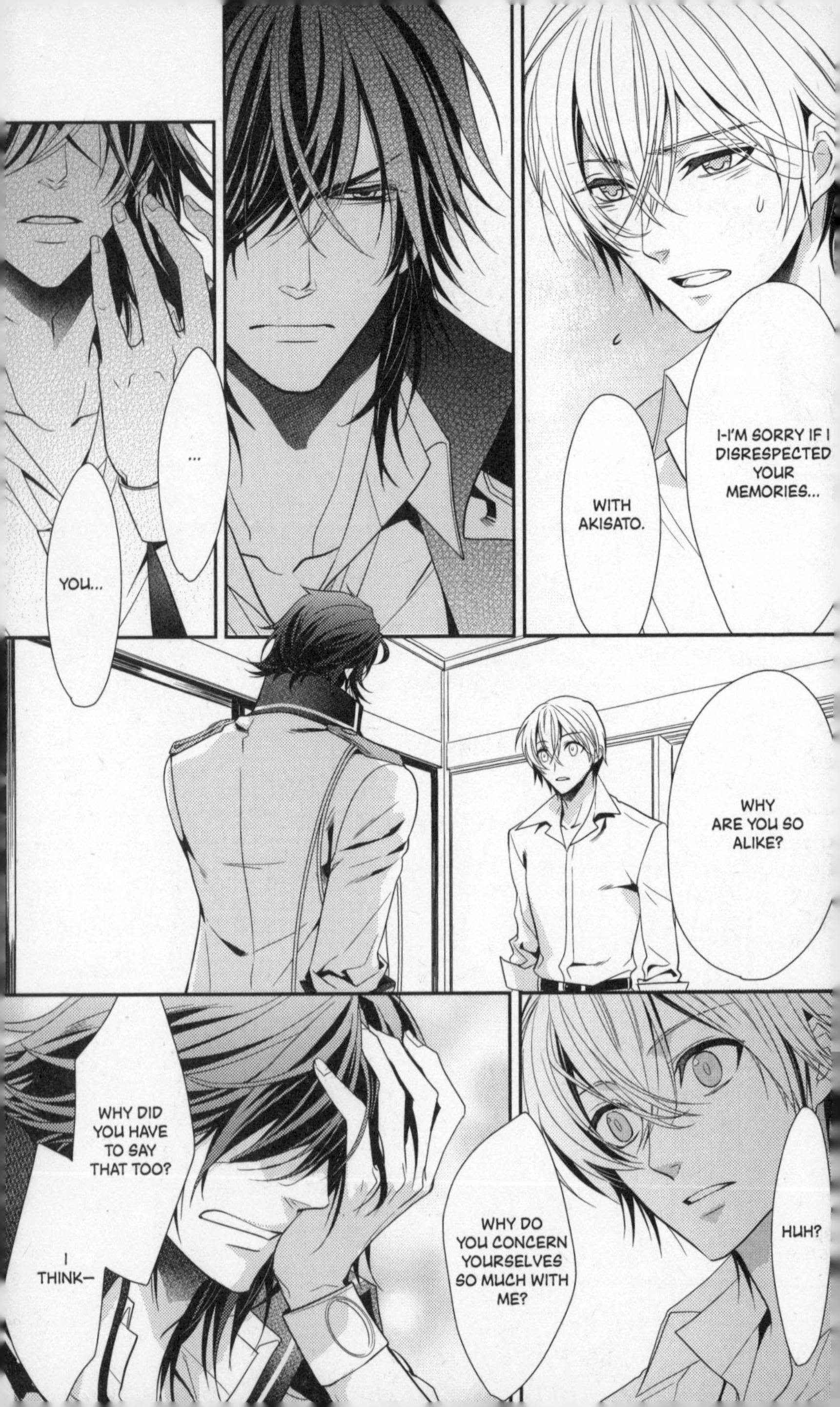
I-I'M SORRY IF I DISRESPECTED YOUR MEMORIES...
WITH AKISATO.
...
YOU...
WHY ARE YOU SO ALIKE?
HUH?
WHY DO YOU CONCERN YOURSELVES SO MUCH WITH ME?
WHY DID YOU HAVE TO SAY THAT TOO?
I THINK—

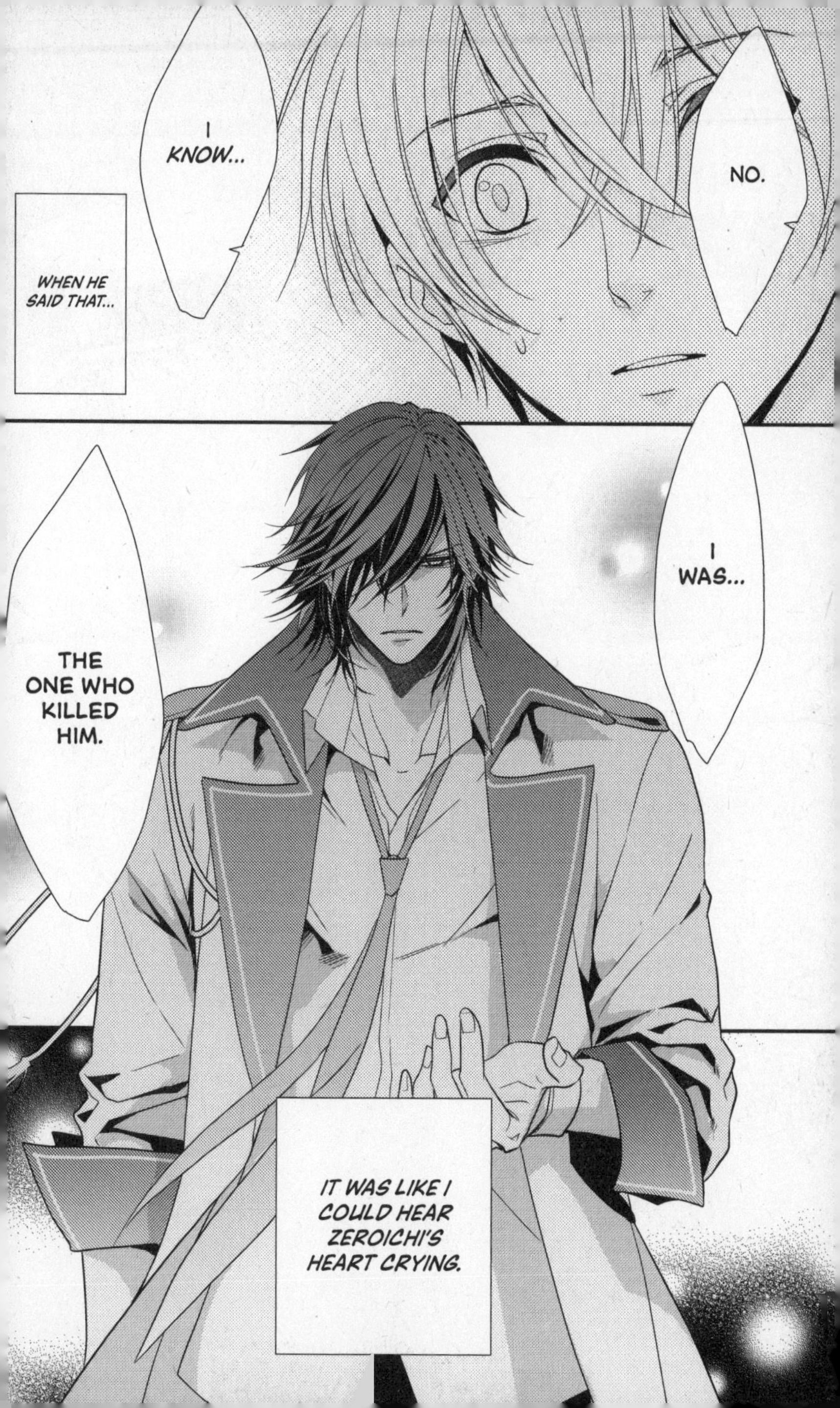
NO.
I KNOW...
WHEN HE SAID THAT...
I WAS...
THE ONE WHO KILLED HIM.
IT WAS LIKE I COULD HEAR ZEROICHI'S HEART CRYING.

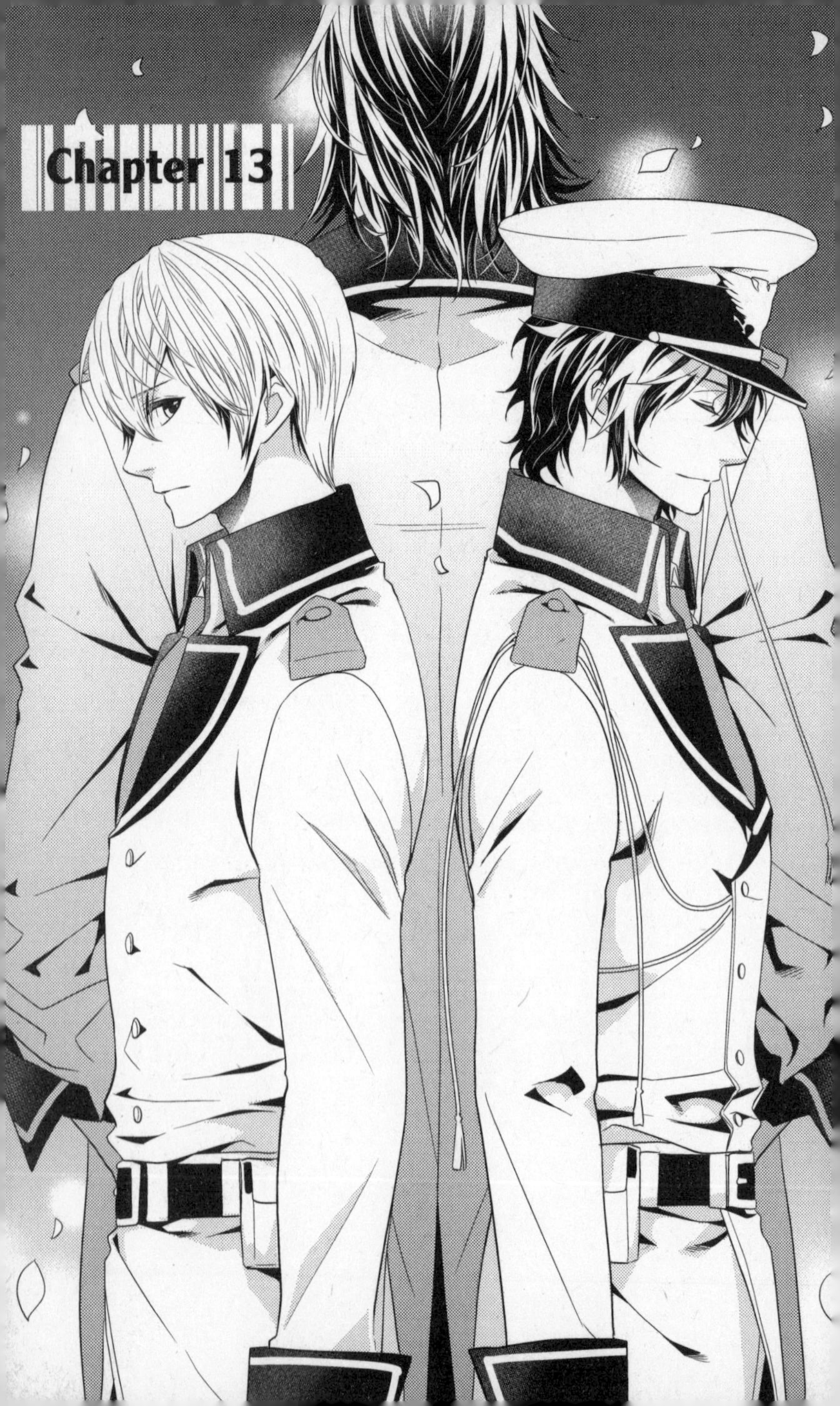
Chapter 13

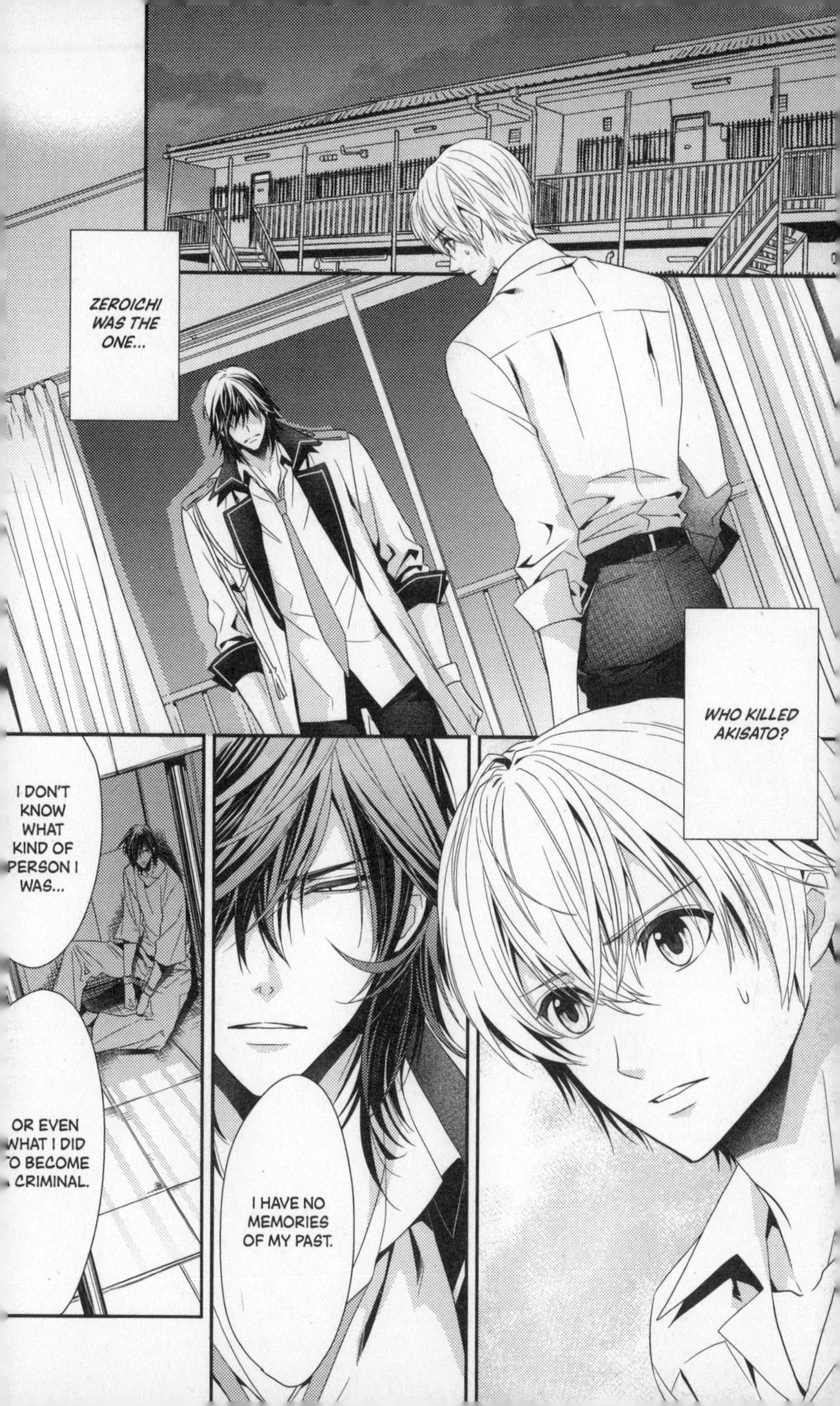
ZEROICHI WAS THE ONE...
WHO KILLED AKISATO?
I HAVE NO MEMORIES OF MY PAST.
I DON'T KNOW WHAT KIND OF PERSON I WAS...
OR EVEN WHAT I DID TO BECOME A CRIMINAL.

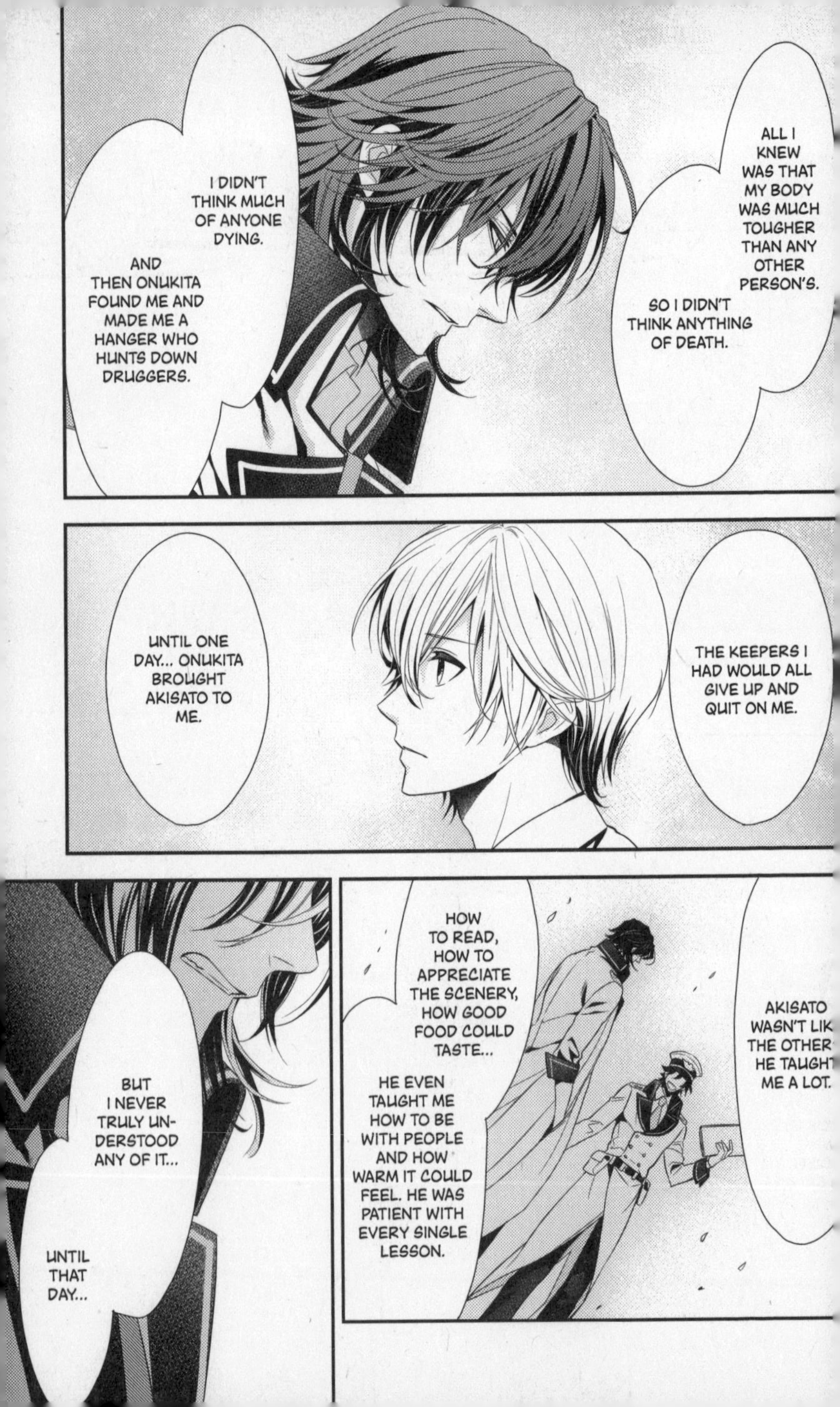
ALL I KNEW WAS THAT MY BODY WAS MUCH TOUGHER THAN ANY OTHER PERSON'S.
SO I DIDN'T THINK ANYTHING OF DEATH.
I DIDN'T THINK MUCH OF ANYONE DYING.
AND THEN ONUKITA FOUND ME AND MADE ME A HANGER WHO HUNTS DOWN DRUGGERS.
THE KEEPERS I HAD WOULD ALL GIVE UP AND QUIT ON ME.
UNTIL ONE DAY... ONUKITA BROUGHT AKISATO TO ME.
AKISATO WASN'T LIK THE OTHER HE TAUGHT ME A LOT.
HOW TO READ, HOW TO APPRECIATE THE SCENERY, HOW GOOD FOOD COULD TASTE...
HE EVEN TAUGHT ME HOW TO BE WITH PEOPLE AND HOW WARM IT COULD FEEL. HE WAS PATIENT WITH EVERY SINGLE LESSON.
BUT I NEVER TRULY UN-DERSTOOD ANY OF IT...
UNTIL THAT DAY...

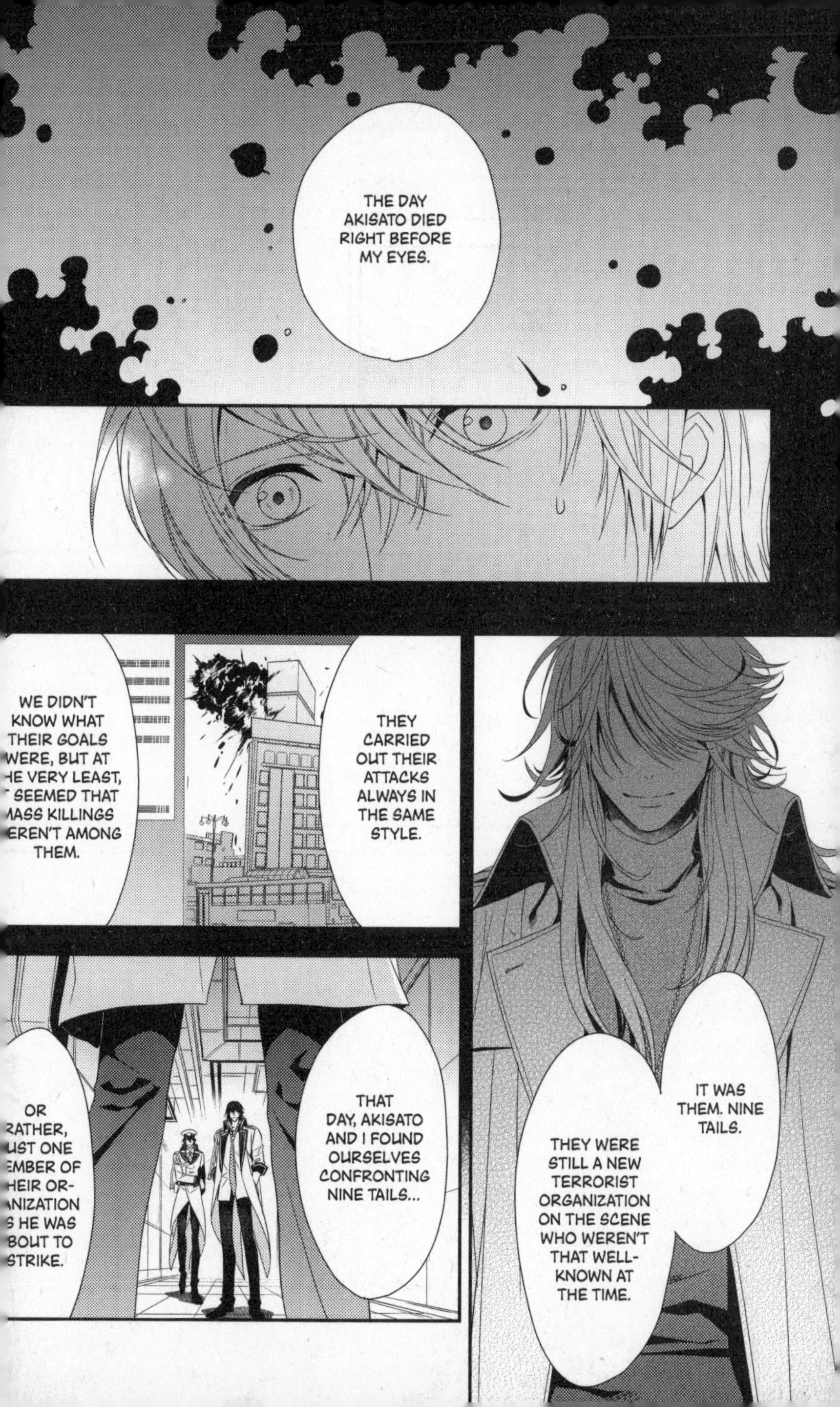
THE DAY AKISATO DIED RIGHT BEFORE MY EYES.
IT WAS THEM. NINE TAILS.
THEY WERE STILL A NEW TERRORIST ORGANIZATION ON THE SCENE WHO WEREN'T THAT WELL-KNOWN AT THE TIME.
THEY CARRIED OUT THEIR ATTACKS ALWAYS IN THE SAME STYLE.
WE DIDN'T KNOW WHAT THEIR GOALS WERE, BUT AT HE VERY LEAST, SEEMED THAT MASS KILLINGS EREN'T AMONG THEM.
THAT DAY, AKISATO AND I FOUND OURSELVES CONFRONTING NINE TAILS...
OR ZATHER, UST ONE EMBER OF HEIR OR- ANIZATION S HE WAS BOUT TO STRIKE.

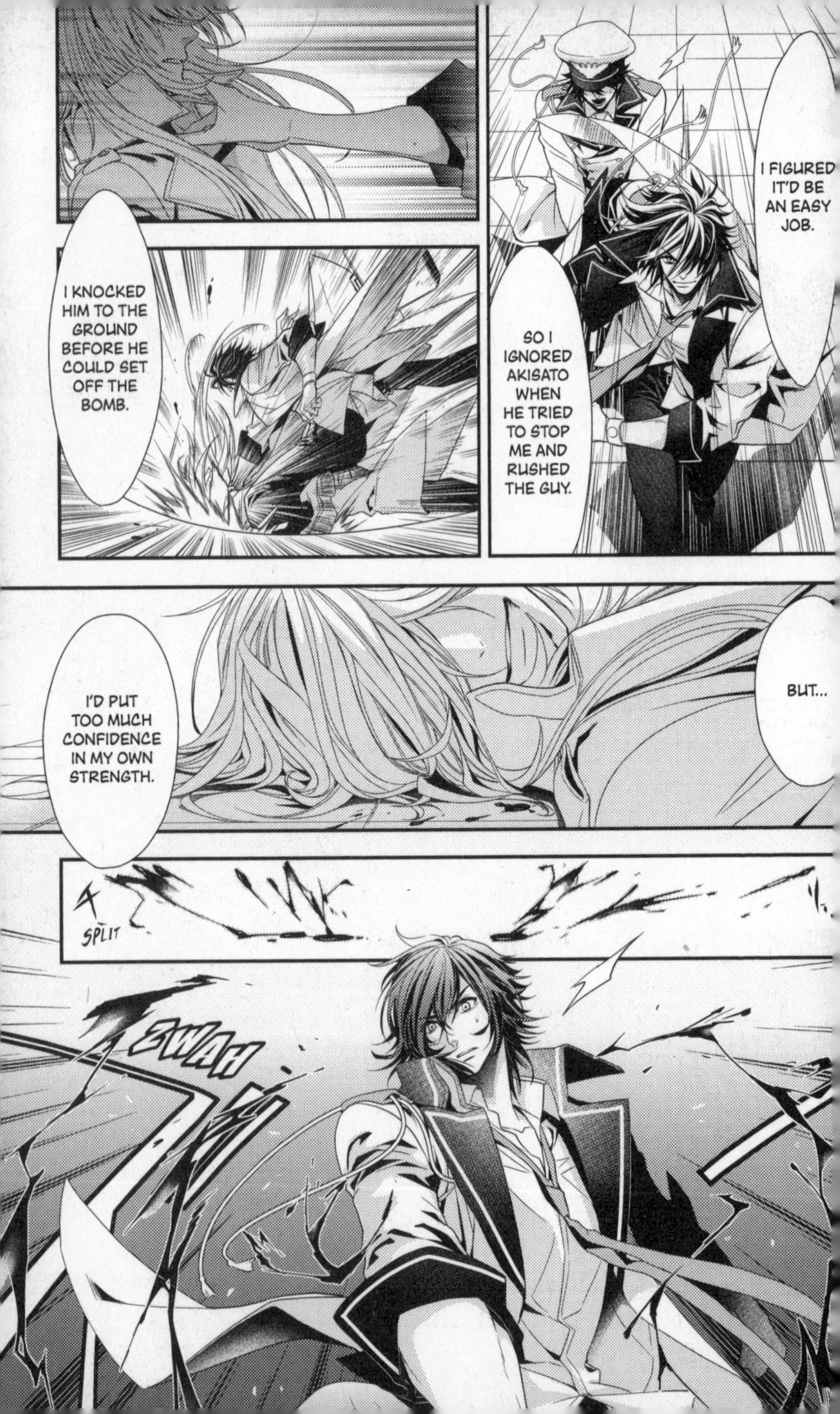
I FIGURED IT'D BE AN EASY JOB.
SO I IGNORED AKISATO WHEN HE TRIED TO STOP ME AND RUSHED THE GUY.
I KNOCKED HIM TO THE GROUND BEFORE HE COULD SET OFF THE BOMB.
BUT...
I'D PUT TOO MUCH CONFIDENCE IN MY OWN STRENGTH.
SPLIT
ZWAH

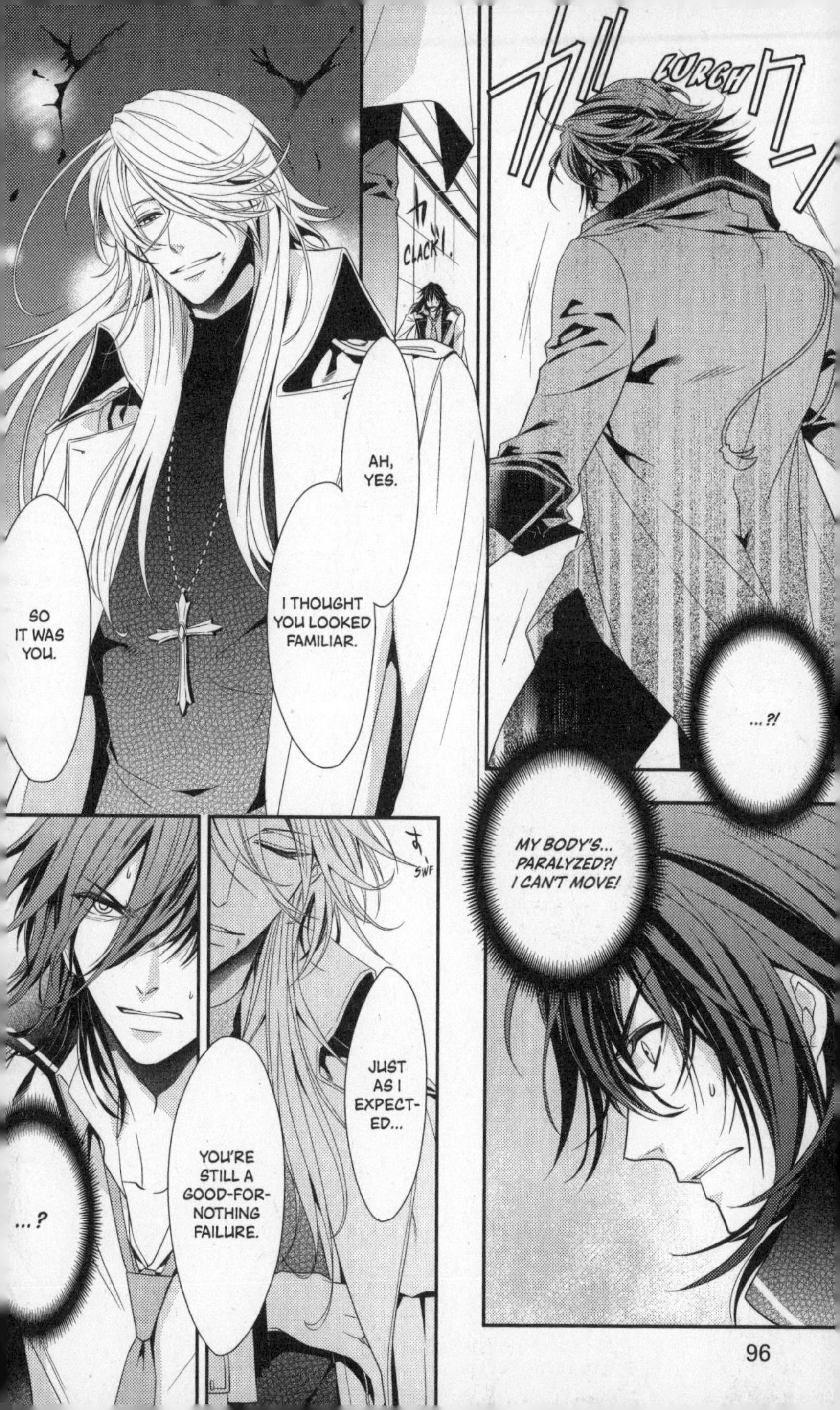

LURCH
...?!
CLACK!
AH, YES.
I THOUGHT YOU LOOKED FAMILIAR.
SO IT WAS YOU.
MY BODY'S... PARALYZED?! I CAN'T MOVE!
SWF
JUST AS I EXPECTED...
YOU'RE STILL A GOOD-FOR-NOTHING FAILURE.
...?

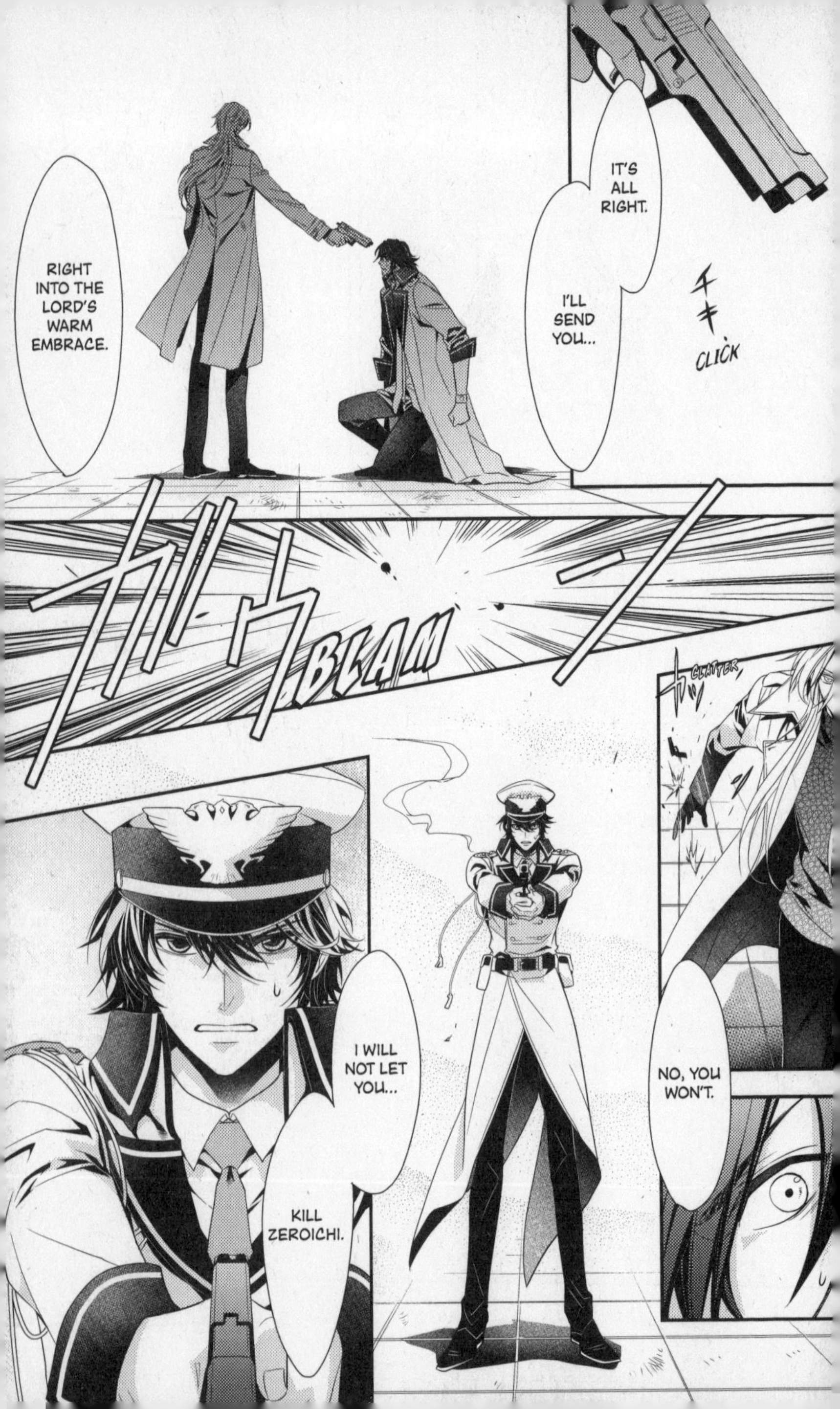
IT'S ALL RIGHT.
I'LL SEND YOU...
チキ
CLICK
RIGHT INTO THE LORD'S WARM EMBRACE.
BLAM
CLATTER
NO, YOU WON'T.
I WILL NOT LET YOU...
KILL ZEROICHI.

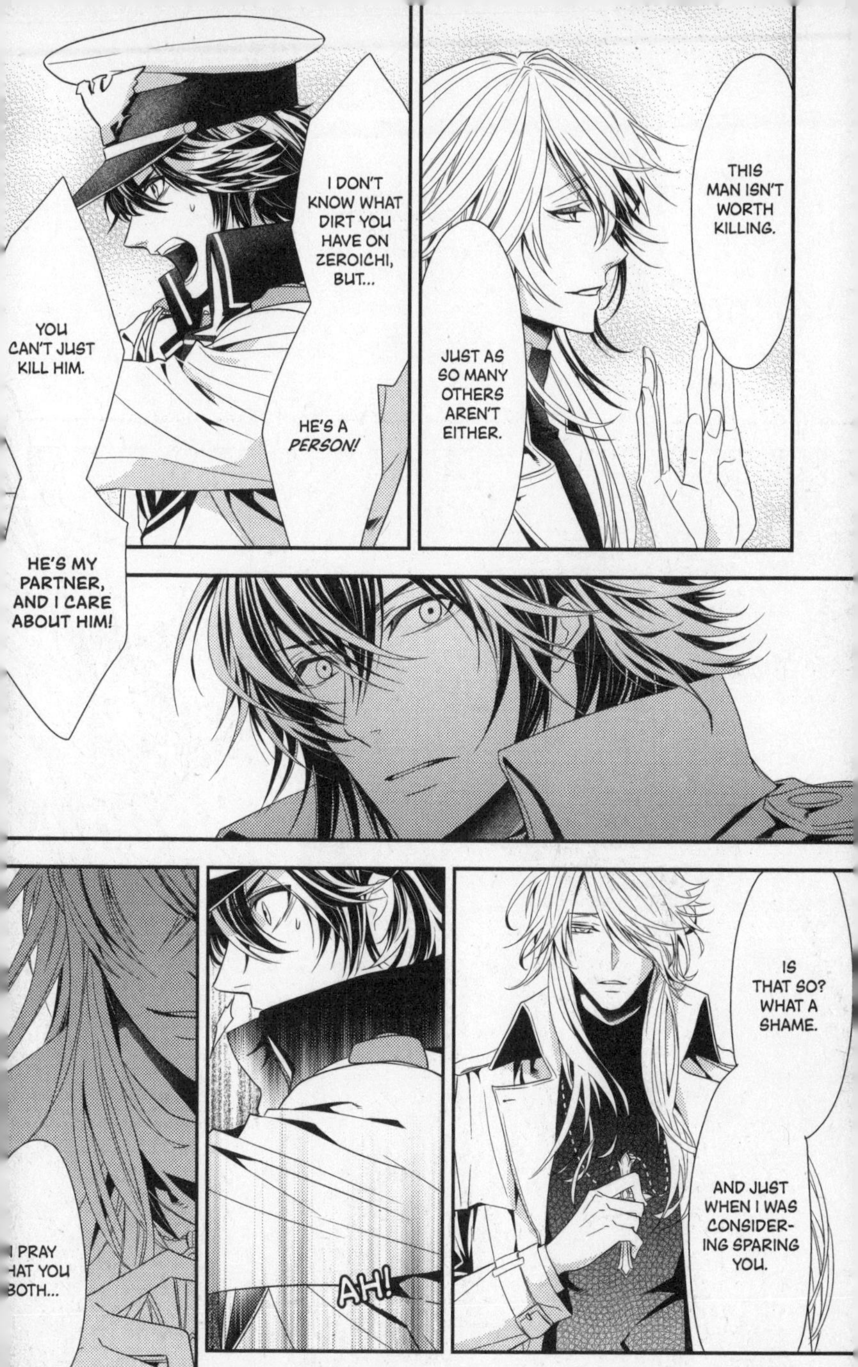
THIS MAN ISN'T WORTH KILLING.
JUST AS SO MANY OTHERS AREN'T EITHER.
I DON'T KNOW WHAT DIRT YOU HAVE ON ZEROICHI, BUT...
HE'S A *PERSON!*
YOU CAN'T JUST KILL HIM.
HE'S MY PARTNER, AND I CARE ABOUT HIM!
IS THAT SO? WHAT A SHAME.
AND JUST WHEN I WAS CONSIDER-ING SPARING YOU.
AH!
I PRAY HAT YOU BOTH...

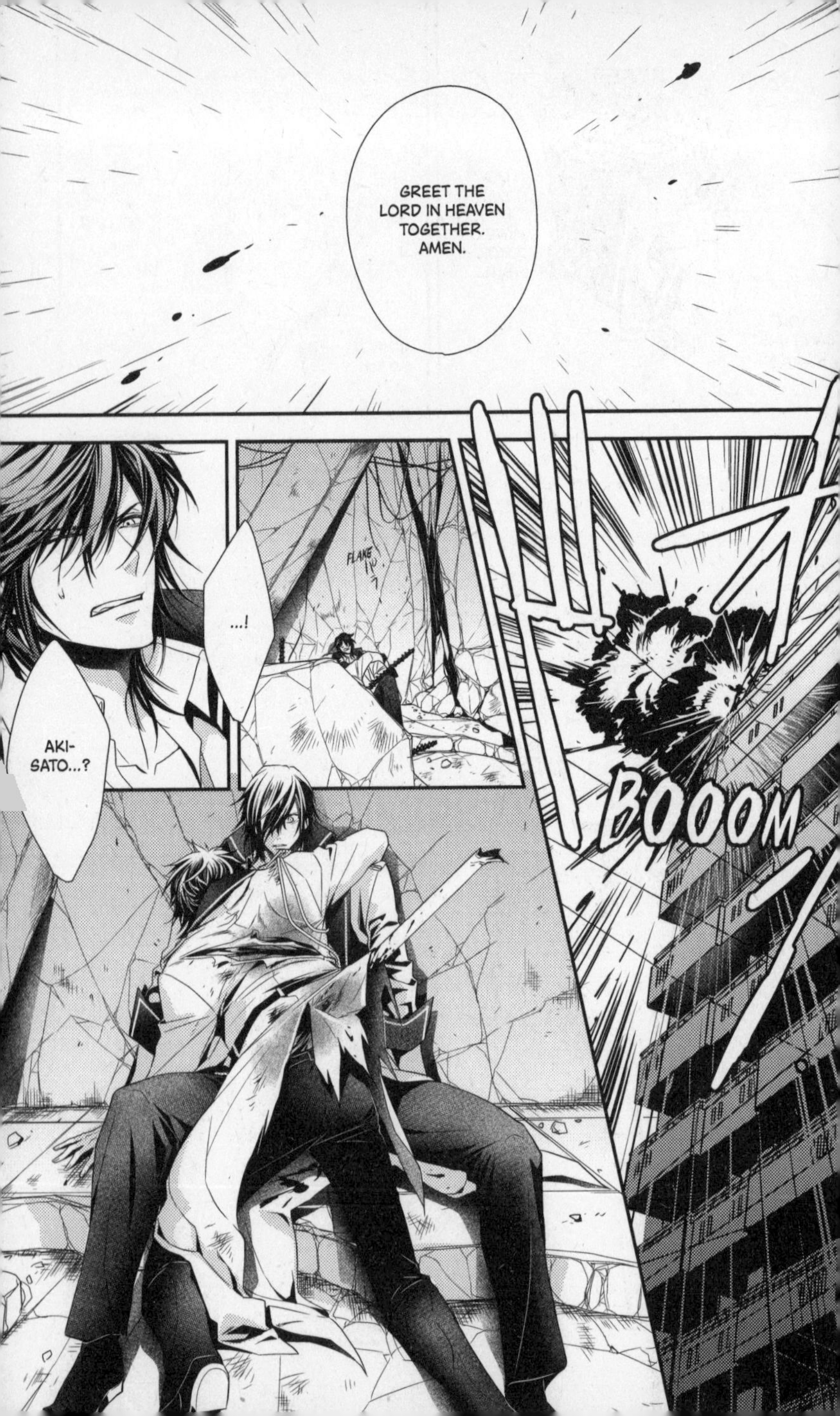
GREET THE LORD IN HEAVEN TOGETHER. AMEN.
BOOOM
FLAKE
...!
AKI-SATO...?

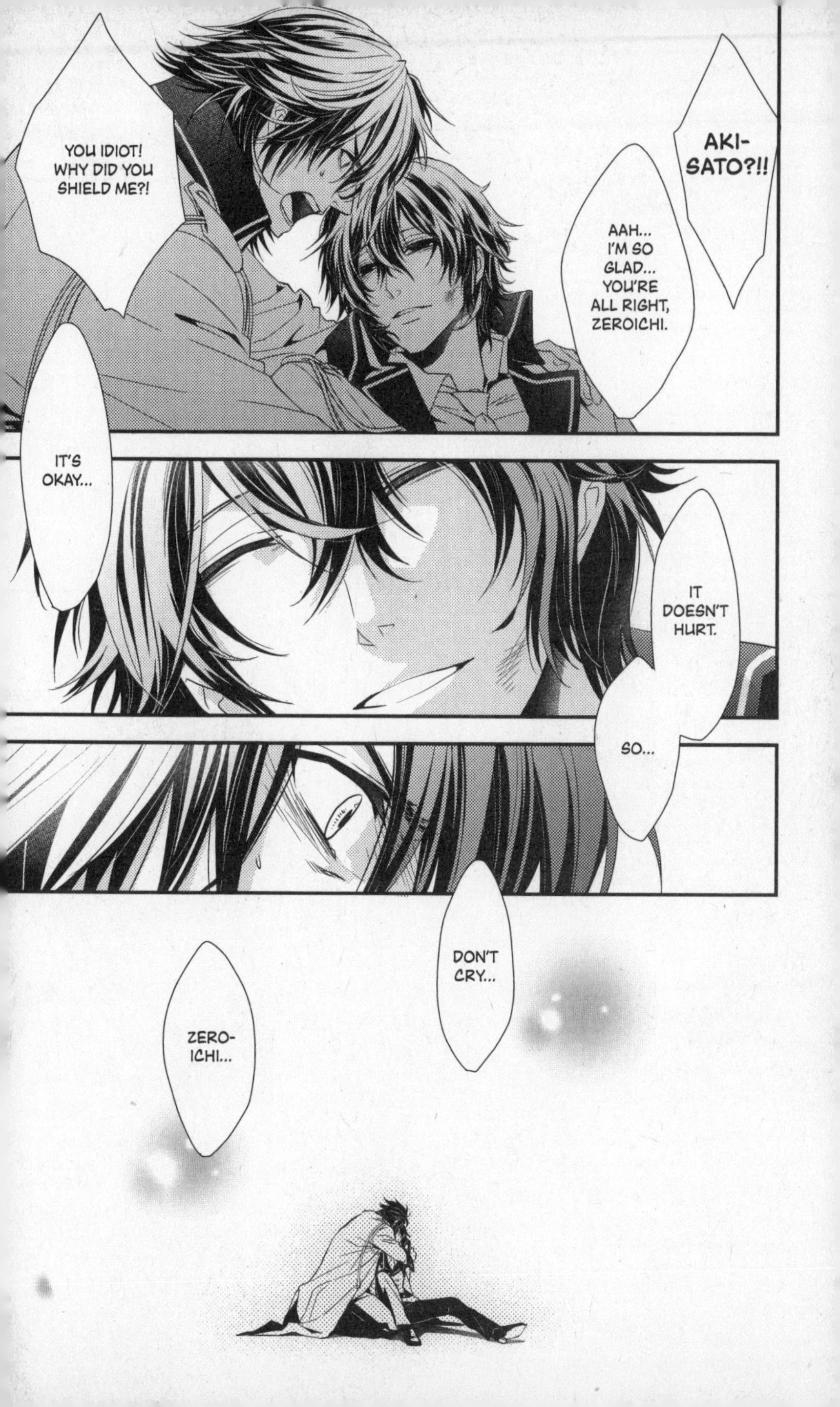
AKI-SATO?!!
AAH... I'M SO GLAD... YOU'RE ALL RIGHT, ZEROICHI.
YOU IDIOT! WHY DID YOU SHIELD ME?!
IT'S OKAY...
IT DOESN'T HURT.
SO...
DON'T CRY...
ZERO-ICHI...

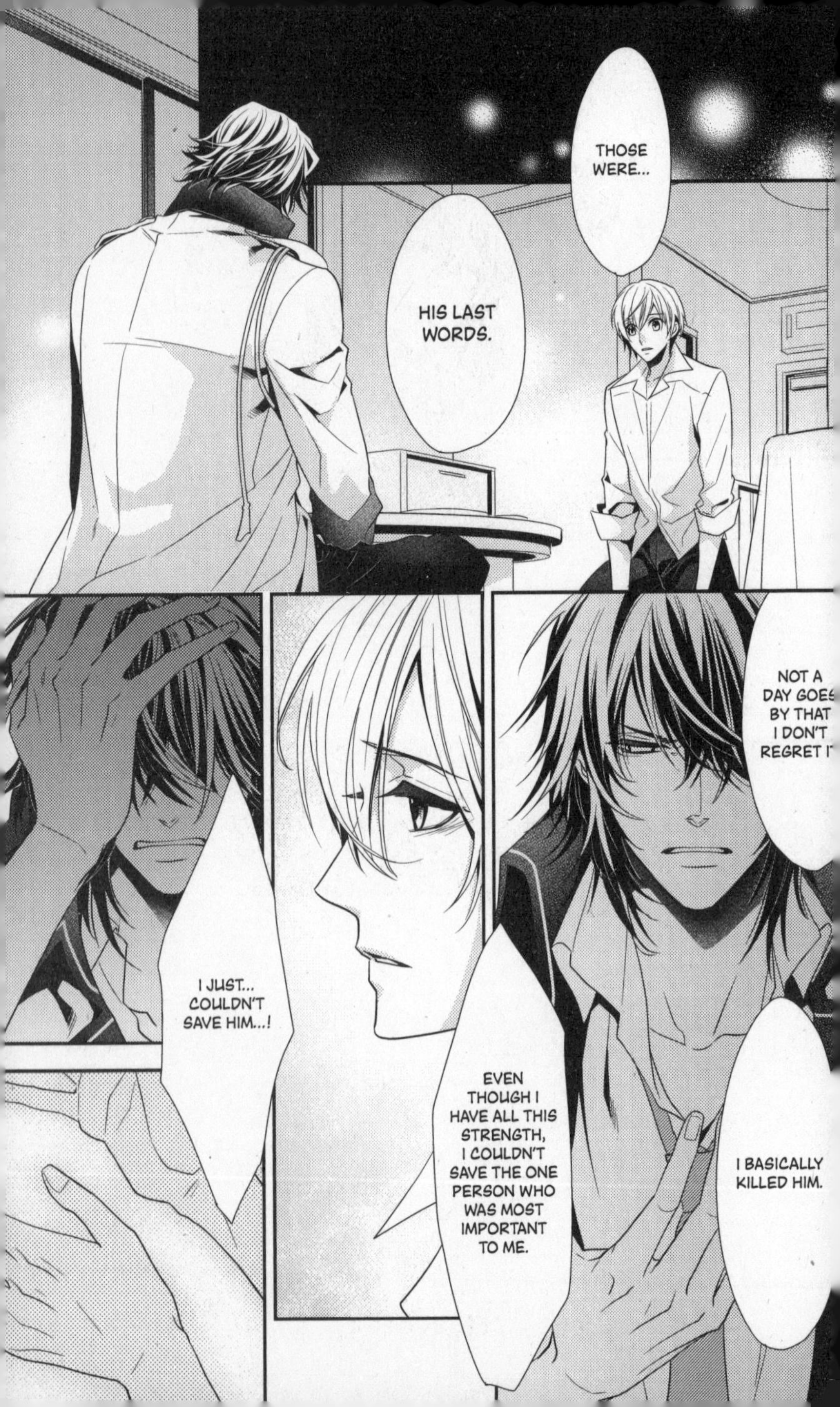
THOSE WERE...
HIS LAST WORDS.
NOT A DAY GOES BY THAT I DON'T REGRET IT
I BASICALLY KILLED HIM.
EVEN THOUGH I HAVE ALL THIS STRENGTH, I COULDN'T SAVE THE ONE PERSON WHO WAS MOST IMPORTANT TO ME.
I JUST... COULDN'T SAVE HIM...!

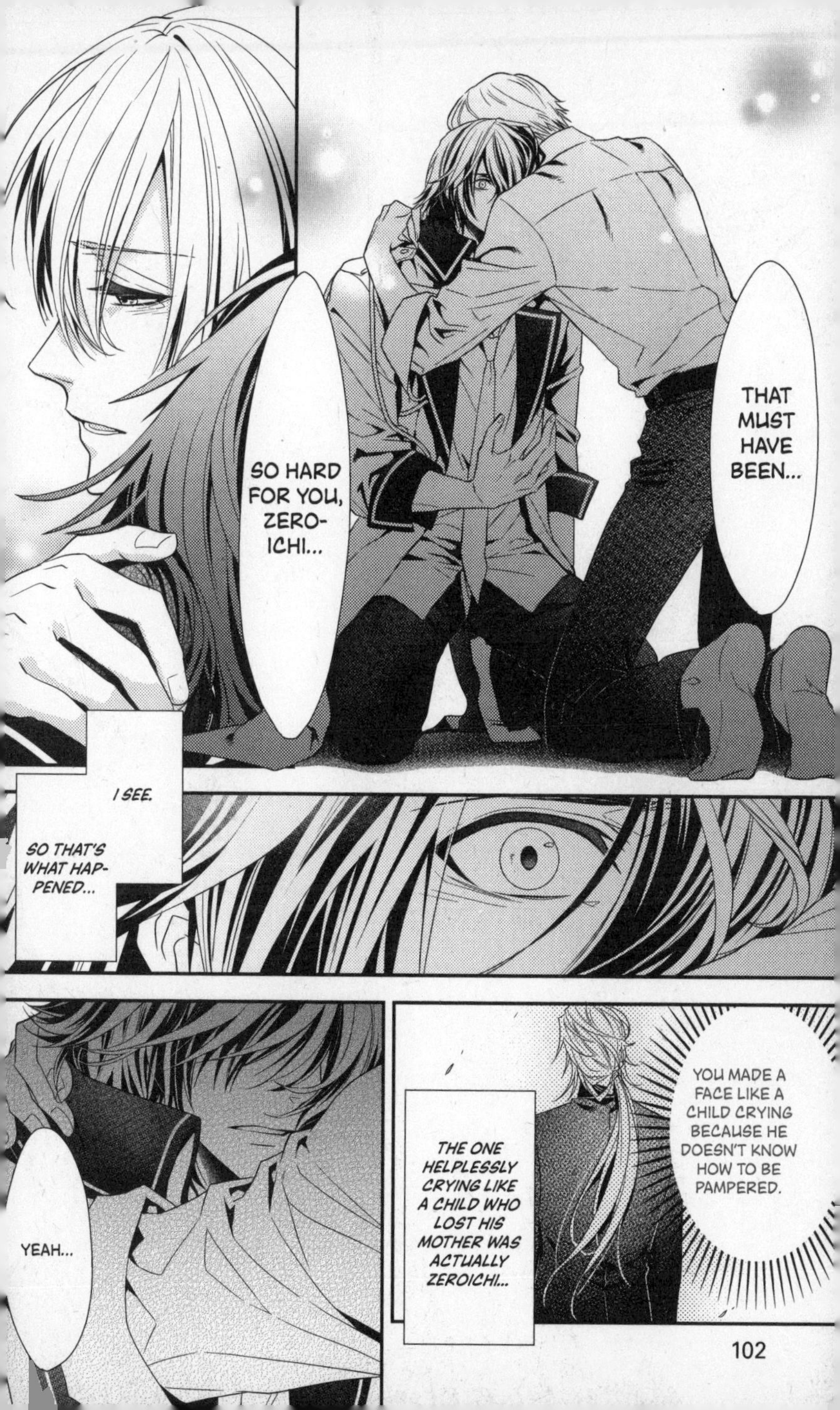

THAT MUST HAVE BEEN...
SO HARD FOR YOU, ZERO-ICHI...
I SEE.
SO THAT'S WHAT HAP-PENED...
YOU MADE A FACE LIKE A CHILD CRYING BECAUSE HE DOESN'T KNOW HOW TO BE PAMPERED.
THE ONE HELPLESSLY CRYING LIKE A CHILD WHO LOST HIS MOTHER WAS ACTUALLY ZEROICHI...
YEAH...

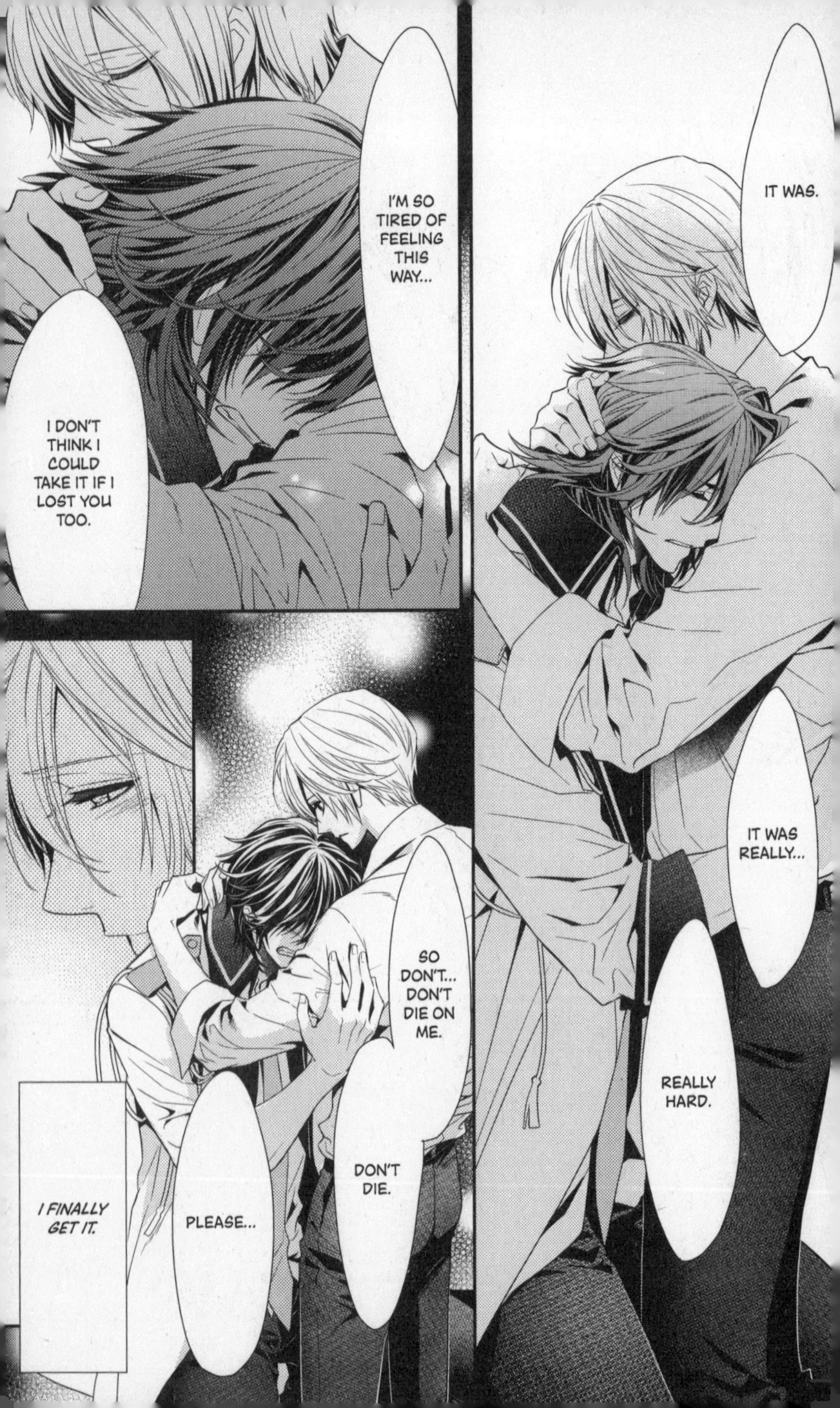
IT WAS.
IT WAS REALLY...
REALLY HARD.
I'M SO TIRED OF FEELING THIS WAY...
I DON'T THINK I COULD TAKE IT IF I LOST YOU TOO.
SO DON'T... DON'T DIE ON ME.
DON'T DIE.
PLEASE...
I FINALLY GET IT.

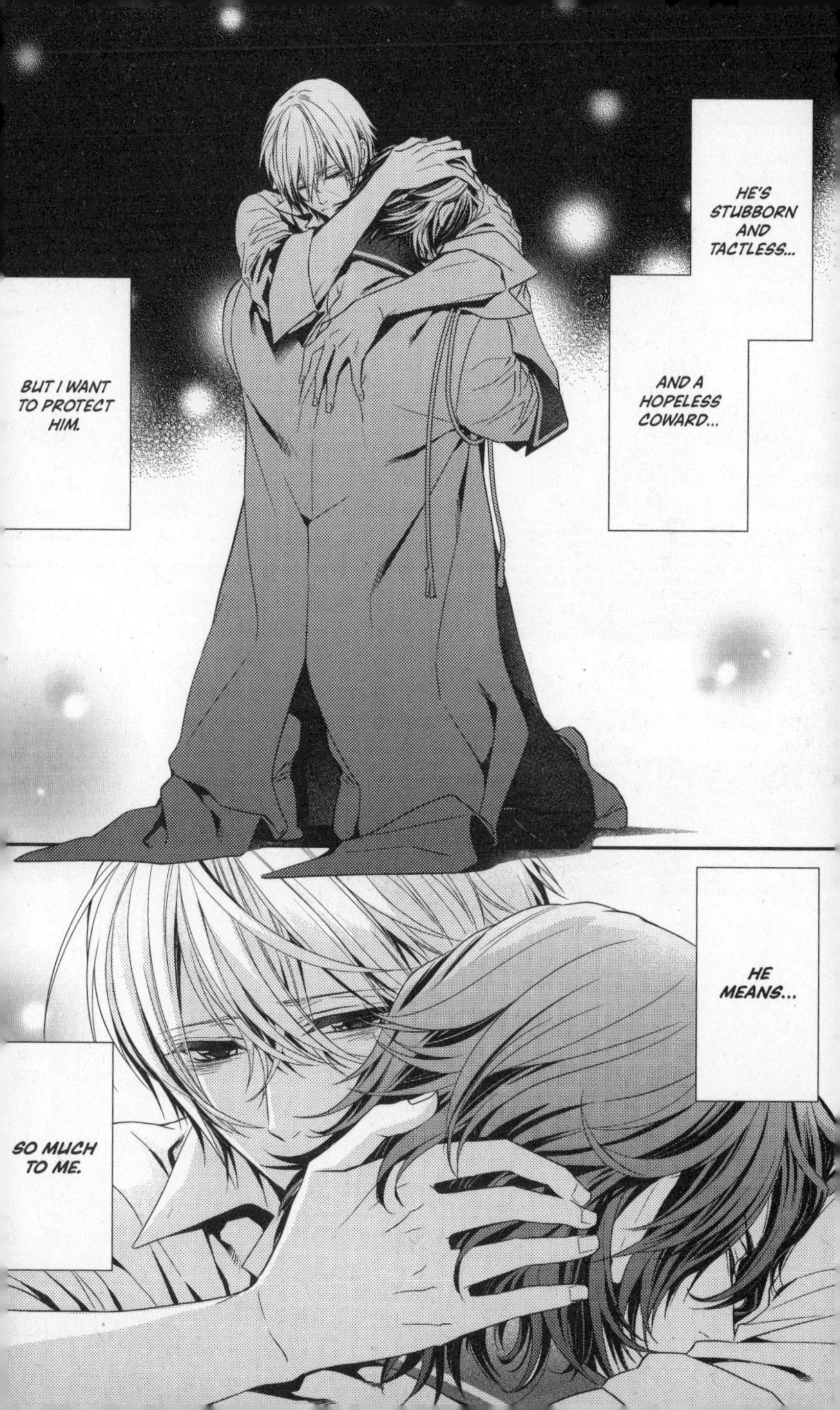
HE'S STUBBORN AND TACTLESS...
AND A HOPELESS COWARD...
BUT I WANT TO PROTECT HIM.
HE MEANS...
SO MUCH TO ME.

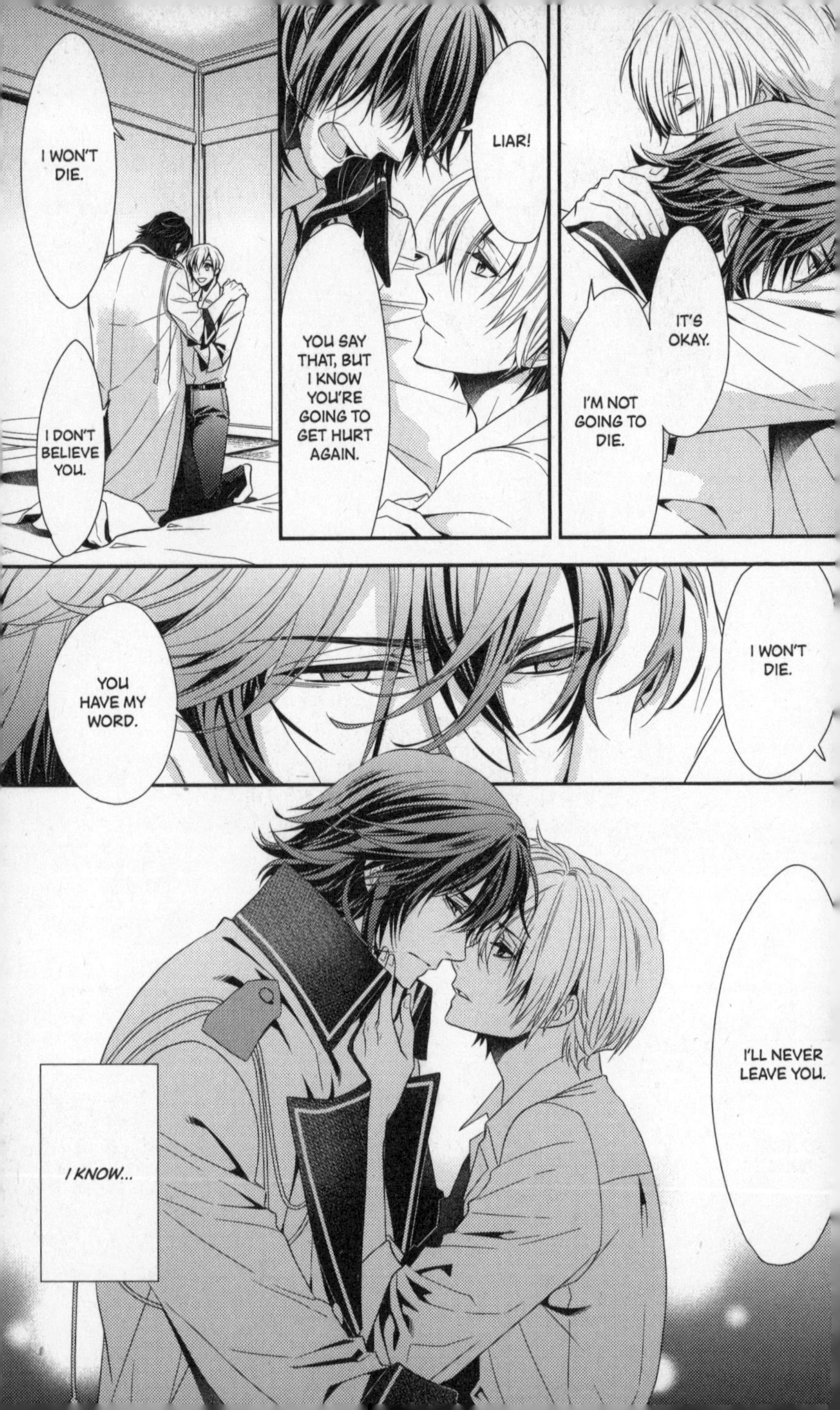
IT'S OKAY.
I'M NOT GOING TO DIE.
LIAR!
YOU SAY THAT, BUT I KNOW YOU'RE GOING TO GET HURT AGAIN.
I WON'T DIE.
I DON'T BELIEVE YOU.
I WON'T DIE.
YOU HAVE MY WORD.
I'LL NEVER LEAVE YOU.
I KNOW...

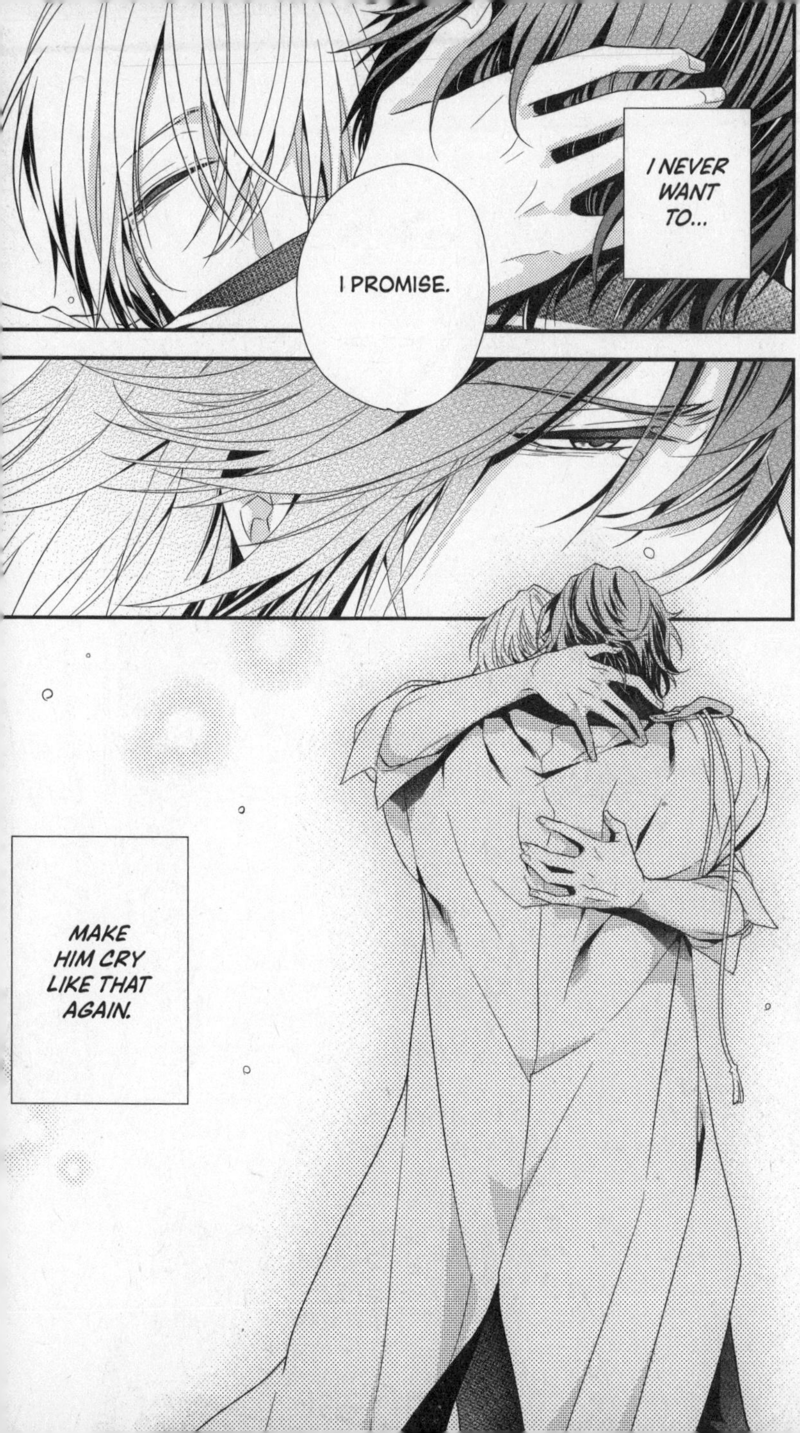
I NEVER WANT TO...
I PROMISE.
MAKE HIM CRY LIKE THAT AGAIN.

Chapter 14

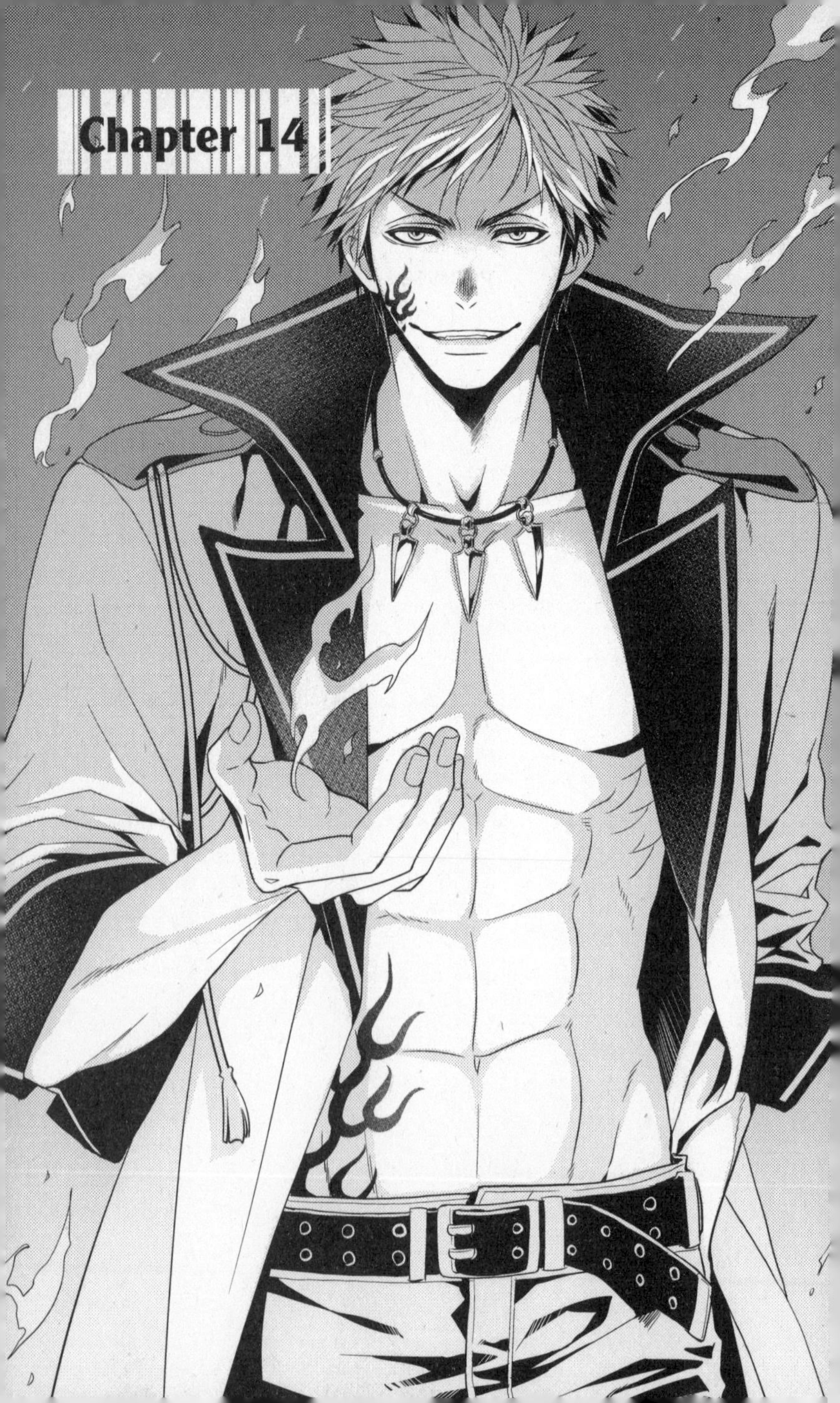

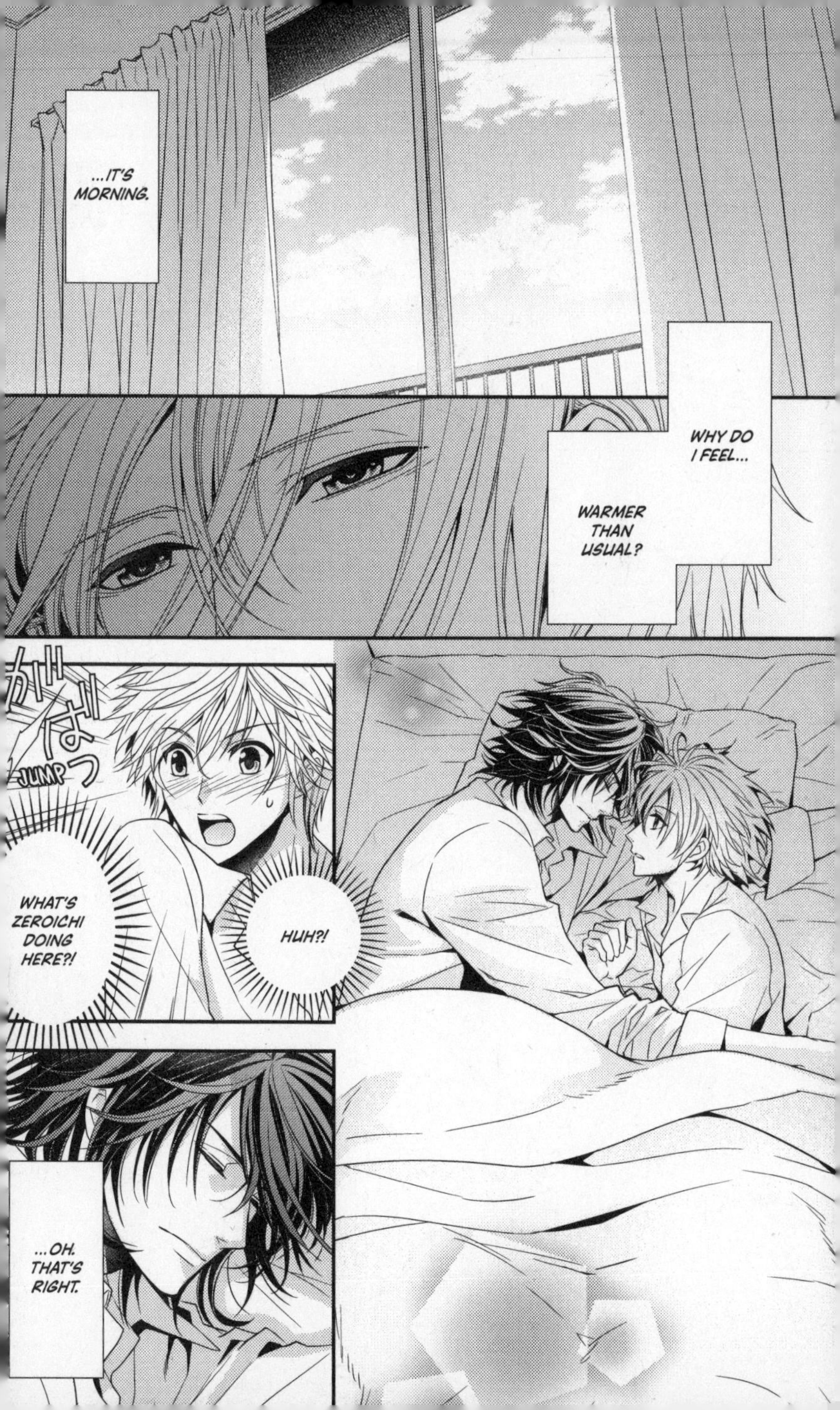
...IT'S MORNING.
WHY DO I FEEL...
WARMER THAN USUAL?
JUMP
HUH?!
WHAT'S ZEROICHI DOING HERE?!
...OH. THAT'S RIGHT.

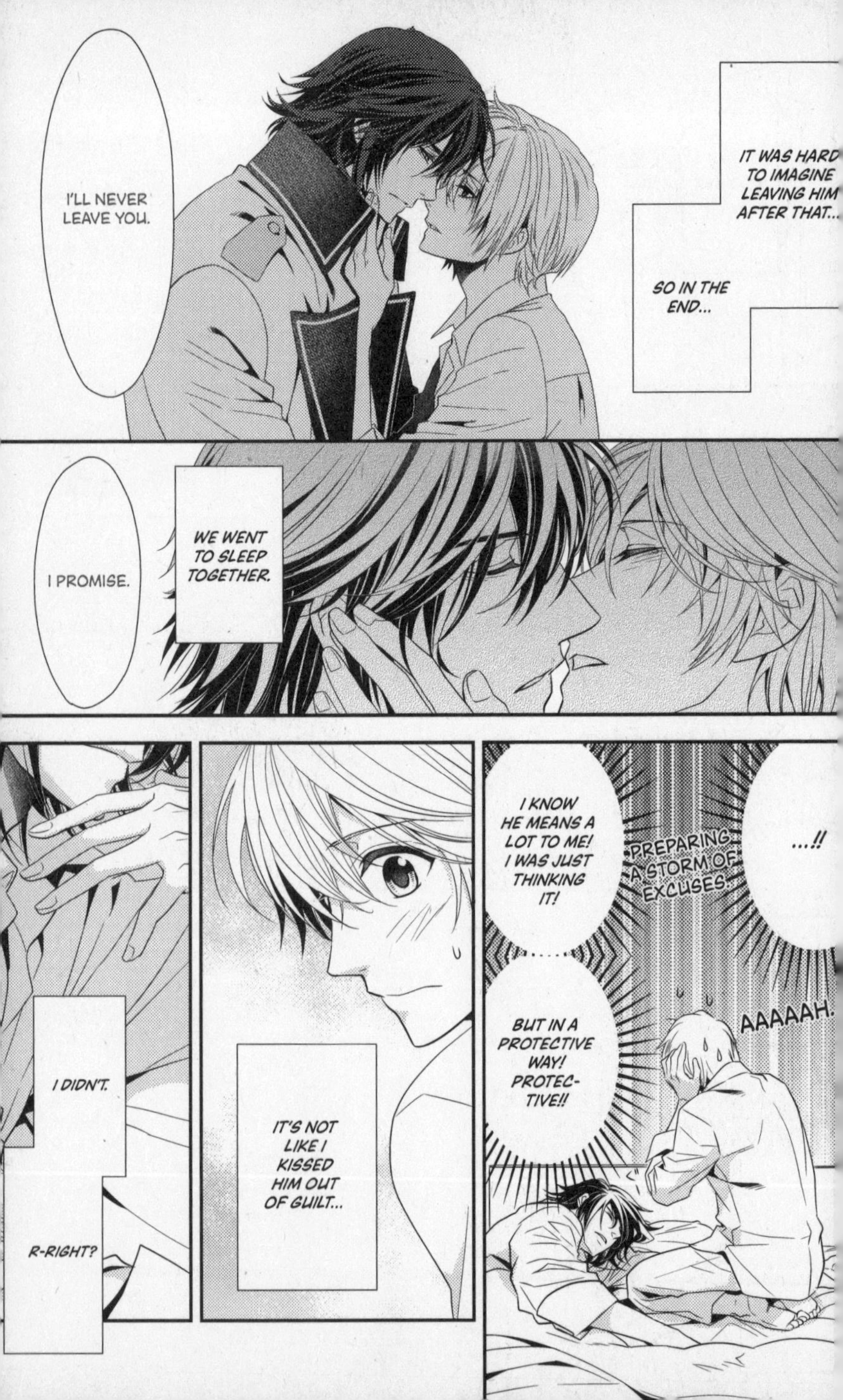
IT WAS HARD TO IMAGINE LEAVING HIM AFTER THAT...
SO IN THE END...
I'LL NEVER LEAVE YOU.
WE WENT TO SLEEP TOGETHER.
I PROMISE.
...!!
PREPARING A STORM OF EXCUSES.
I KNOW HE MEANS A LOT TO ME! I WAS JUST THINKING IT!
AAAAAH.
BUT IN A PROTECTIVE WAY! PROTEC-TIVE!!
IT'S NOT LIKE I KISSED HIM OUT OF GUILT...
I DIDN'T.
R-RIGHT?

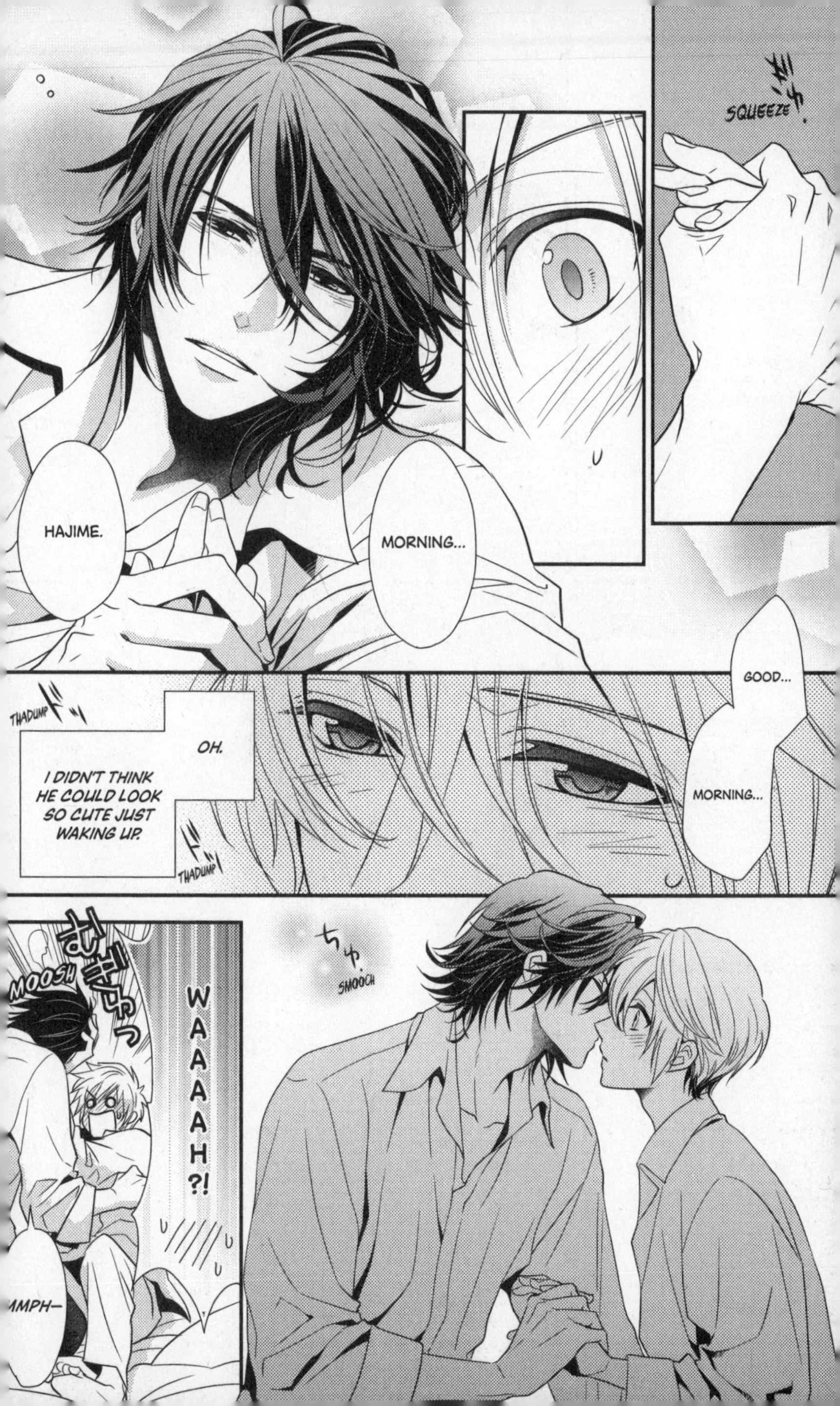

SQUEEZE
MORNING...
HAJIME.
GOOD... MORNING...
THADUMP
OH.
I DIDN'T THINK HE COULD LOOK SO CUTE JUST WAKING UP.
THADUMP
SMOOCH
WAAAAAH?!
MOOSH
MMPH—

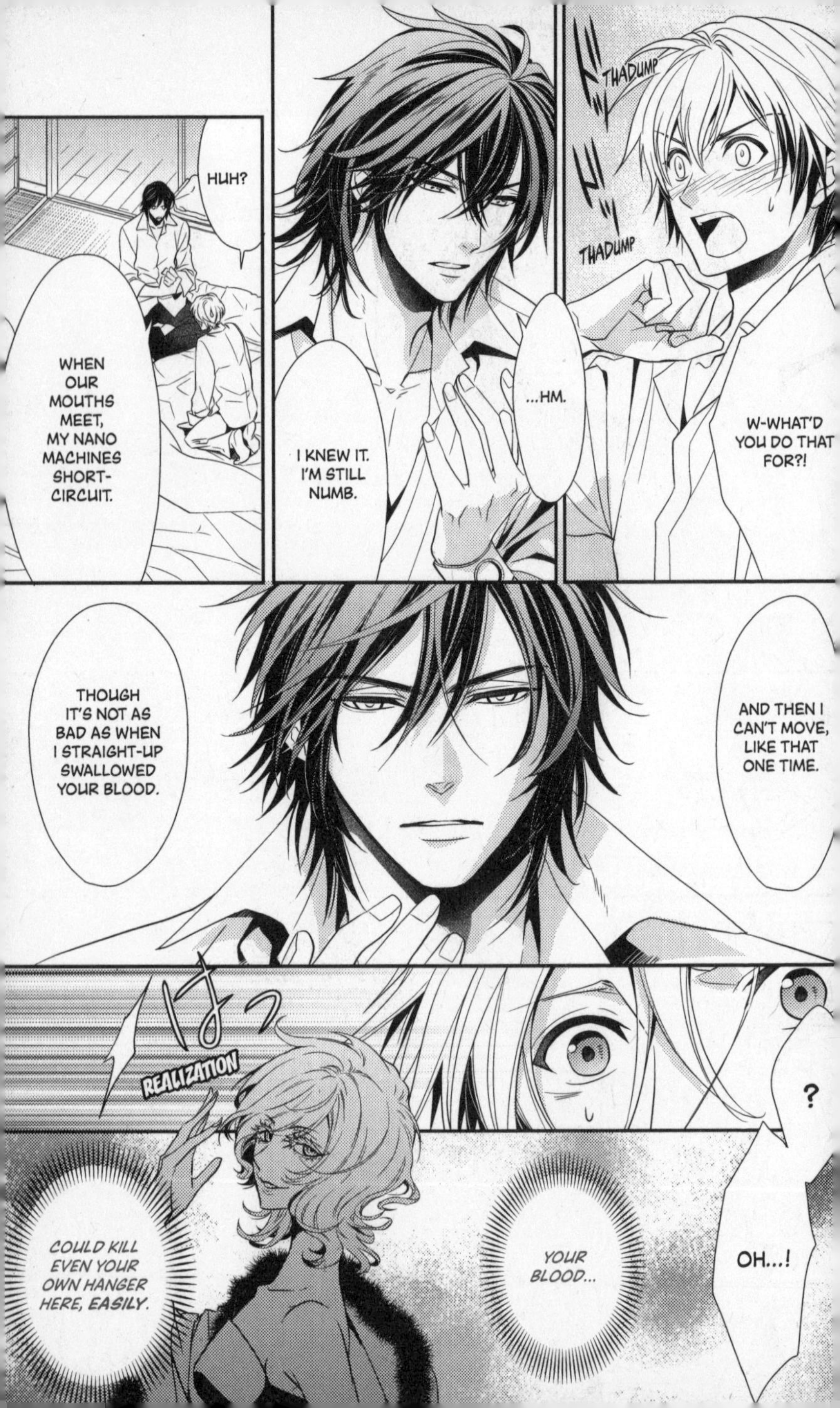
THADUMP
THADUMP
W-WHAT'D YOU DO THAT FOR?!
...HM.
I KNEW IT. I'M STILL NUMB.
HUH?
WHEN OUR MOUTHS MEET, MY NANO MACHINES SHORT-CIRCUIT.
AND THEN I CAN'T MOVE, LIKE THAT ONE TIME.
THOUGH IT'S NOT AS BAD AS WHEN I STRAIGHT-UP SWALLOWED YOUR BLOOD.
?
はっ
REALIZATION
OH...!
YOUR BLOOD...
COULD KILL EVEN YOUR OWN HANGER HERE, EASILY.

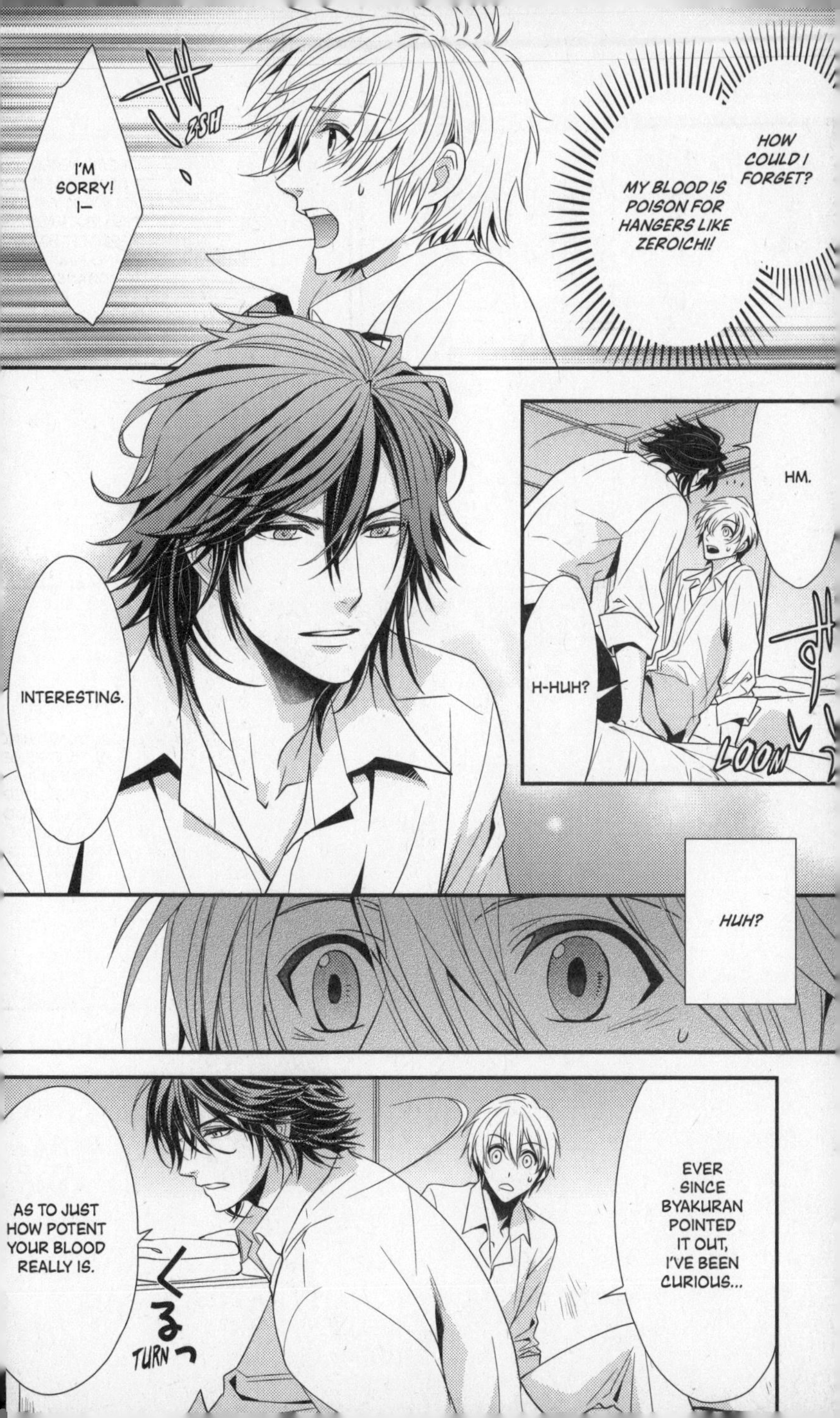
HOW COULD I FORGET?
MY BLOOD IS POISON FOR HANGERS LIKE ZEROICHI!
ZSH
I'M SORRY! I—
HM.
H-HUH?
LOOM
INTERESTING.
HUH?
EVER SINCE BYAKURAN POINTED IT OUT, I'VE BEEN CURIOUS...
AS TO JUST HOW POTENT YOUR BLOOD REALLY IS.
TURN

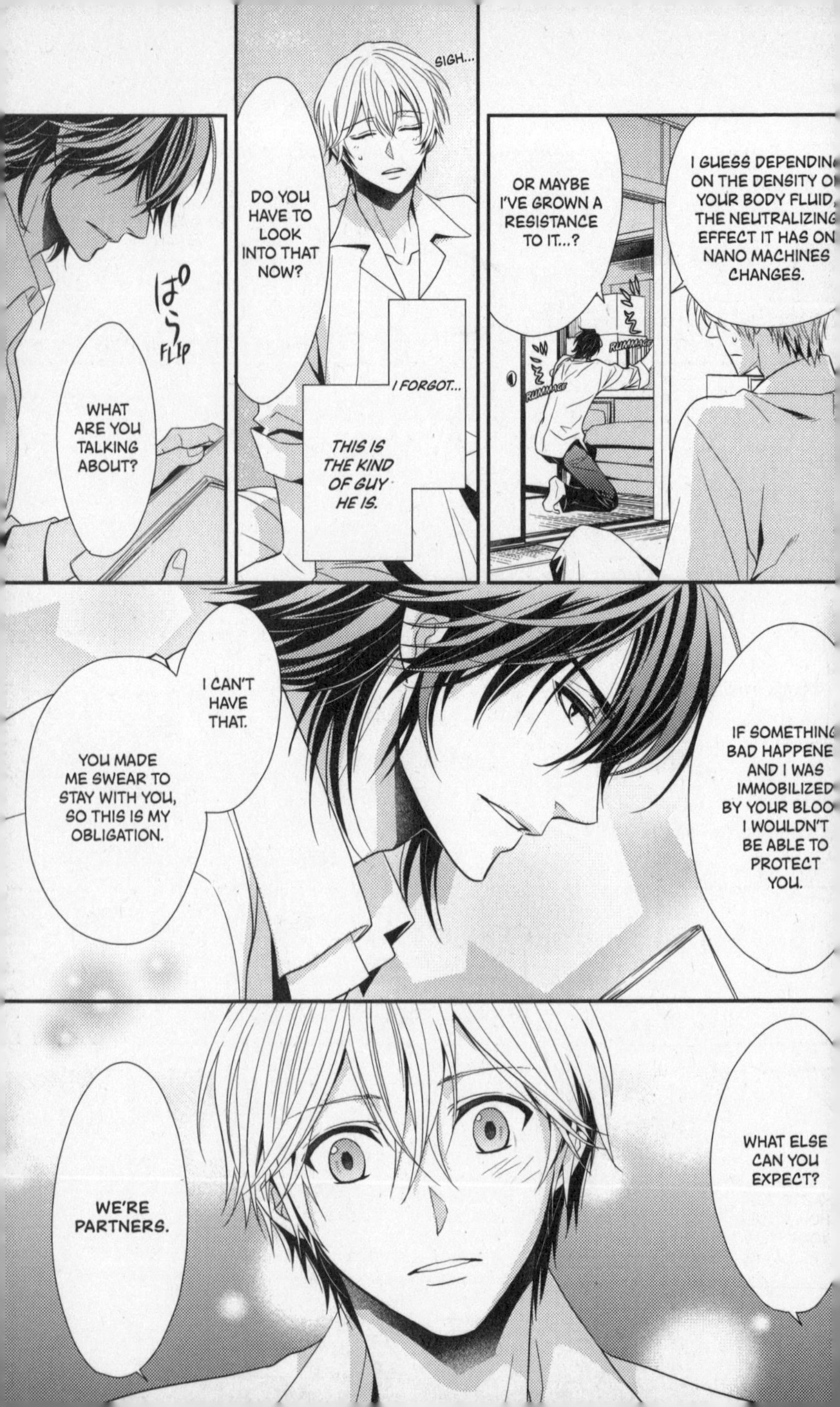

I GUESS DEPENDIN ON THE DENSITY O YOUR BODY FLUID, THE NEUTRALIZING EFFECT IT HAS ON NANO MACHINES CHANGES.
OR MAYBE I'VE GROWN A RESISTANCE TO IT...?
RUMMAGE
RUMMAGE
SIGH...
DO YOU HAVE TO LOOK INTO THAT NOW?
I FORGOT...
THIS IS THE KIND OF GUY HE IS.
ぱら
FLIP
WHAT ARE YOU TALKING ABOUT?
IF SOMETHIN BAD HAPPENE AND I WAS IMMOBILIZED BY YOUR BLOO I WOULDN'T BE ABLE TO PROTECT YOU.
I CAN'T HAVE THAT.
YOU MADE ME SWEAR TO STAY WITH YOU, SO THIS IS MY OBLIGATION.
WHAT ELSE CAN YOU EXPECT?
WE'RE PARTNERS.

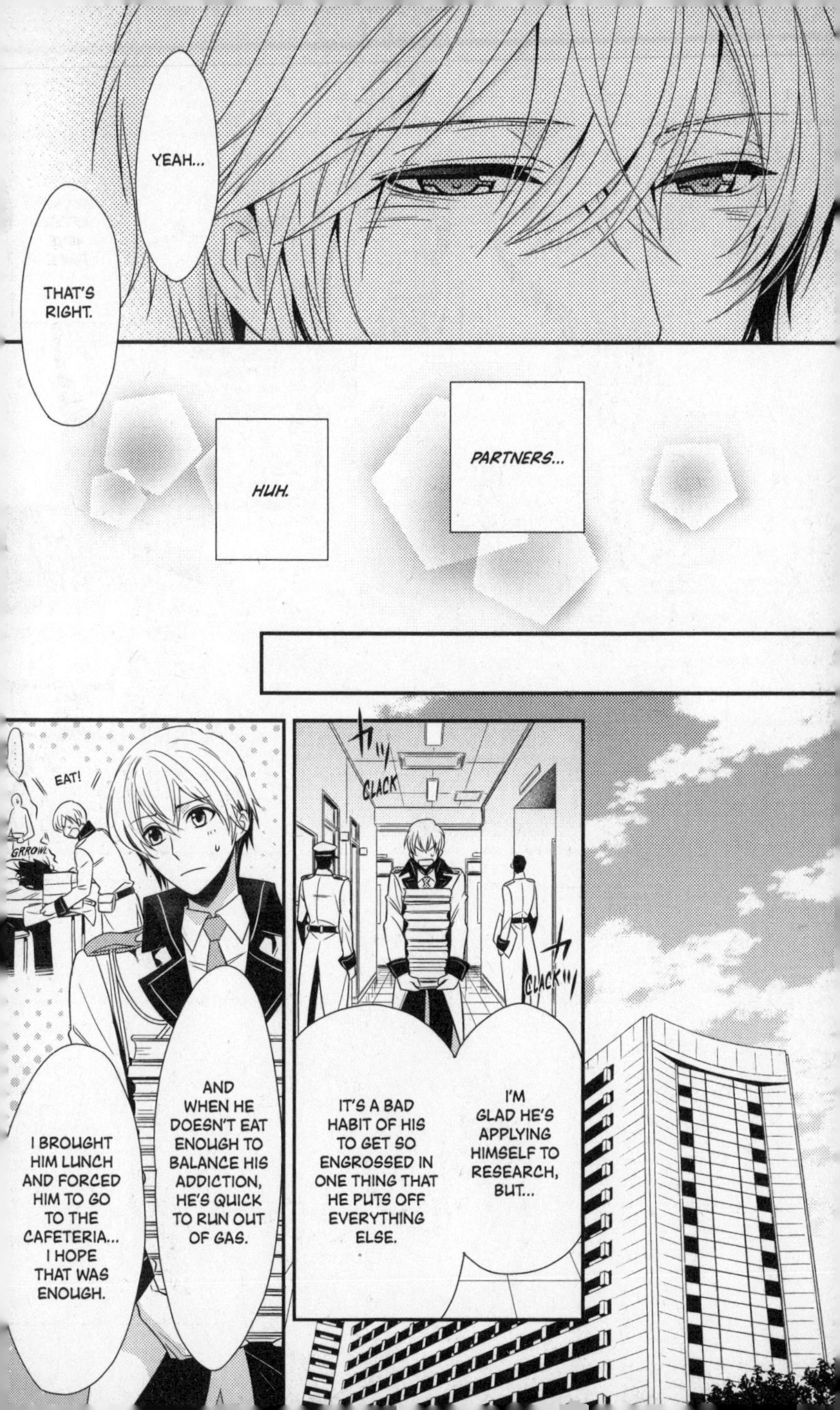
YEAH...
THAT'S RIGHT.
PARTNERS...
HUH.
I'M GLAD HE'S APPLYING HIMSELF TO RESEARCH, BUT...
CLACK
CLACK
IT'S A BAD HABIT OF HIS TO GET SO ENGROSSED IN ONE THING THAT HE PUTS OFF EVERYTHING ELSE.
...
EAT!
GRROWL
AND WHEN HE DOESN'T EAT ENOUGH TO BALANCE HIS ADDICTION, HE'S QUICK TO RUN OUT OF GAS.
I BROUGHT HIM LUNCH AND FORCED HIM TO GO TO THE CAFETERIA... I HOPE THAT WAS ENOUGH.

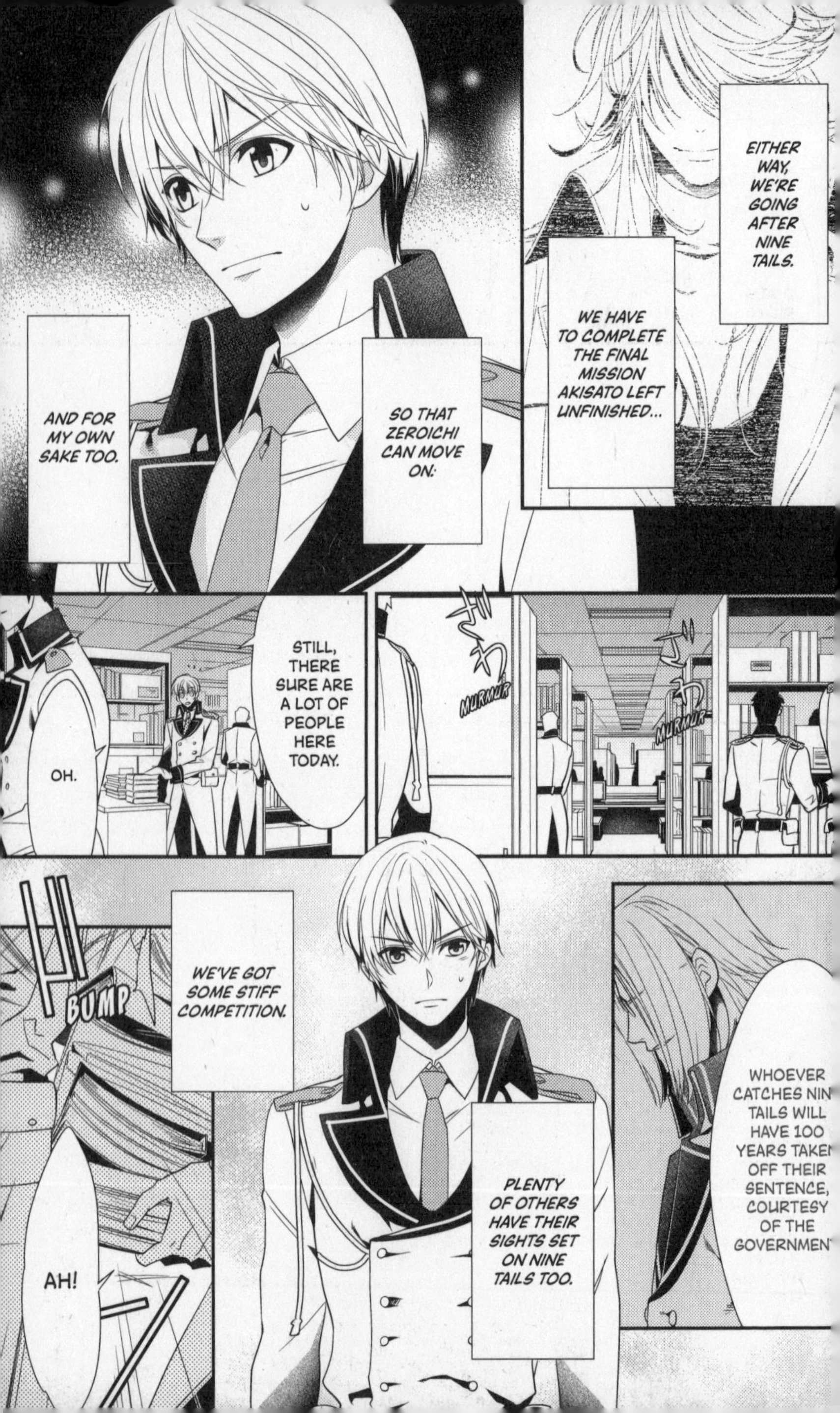
EITHER WAY, WE'RE GOING AFTER NINE TAILS.
WE HAVE TO COMPLETE THE FINAL MISSION AKISATO LEFT UNFINISHED...
SO THAT ZEROICHI CAN MOVE ON:
AND FOR MY OWN SAKE TOO.
MURMUR
MURMUR
STILL, THERE SURE ARE A LOT OF PEOPLE HERE TODAY.
OH.
WHOEVER CATCHES NIN TAILS WILL HAVE 100 YEARS TAKEN OFF THEIR SENTENCE, COURTESY OF THE GOVERNMEN
PLENTY OF OTHERS HAVE THEIR SIGHTS SET ON NINE TAILS TOO.
WE'VE GOT SOME STIFF COMPETITION.
BUMP
AH!

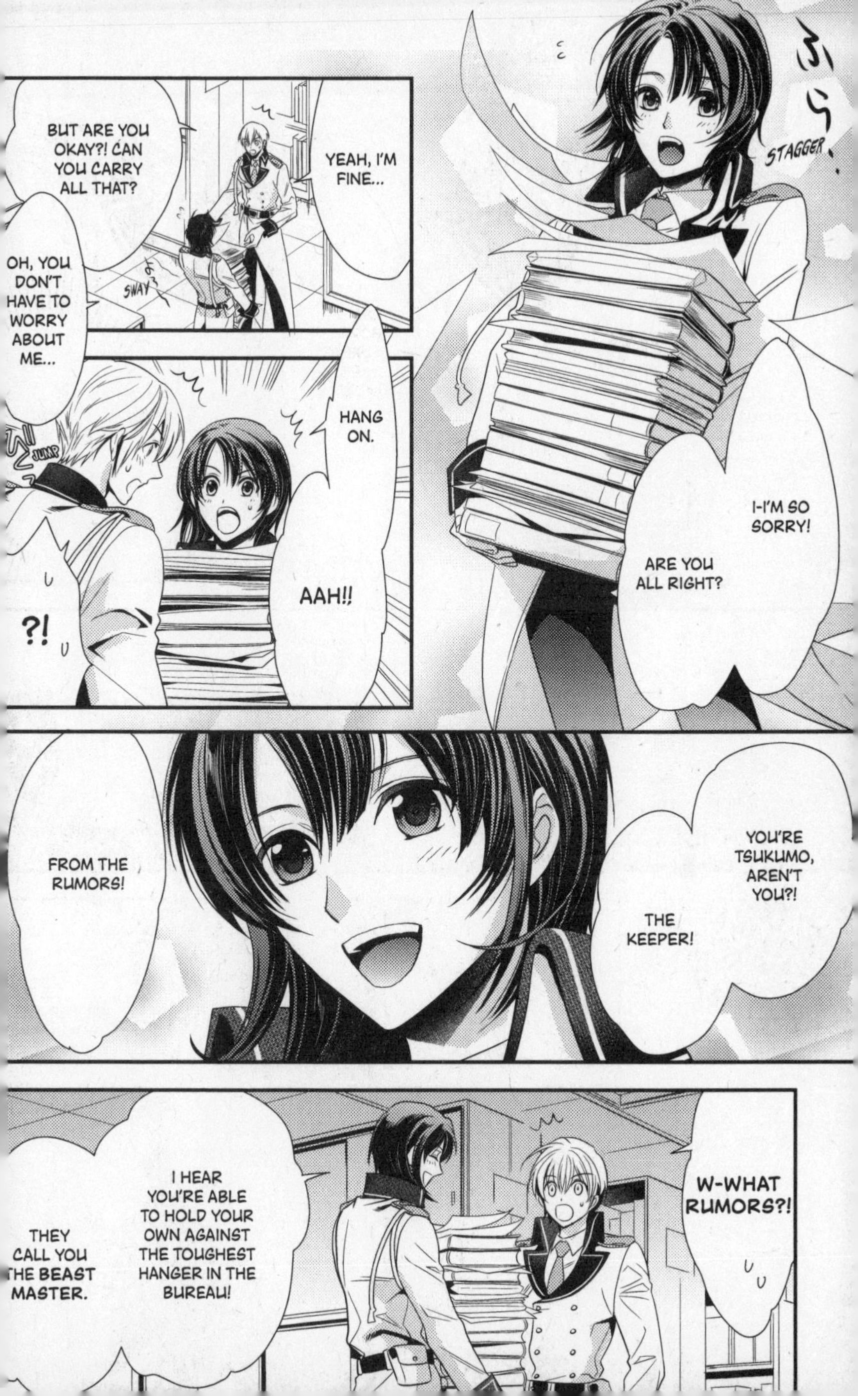
ふら
STAGGER
I-I'M SO SORRY!
ARE YOU ALL RIGHT?
YEAH, I'M FINE...
BUT ARE YOU OKAY?! CAN YOU CARRY ALL THAT?
OH, YOU DON'T HAVE TO WORRY ABOUT ME...
SWAY
HANG ON.
AAH!!
JUMP
?!
YOU'RE TSUKUMO, AREN'T YOU?!
THE KEEPER!
FROM THE RUMORS!
W-WHAT RUMORS?!
I HEAR YOU'RE ABLE TO HOLD YOUR OWN AGAINST THE TOUGHEST HANGER IN THE BUREAU!
THEY CALL YOU THE BEAST MASTER.

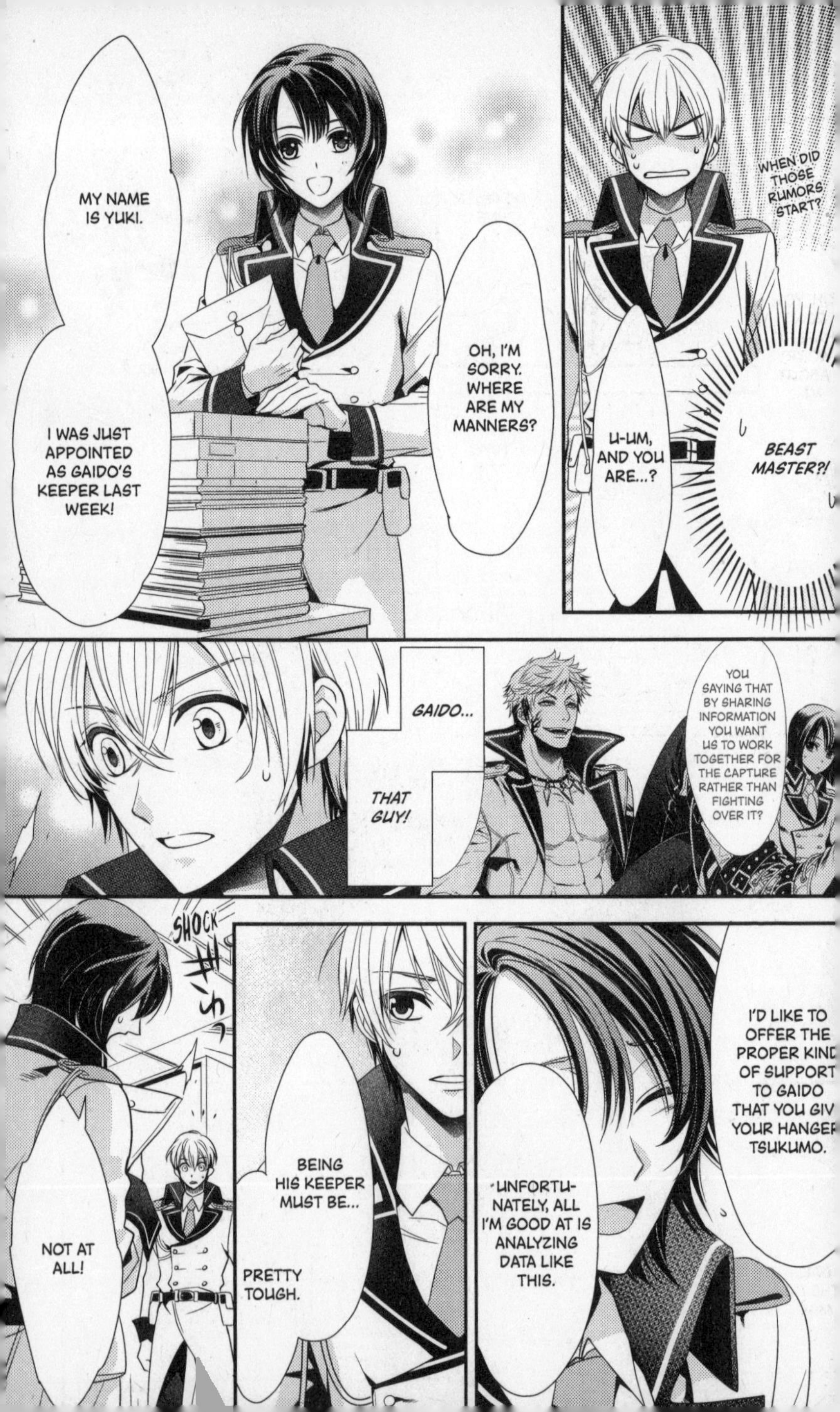
WHEN DID THOSE RUMORS START?
BEAST MASTER?!
U-UM, AND YOU ARE...?
OH, I'M SORRY. WHERE ARE MY MANNERS?
MY NAME IS YUKI.
I WAS JUST APPOINTED AS GAIDO'S KEEPER LAST WEEK!
YOU SAYING THAT BY SHARING INFORMATION YOU WANT US TO WORK TOGETHER FOR THE CAPTURE RATHER THAN FIGHTING OVER IT?
GAIDO...
THAT GUY!
I'D LIKE TO OFFER THE PROPER KIND OF SUPPORT TO GAIDO THAT YOU GIV YOUR HANGEF TSUKUMO.
UNFORTU-NATELY, ALL I'M GOOD AT IS ANALYZING DATA LIKE THIS.
BEING HIS KEEPER MUST BE...
PRETTY TOUGH.
SHOCK
NOT AT ALL!

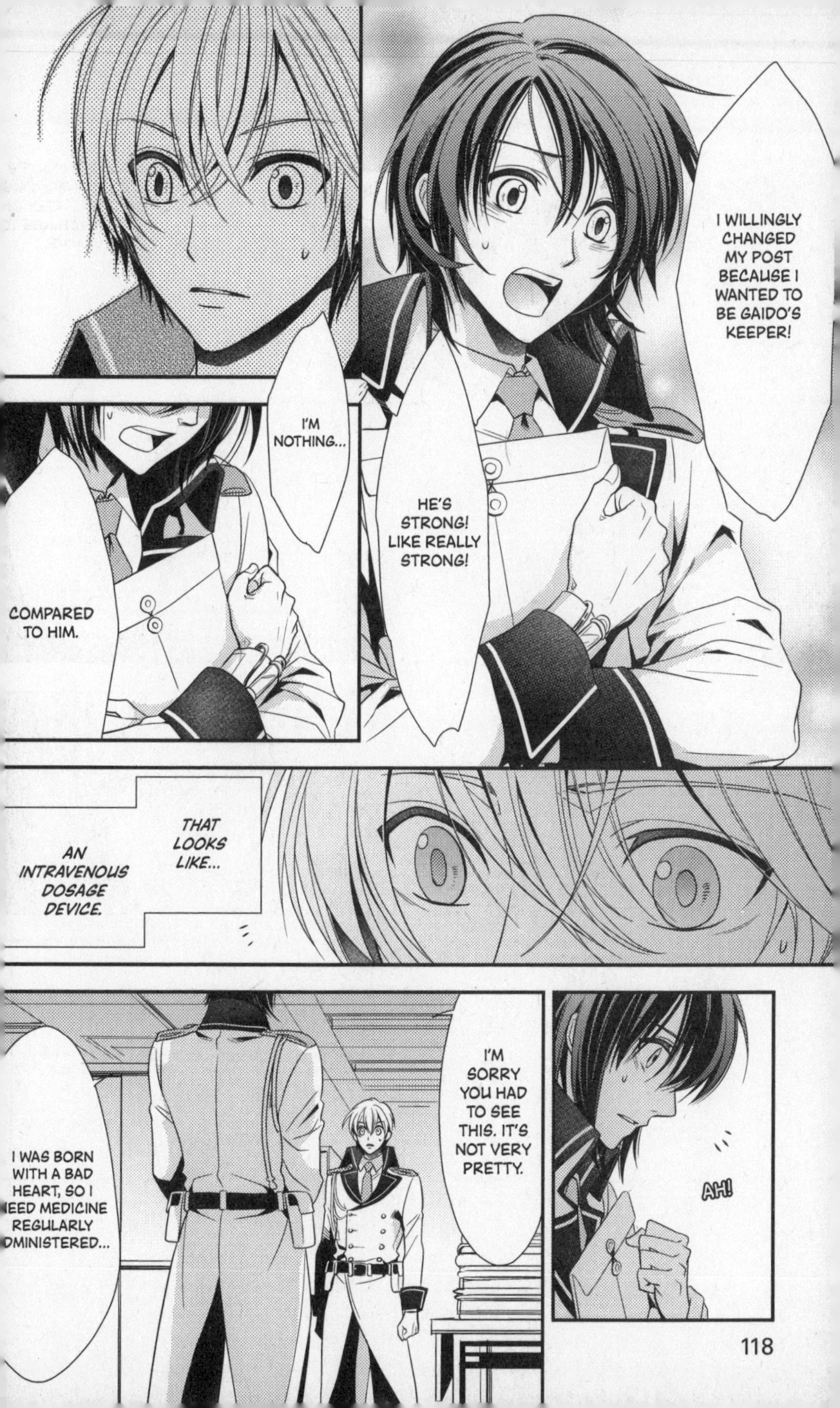
I WILLINGLY CHANGED MY POST BECAUSE I WANTED TO BE GAIDO'S KEEPER!
HE'S STRONG! LIKE REALLY STRONG!
I'M NOTHING...
COMPARED TO HIM.
THAT LOOKS LIKE...
AN INTRAVENOUS DOSAGE DEVICE.
AH!
I'M SORRY YOU HAD TO SEE THIS. IT'S NOT VERY PRETTY.
I WAS BORN WITH A BAD HEART, SO I EED MEDICINE REGULARLY DMINISTERED...

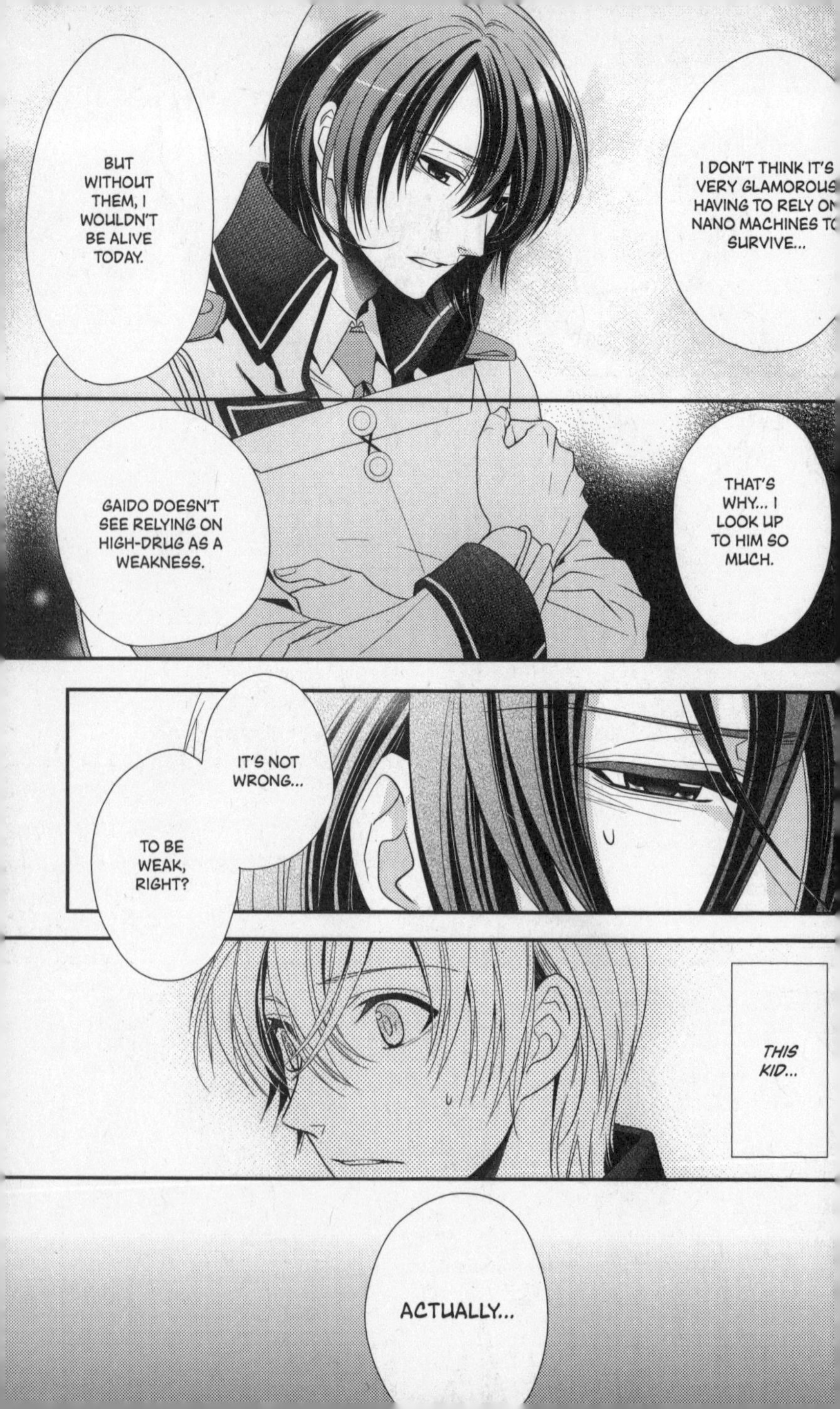
I DON'T THINK IT'S VERY GLAMOROUS HAVING TO RELY ON NANO MACHINES TO SURVIVE...
BUT WITHOUT THEM, I WOULDN'T BE ALIVE TODAY.
THAT'S WHY... I LOOK UP TO HIM SO MUCH.
GAIDO DOESN'T SEE RELYING ON HIGH-DRUG AS A WEAKNESS.
IT'S NOT WRONG...
TO BE WEAK, RIGHT?
THIS KID...
ACTUALLY...

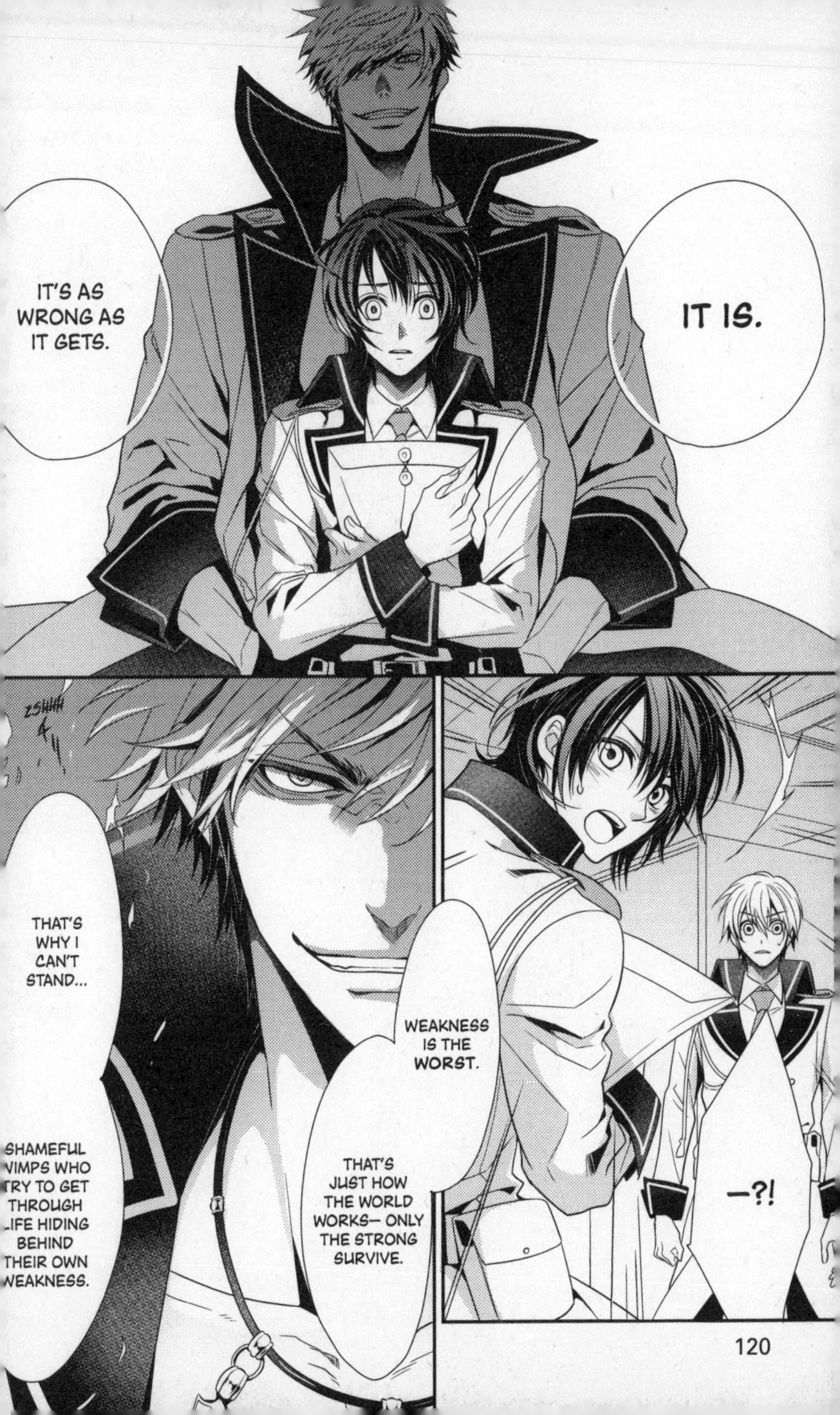
IT IS.
IT'S AS WRONG AS IT GETS.
—?!
ZSHHH
THAT'S WHY I CAN'T STAND...
SHAMEFUL VIMPS WHO TRY TO GET THROUGH LIFE HIDING BEHIND THEIR OWN VEAKNESS.
WEAKNESS IS THE WORST.
THAT'S JUST HOW THE WORLD WORKS— ONLY THE STRONG SURVIVE.

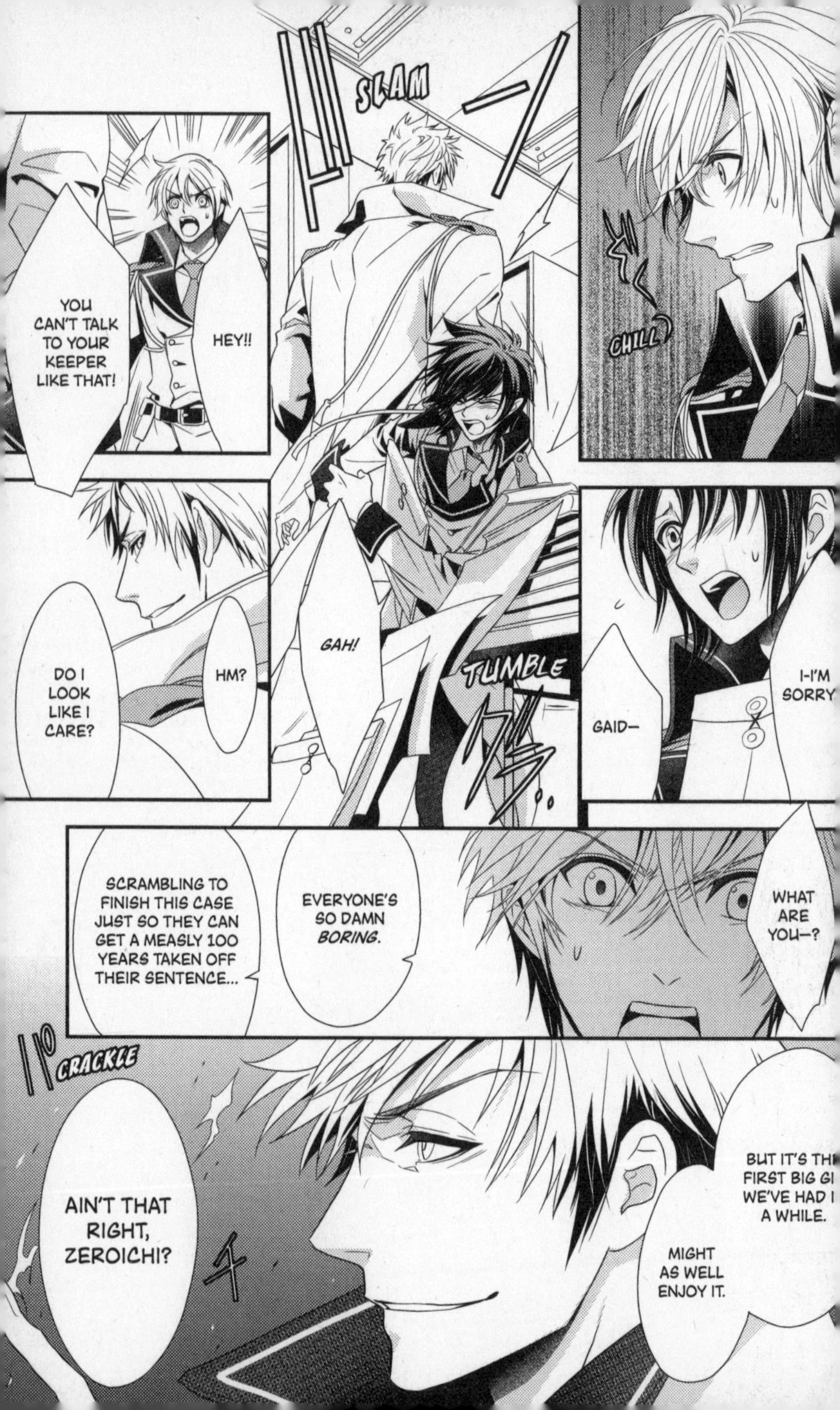
CHILL
SLAM
HEY!!
YOU CAN'T TALK TO YOUR KEEPER LIKE THAT!
HM?
DO I LOOK LIKE I CARE?
GAH!
TUMBLE
I-I'M SORRY
GAID—
WHAT ARE YOU—?
EVERYONE'S SO DAMN *BORING*.
SCRAMBLING TO FINISH THIS CASE JUST SO THEY CAN GET A MEASLY 100 YEARS TAKEN OFF THEIR SENTENCE...
BUT IT'S TH FIRST BIG GI WE'VE HAD I A WHILE.
MIGHT AS WELL ENJOY IT.
CRACKLE
AIN'T THAT RIGHT, ZEROICHI?

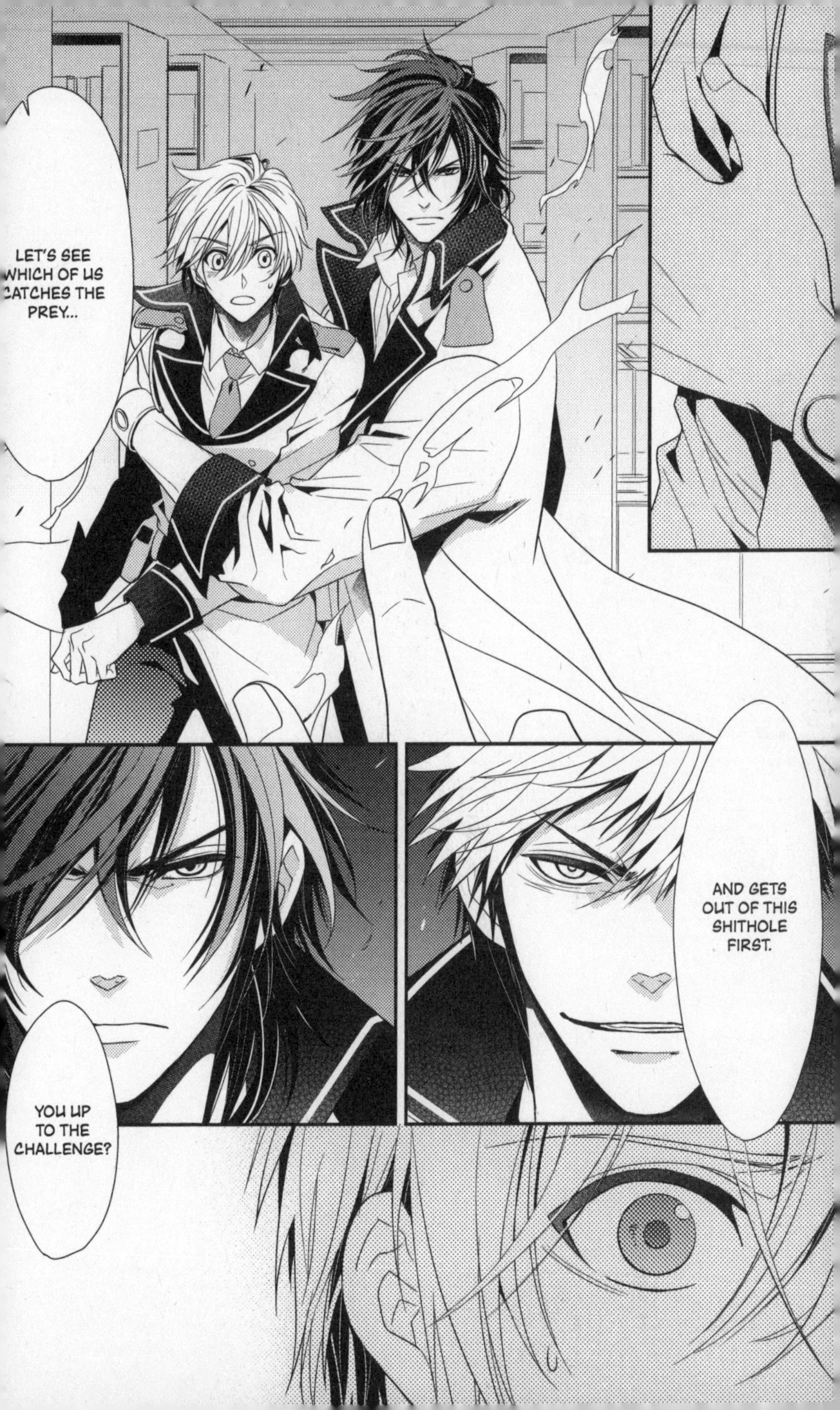
LET'S SEE WHICH OF US CATCHES THE PREY...
AND GETS OUT OF THIS SHITHOLE FIRST.
YOU UP TO THE CHALLENGE?

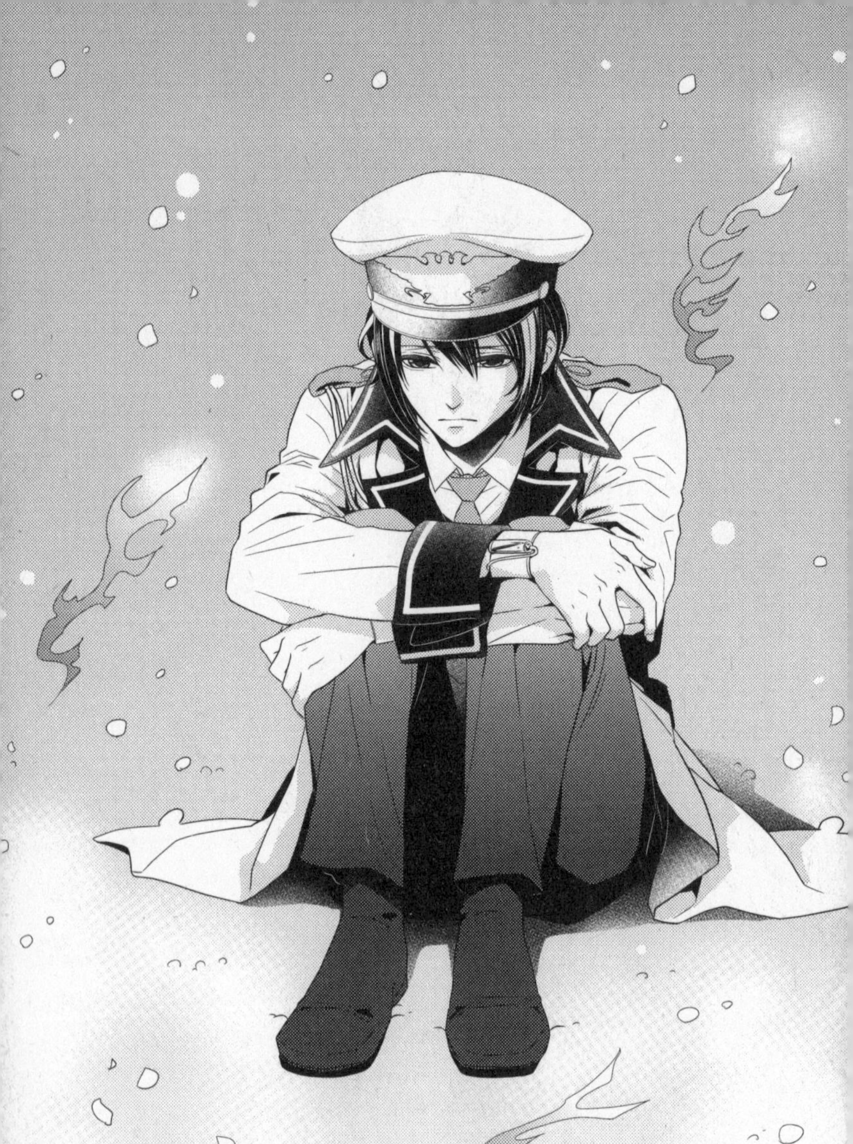

Chapter 15

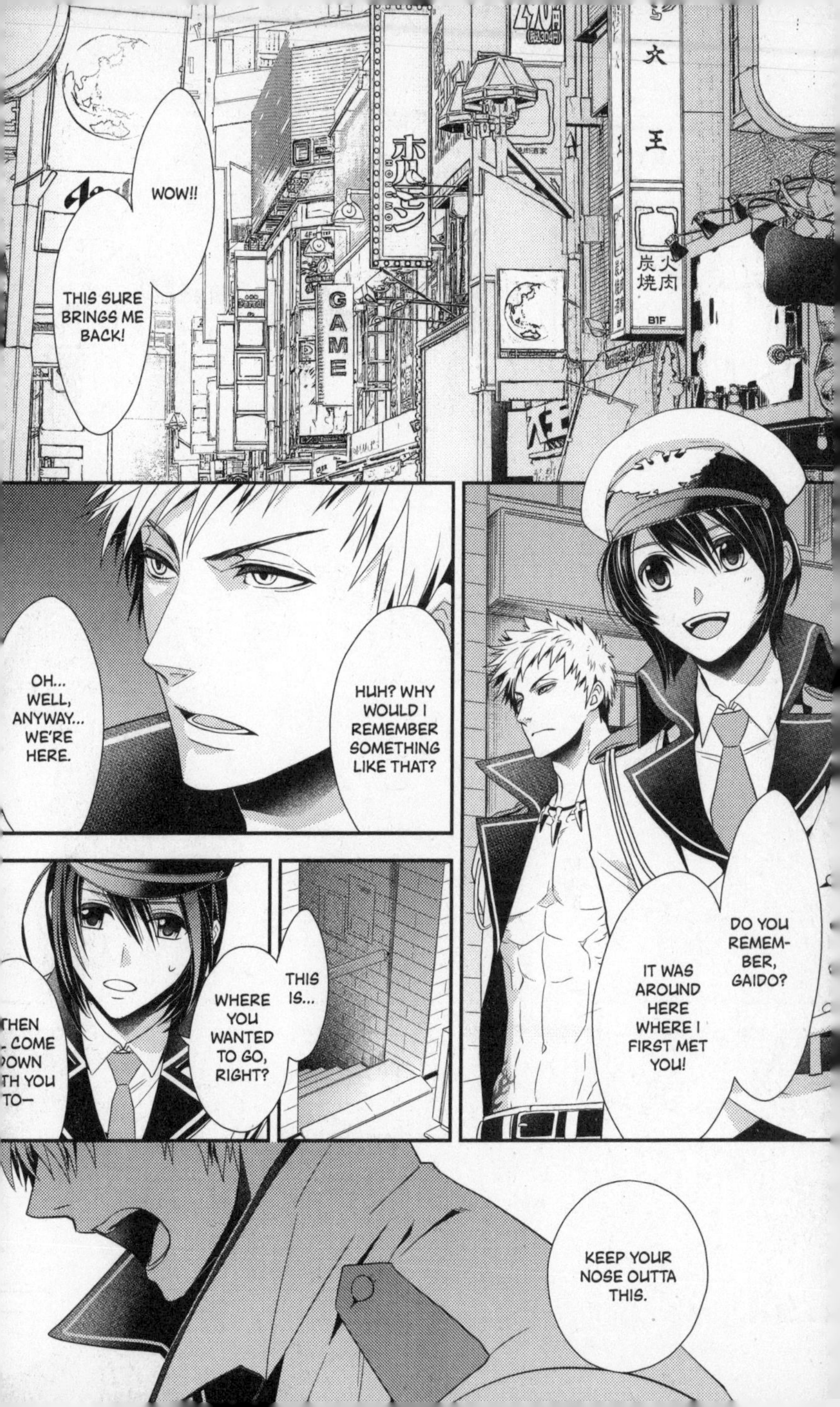
WOW!!
THIS SURE BRINGS ME BACK!
DO YOU REMEMBER, GAIDO?
IT WAS AROUND HERE WHERE I FIRST MET YOU!
HUH? WHY WOULD I REMEMBER SOMETHING LIKE THAT?
OH... WELL, ANYWAY... WE'RE HERE.
THIS IS...
WHERE YOU WANTED TO GO, RIGHT?
THEN L COME OWN TH YOU TO—
KEEP YOUR NOSE OUTTA THIS.

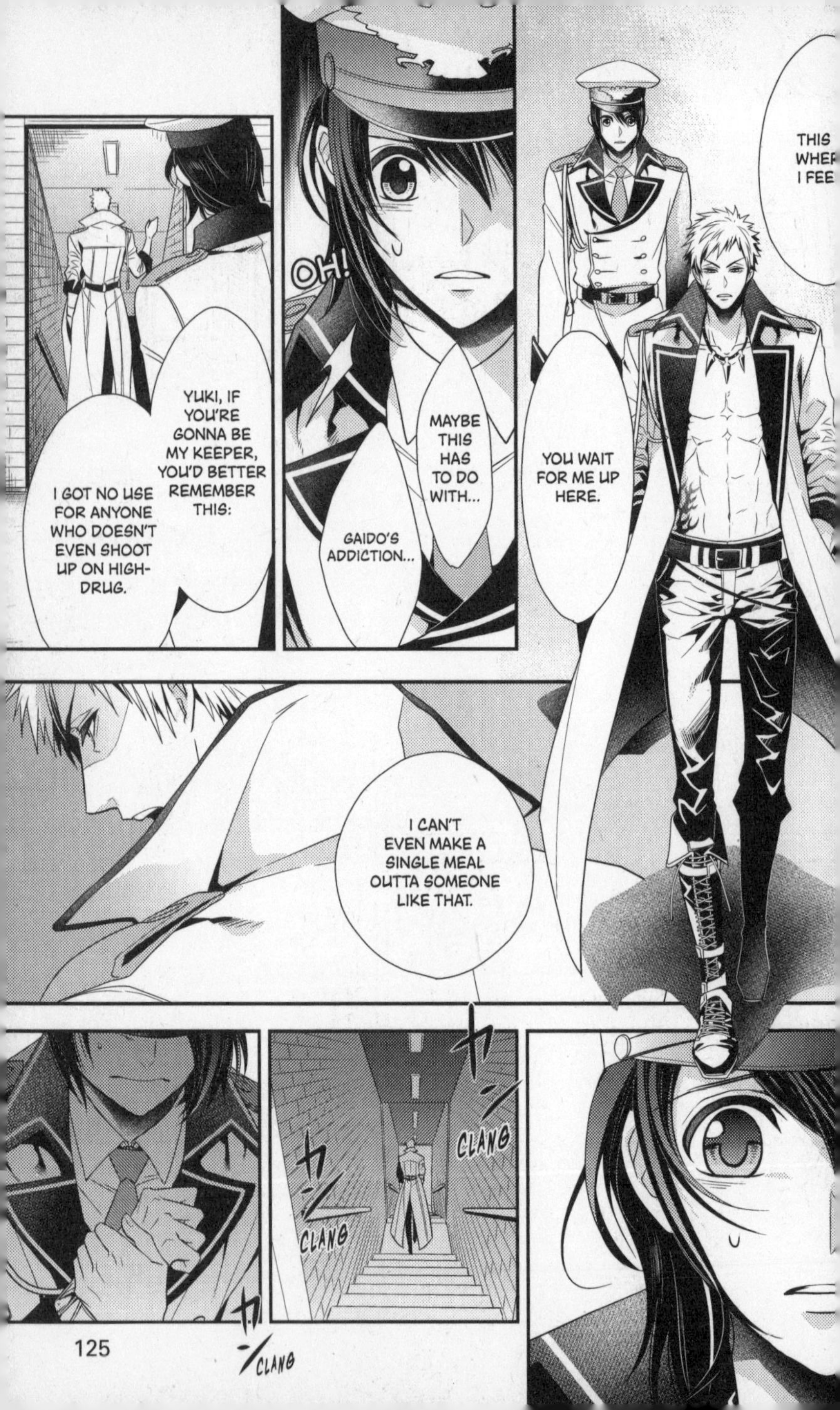

THIS
WHEF
I FEE
YOU WAIT FOR ME UP HERE.
OH!
MAYBE THIS HAS TO DO WITH...
GAIDO'S ADDICTION...
YUKI, IF YOU'RE GONNA BE MY KEEPER, YOU'D BETTER REMEMBER THIS:
I GOT NO USE FOR ANYONE WHO DOESN'T EVEN SHOOT UP ON HIGH-DRUG.
I CAN'T EVEN MAKE A SINGLE MEAL OUTTA SOMEONE LIKE THAT.
CLANG
CLANG
CLANG

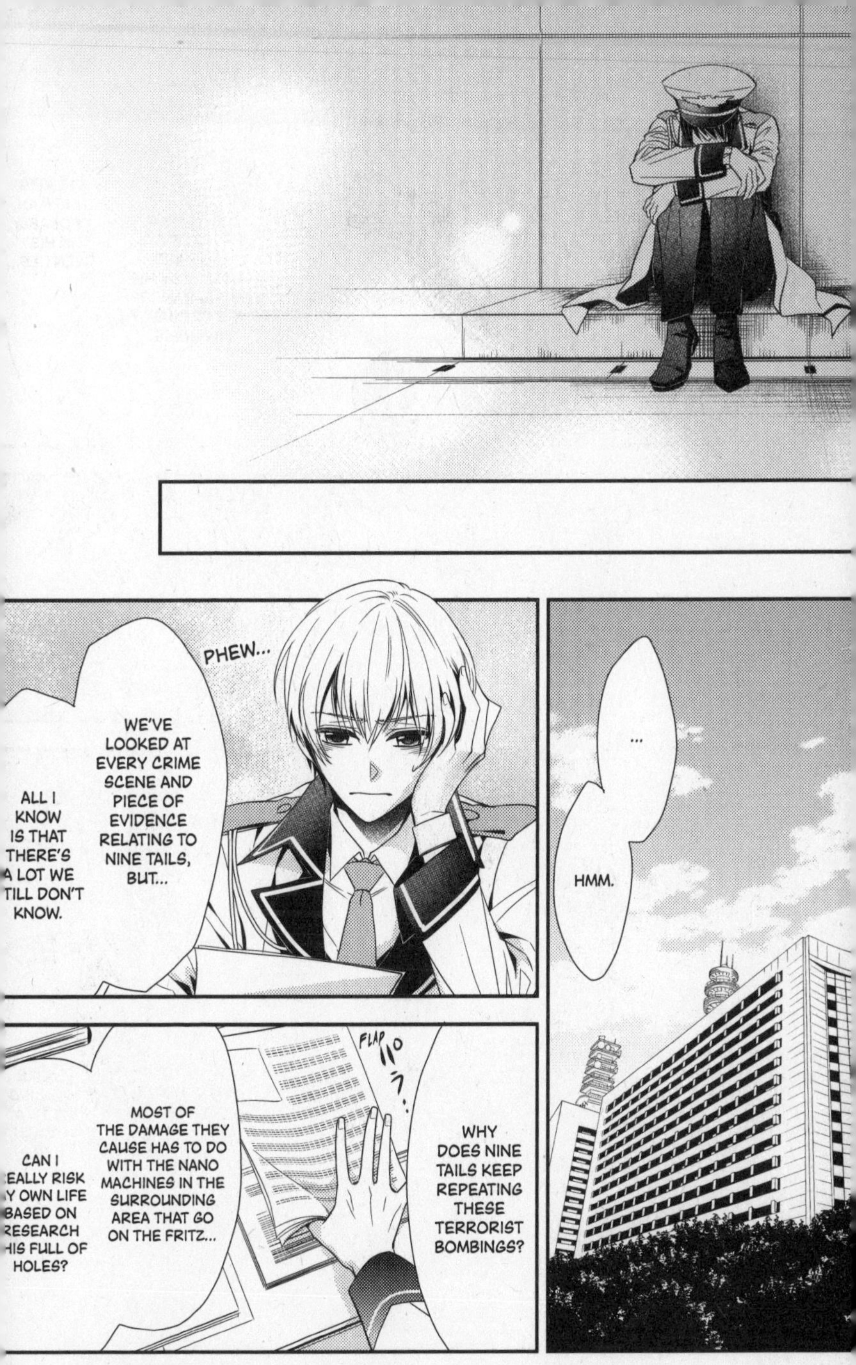
...
HMM.
PHEW...
WE'VE LOOKED AT EVERY CRIME SCENE AND PIECE OF EVIDENCE RELATING TO NINE TAILS, BUT...
ALL I KNOW IS THAT THERE'S A LOT WE TILL DON'T KNOW.
FLAP
WHY DOES NINE TAILS KEEP REPEATING THESE TERRORIST BOMBINGS?
MOST OF THE DAMAGE THEY CAUSE HAS TO DO WITH THE NANO MACHINES IN THE SURROUNDING AREA THAT GO ON THE FRITZ...
CAN I EALLY RISK Y OWN LIFE BASED ON ESEARCH HIS FULL OF HOLES?

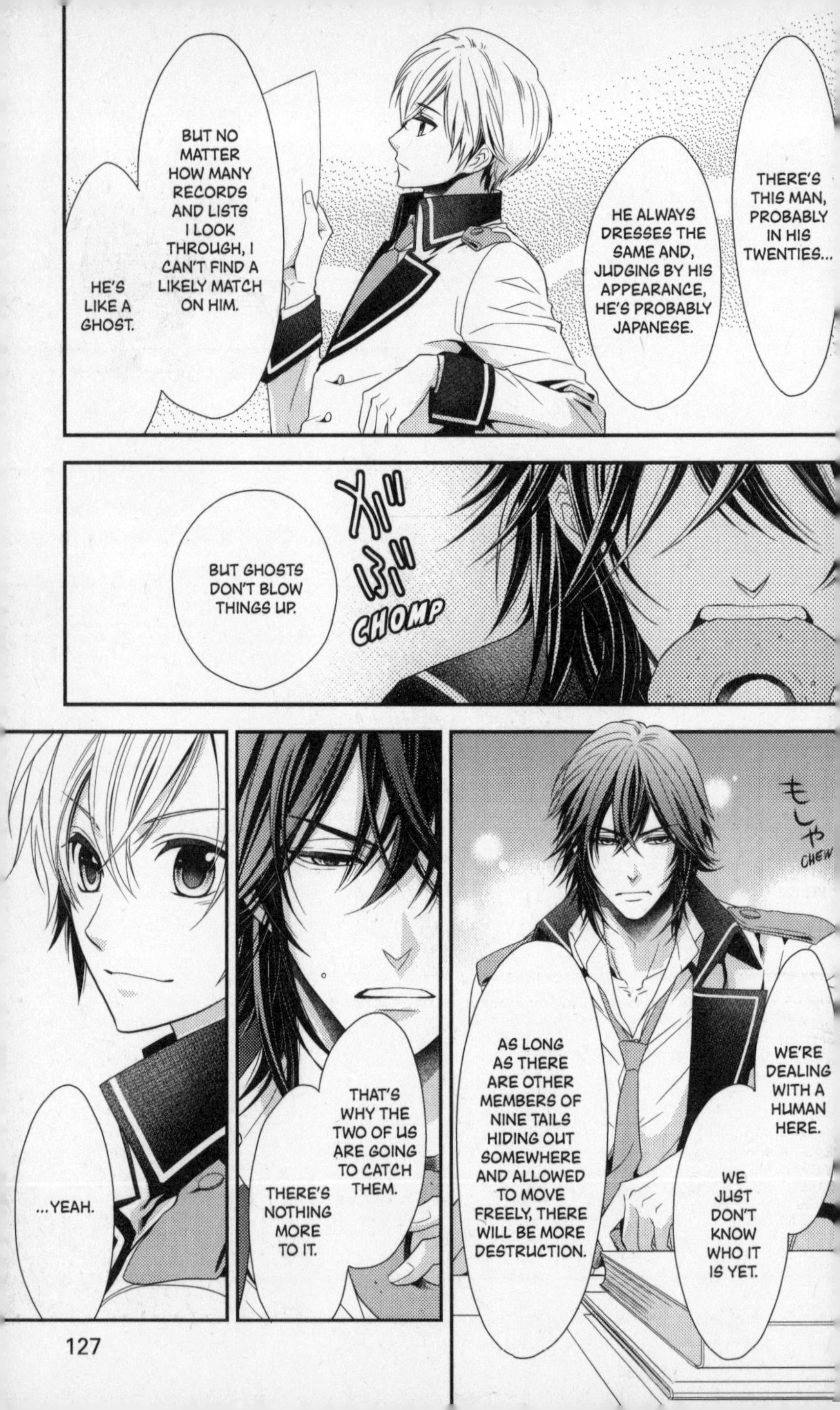
THERE'S THIS MAN, PROBABLY IN HIS TWENTIES...
HE ALWAYS DRESSES THE SAME AND, JUDGING BY HIS APPEARANCE, HE'S PROBABLY JAPANESE.
BUT NO MATTER HOW MANY RECORDS AND LISTS I LOOK THROUGH, I CAN'T FIND A LIKELY MATCH ON HIM.
HE'S LIKE A GHOST.
CHOMP
BUT GHOSTS DON'T BLOW THINGS UP.
もしゃ
CHEW
WE'RE DEALING WITH A HUMAN HERE.
WE JUST DON'T KNOW WHO IT IS YET.
AS LONG AS THERE ARE OTHER MEMBERS OF NINE TAILS HIDING OUT SOMEWHERE AND ALLOWED TO MOVE FREELY, THERE WILL BE MORE DESTRUCTION.
THAT'S WHY THE TWO OF US ARE GOING TO CATCH THEM.
THERE'S NOTHING MORE TO IT.
...YEAH.

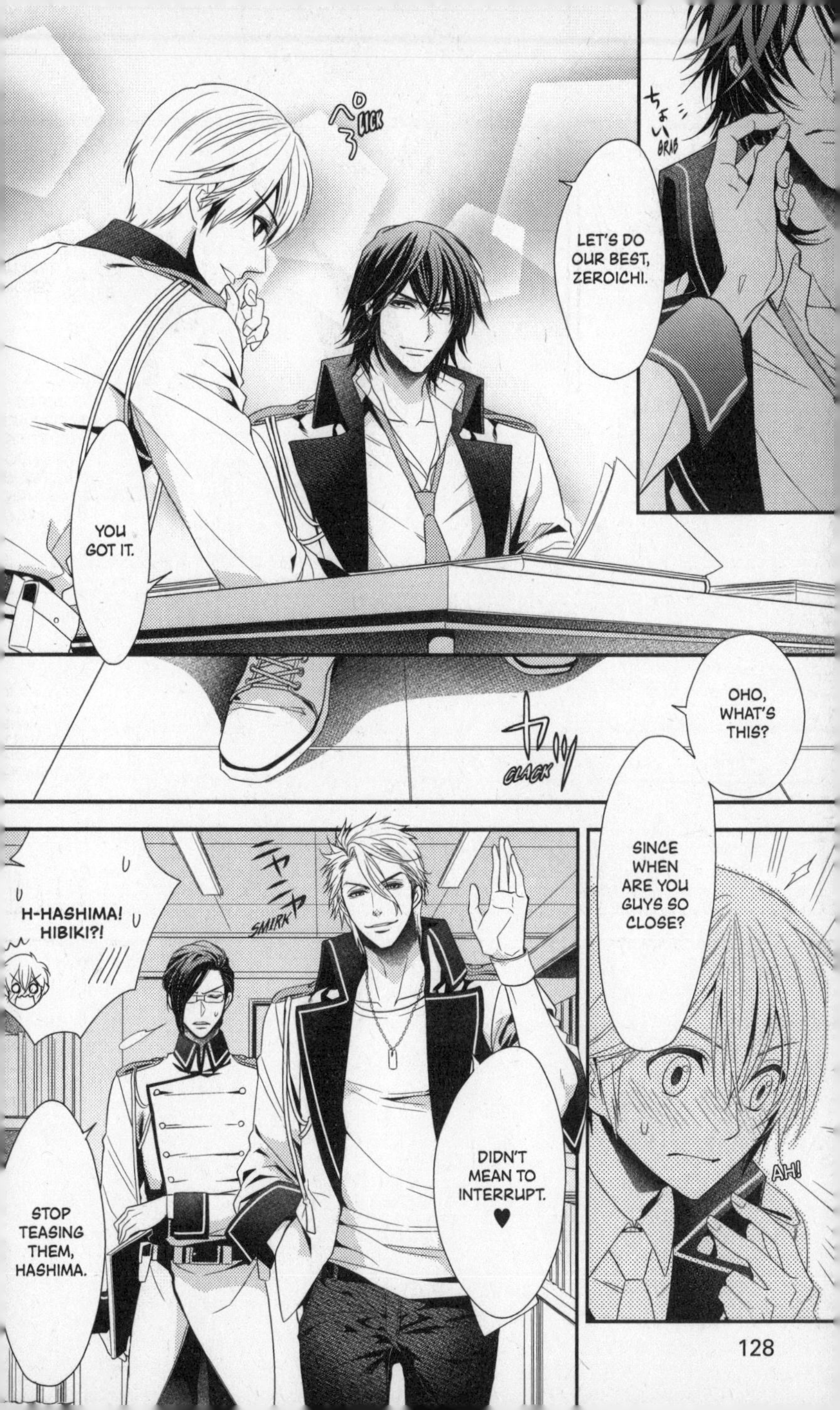
ちょい
GRAB
LET'S DO OUR BEST, ZEROICHI.
ぺろ
LICK
YOU GOT IT.
OHO, WHAT'S THIS?
カッ
CLACK
SINCE WHEN ARE YOU GUYS SO CLOSE?
AH!
ニヤニヤ
SMIRK
DIDN'T MEAN TO INTERRUPT. ♥
H-HASHIMA! HIBIKI?!
STOP TEASING THEM, HASHIMA.

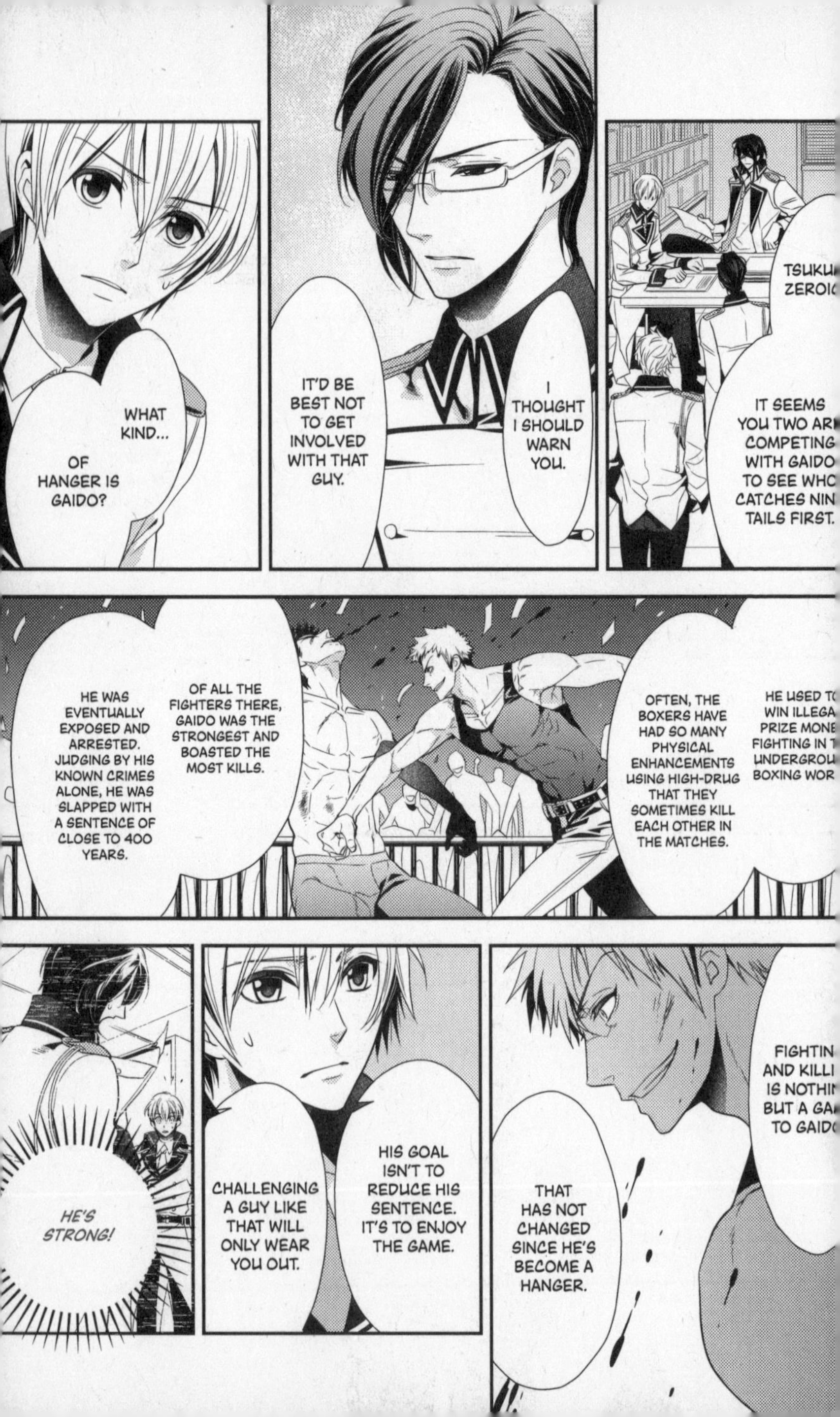
TSUKU ZEROI
IT SEEMS YOU TWO AR COMPETING WITH GAIDO TO SEE WHO CATCHES NIN TAILS FIRST.
I THOUGHT I SHOULD WARN YOU.
IT'D BE BEST NOT TO GET INVOLVED WITH THAT GUY.
WHAT KIND...
OF HANGER IS GAIDO?
HE USED T WIN ILLEGA PRIZE MONE FIGHTING IN T UNDERGROU BOXING WOR
OFTEN, THE BOXERS HAVE HAD SO MANY PHYSICAL ENHANCEMENTS USING HIGH-DRUG THAT THEY SOMETIMES KILL EACH OTHER IN THE MATCHES.
OF ALL THE FIGHTERS THERE, GAIDO WAS THE STRONGEST AND BOASTED THE MOST KILLS.
HE WAS EVENTUALLY EXPOSED AND ARRESTED. JUDGING BY HIS KNOWN CRIMES ALONE, HE WAS SLAPPED WITH A SENTENCE OF CLOSE TO 400 YEARS.
FIGHTIN AND KILLI IS NOTHIN BUT A GA TO GAID
THAT HAS NOT CHANGED SINCE HE'S BECOME A HANGER.
HIS GOAL ISN'T TO REDUCE HIS SENTENCE. IT'S TO ENJOY THE GAME.
CHALLENGING A GUY LIKE THAT WILL ONLY WEAR YOU OUT.
HE'S STRONG!

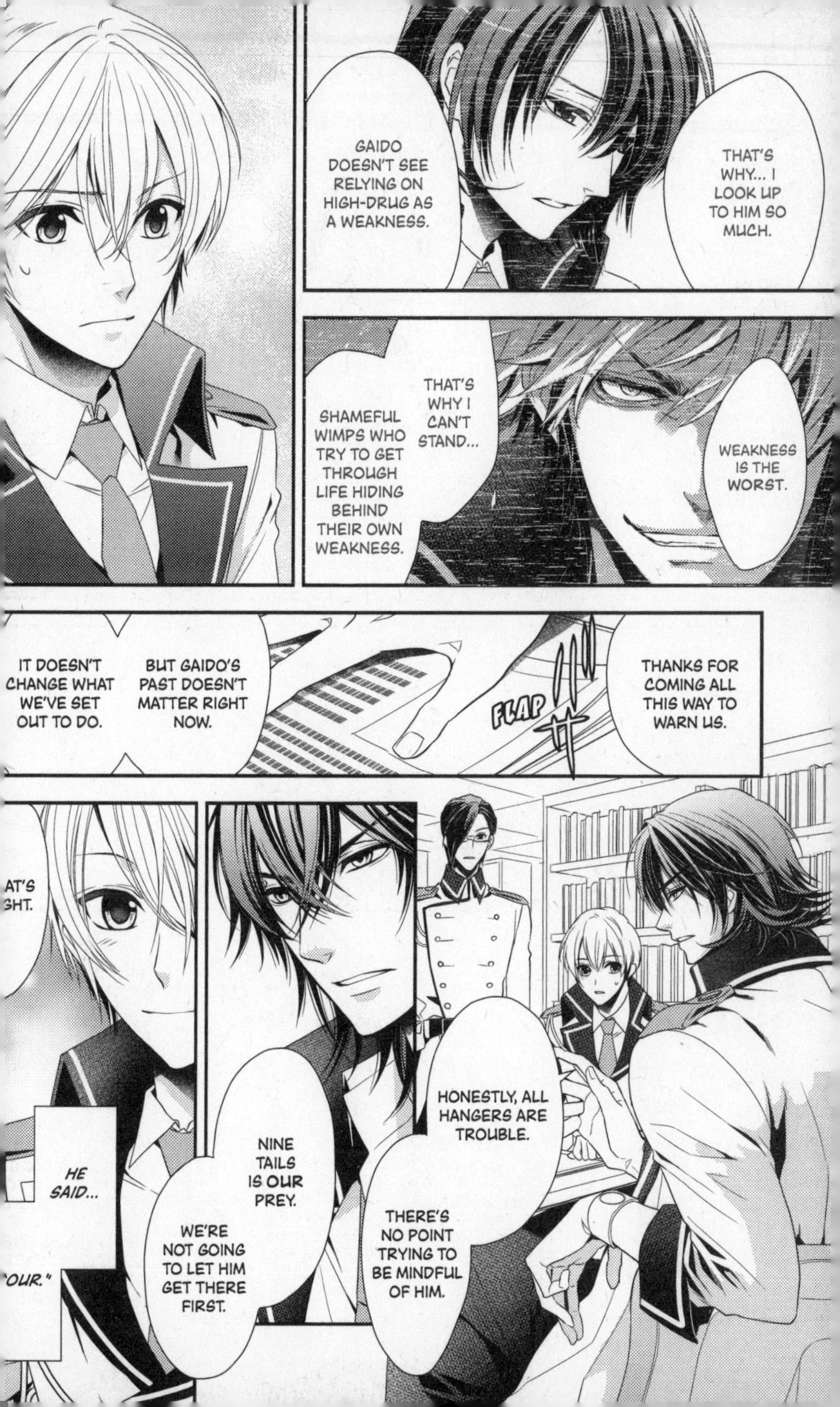
GAIDO DOESN'T SEE RELYING ON HIGH-DRUG AS A WEAKNESS.
THAT'S WHY... I LOOK UP TO HIM SO MUCH.
WEAKNESS IS THE WORST.
THAT'S WHY I CAN'T STAND...
SHAMEFUL WIMPS WHO TRY TO GET THROUGH LIFE HIDING BEHIND THEIR OWN WEAKNESS.
THANKS FOR COMING ALL THIS WAY TO WARN US.
FLAP
BUT GAIDO'S PAST DOESN'T MATTER RIGHT NOW.
IT DOESN'T CHANGE WHAT WE'VE SET OUT TO DO.
HONESTLY, ALL HANGERS ARE TROUBLE.
THERE'S NO POINT TRYING TO BE MINDFUL OF HIM.
NINE TAILS IS OUR PREY.
WE'RE NOT GOING TO LET HIM GET THERE FIRST.
AT'S GHT.
HE SAID...
OUR."

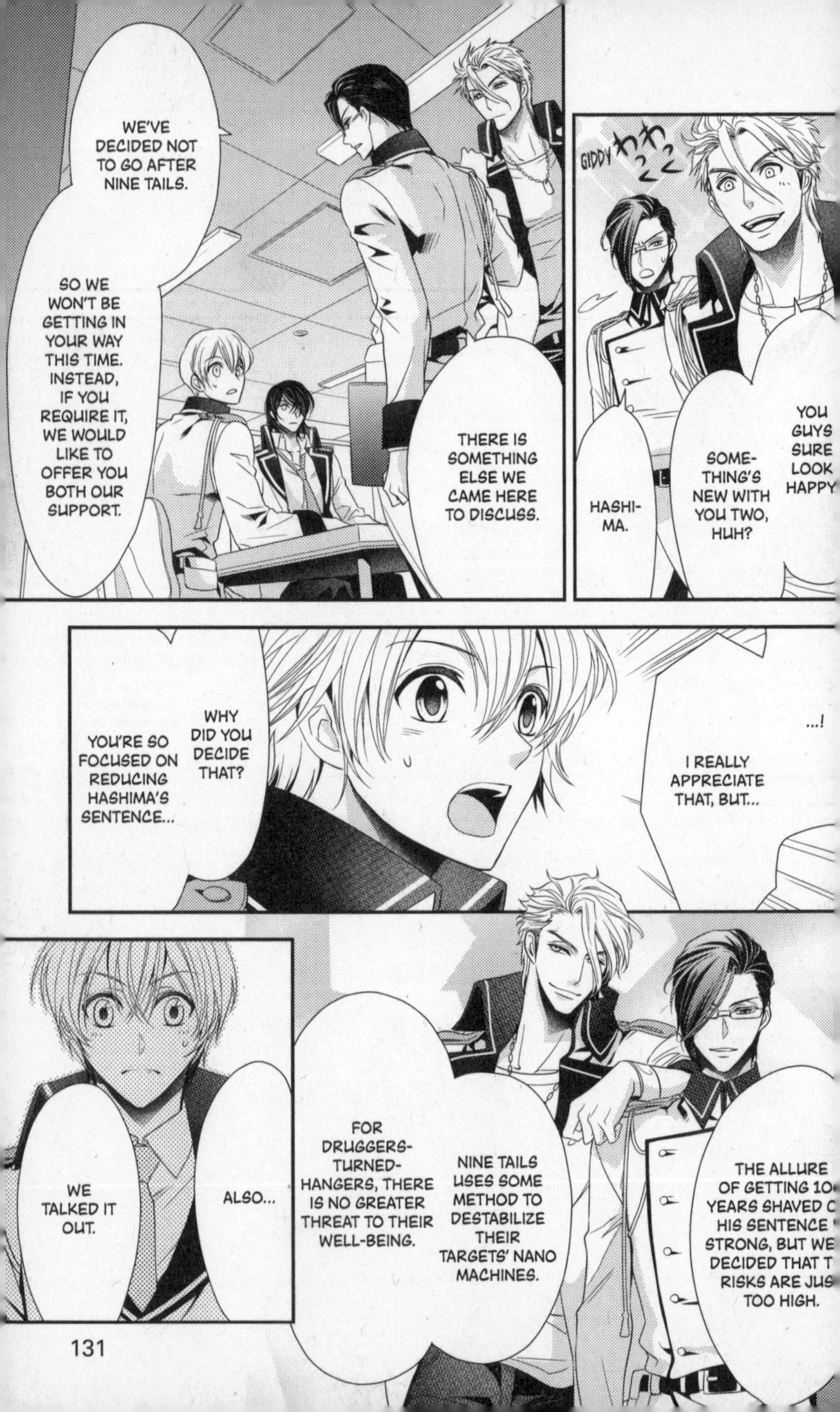
GIDDY
YOU GUYS SURE LOOK HAPPY
SOME-THING'S NEW WITH YOU TWO, HUH?
HASHI-MA.
THERE IS SOMETHING ELSE WE CAME HERE TO DISCUSS.
WE'VE DECIDED NOT TO GO AFTER NINE TAILS.
SO WE WON'T BE GETTING IN YOUR WAY THIS TIME. INSTEAD, IF YOU REQUIRE IT, WE WOULD LIKE TO OFFER YOU BOTH OUR SUPPORT.
...!
I REALLY APPRECIATE THAT, BUT...
WHY DID YOU DECIDE THAT?
YOU'RE SO FOCUSED ON REDUCING HASHIMA'S SENTENCE...
THE ALLURE OF GETTING 10 YEARS SHAVED O HIS SENTENCE STRONG, BUT WE DECIDED THAT T RISKS ARE JUS TOO HIGH.
NINE TAILS USES SOME METHOD TO DESTABILIZE THEIR TARGETS' NANO MACHINES.
FOR DRUGGERS-TURNED-HANGERS, THERE IS NO GREATER THREAT TO THEIR WELL-BEING.
ALSO...
WE TALKED IT OUT.

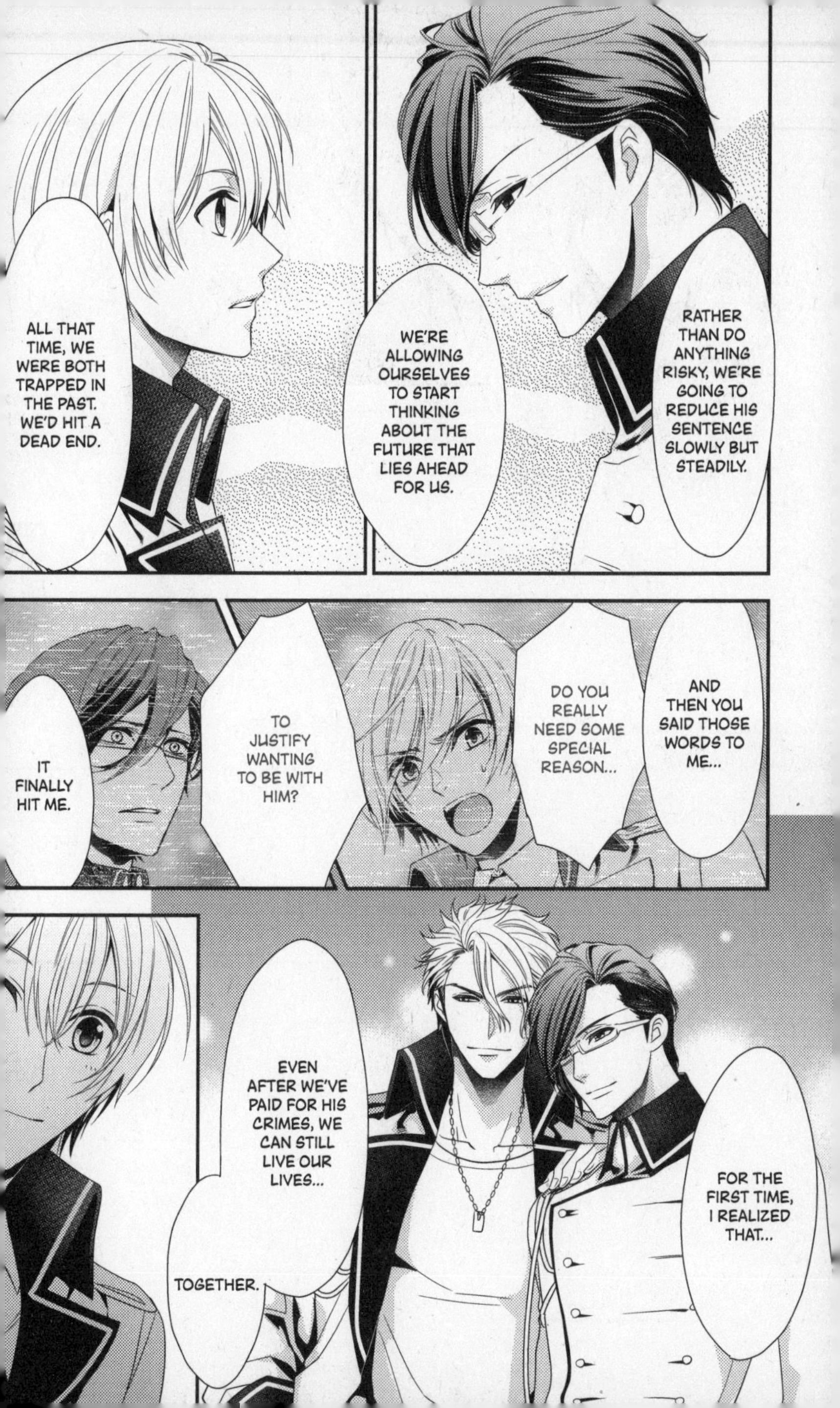
RATHER THAN DO ANYTHING RISKY, WE'RE GOING TO REDUCE HIS SENTENCE SLOWLY BUT STEADILY.
WE'RE ALLOWING OURSELVES TO START THINKING ABOUT THE FUTURE THAT LIES AHEAD FOR US.
ALL THAT TIME, WE WERE BOTH TRAPPED IN THE PAST. WE'D HIT A DEAD END.
AND THEN YOU SAID THOSE WORDS TO ME...
DO YOU REALLY NEED SOME SPECIAL REASON...
TO JUSTIFY WANTING TO BE WITH HIM?
IT FINALLY HIT ME.
FOR THE FIRST TIME, I REALIZED THAT...
EVEN AFTER WE'VE PAID FOR HIS CRIMES, WE CAN STILL LIVE OUR LIVES...
TOGETHER.

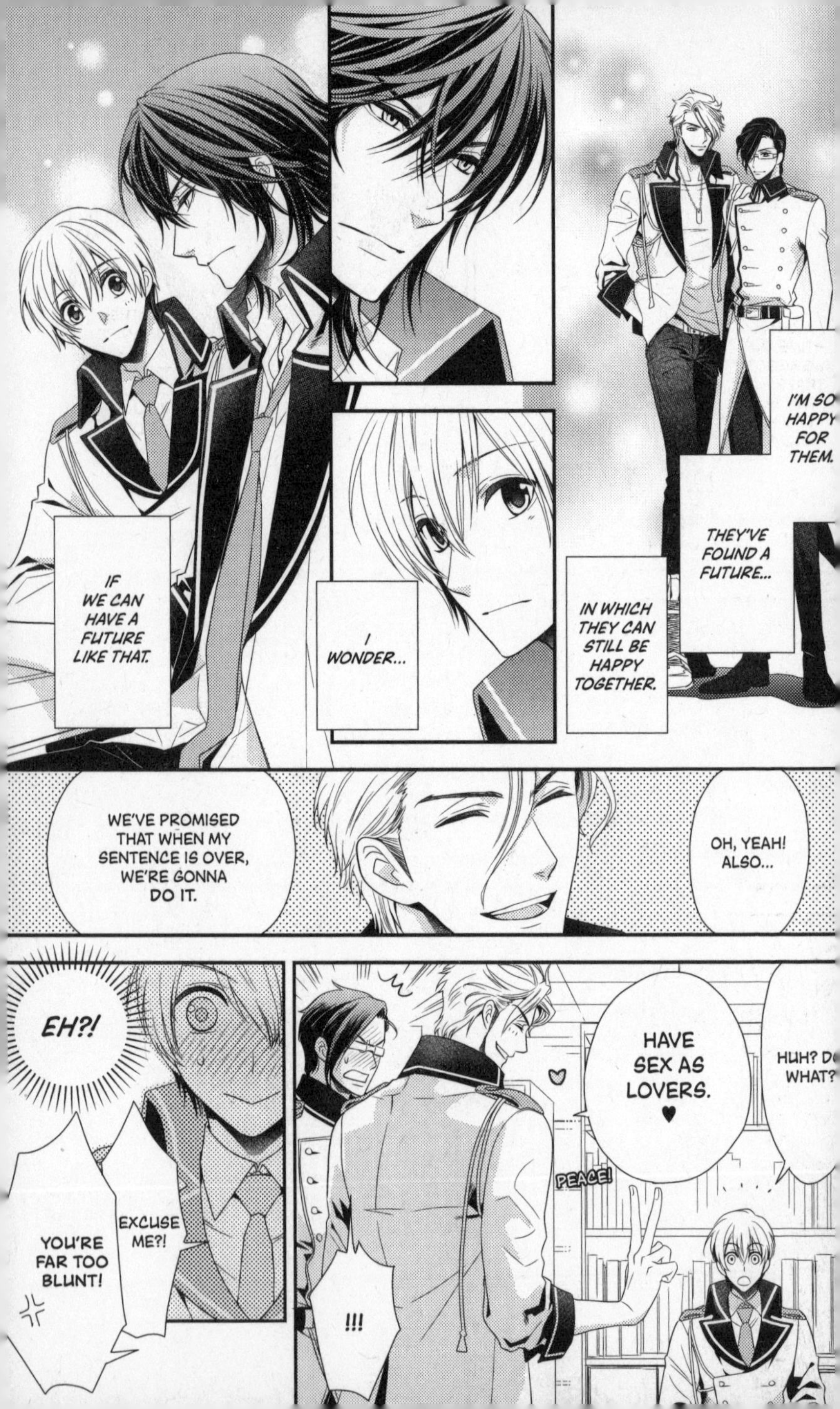
I'M SO HAPPY FOR THEM.
THEY'VE FOUND A FUTURE...
IN WHICH THEY CAN STILL BE HAPPY TOGETHER.
I WONDER...
IF WE CAN HAVE A FUTURE LIKE THAT.
OH, YEAH! ALSO...
WE'VE PROMISED THAT WHEN MY SENTENCE IS OVER, WE'RE GONNA DO IT.
HUH? DO WHAT?
HAVE SEX AS LOVERS. ♥
PEACE!
!!!
EH?!
EXCUSE ME?!
YOU'RE FAR TOO BLUNT!

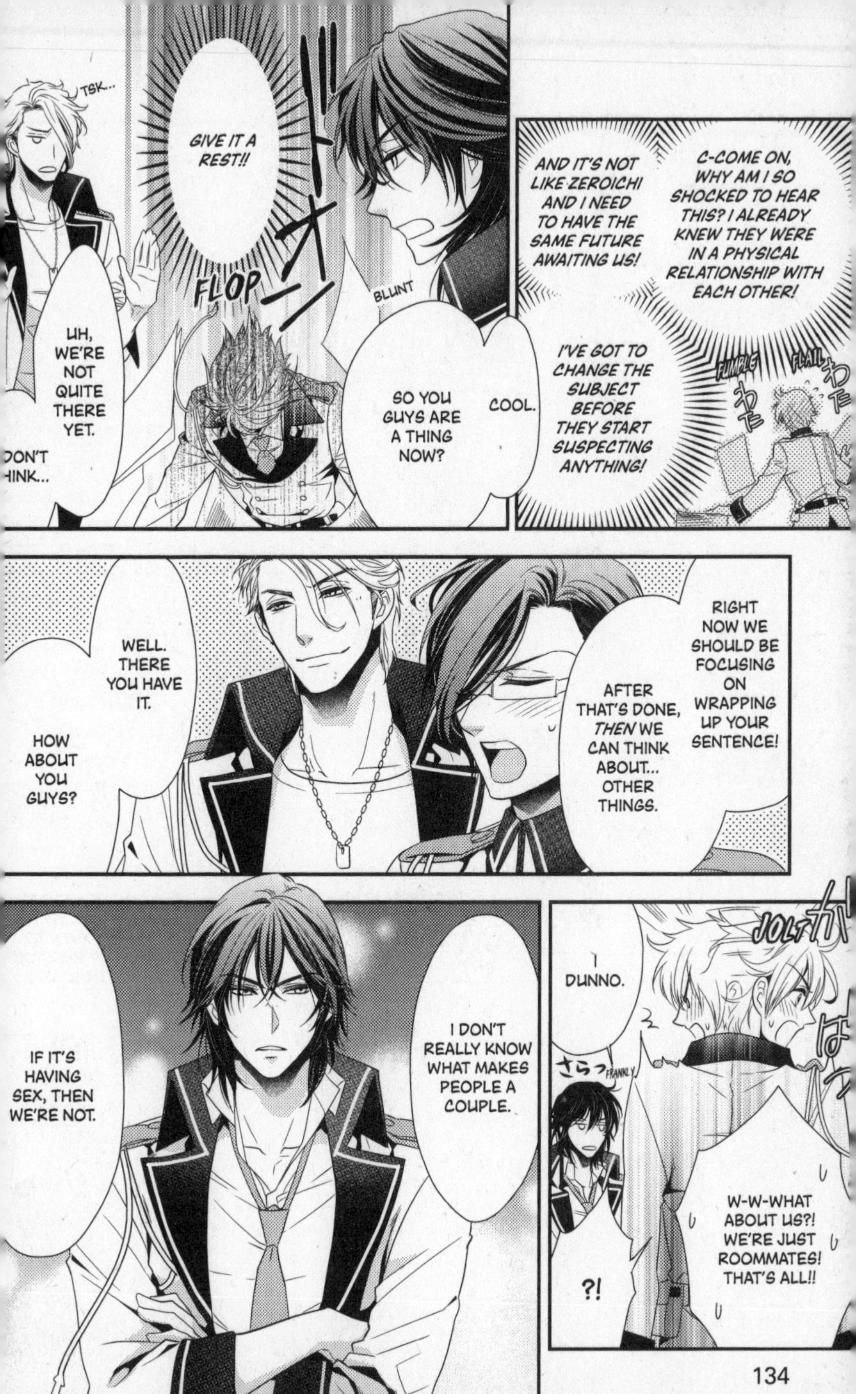
C-COME ON, WHY AM I SO SHOCKED TO HEAR THIS? I ALREADY KNEW THEY WERE IN A PHYSICAL RELATIONSHIP WITH EACH OTHER!
AND IT'S NOT LIKE ZEROICHI AND I NEED TO HAVE THE SAME FUTURE AWAITING US!
FLAIL わた
FUMBLE わた
I'VE GOT TO CHANGE THE SUBJECT BEFORE THEY START SUSPECTING ANYTHING!
BLUNT
COOL.
SO YOU GUYS ARE A THING NOW?
GIVE IT A REST!!
FLOP
TSK...
UH, WE'RE NOT QUITE THERE YET.
DON'T HINK...
RIGHT NOW WE SHOULD BE FOCUSING ON WRAPPING UP YOUR SENTENCE!
AFTER THAT'S DONE, THEN WE CAN THINK ABOUT... OTHER THINGS.
WELL. THERE YOU HAVE IT.
HOW ABOUT YOU GUYS?
JOLT
はっ
I DUNNO.
さらっ FRANKLY
W-W-WHAT ABOUT US?! WE'RE JUST ROOMMATES! THAT'S ALL!!
?!
I DON'T REALLY KNOW WHAT MAKES PEOPLE A COUPLE.
IF IT'S HAVING SEX, THEN WE'RE NOT.

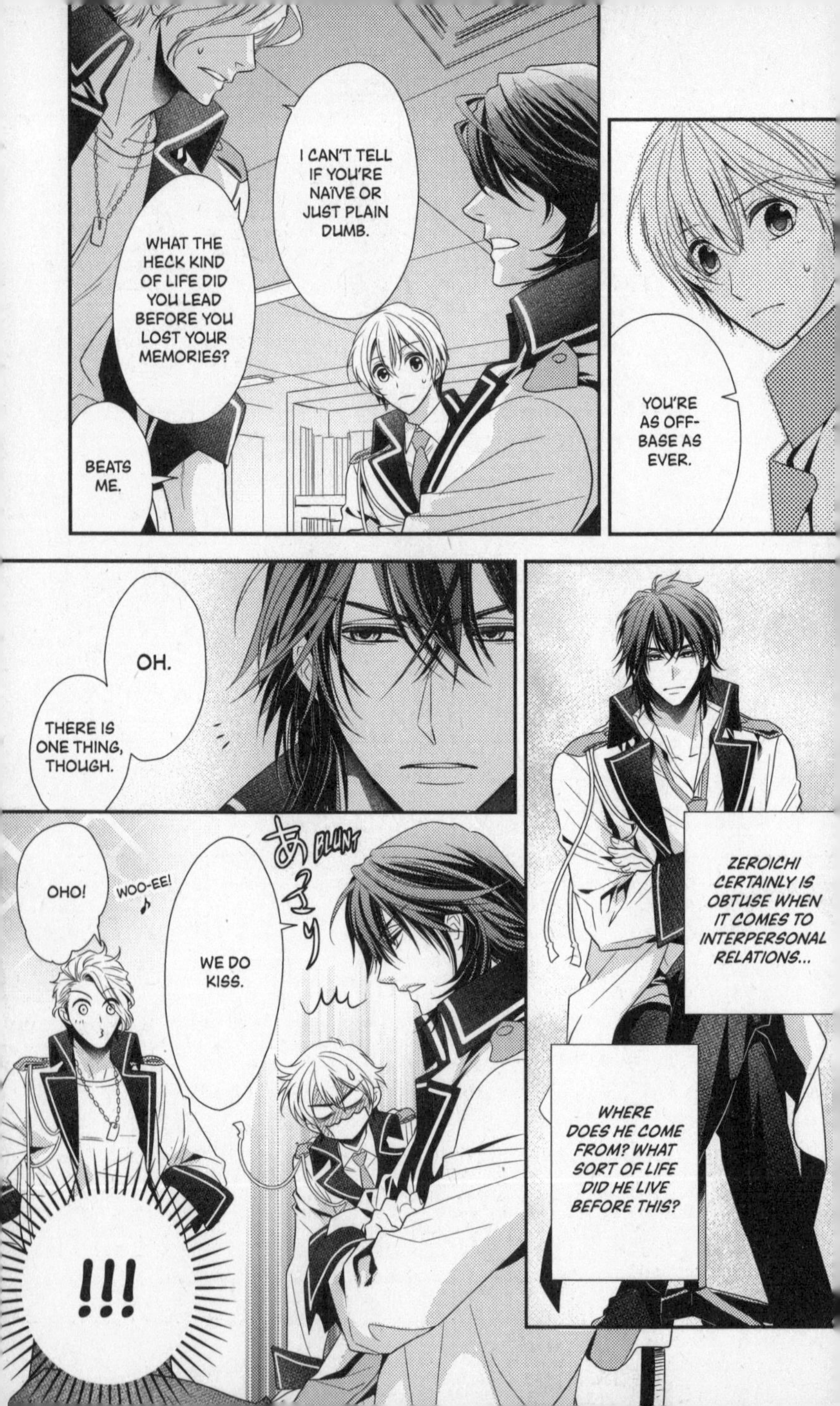
YOU'RE AS OFF-BASE AS EVER.
I CAN'T TELL IF YOU'RE NAÏVE OR JUST PLAIN DUMB.
WHAT THE HECK KIND OF LIFE DID YOU LEAD BEFORE YOU LOST YOUR MEMORIES?
BEATS ME.
ZEROICHI CERTAINLY IS OBTUSE WHEN IT COMES TO INTERPERSONAL RELATIONS...
WHERE DOES HE COME FROM? WHAT SORT OF LIFE DID HE LIVE BEFORE THIS?
OH.
THERE IS ONE THING, THOUGH.
あっさり
BLUNT
WE DO KISS.
OHO!
WOO-EE! ♪
!!!

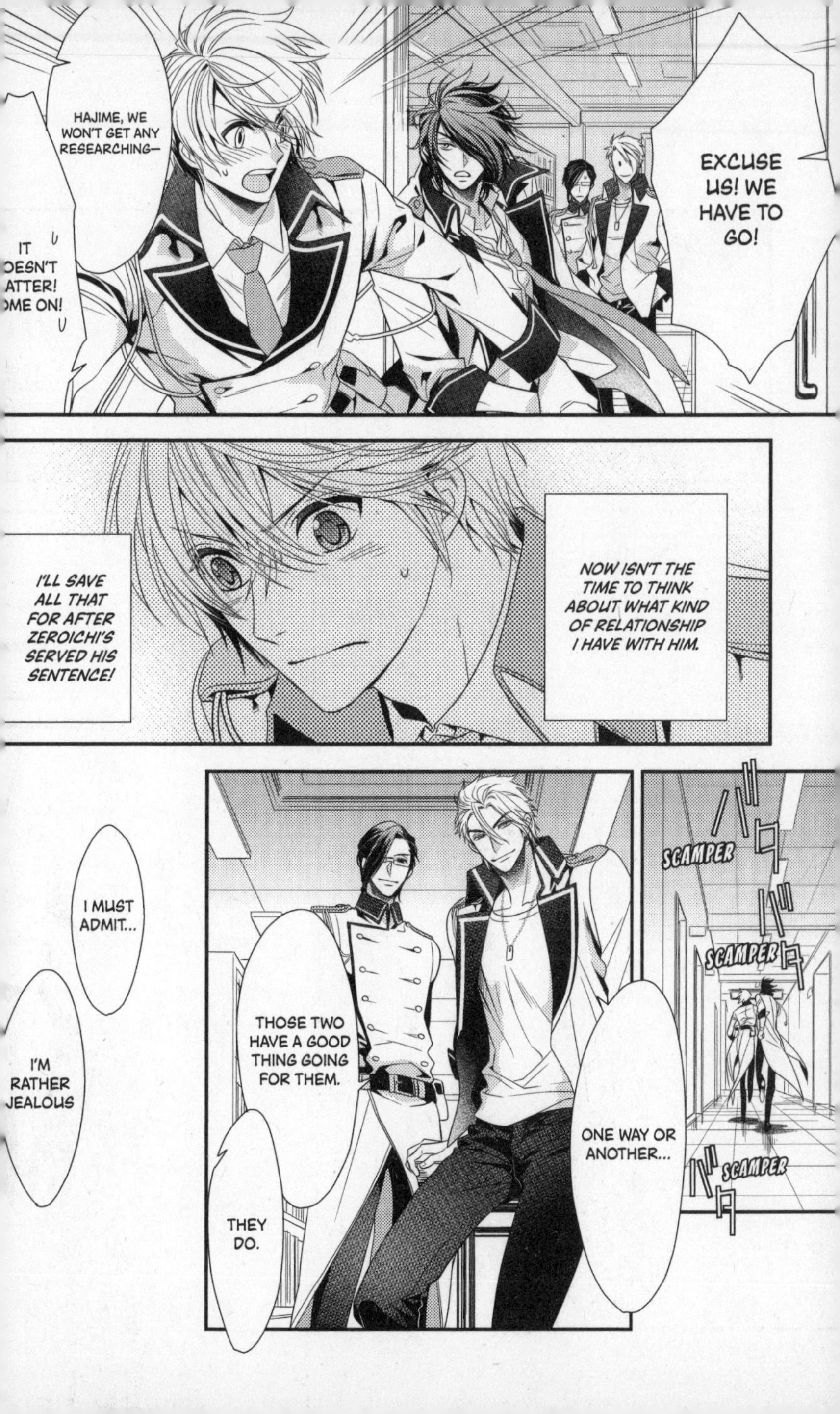
EXCUSE US! WE HAVE TO GO!
HAJIME, WE WON'T GET ANY RESEARCHING—
IT OESN'T ATTER! OME ON!
NOW ISN'T THE TIME TO THINK ABOUT WHAT KIND OF RELATIONSHIP I HAVE WITH HIM.
I'LL SAVE ALL THAT FOR AFTER ZEROICHI'S SERVED HIS SENTENCE!
SCAMPER
SCAMPER
SCAMPER
ONE WAY OR ANOTHER...
THOSE TWO HAVE A GOOD THING GOING FOR THEM.
THEY DO.
I MUST ADMIT...
I'M RATHER JEALOUS

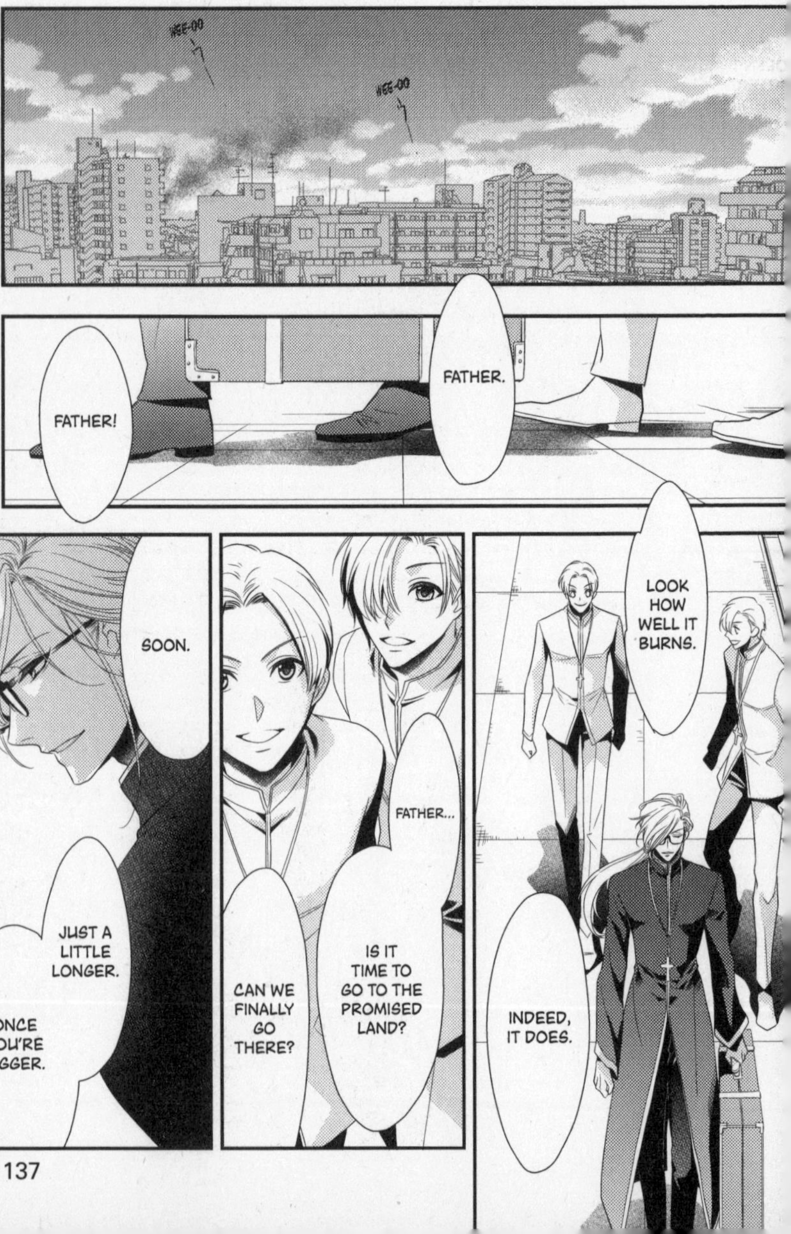

WEE-OO
WEE-OO
FATHER.
FATHER!
LOOK HOW WELL IT BURNS.
INDEED, IT DOES.
FATHER...
IS IT TIME TO GO TO THE PROMISED LAND?
CAN WE FINALLY GO THERE?
SOON.
JUST A LITTLE LONGER.
ONCE YOU'RE BIGGER.

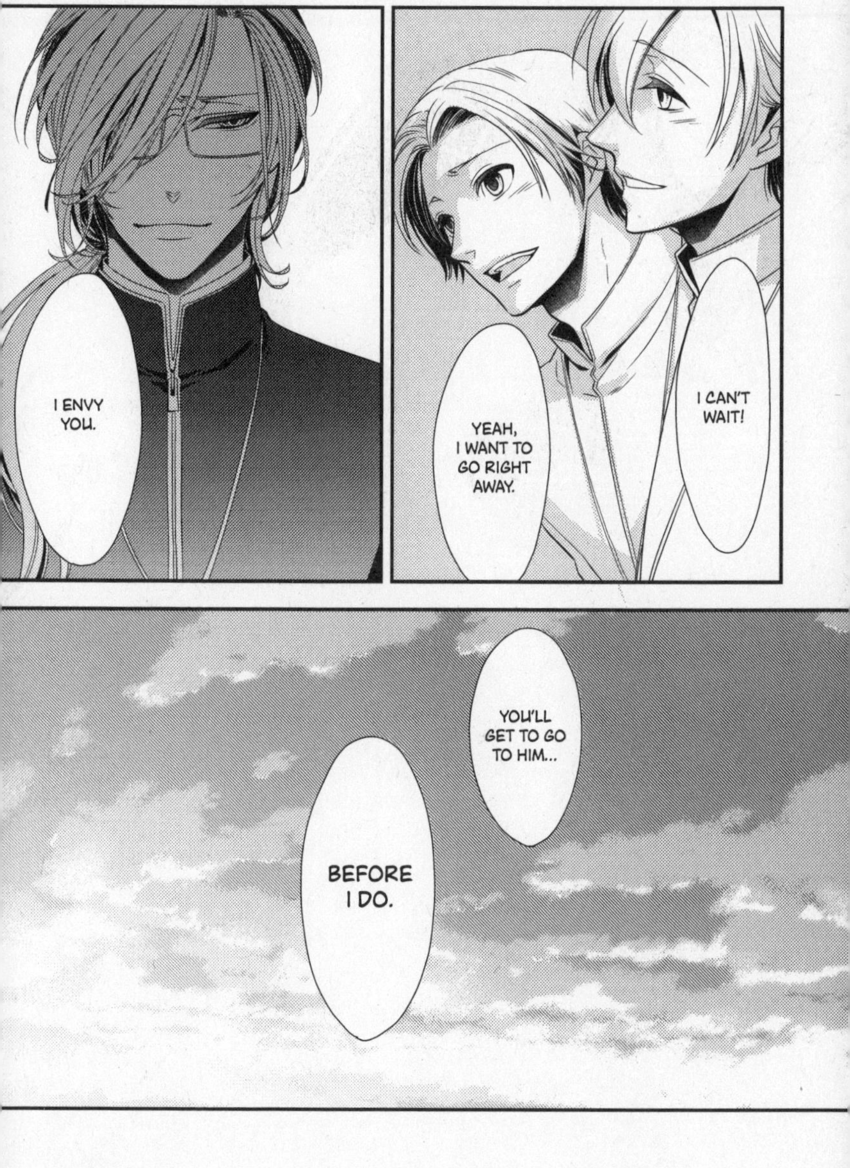
I CAN'T WAIT!
YEAH, I WANT TO GO RIGHT AWAY.
I ENVY YOU.
YOU'LL GET TO GO TO HIM...
BEFORE I DO.

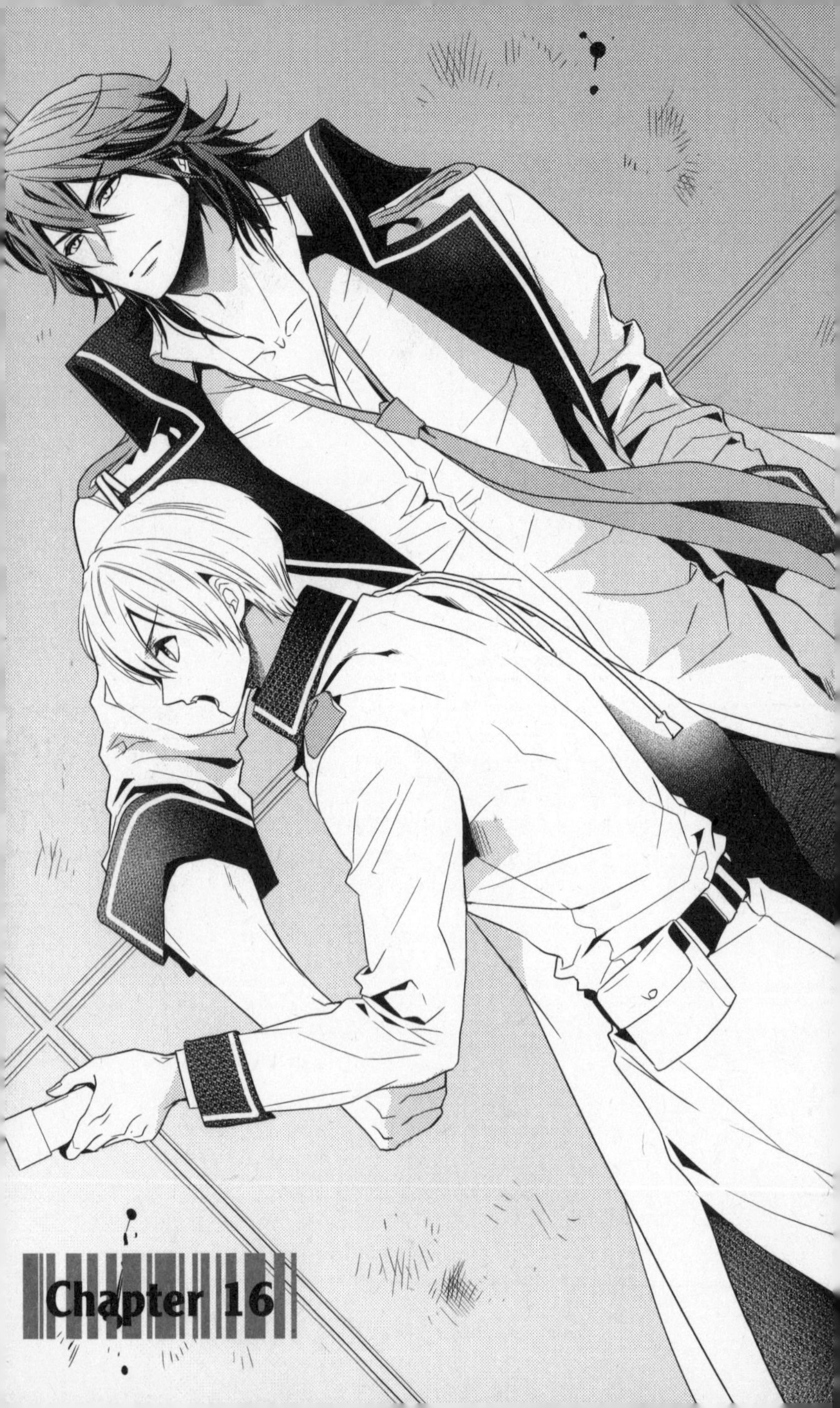
Chapter 16

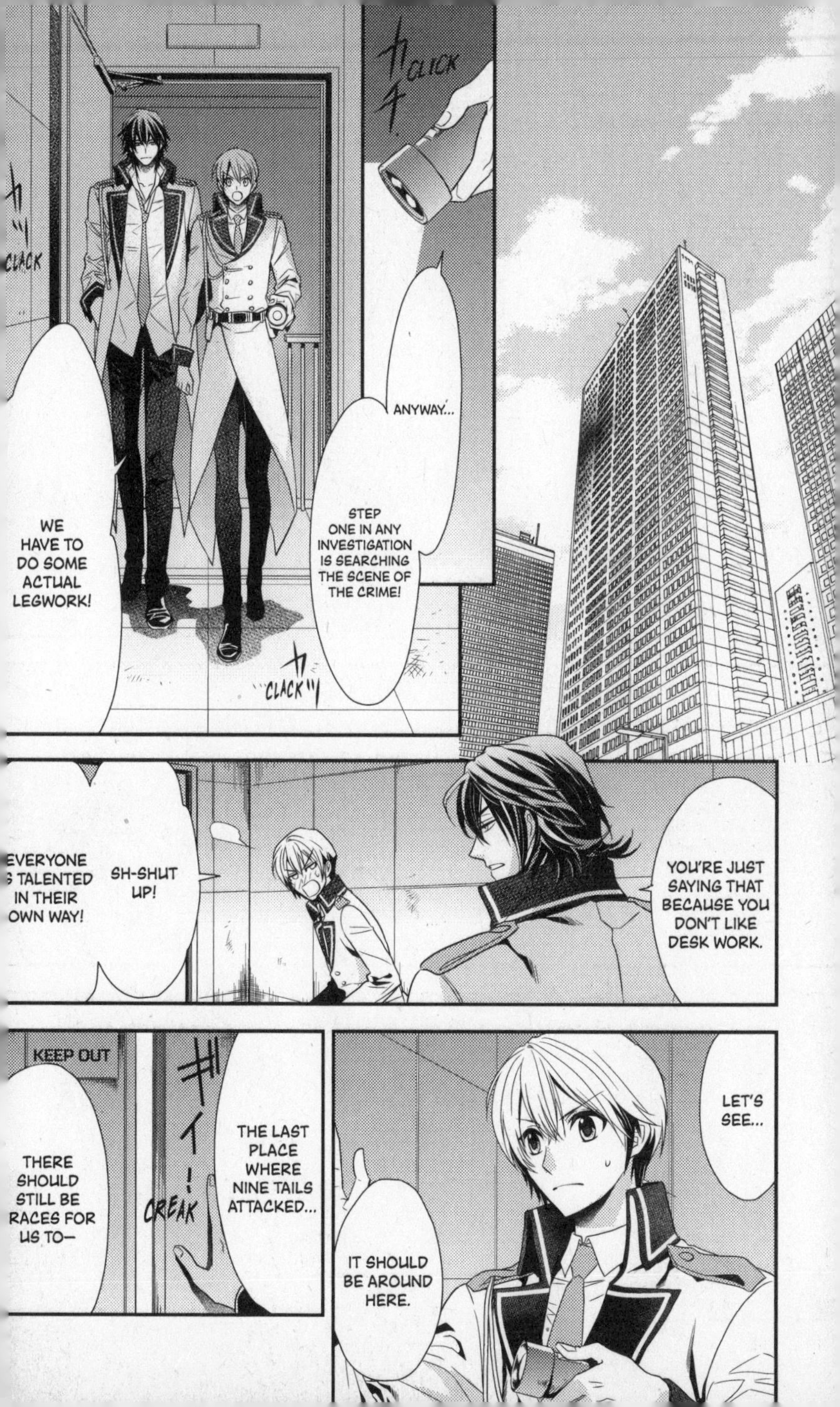
CLICK
ANYWAY...
STEP ONE IN ANY INVESTIGATION IS SEARCHING THE SCENE OF THE CRIME!
CLACK
WE HAVE TO DO SOME ACTUAL LEGWORK!
CLACK
YOU'RE JUST SAYING THAT BECAUSE YOU DON'T LIKE DESK WORK.
SH-SHUT UP!
EVERYONE S TALENTED IN THEIR OWN WAY!
LET'S SEE...
IT SHOULD BE AROUND HERE.
THE LAST PLACE WHERE NINE TAILS ATTACKED...
CREAK
KEEP OUT
THERE SHOULD STILL BE RACES FOR US TO—

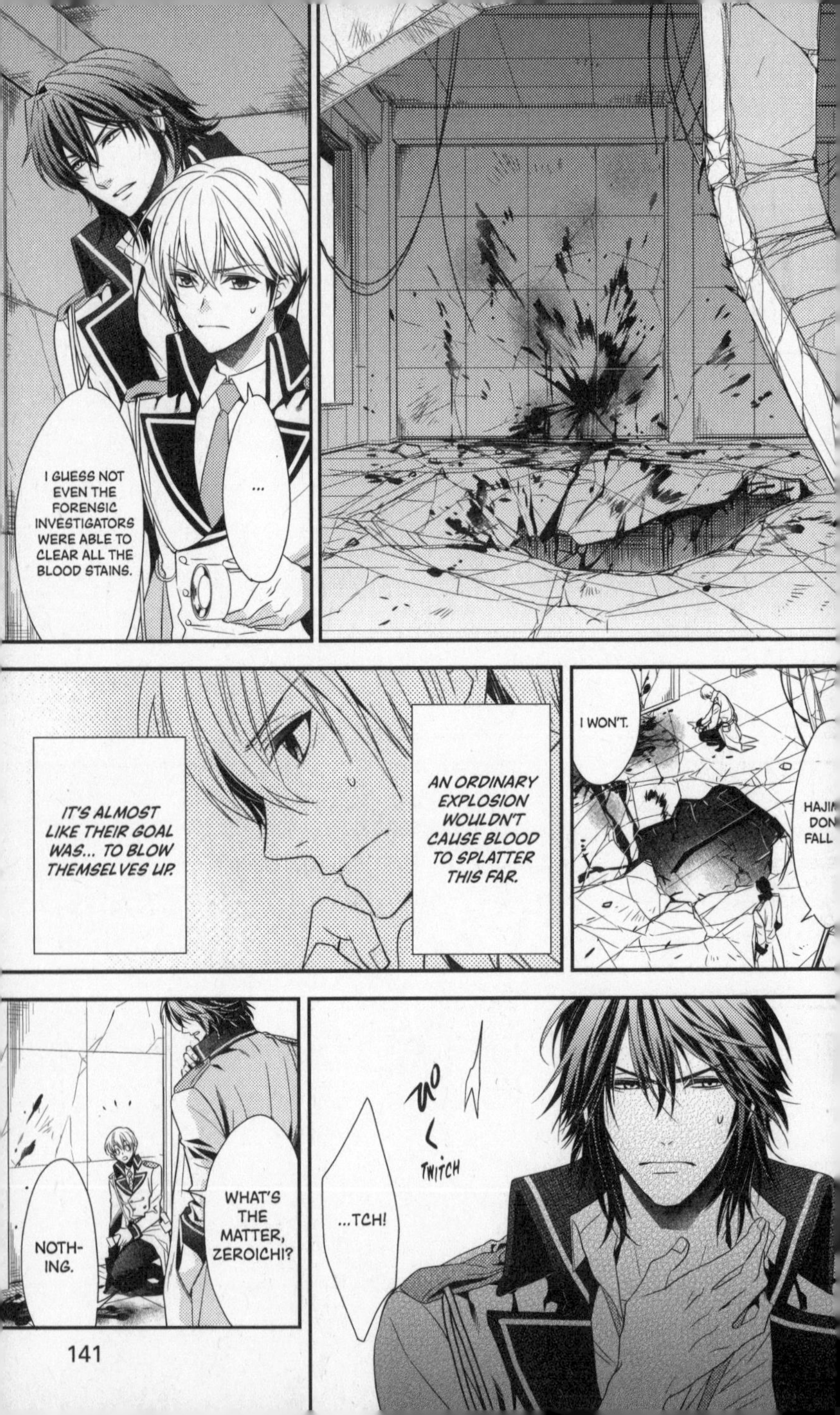
...
I GUESS NOT EVEN THE FORENSIC INVESTIGATORS WERE ABLE TO CLEAR ALL THE BLOOD STAINS.
HAJI DON FALL
I WON'T.
AN ORDINARY EXPLOSION WOULDN'T CAUSE BLOOD TO SPLATTER THIS FAR.
IT'S ALMOST LIKE THEIR GOAL WAS... TO BLOW THEMSELVES UP.
ぴく
TWITCH
...TCH!
WHAT'S THE MATTER, ZEROICHI?
NOTH-ING.

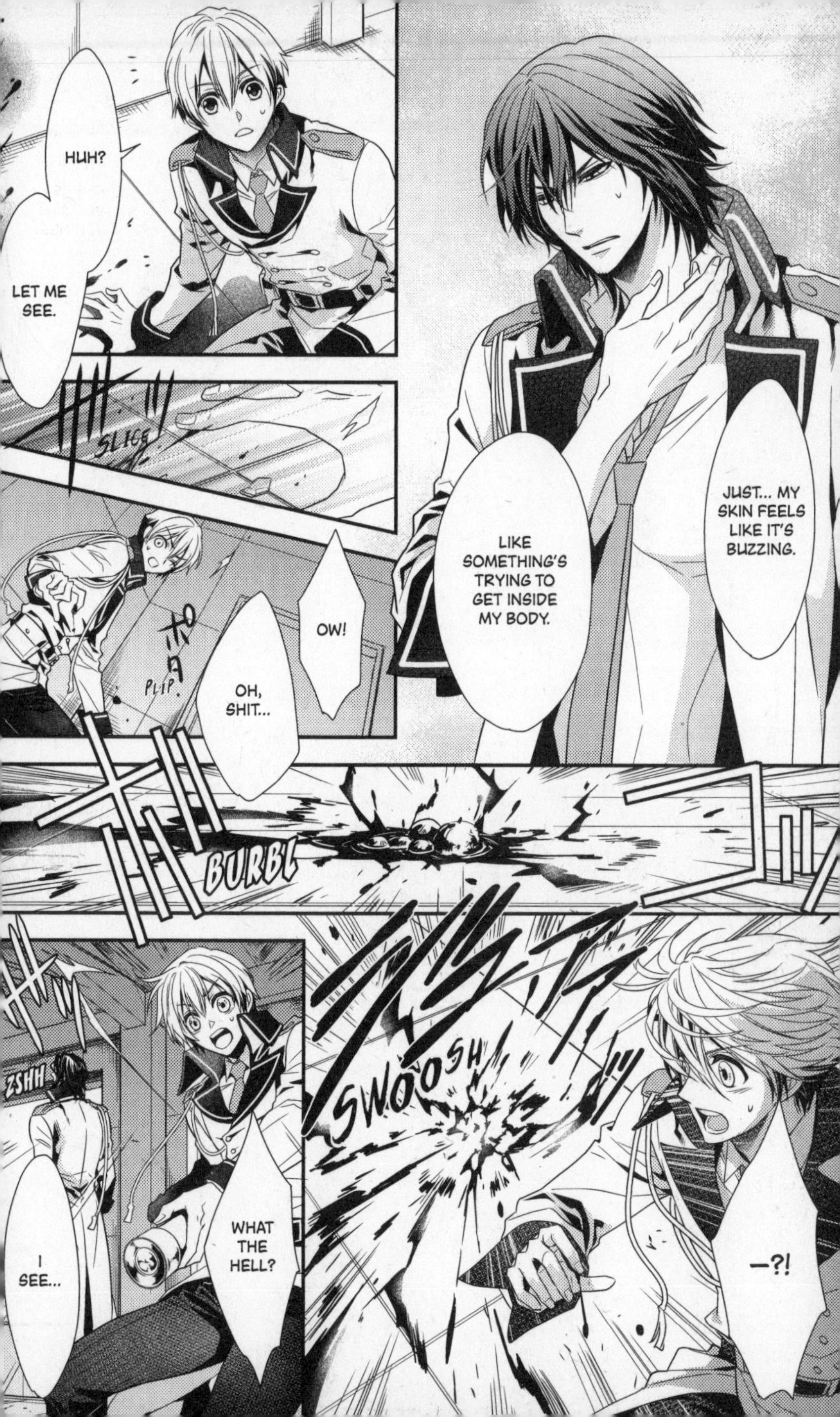
JUST... MY SKIN FEELS LIKE IT'S BUZZING.
LIKE SOMETHING'S TRYING TO GET INSIDE MY BODY.
HUH?
LET ME SEE.
SLICE
OW!
OH, SHIT...
PLIP
BURBL
SWOOSH
—?!
ZSHH
WHAT THE HELL?
I SEE...

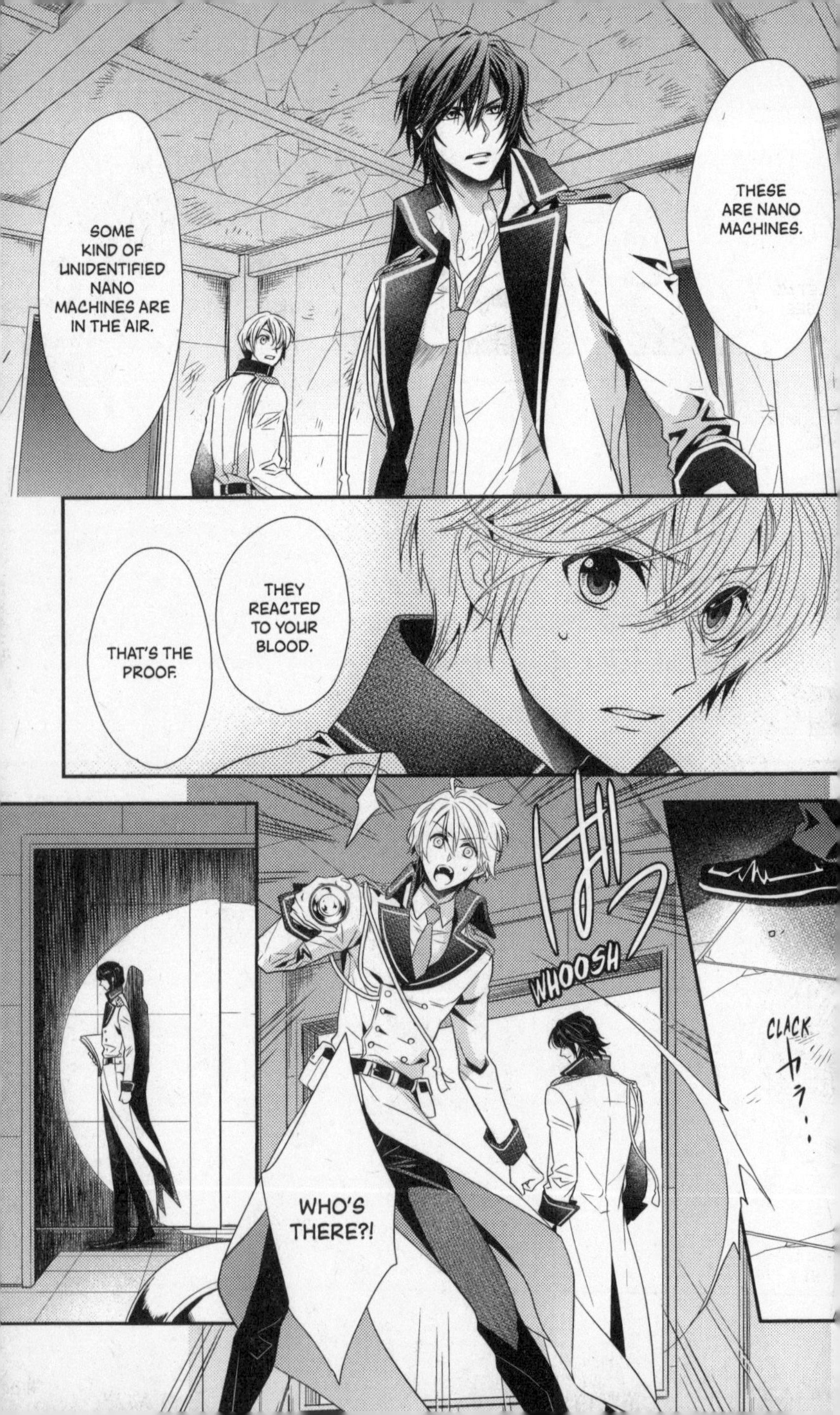
THESE ARE NANO MACHINES.
SOME KIND OF UNIDENTIFIED NANO MACHINES ARE IN THE AIR.
THEY REACTED TO YOUR BLOOD.
THAT'S THE PROOF.
はっ
WHOOSH
CLACK
カラ・・
WHO'S THERE?!

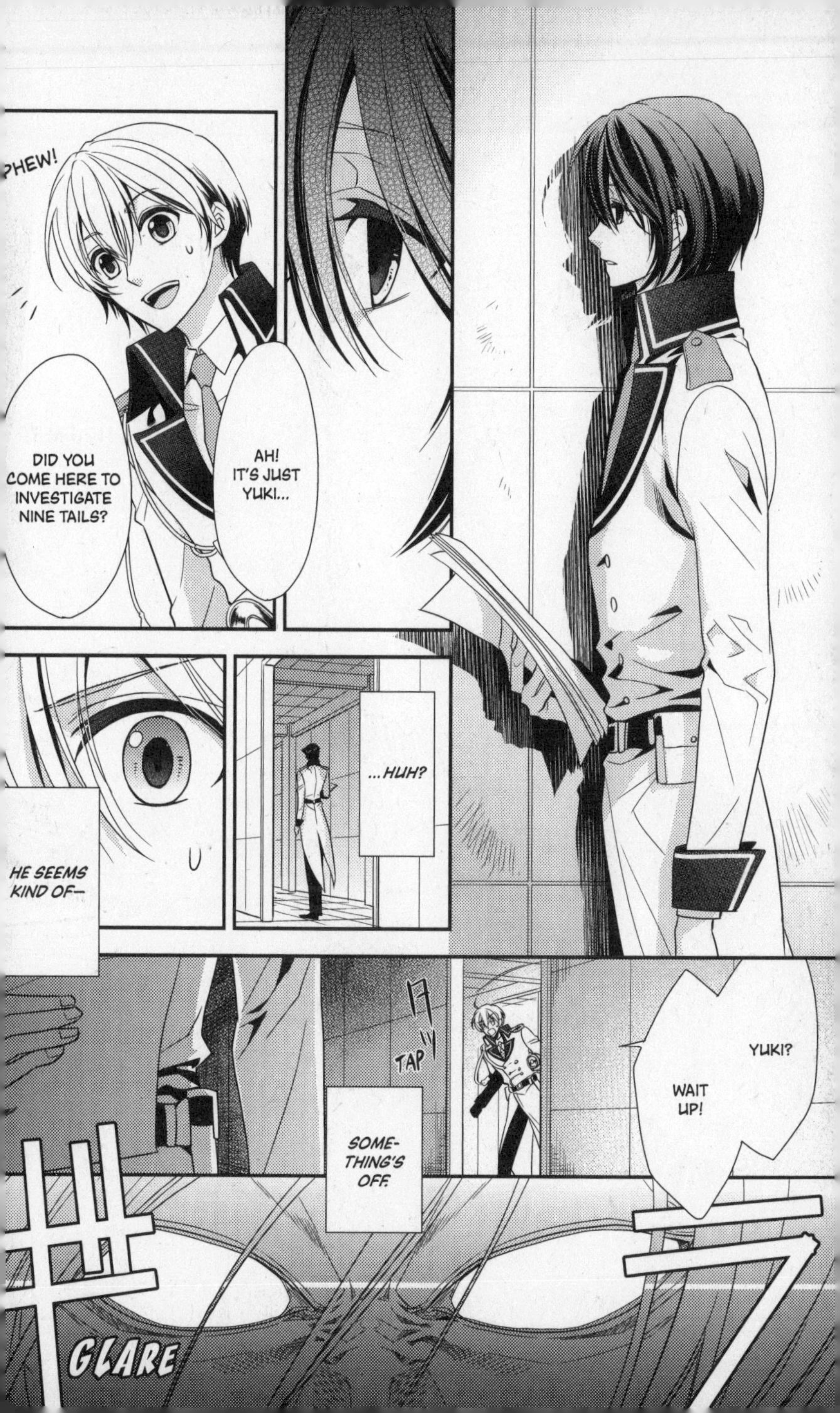
PHEW!
AH! IT'S JUST YUKI...
DID YOU COME HERE TO INVESTIGATE NINE TAILS?
...HUH?
HE SEEMS KIND OF—
YUKI?
WAIT UP!
TAP
SOME-THING'S OFF.
GLARE

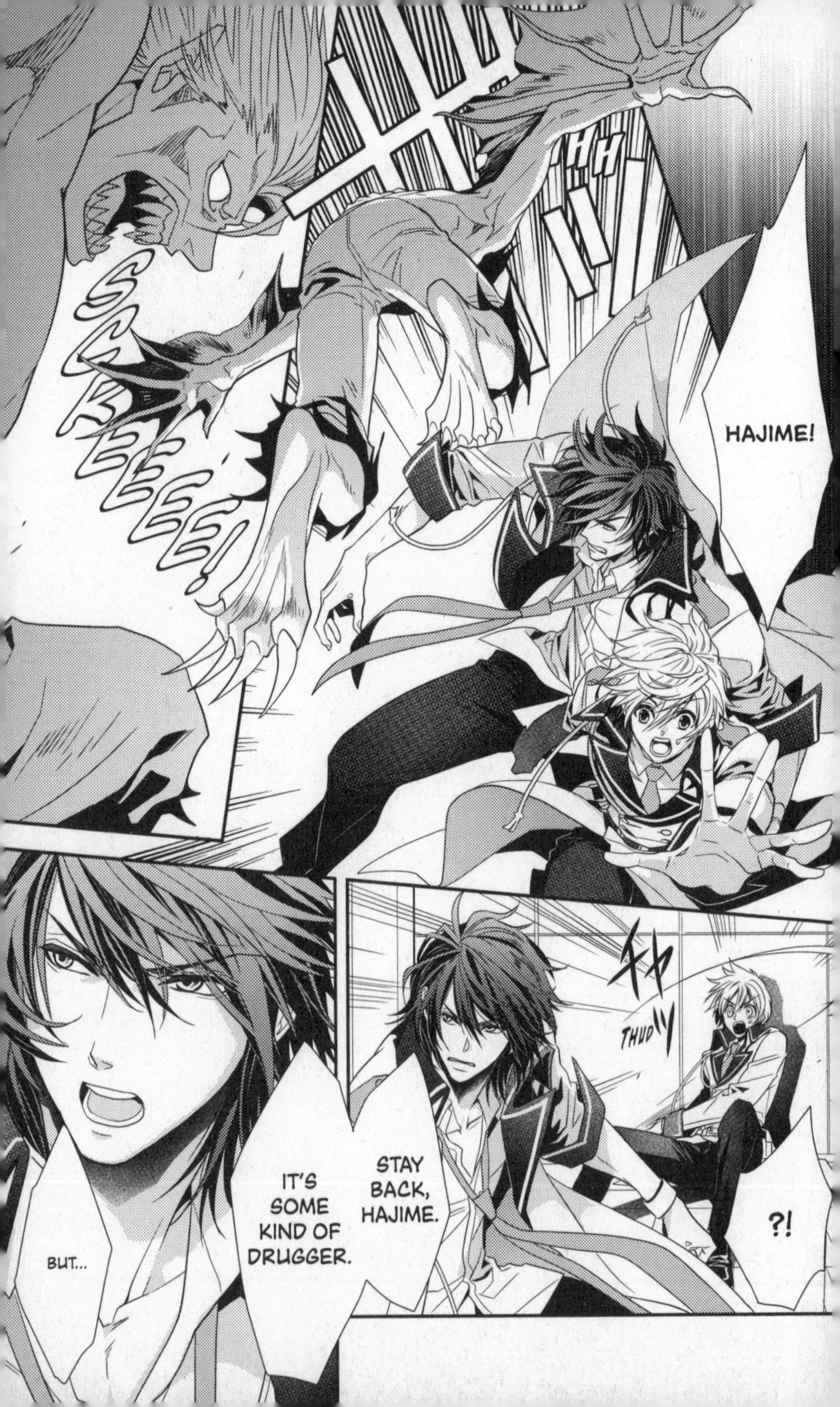
HAJIME!
SCREEEEE!
THUD
?!
STAY BACK, HAJIME.
IT'S SOME KIND OF DRUGGER.
BUT...

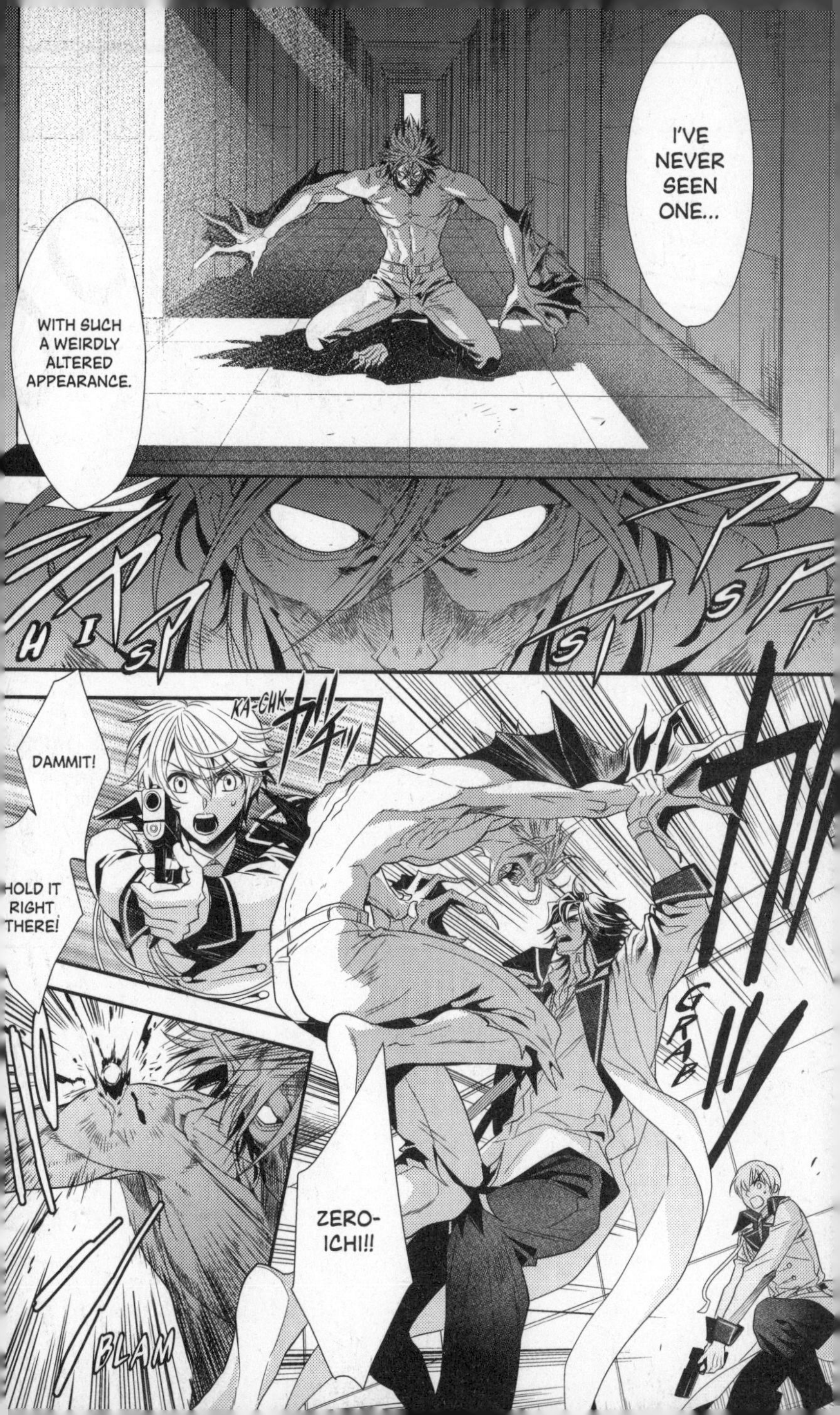
I'VE NEVER SEEN ONE...
WITH SUCH A WEIRDLY ALTERED APPEARANCE.
HISSS
GRAB
KA-CHK
DAMMIT!
HOLD IT RIGHT THERE!
ZERO-ICHI!!
BLAM

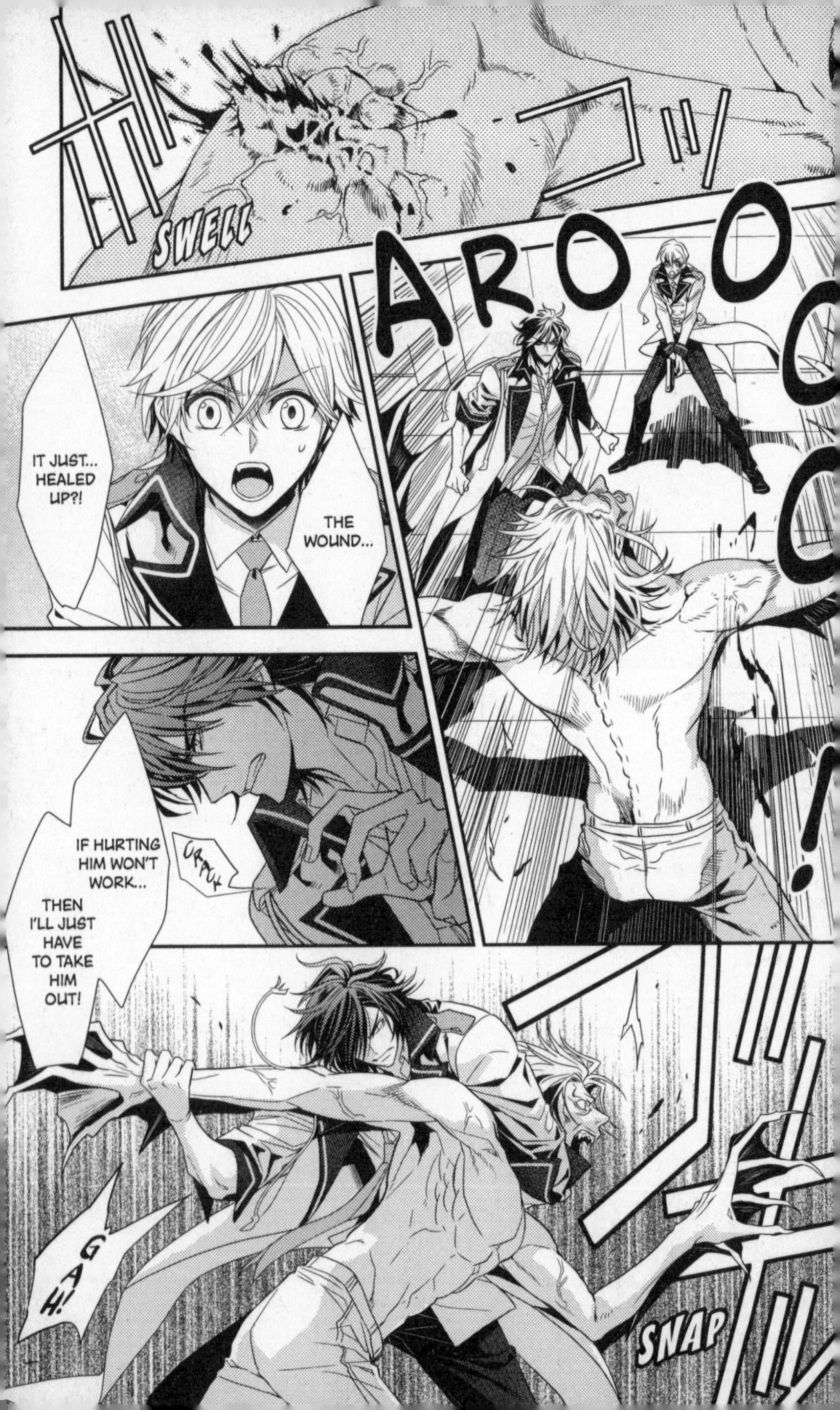
SWELL
AROOOO!
THE WOUND...
IT JUST... HEALED UP?!
IF HURTING HIM WON'T WORK...
URPUK
THEN I'LL JUST HAVE TO TAKE HIM OUT!
SNAP
GAH!

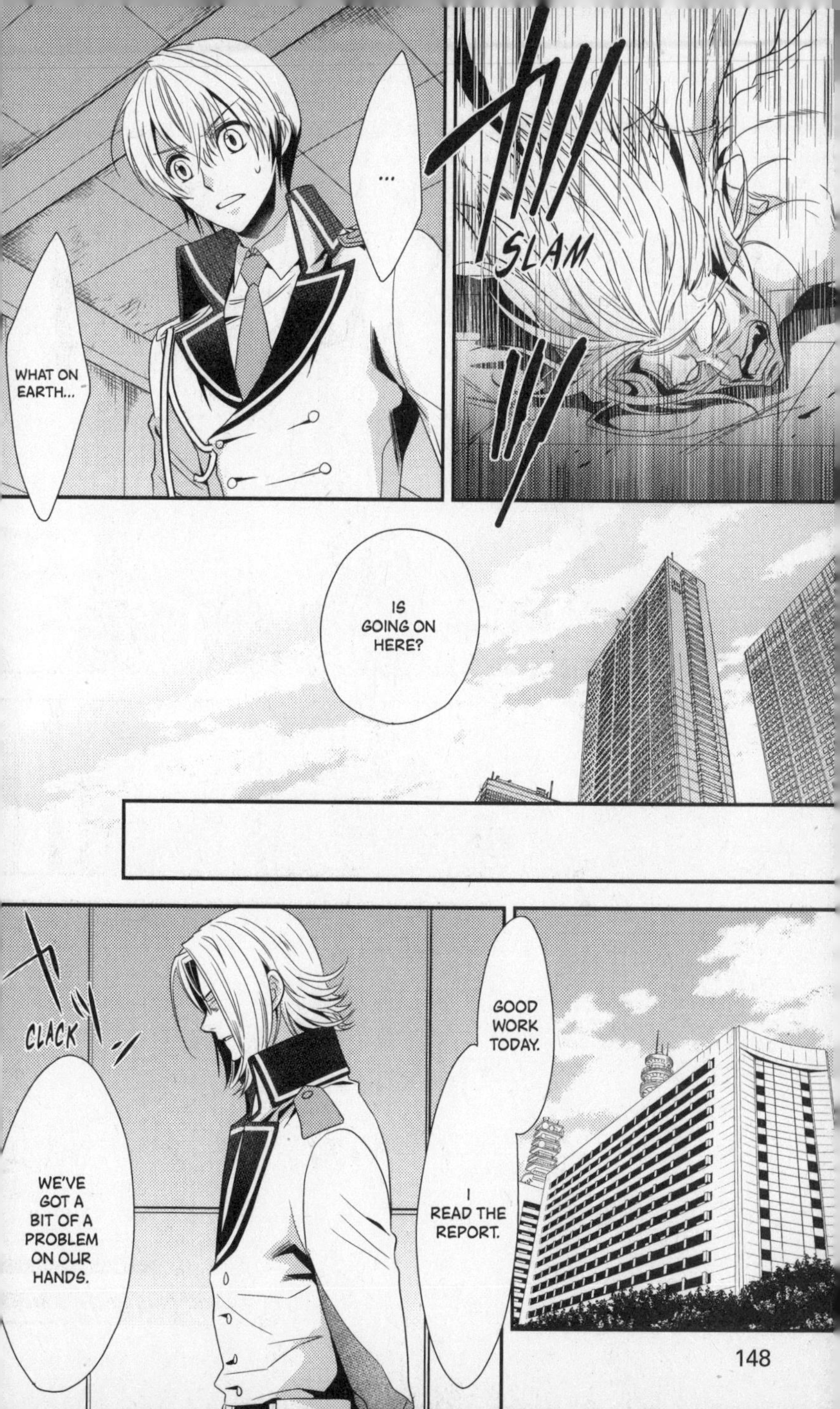
SLAM
...
WHAT ON EARTH...
IS GOING ON HERE?
GOOD WORK TODAY.
I READ THE REPORT.
CLACK
WE'VE GOT A BIT OF A PROBLEM ON OUR HANDS.

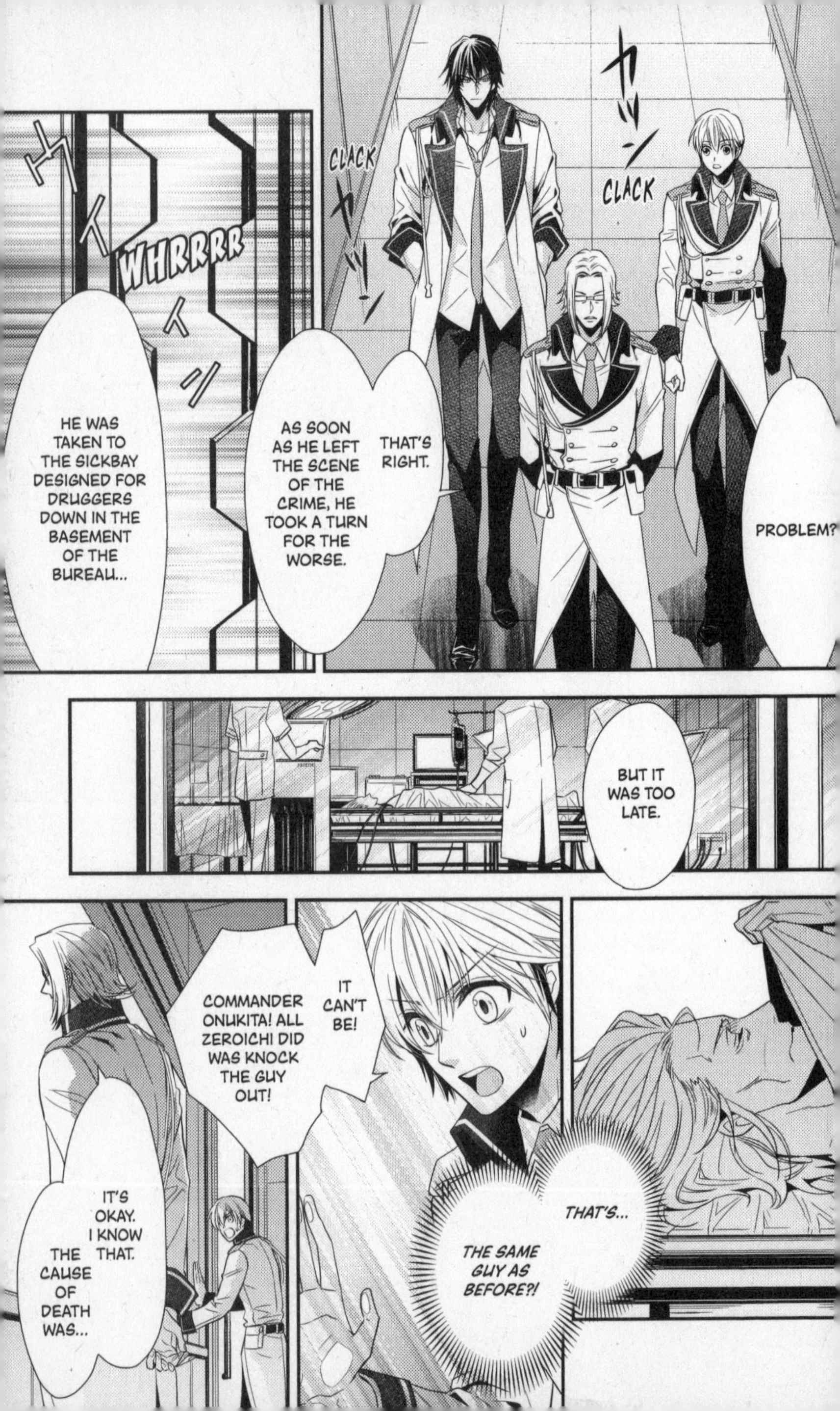
CLACK
CLACK
PROBLEM?
THAT'S RIGHT.
AS SOON AS HE LEFT THE SCENE OF THE CRIME, HE TOOK A TURN FOR THE WORSE.
WHRRRR
HE WAS TAKEN TO THE SICKBAY DESIGNED FOR DRUGGERS DOWN IN THE BASEMENT OF THE BUREAU...
BUT IT WAS TOO LATE.
THAT'S...
THE SAME GUY AS BEFORE?!
IT CAN'T BE!
COMMANDER ONUKITA! ALL ZEROICHI DID WAS KNOCK THE GUY OUT!
IT'S OKAY. I KNOW THAT.
THE CAUSE OF DEATH WAS...

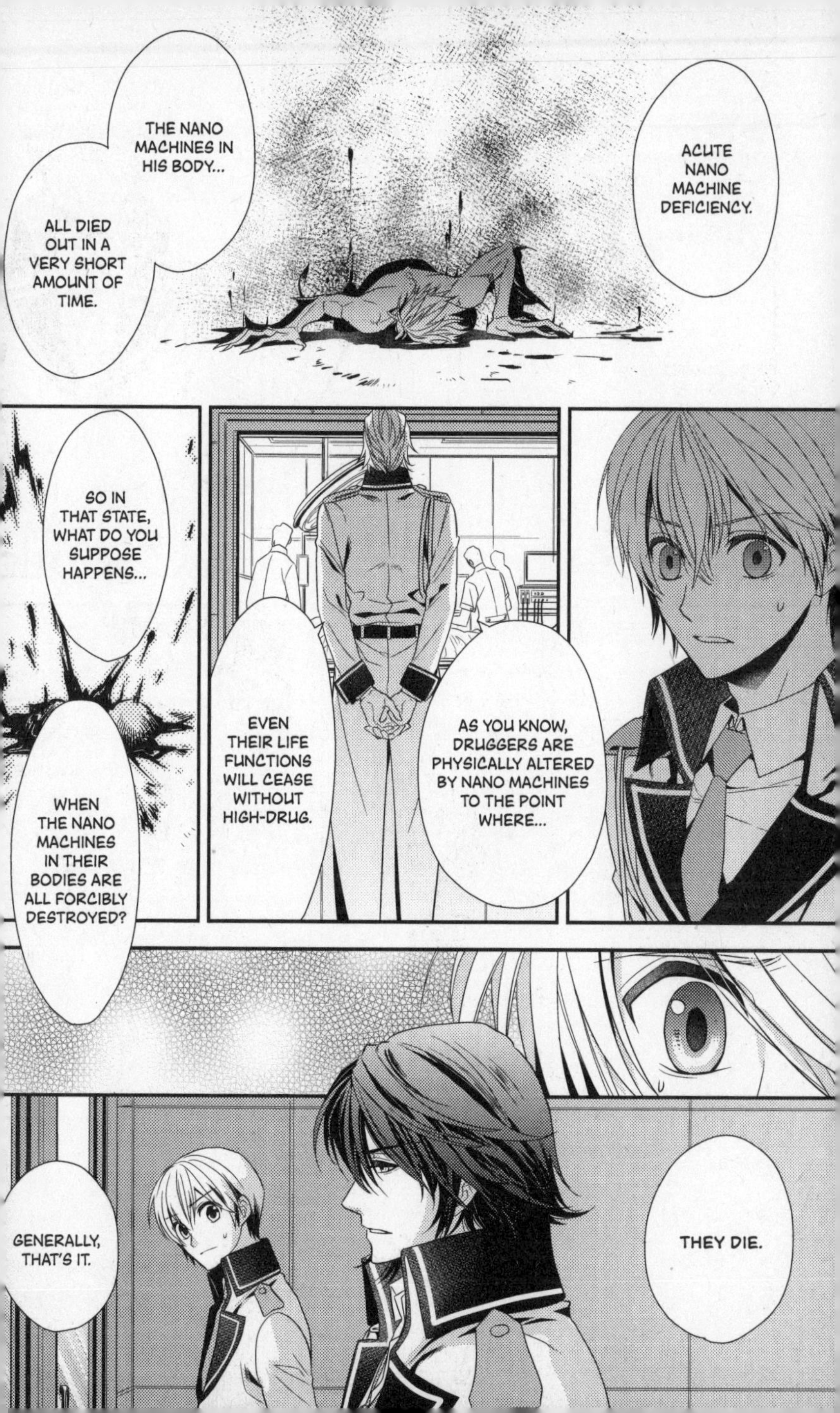
ACUTE NANO MACHINE DEFICIENCY.
THE NANO MACHINES IN HIS BODY...
ALL DIED OUT IN A VERY SHORT AMOUNT OF TIME.
AS YOU KNOW, DRUGGERS ARE PHYSICALLY ALTERED BY NANO MACHINES TO THE POINT WHERE...
EVEN THEIR LIFE FUNCTIONS WILL CEASE WITHOUT HIGH-DRUG.
SO IN THAT STATE, WHAT DO YOU SUPPOSE HAPPENS...
WHEN THE NANO MACHINES IN THEIR BODIES ARE ALL FORCIBLY DESTROYED?
THEY DIE.
GENERALLY, THAT'S IT.

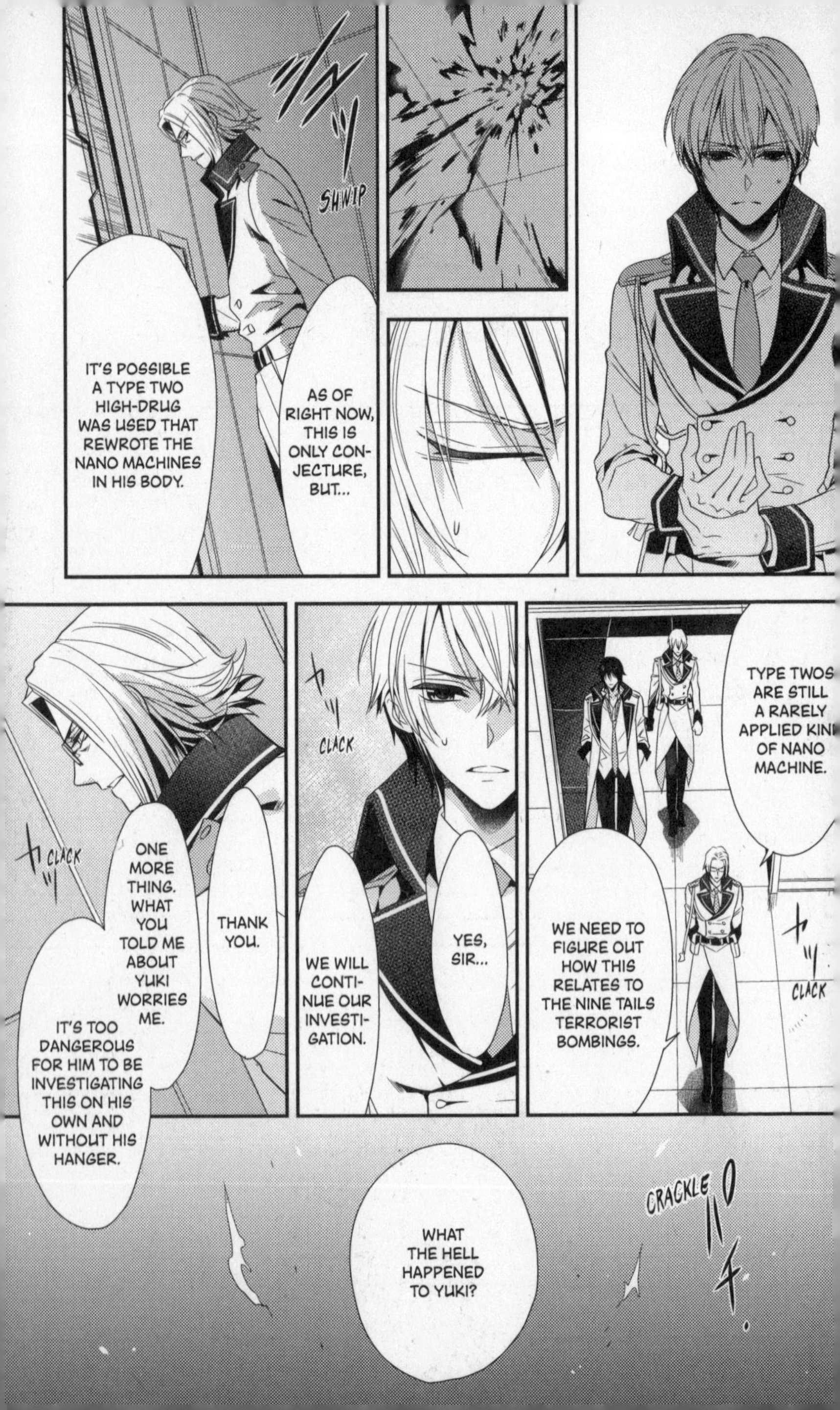
SHWIP
AS OF RIGHT NOW, THIS IS ONLY CONJECTURE, BUT...
IT'S POSSIBLE A TYPE TWO HIGH-DRUG WAS USED THAT REWROTE THE NANO MACHINES IN HIS BODY.
TYPE TWOS ARE STILL A RARELY APPLIED KIND OF NANO MACHINE.
WE NEED TO FIGURE OUT HOW THIS RELATES TO THE NINE TAILS TERRORIST BOMBINGS.
CLACK
YES, SIR...
WE WILL CONTINUE OUR INVESTIGATION.
CLACK
THANK YOU.
ONE MORE THING. WHAT YOU TOLD ME ABOUT YUKI WORRIES ME.
IT'S TOO DANGEROUS FOR HIM TO BE INVESTIGATING THIS ON HIS OWN AND WITHOUT HIS HANGER.
CLACK
CRACKLE
WHAT THE HELL HAPPENED TO YUKI?

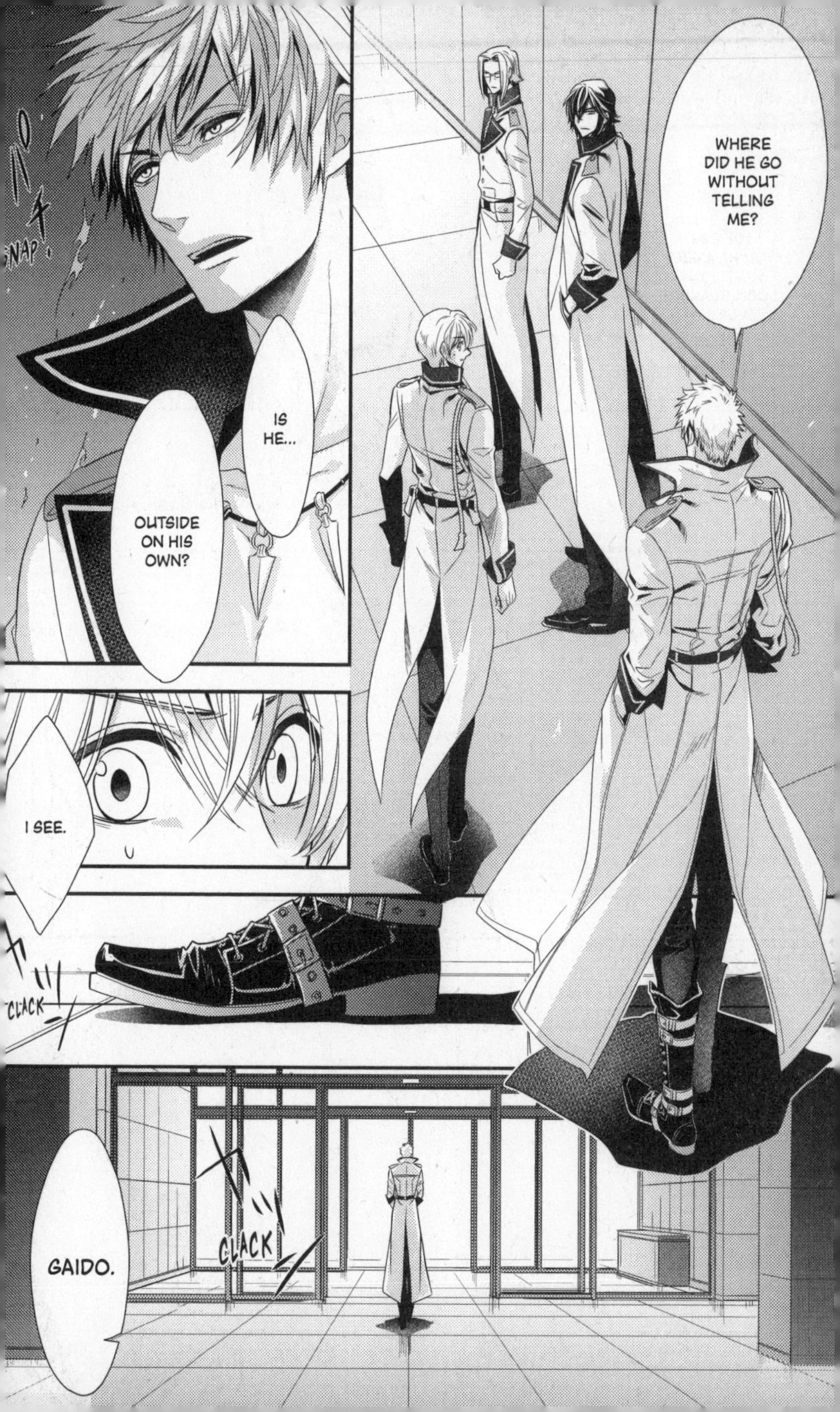
WHERE DID HE GO WITHOUT TELLING ME?
SNAP
IS HE...
OUTSIDE ON HIS OWN?
I SEE.
CLACK
CLACK
GAIDO.

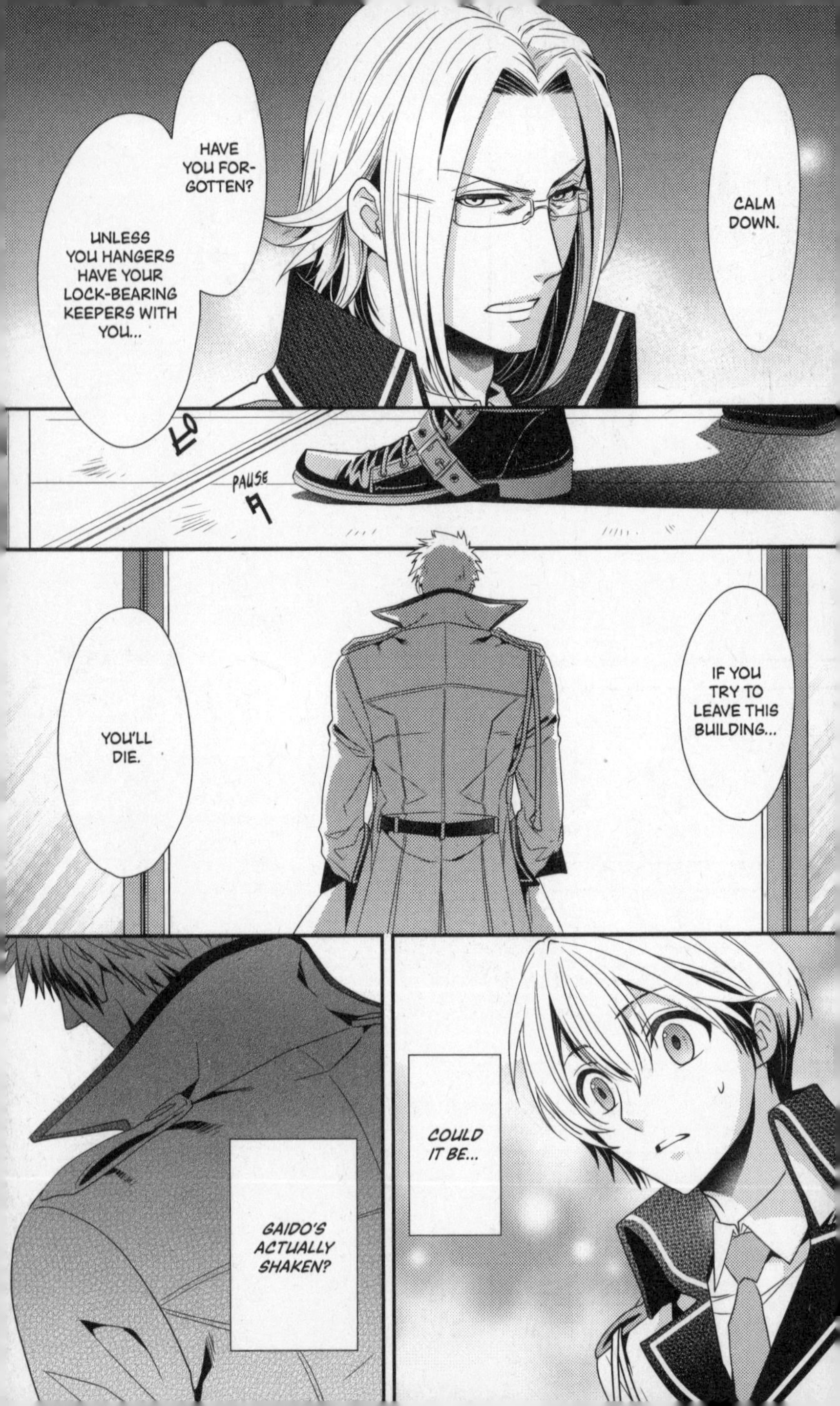
CALM DOWN.
HAVE YOU FOR-GOTTEN?
UNLESS YOU HANGERS HAVE YOUR LOCK-BEARING KEEPERS WITH YOU...
PAUSE
IF YOU TRY TO LEAVE THIS BUILDING...
YOU'LL DIE.
COULD IT BE...
GAIDO'S ACTUALLY SHAKEN?

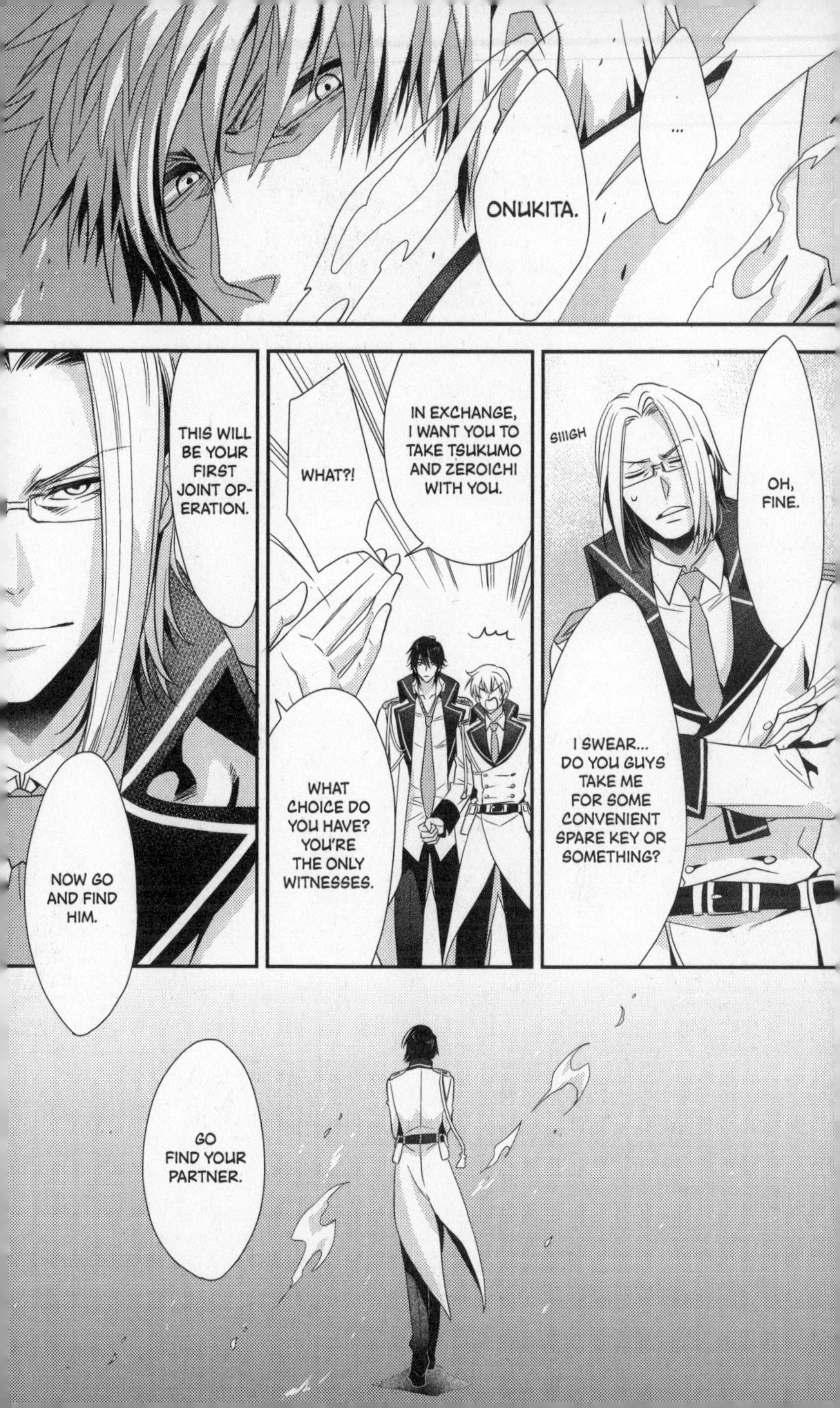
...
ONUKITA.
OH, FINE.
SIIIGH
I SWEAR... DO YOU GUYS TAKE ME FOR SOME CONVENIENT SPARE KEY OR SOMETHING?
IN EXCHANGE, I WANT YOU TO TAKE TSUKUMO AND ZEROICHI WITH YOU.
WHAT?!
WHAT CHOICE DO YOU HAVE? YOU'RE THE ONLY WITNESSES.
THIS WILL BE YOUR FIRST JOINT OPERATION.
NOW GO AND FIND HIM.
GO FIND YOUR PARTNER.

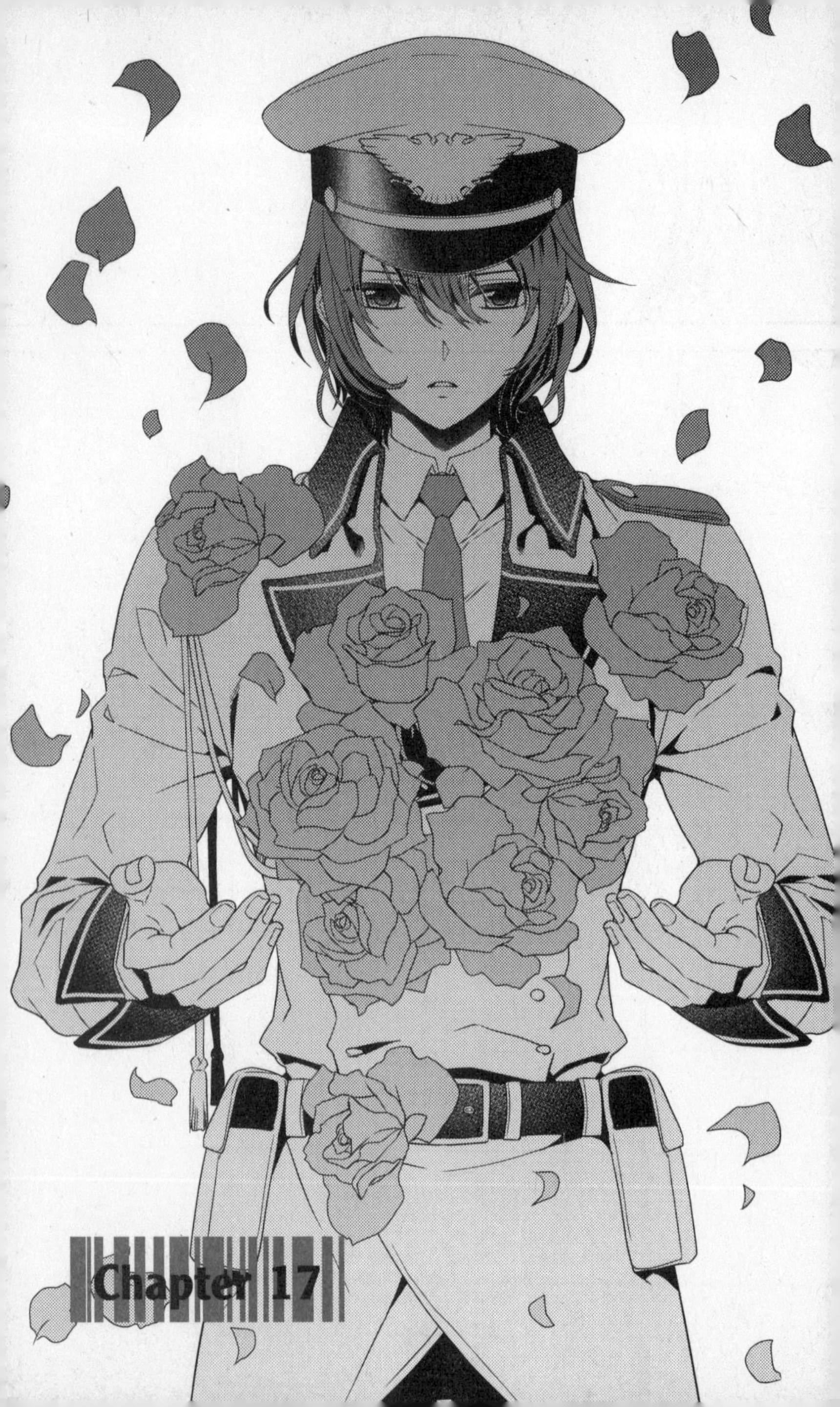
Chapter 17

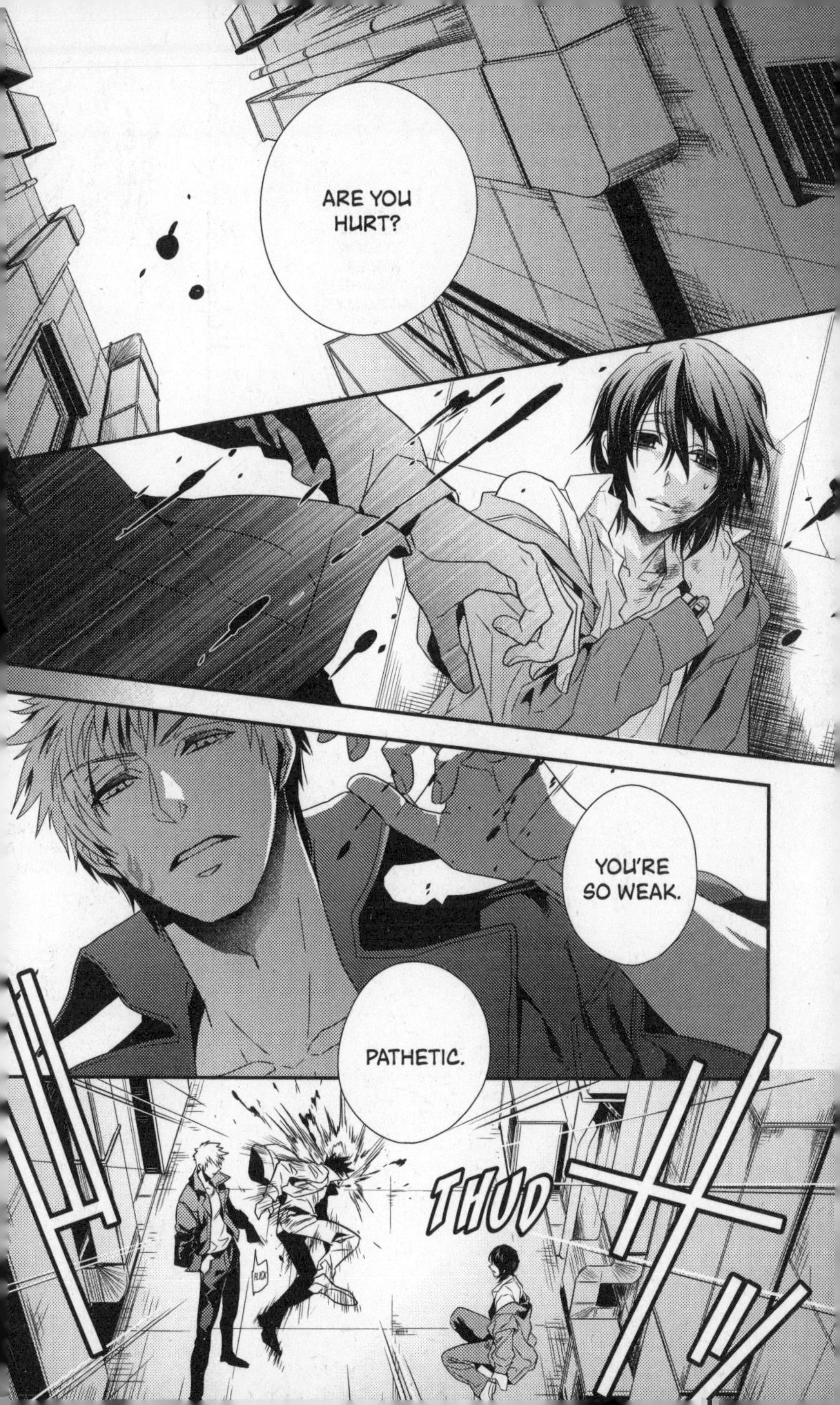
ARE YOU HURT?
YOU'RE SO WEAK.
PATHETIC.
THUD
FLICK

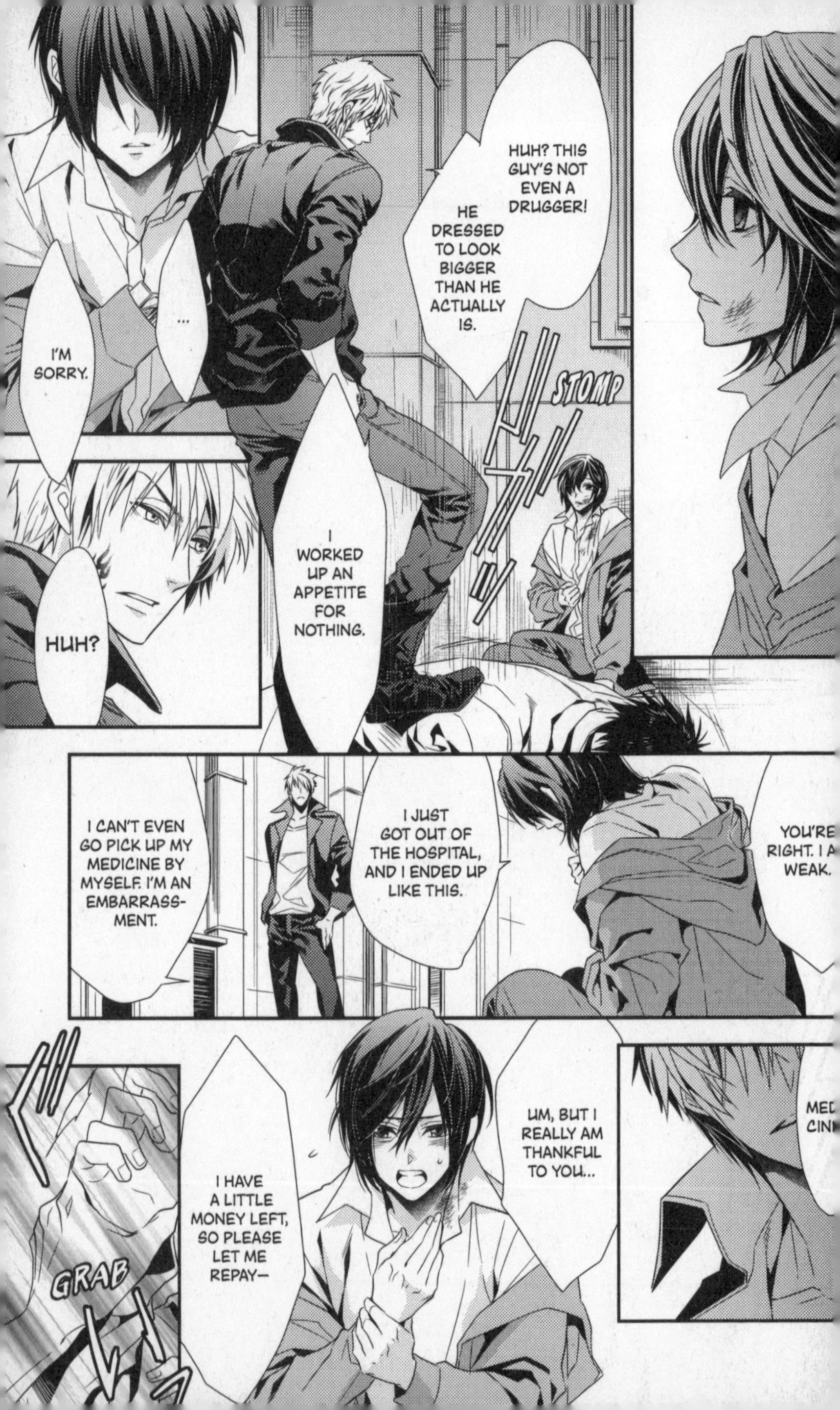
HUH? THIS GUY'S NOT EVEN A DRUGGER!
HE DRESSED TO LOOK BIGGER THAN HE ACTUALLY IS.
STOMP
I WORKED UP AN APPETITE FOR NOTHING.
...
I'M SORRY.
HUH?
YOU'RE RIGHT. I A
WEAK.
I JUST GOT OUT OF THE HOSPITAL, AND I ENDED UP LIKE THIS.
I CAN'T EVEN GO PICK UP MY MEDICINE BY MYSELF. I'M AN EMBARRASS-MENT.
MED CIN
UM, BUT I REALLY AM THANKFUL TO YOU...
I HAVE A LITTLE MONEY LEFT, SO PLEASE LET ME REPAY—
GRAB

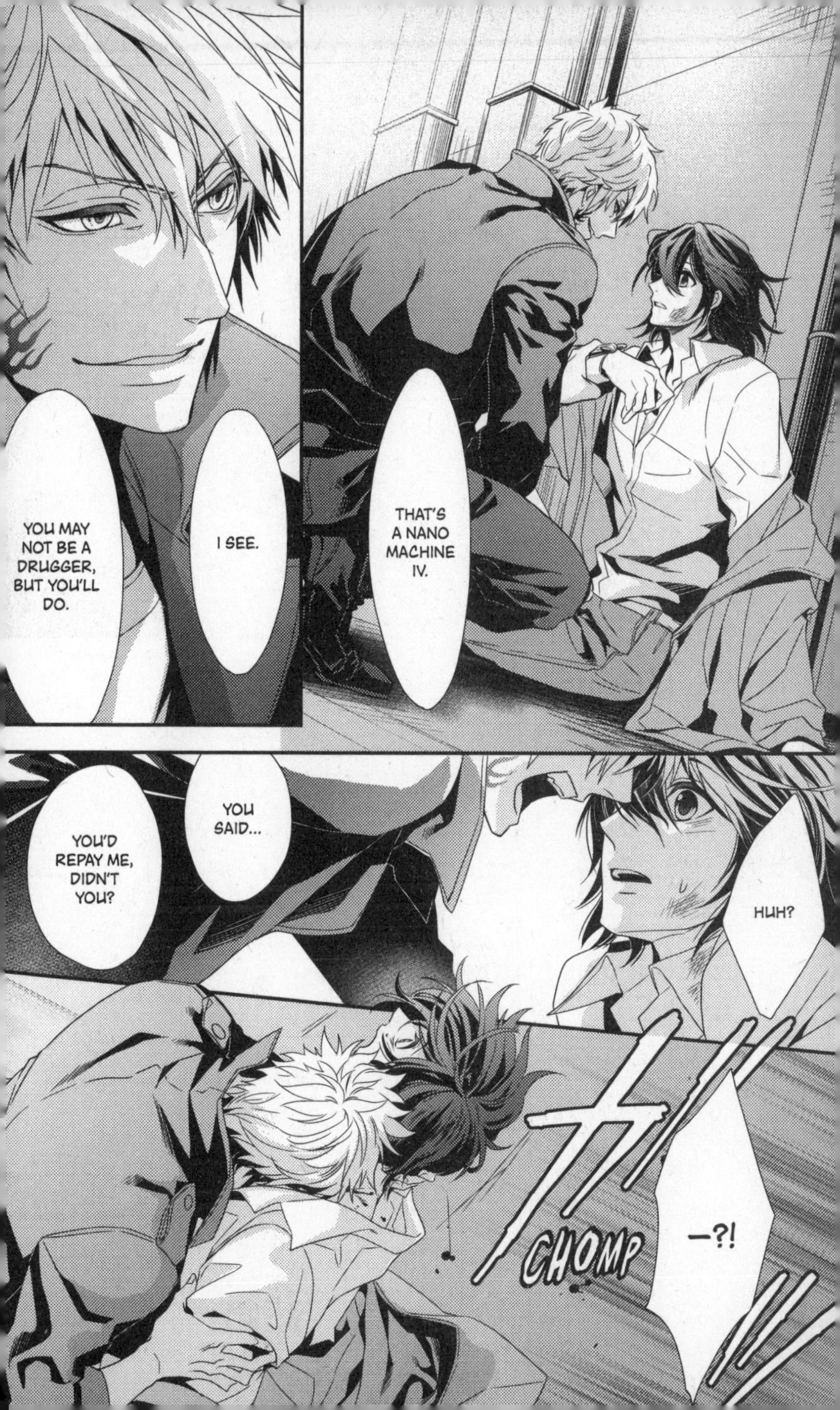
THAT'S A NANO MACHINE IV.
I SEE.
YOU MAY NOT BE A DRUGGER, BUT YOU'LL DO.
YOU SAID...
YOU'D REPAY ME, DIDN'T YOU?
HUH?
—?!
CHOMP

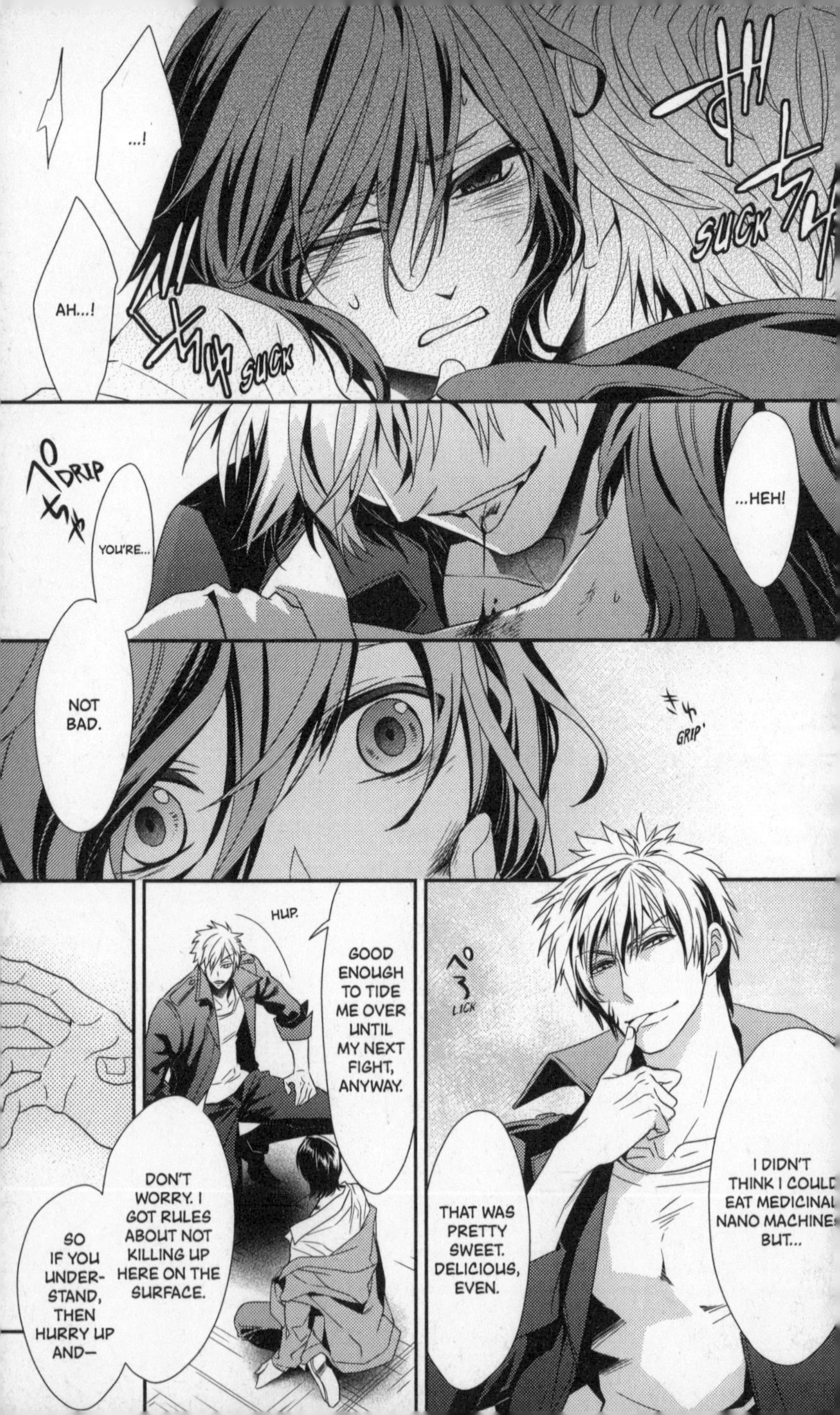
SUCK
...!
AH...!
SUCK
...HEH!
DRIP
YOU'RE...
NOT BAD.
GRIP
I DIDN'T THINK I COULD EAT MEDICINAL NANO MACHINES BUT...
LICK
THAT WAS PRETTY SWEET. DELICIOUS, EVEN.
HUP.
GOOD ENOUGH TO TIDE ME OVER UNTIL MY NEXT FIGHT, ANYWAY.
DON'T WORRY. I GOT RULES ABOUT NOT KILLING UP HERE ON THE SURFACE.
SO IF YOU UNDER-STAND, THEN HURRY UP AND—

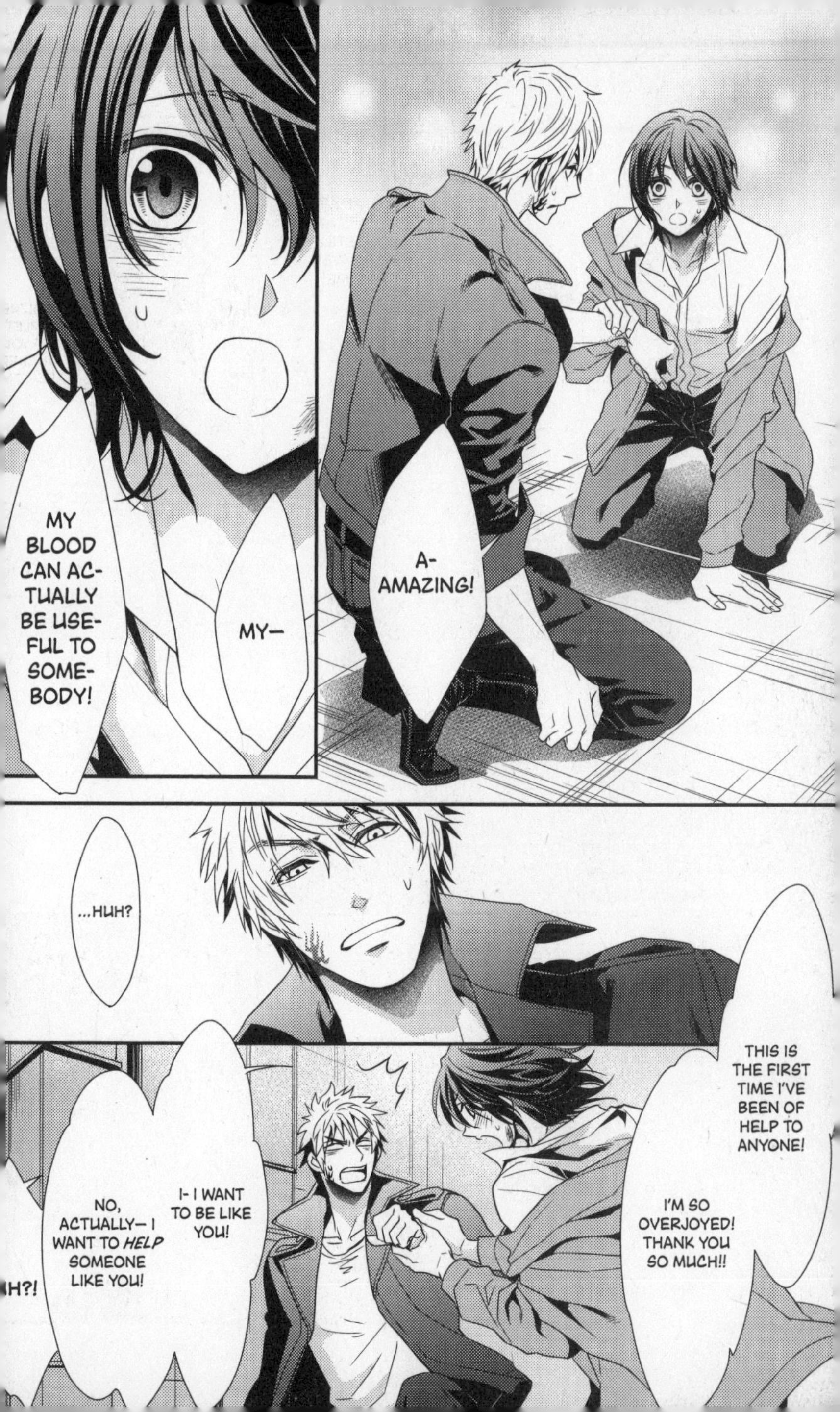
A- AMAZING!
MY—
MY BLOOD CAN ACTUALLY BE USEFUL TO SOMEBODY!
...HUH?
THIS IS THE FIRST TIME I'VE BEEN OF HELP TO ANYONE!
I'M SO OVERJOYED! THANK YOU SO MUCH!!
I- I WANT TO BE LIKE YOU!
NO, ACTUALLY— I WANT TO *HELP* SOMEONE LIKE YOU!
H?!

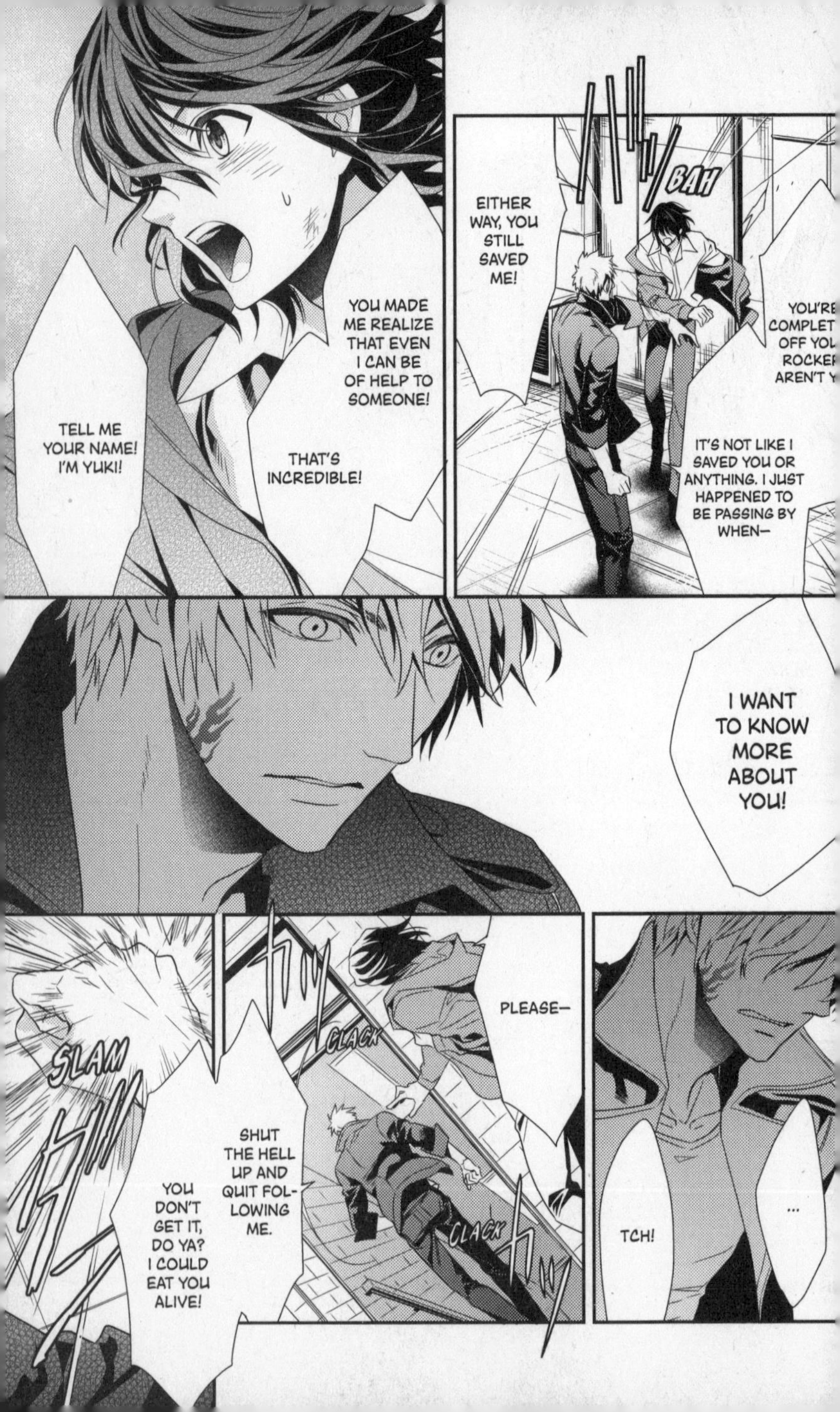
BAH
YOU'RE COMPLET OFF YO ROCKER AREN'T Y
IT'S NOT LIKE I SAVED YOU OR ANYTHING. I JUST HAPPENED TO BE PASSING BY WHEN—
EITHER WAY, YOU STILL SAVED ME!
YOU MADE ME REALIZE THAT EVEN I CAN BE OF HELP TO SOMEONE!
THAT'S INCREDIBLE!
TELL ME YOUR NAME! I'M YUKI!
I WANT TO KNOW MORE ABOUT YOU!
...
TCH!
PLEASE—
CLACK
SHUT THE HELL UP AND QUIT FOL-LOWING ME.
CLACK
SLAM
YOU DON'T GET IT, DO YA? I COULD EAT YOU ALIVE!

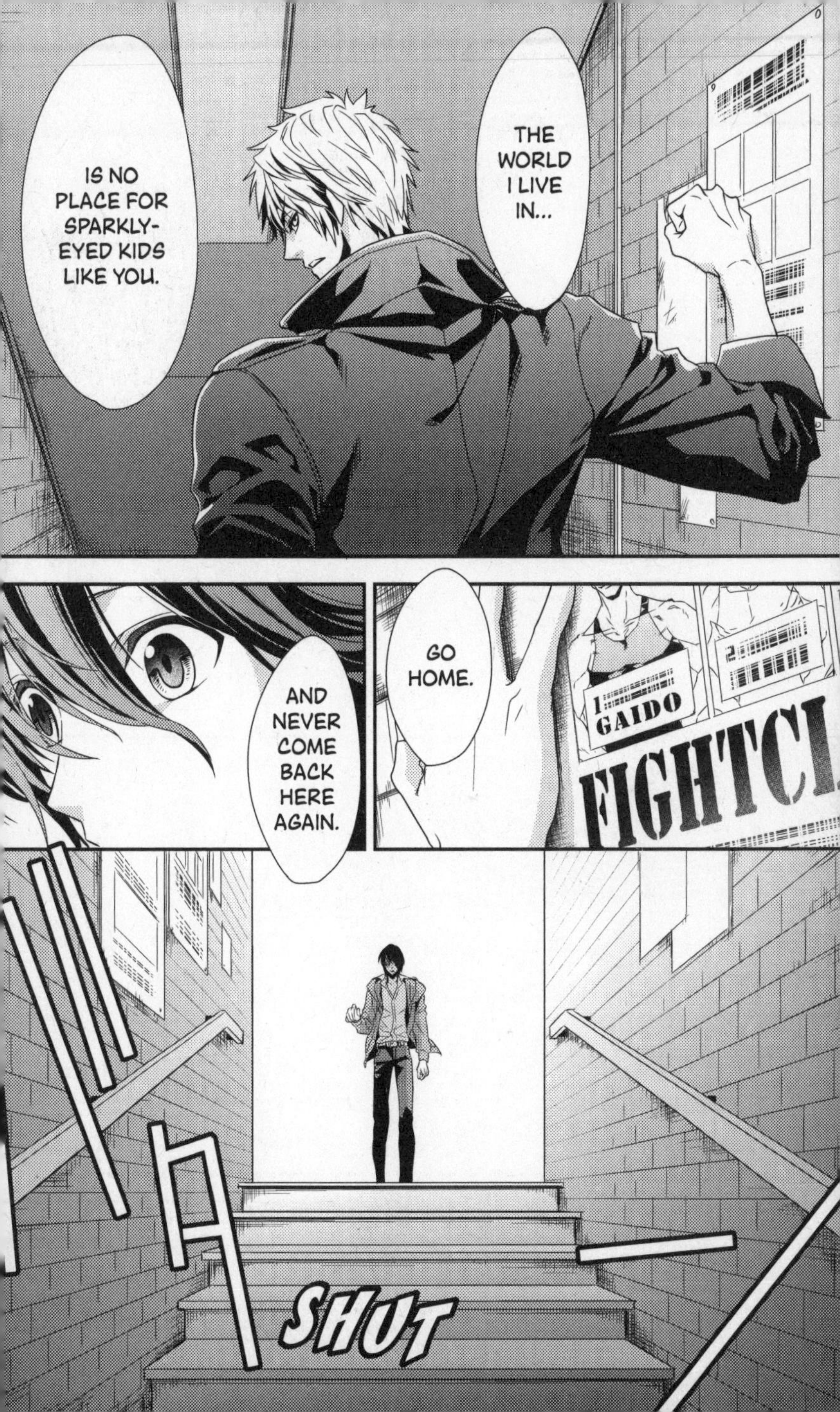
THE WORLD I LIVE IN...
IS NO PLACE FOR SPARKLY-EYED KIDS LIKE YOU.
GO HOME.
1 GAIDO
2
FIGHTC
AND NEVER COME BACK HERE AGAIN.
SHUT

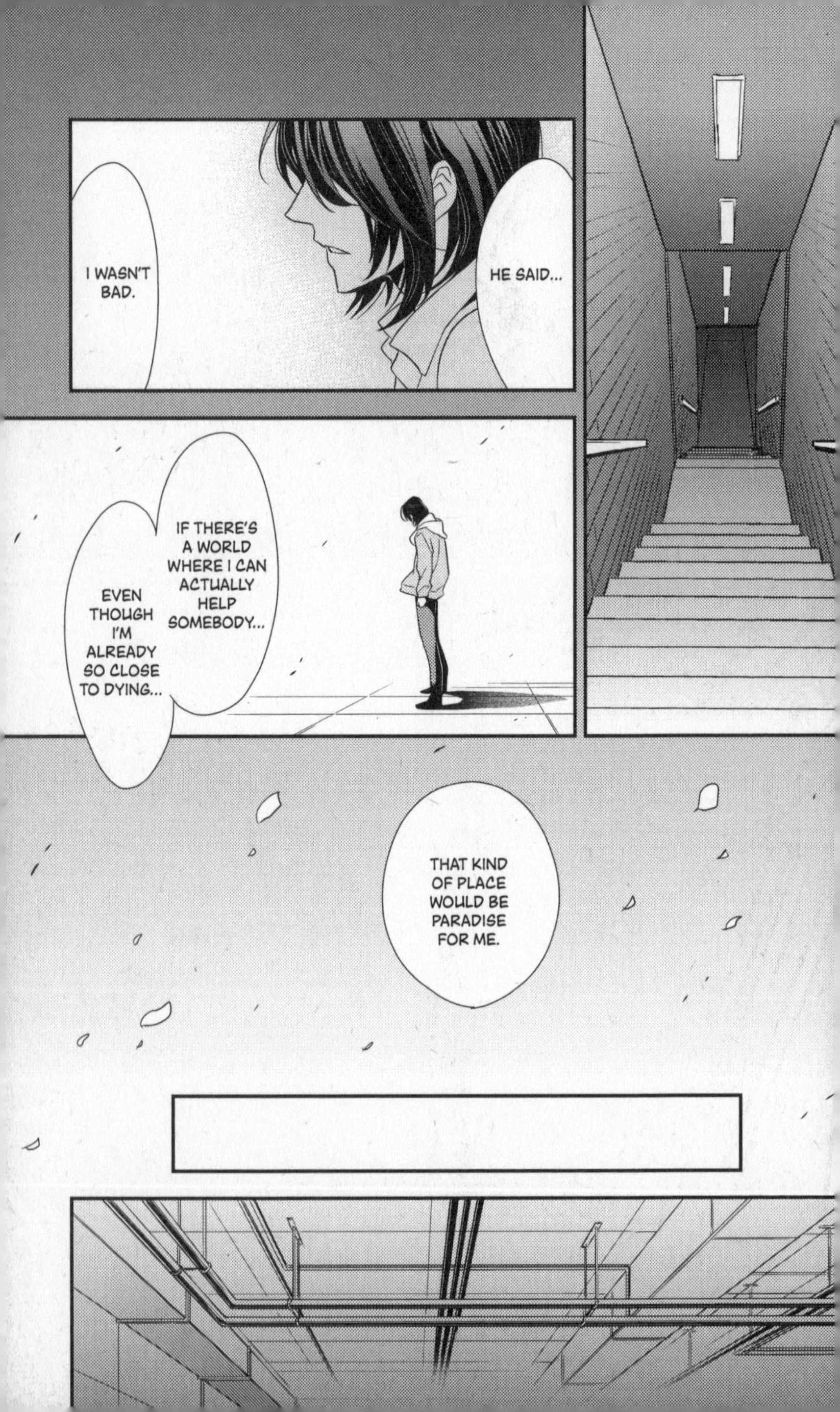
HE SAID...
I WASN'T BAD.
IF THERE'S A WORLD WHERE I CAN ACTUALLY HELP SOMEBODY...
EVEN THOUGH I'M ALREADY SO CLOSE TO DYING...
THAT KIND OF PLACE WOULD BE PARADISE FOR ME.

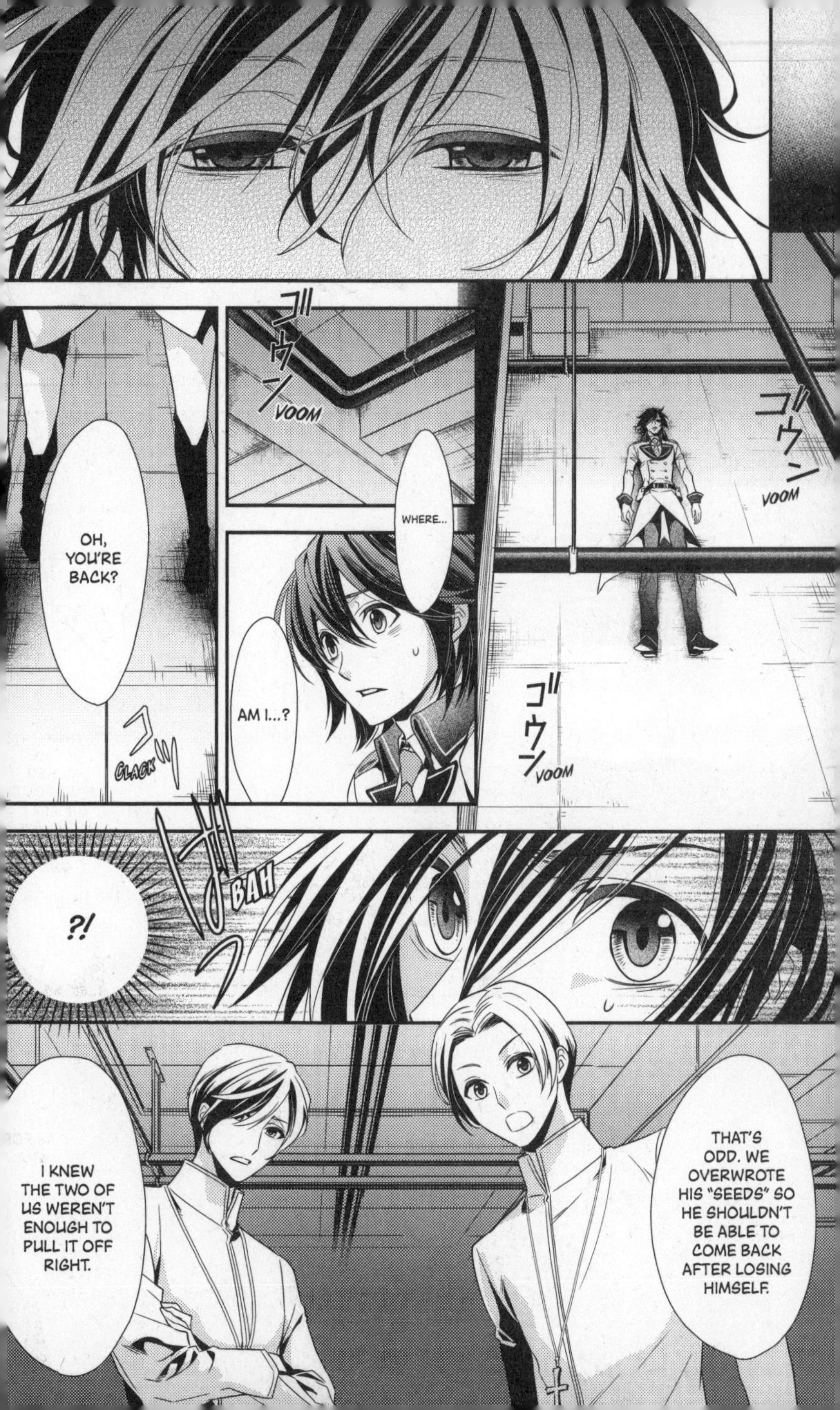
ゴウン
VOOM
ゴウン
VOOM
ゴウン
VOOM
WHERE...
AM I...?
OH, YOU'RE BACK?
コッ
CLACK
バッ
BAH
?!
THAT'S ODD. WE OVERWROTE HIS "SEEDS" SO HE SHOULDN'T BE ABLE TO COME BACK AFTER LOSING HIMSELF.
I KNEW THE TWO OF US WEREN'T ENOUGH TO PULL IT OFF RIGHT.

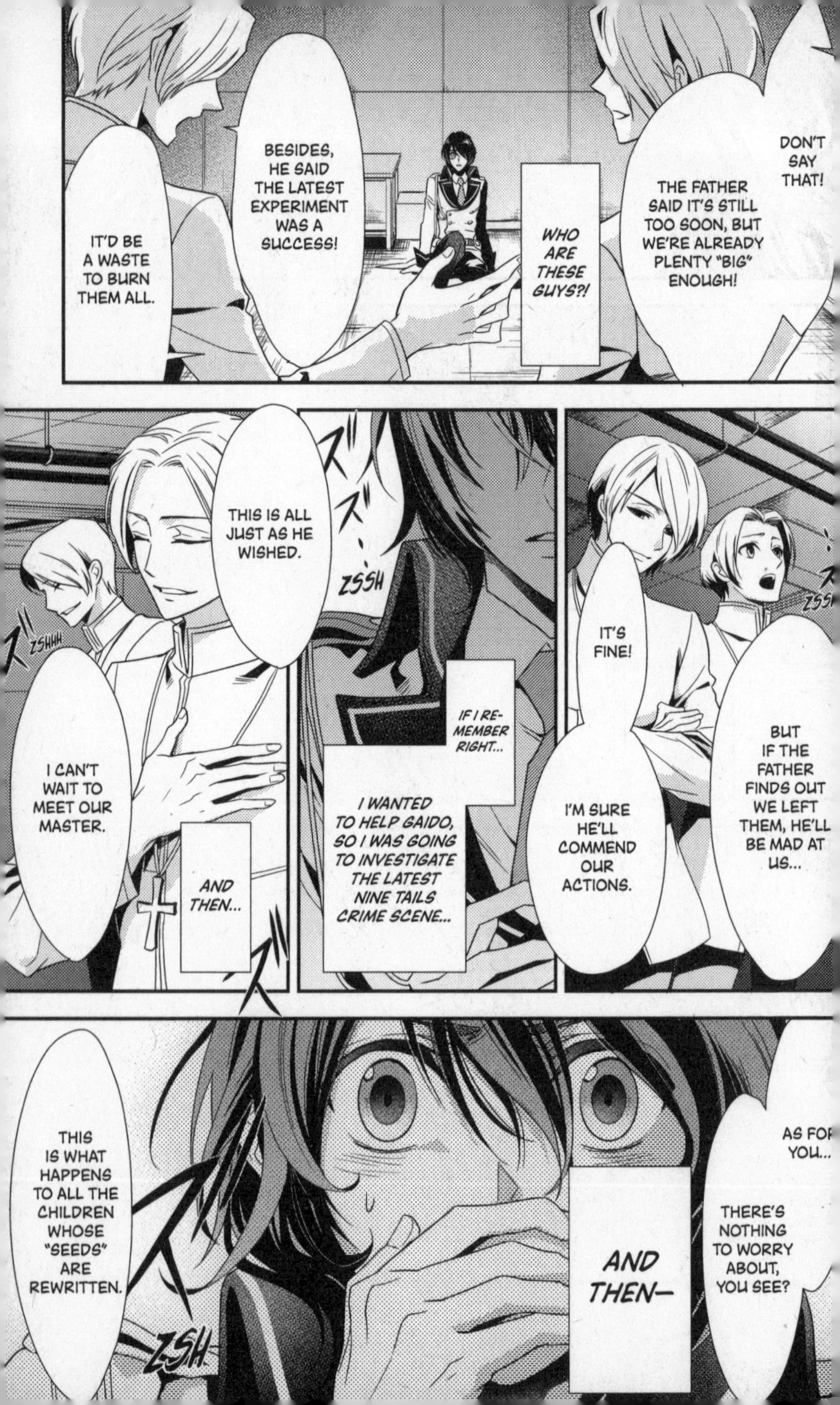
DON'T SAY THAT!
THE FATHER SAID IT'S STILL TOO SOON, BUT WE'RE ALREADY PLENTY "BIG" ENOUGH!
WHO ARE THESE GUYS?!
BESIDES, HE SAID THE LATEST EXPERIMENT WAS A SUCCESS!
IT'D BE A WASTE TO BURN THEM ALL.
ZSSH
BUT IF THE FATHER FINDS OUT WE LEFT THEM, HE'LL BE MAD AT US...
IT'S FINE!
I'M SURE HE'LL COMMEND OUR ACTIONS.
IF I RE-MEMBER RIGHT...
I WANTED TO HELP GAIDO, SO I WAS GOING TO INVESTIGATE THE LATEST NINE TAILS CRIME SCENE...
ZSSH
THIS IS ALL JUST AS HE WISHED.
I CAN'T WAIT TO MEET OUR MASTER.
AND THEN...
ZSHHH
AS FOR YOU...
THERE'S NOTHING TO WORRY ABOUT, YOU SEE?
AND THEN—
THIS IS WHAT HAPPENS TO ALL THE CHILDREN WHOSE "SEEDS" ARE REWRITTEN.
ZSH

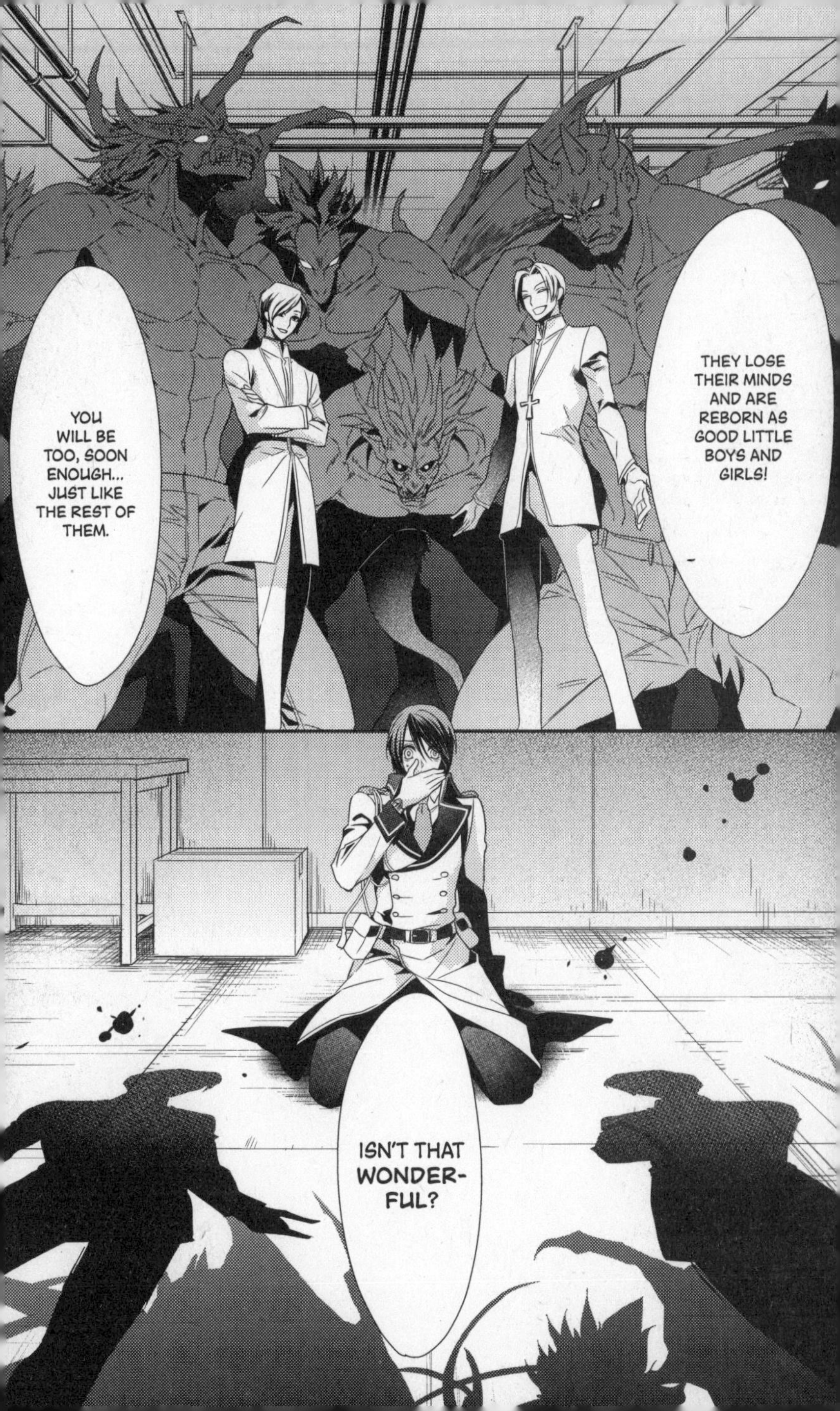
THEY LOSE THEIR MINDS AND ARE REBORN AS GOOD LITTLE BOYS AND GIRLS!
YOU WILL BE TOO, SOON ENOUGH... JUST LIKE THE REST OF THEM.
ISN'T THAT WONDER-FUL?

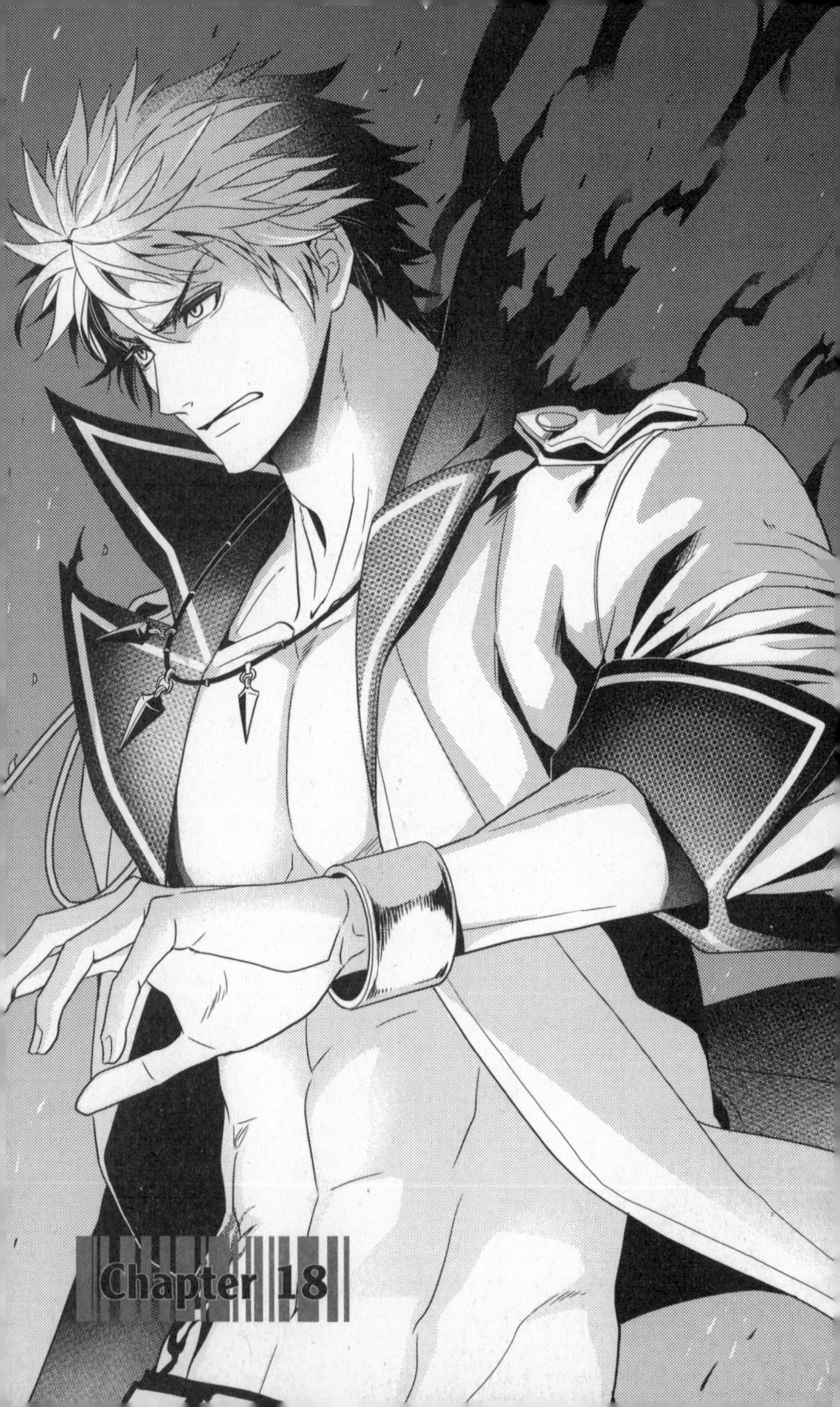
Chapter 18

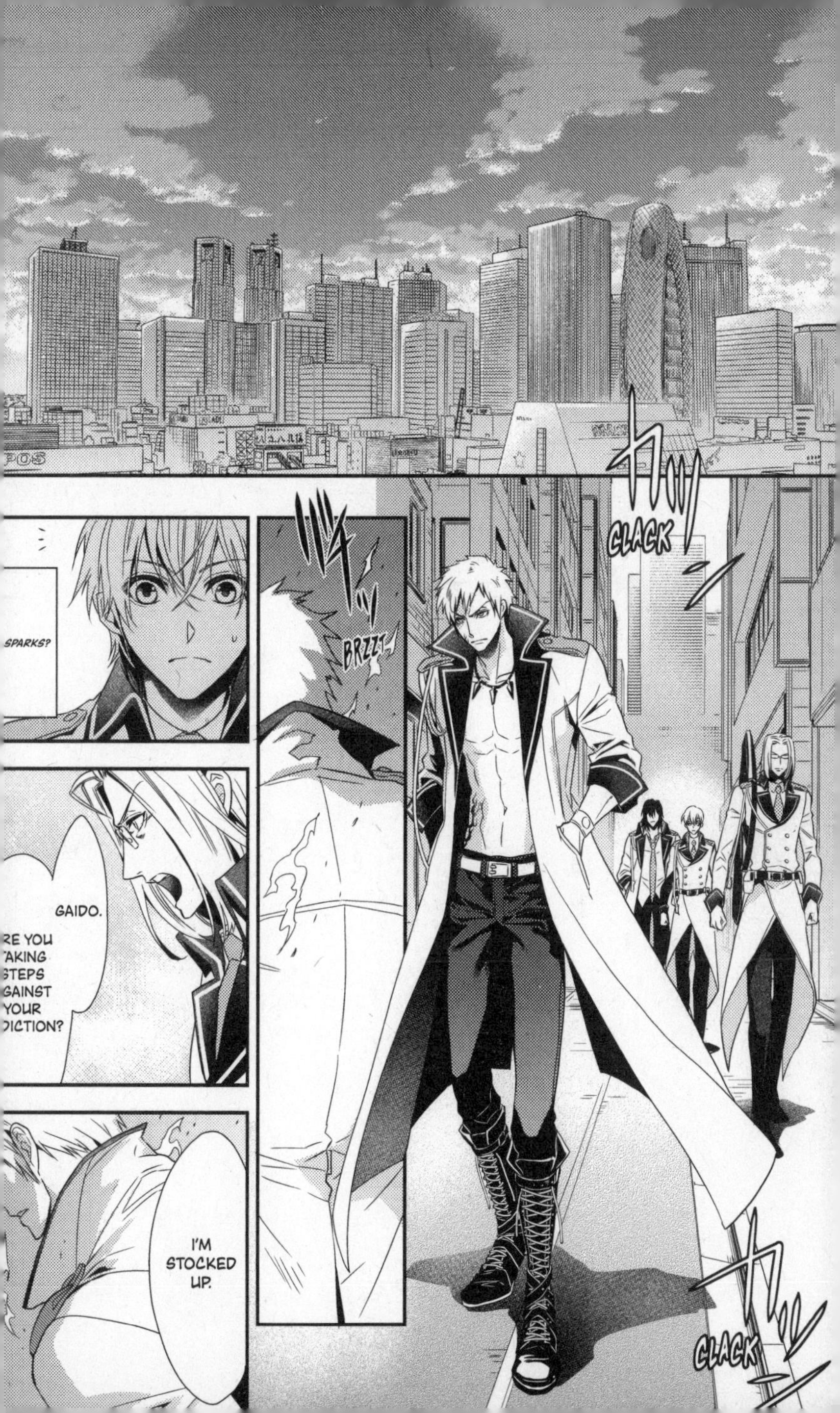
CLACK
CLACK
BRZZT
SPARKS?
GAIDO.
RE YOU TAKING STEPS GAINST YOUR DICTION?
I'M STOCKED UP.

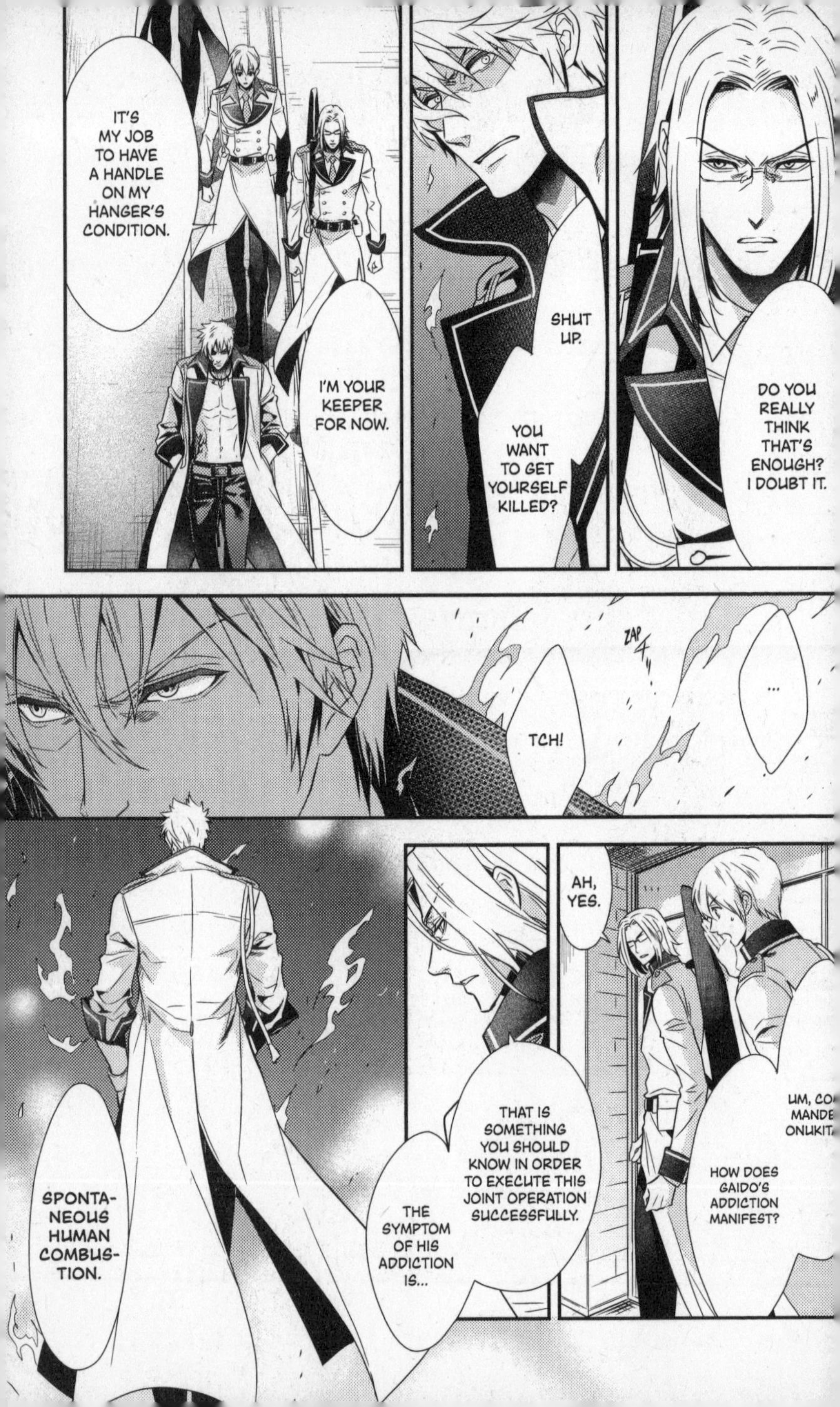
DO YOU REALLY THINK THAT'S ENOUGH? I DOUBT IT.
SHUT UP.
YOU WANT TO GET YOURSELF KILLED?
I'M YOUR KEEPER FOR NOW.
IT'S MY JOB TO HAVE A HANDLE ON MY HANGER'S CONDITION.
...
ZAP
TCH!
UM, CO MANDE ONUKIT
HOW DOES GAIDO'S ADDICTION MANIFEST?
AH, YES.
THAT IS SOMETHING YOU SHOULD KNOW IN ORDER TO EXECUTE THIS JOINT OPERATION SUCCESSFULLY.
THE SYMPTOM OF HIS ADDICTION IS...
SPONTANEOUS HUMAN COMBUSTION.

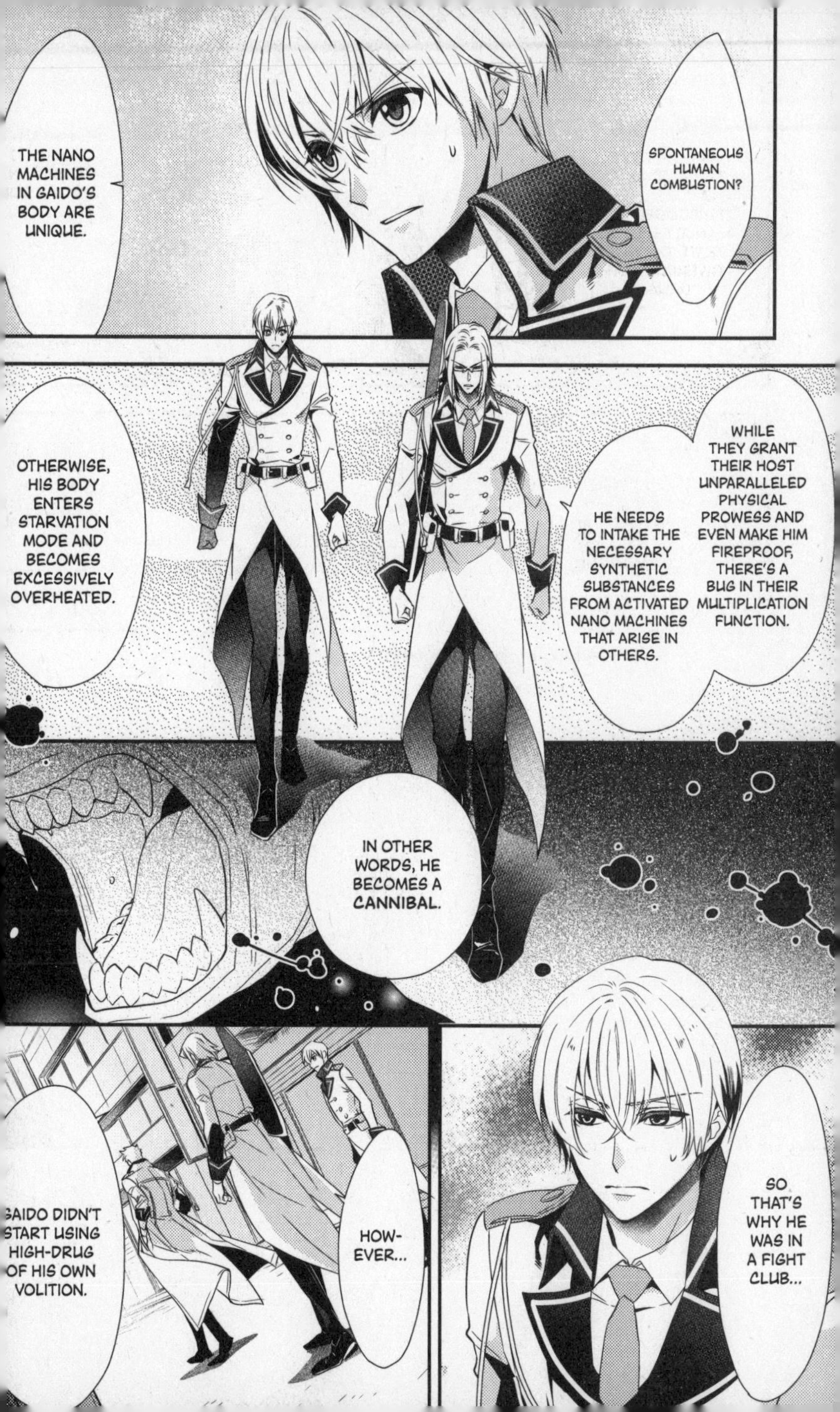
SPONTANEOUS HUMAN COMBUSTION?
THE NANO MACHINES IN GAIDO'S BODY ARE UNIQUE.
WHILE THEY GRANT THEIR HOST UNPARALLELED PHYSICAL PROWESS AND EVEN MAKE HIM FIREPROOF, THERE'S A BUG IN THEIR MULTIPLICATION FUNCTION.
HE NEEDS TO INTAKE THE NECESSARY SYNTHETIC SUBSTANCES FROM ACTIVATED NANO MACHINES THAT ARISE IN OTHERS.
OTHERWISE, HIS BODY ENTERS STARVATION MODE AND BECOMES EXCESSIVELY OVERHEATED.
IN OTHER WORDS, HE BECOMES A CANNIBAL.
SO THAT'S WHY HE WAS IN A FIGHT CLUB...
HOW-EVER...
GAIDO DIDN'T START USING HIGH-DRUG OF HIS OWN VOLITION.

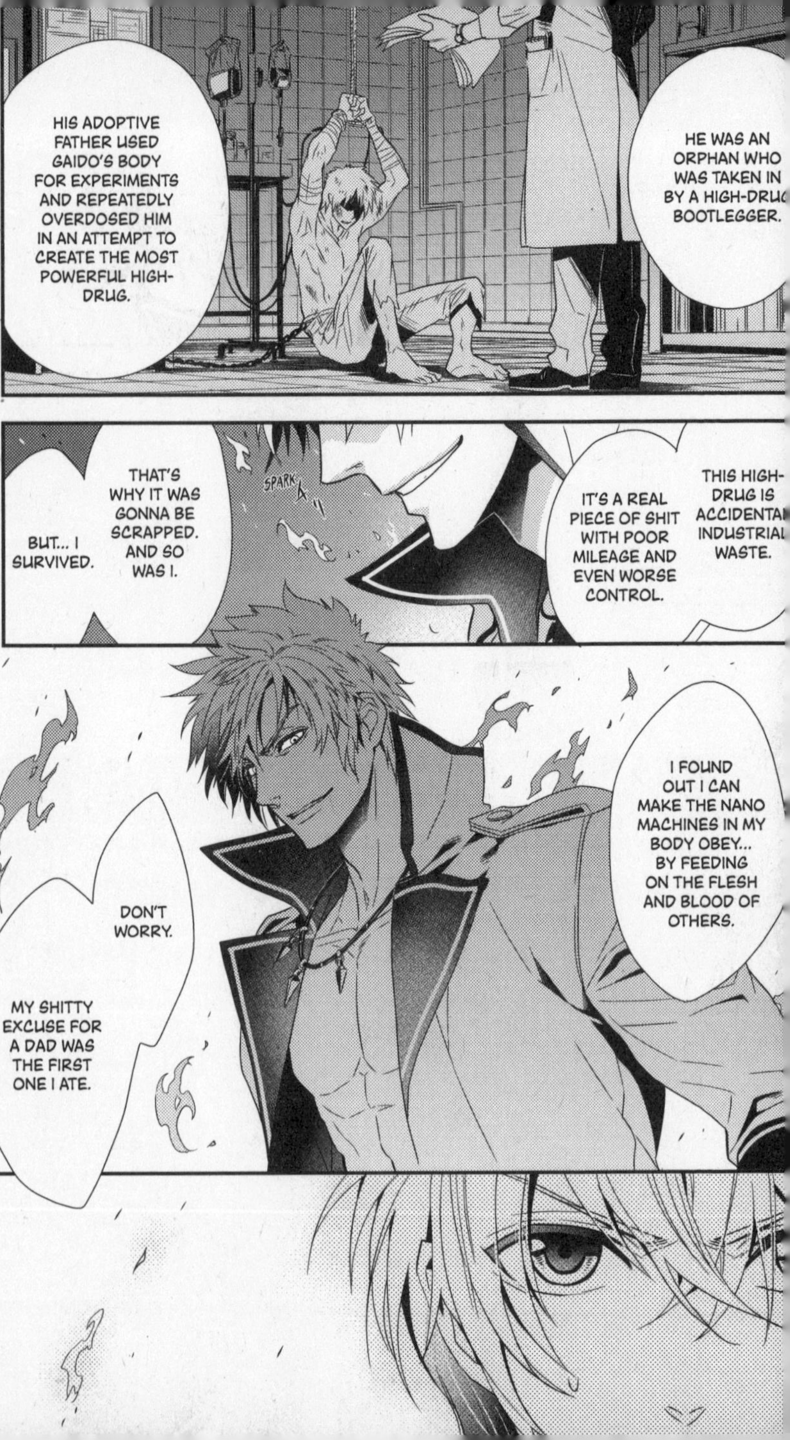
HE WAS AN ORPHAN WHO WAS TAKEN IN BY A HIGH-DRU BOOTLEGGER.
HIS ADOPTIVE FATHER USED GAIDO'S BODY FOR EXPERIMENTS AND REPEATEDLY OVERDOSED HIM IN AN ATTEMPT TO CREATE THE MOST POWERFUL HIGH-DRUG.
THIS HIGH-DRUG IS ACCIDENTA INDUSTRIA WASTE.
IT'S A REAL PIECE OF SHIT WITH POOR MILEAGE AND EVEN WORSE CONTROL.
SPARK
THAT'S WHY IT WAS GONNA BE SCRAPPED. AND SO WAS I.
BUT... I SURVIVED.
I FOUND OUT I CAN MAKE THE NANO MACHINES IN MY BODY OBEY... BY FEEDING ON THE FLESH AND BLOOD OF OTHERS.
DON'T WORRY.
MY SHITTY EXCUSE FOR A DAD WAS THE FIRST ONE I ATE.

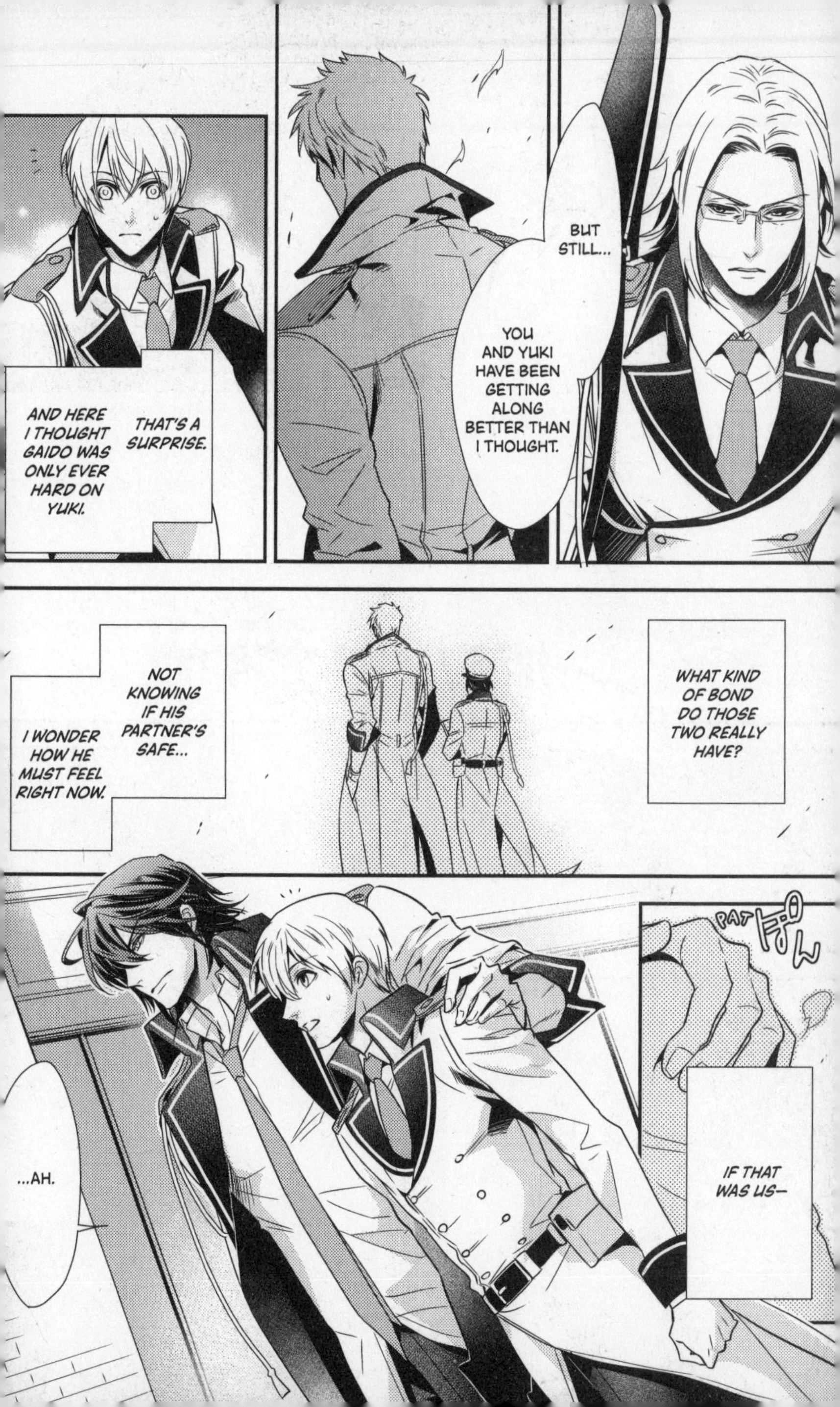
BUT STILL...
YOU AND YUKI HAVE BEEN GETTING ALONG BETTER THAN I THOUGHT.
THAT'S A SURPRISE.
AND HERE I THOUGHT GAIDO WAS ONLY EVER HARD ON YUKI.
WHAT KIND OF BOND DO THOSE TWO REALLY HAVE?
NOT KNOWING IF HIS PARTNER'S SAFE...
I WONDER HOW HE MUST FEEL RIGHT NOW.
PAT
IF THAT WAS US—
...AH.

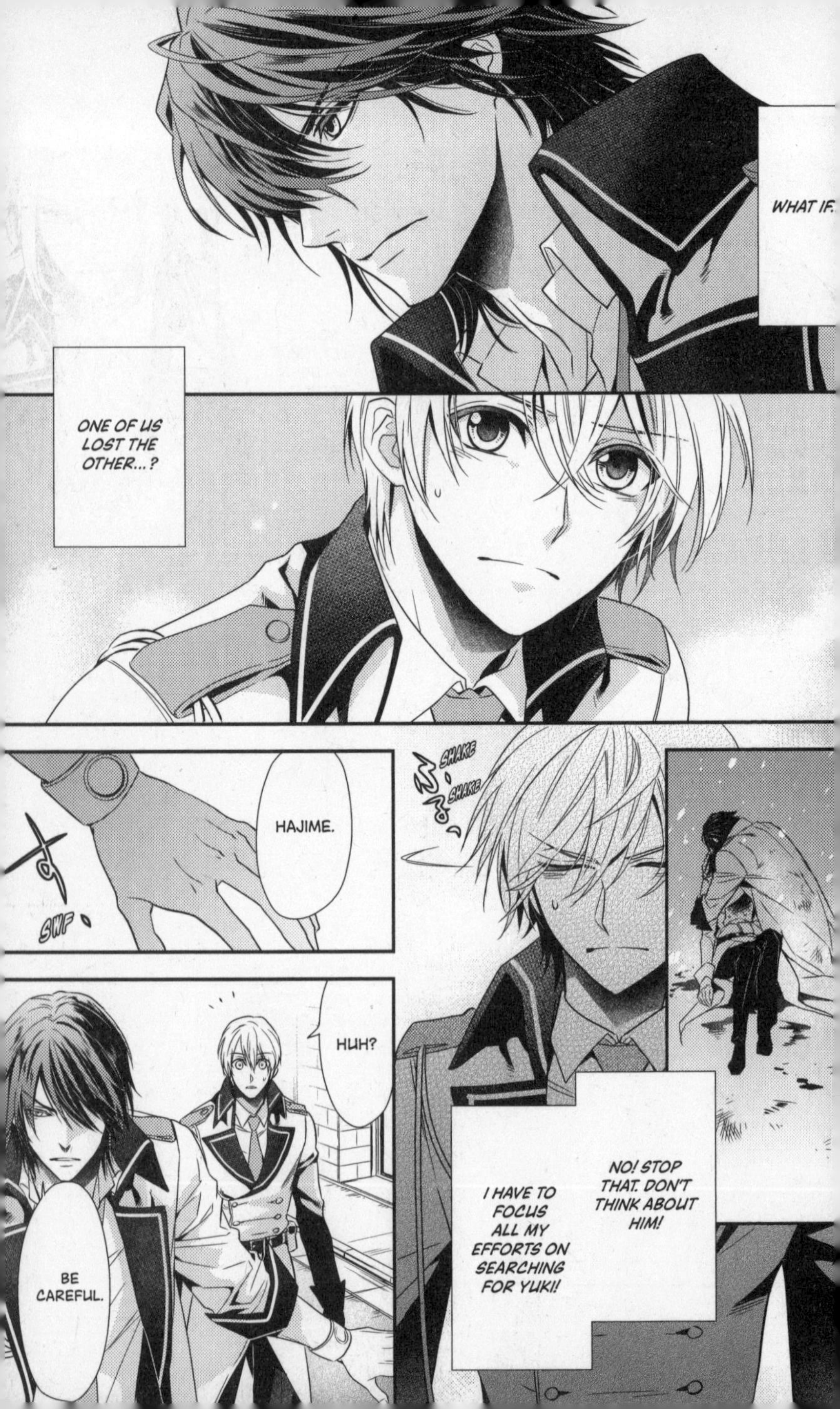
WHAT IF.
ONE OF US LOST THE OTHER...?
SHAKE SHAKE
NO! STOP THAT. DON'T THINK ABOUT HIM!
I HAVE TO FOCUS ALL MY EFFORTS ON SEARCHING FOR YUKI!
HAJIME.
SWF
HUH?
BE CAREFUL.

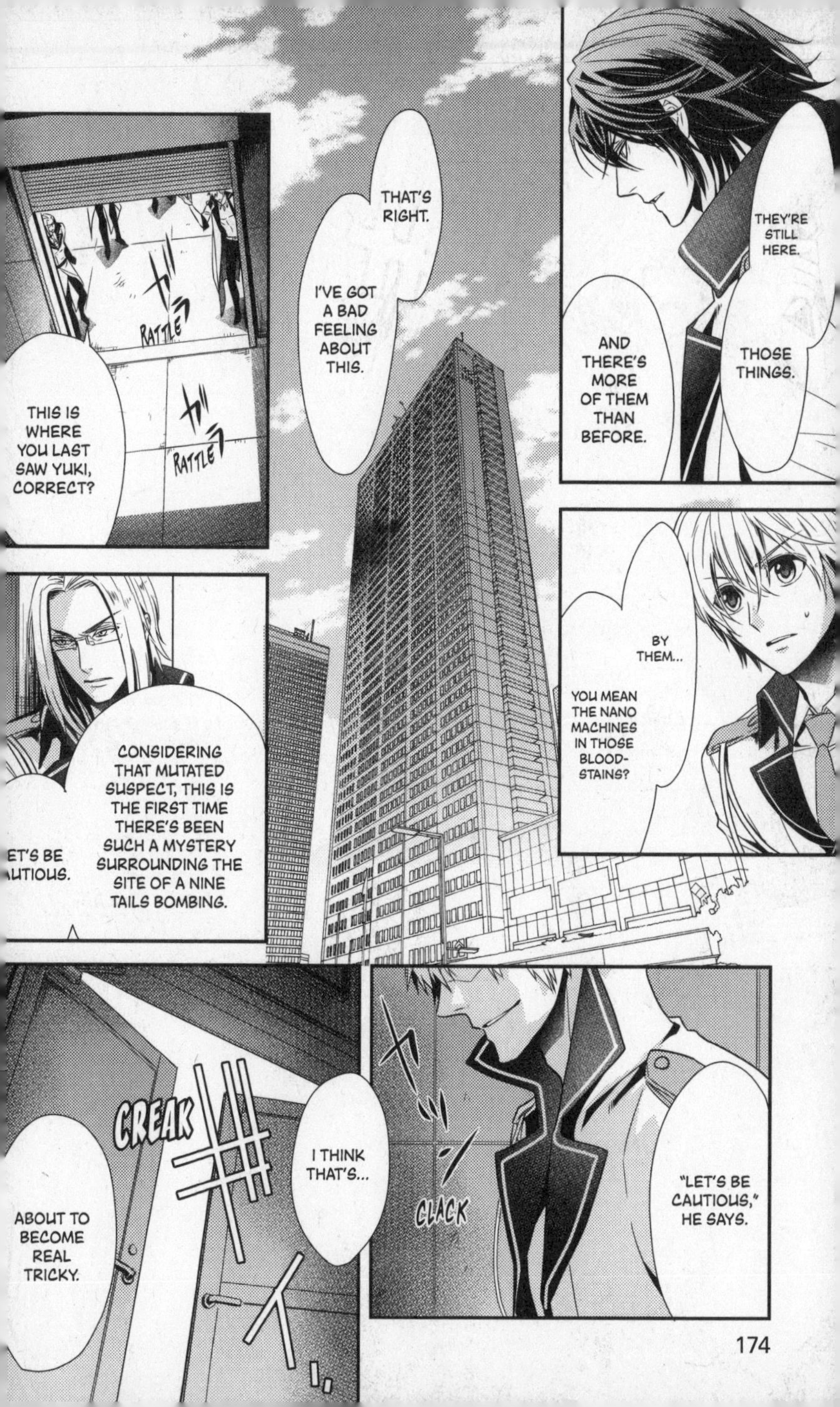
THEY'RE STILL HERE.
THOSE THINGS.
AND THERE'S MORE OF THEM THAN BEFORE.
THAT'S RIGHT.
I'VE GOT A BAD FEELING ABOUT THIS.
RATTLE
RATTLE
THIS IS WHERE YOU LAST SAW YUKI, CORRECT?
BY THEM...
YOU MEAN THE NANO MACHINES IN THOSE BLOOD-STAINS?
CONSIDERING THAT MUTATED SUSPECT, THIS IS THE FIRST TIME THERE'S BEEN SUCH A MYSTERY SURROUNDING THE SITE OF A NINE TAILS BOMBING.
ET'S BE UTIOUS.
CLACK
"LET'S BE CAUTIOUS," HE SAYS.
I THINK THAT'S...
CREAK
ABOUT TO BECOME REAL TRICKY.

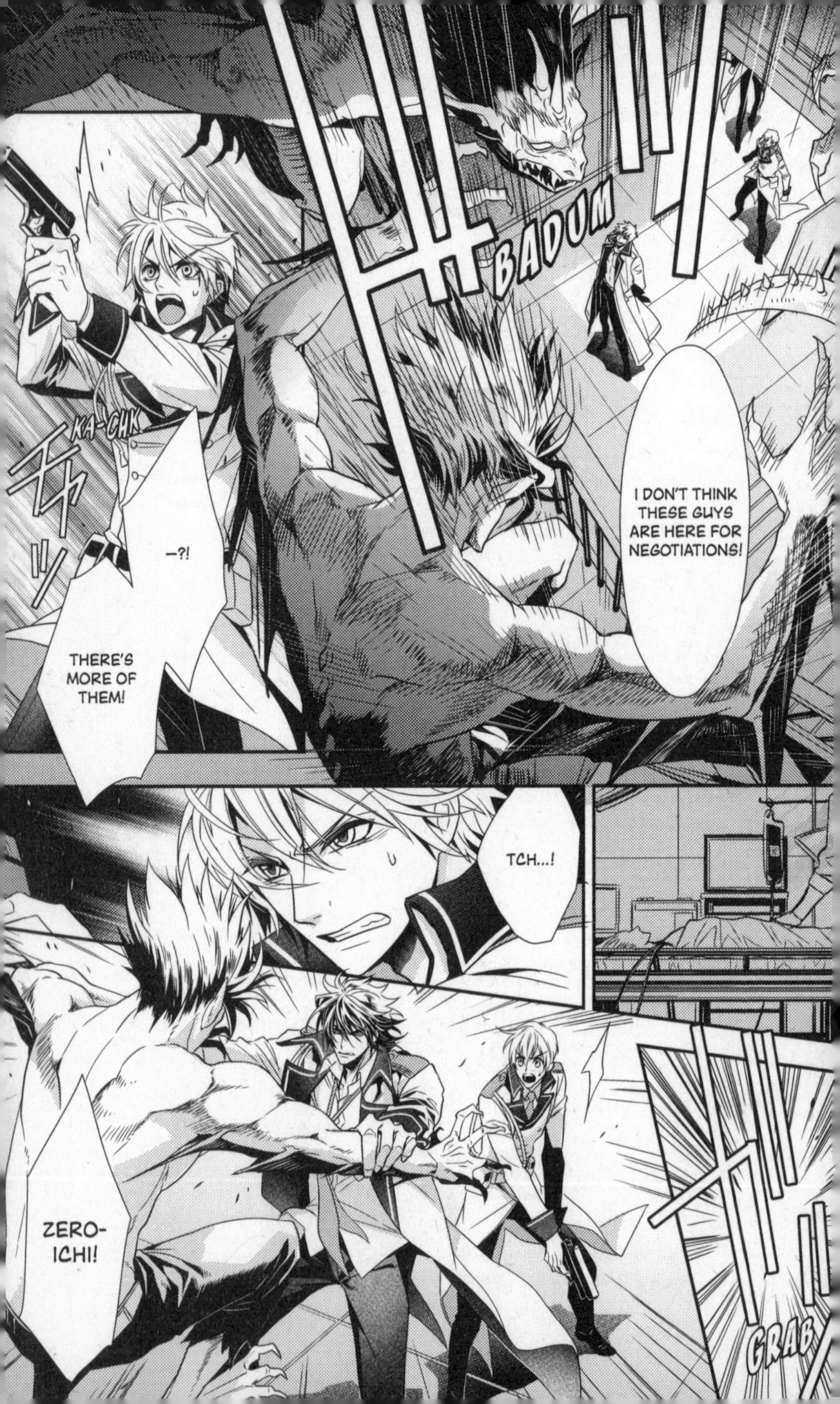
BADUM
I DON'T THINK THESE GUYS ARE HERE FOR NEGOTIATIONS!
KA-CHK
—?!
THERE'S MORE OF THEM!
TCH...!
GRAB
ZERO-ICHI!

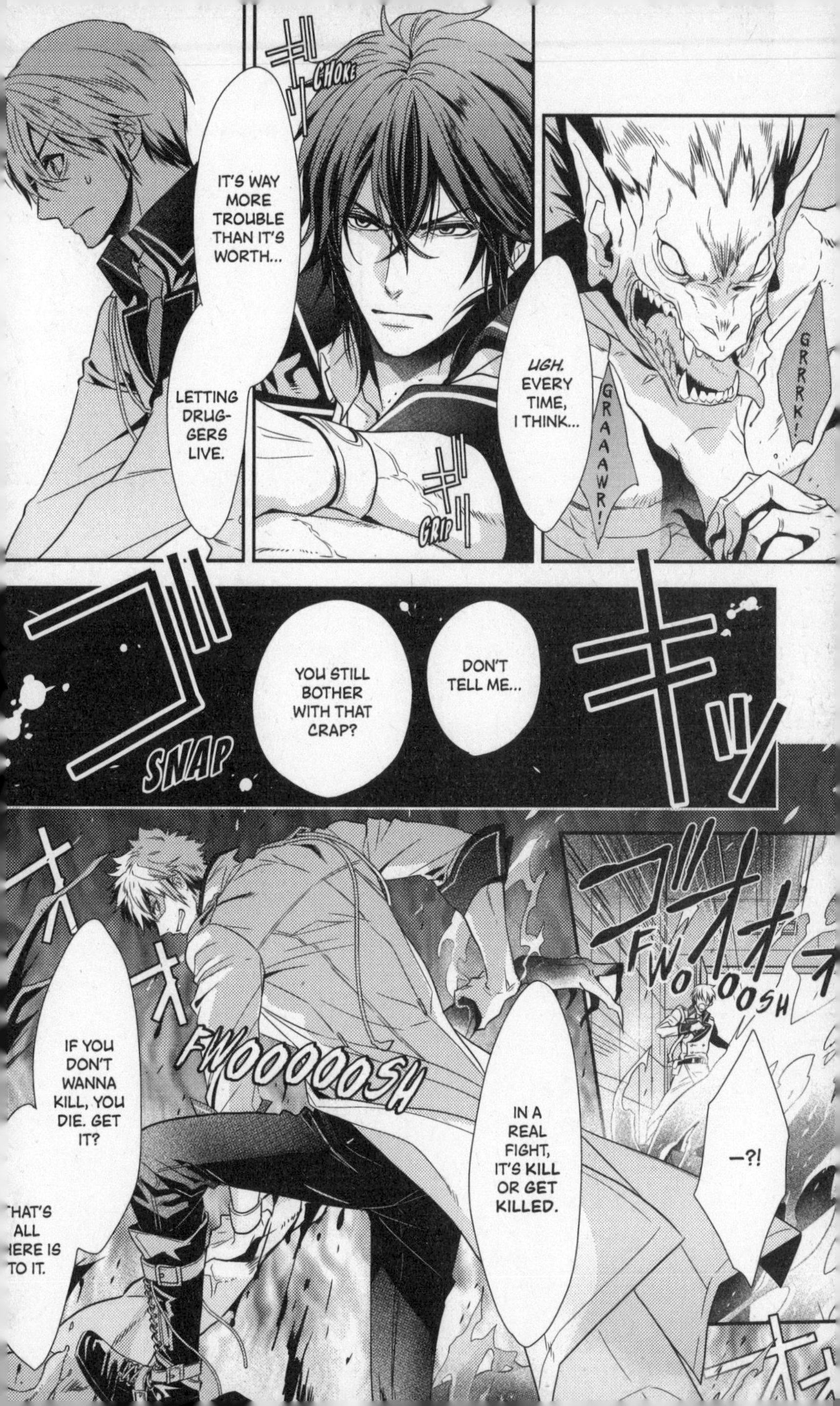
GRRRK!
GRAAAWR!
UGH. EVERY TIME, I THINK...
CHOKE
IT'S WAY MORE TROUBLE THAN IT'S WORTH...
GRIP
LETTING DRUGGERS LIVE.
DON'T TELL ME...
YOU STILL BOTHER WITH THAT CRAP?
SNAP
FWOOOSH
—?!
IN A REAL FIGHT, IT'S KILL OR GET KILLED.
FWOOOOOOSH
IF YOU DON'T WANNA KILL, YOU DIE. GET IT?
'HAT'S ALL HERE IS TO IT.

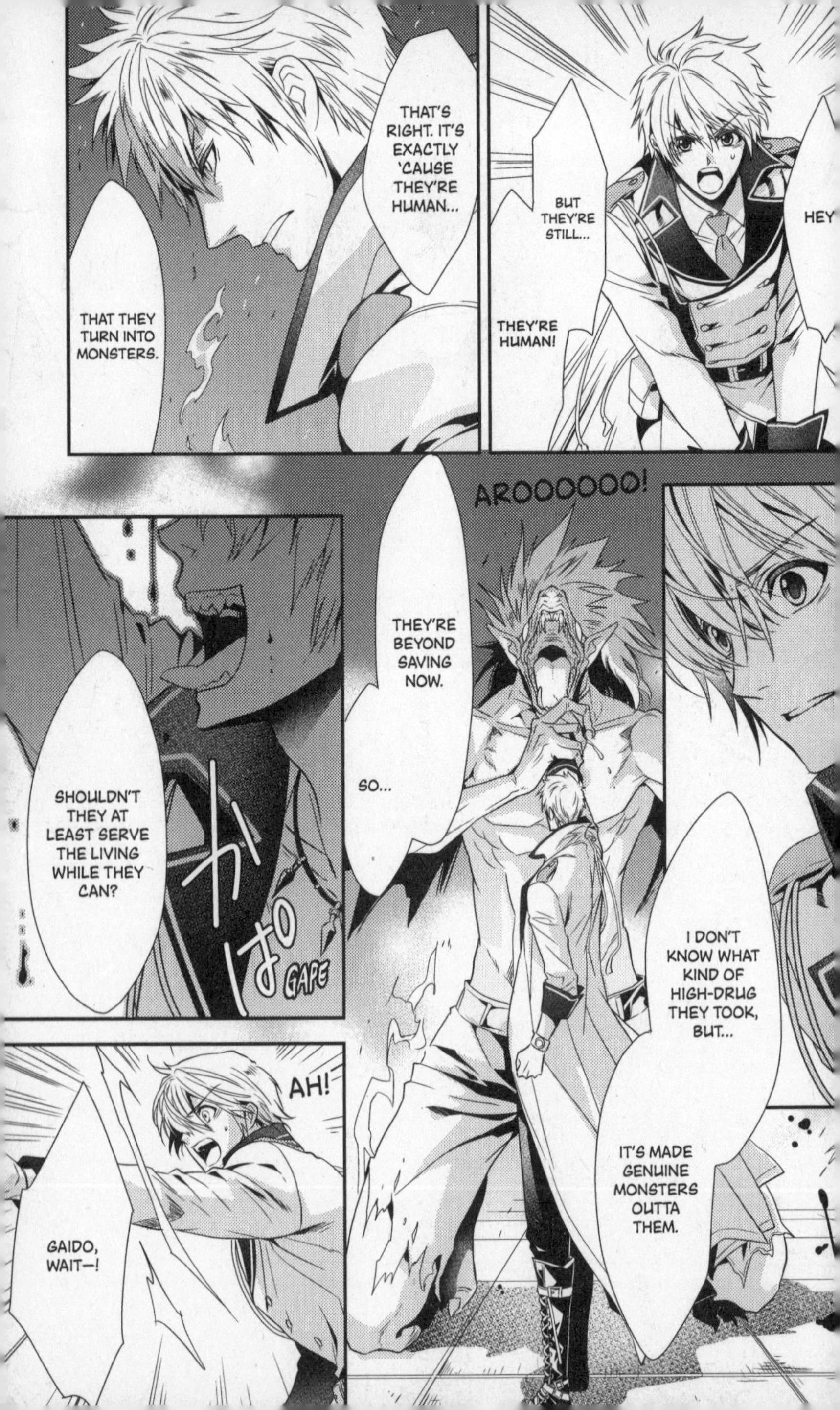
HEY
BUT THEY'RE STILL...
THEY'RE HUMAN!
THAT'S RIGHT. IT'S EXACTLY 'CAUSE THEY'RE HUMAN...
THAT THEY TURN INTO MONSTERS.
I DON'T KNOW WHAT KIND OF HIGH-DRUG THEY TOOK, BUT...
IT'S MADE GENUINE MONSTERS OUTTA THEM.
AROOOOOO!
THEY'RE BEYOND SAVING NOW.
SO...
SHOULDN'T THEY AT LEAST SERVE THE LIVING WHILE THEY CAN?
GAPE
AH!
GAIDO, WAIT—!

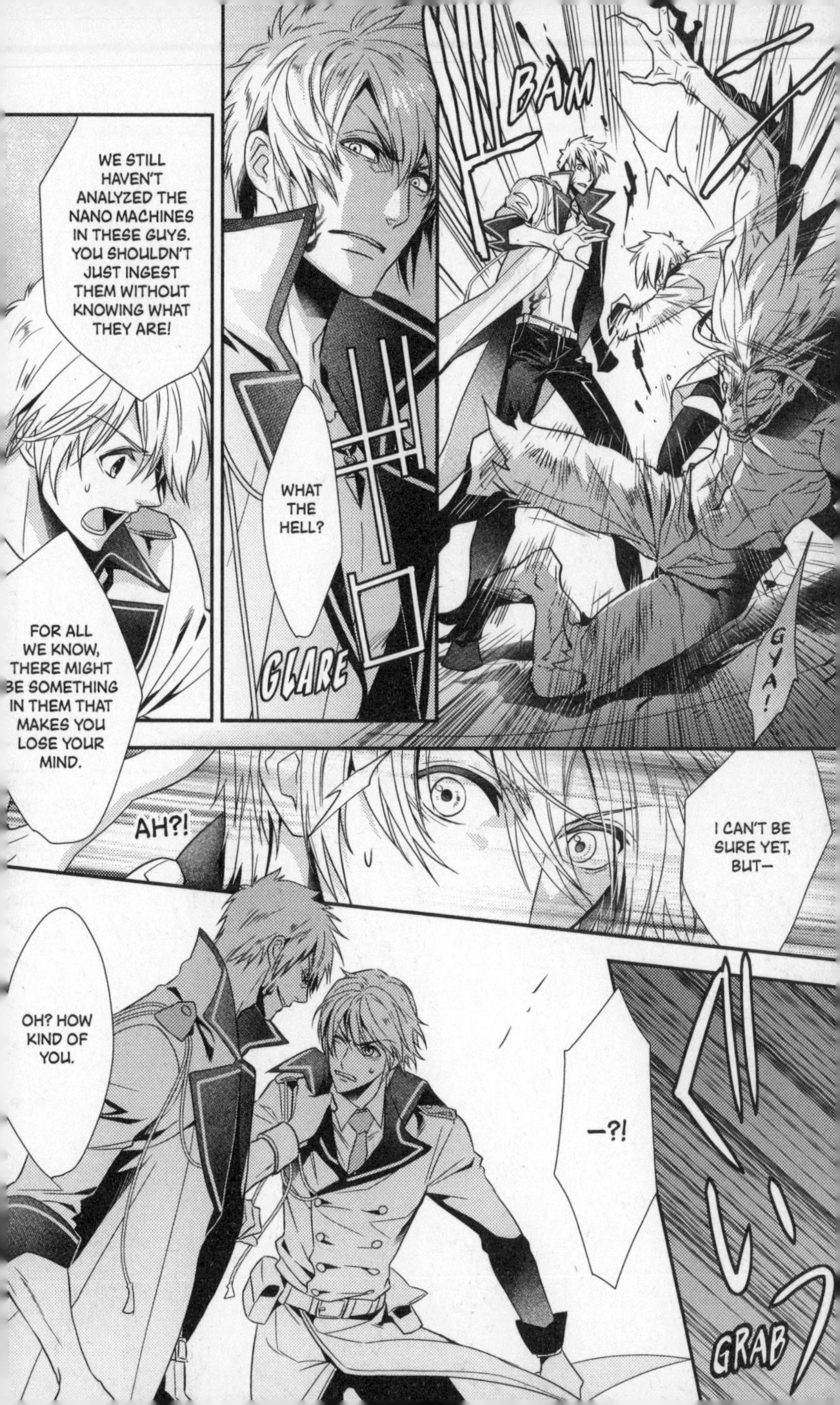
BAM
GYA!
WHAT THE HELL?
GLARE
WE STILL HAVEN'T ANALYZED THE NANO MACHINES IN THESE GUYS. YOU SHOULDN'T JUST INGEST THEM WITHOUT KNOWING WHAT THEY ARE!
FOR ALL WE KNOW, THERE MIGHT BE SOMETHING IN THEM THAT MAKES YOU LOSE YOUR MIND.
AH?!
I CAN'T BE SURE YET, BUT—
—?!
GRAB
OH? HOW KIND OF YOU.

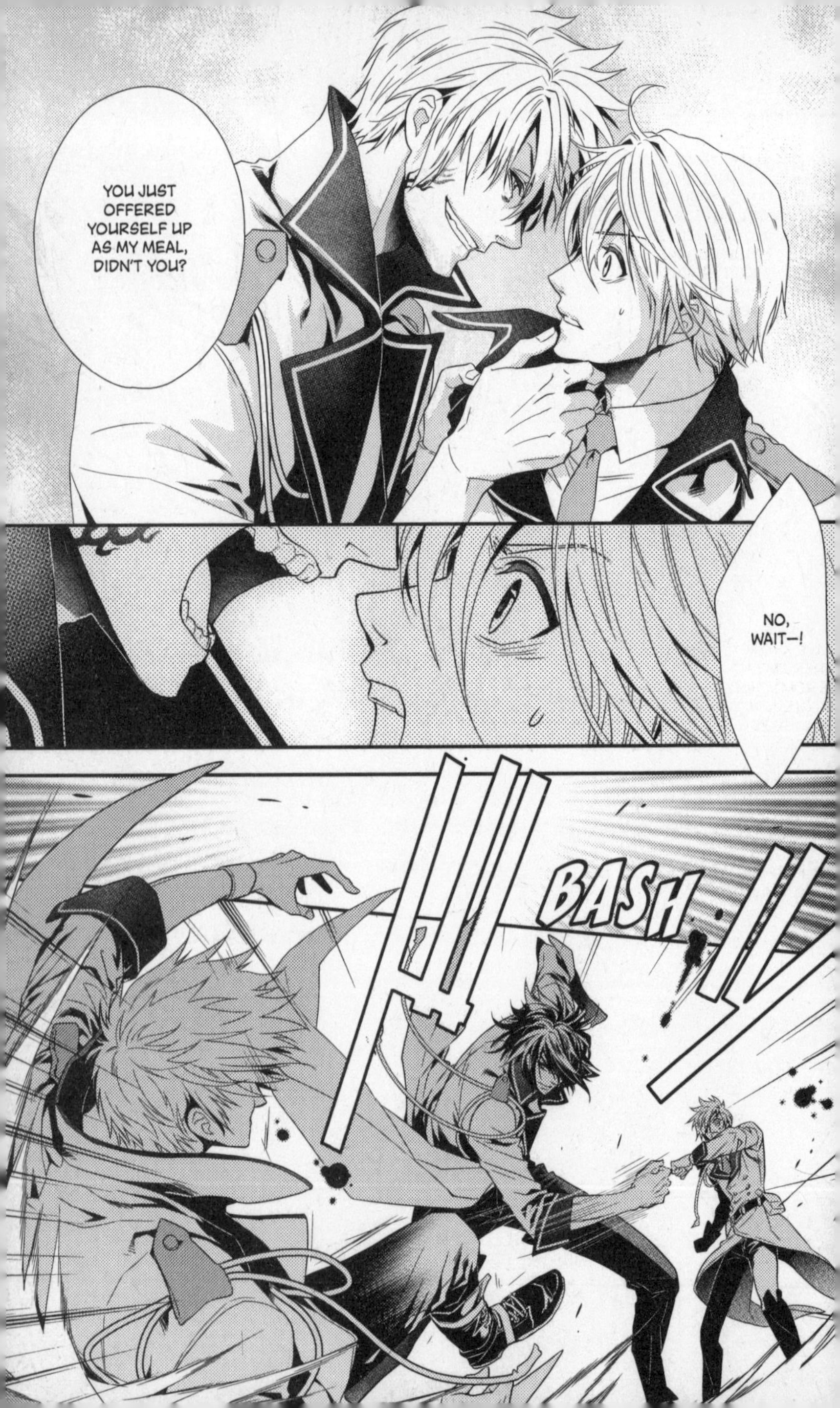
YOU JUST OFFERED YOURSELF UP AS MY MEAL, DIDN'T YOU?
NO, WAIT—!
BASH

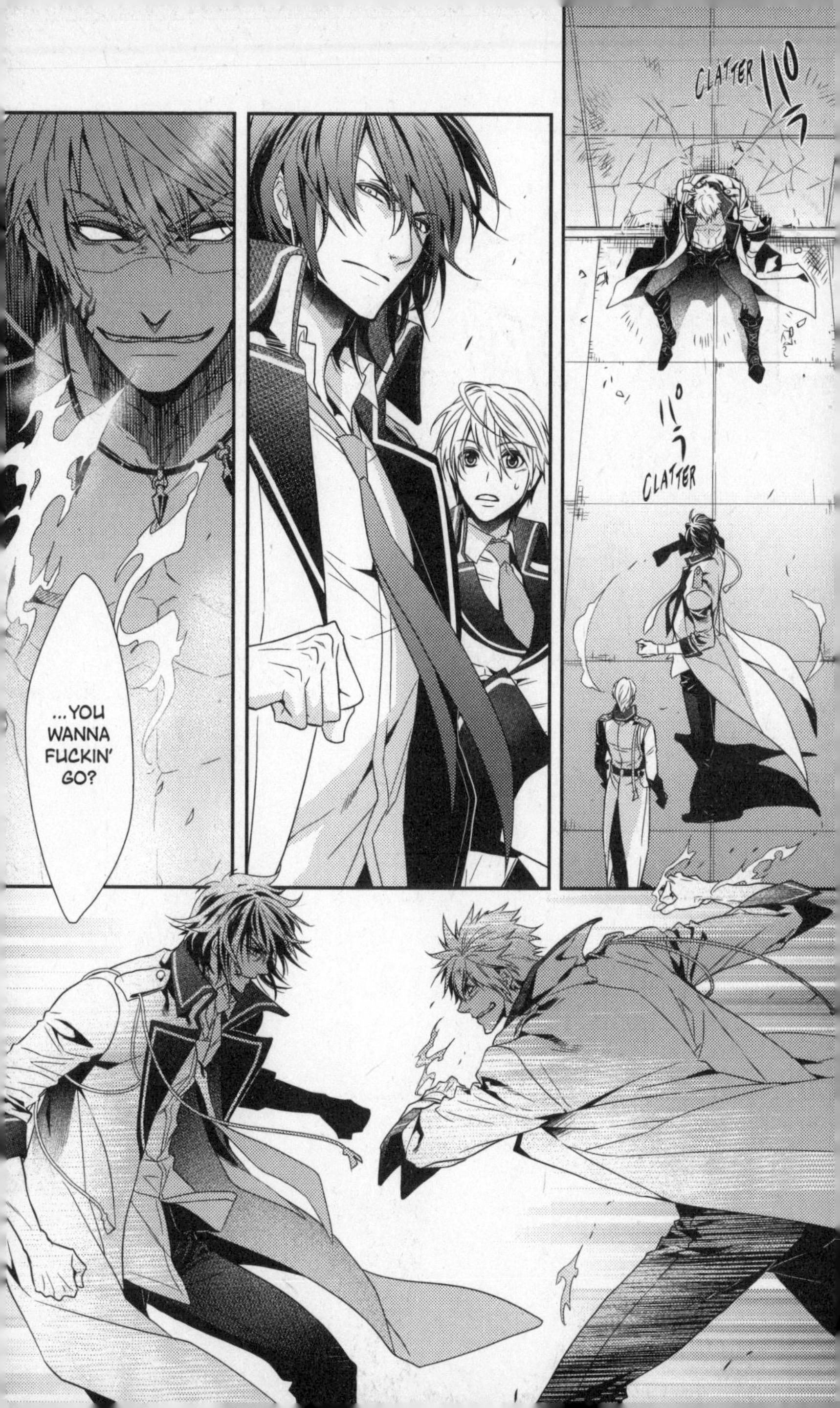
CLATTER
CLATTER
...YOU WANNA FUCKIN' GO?

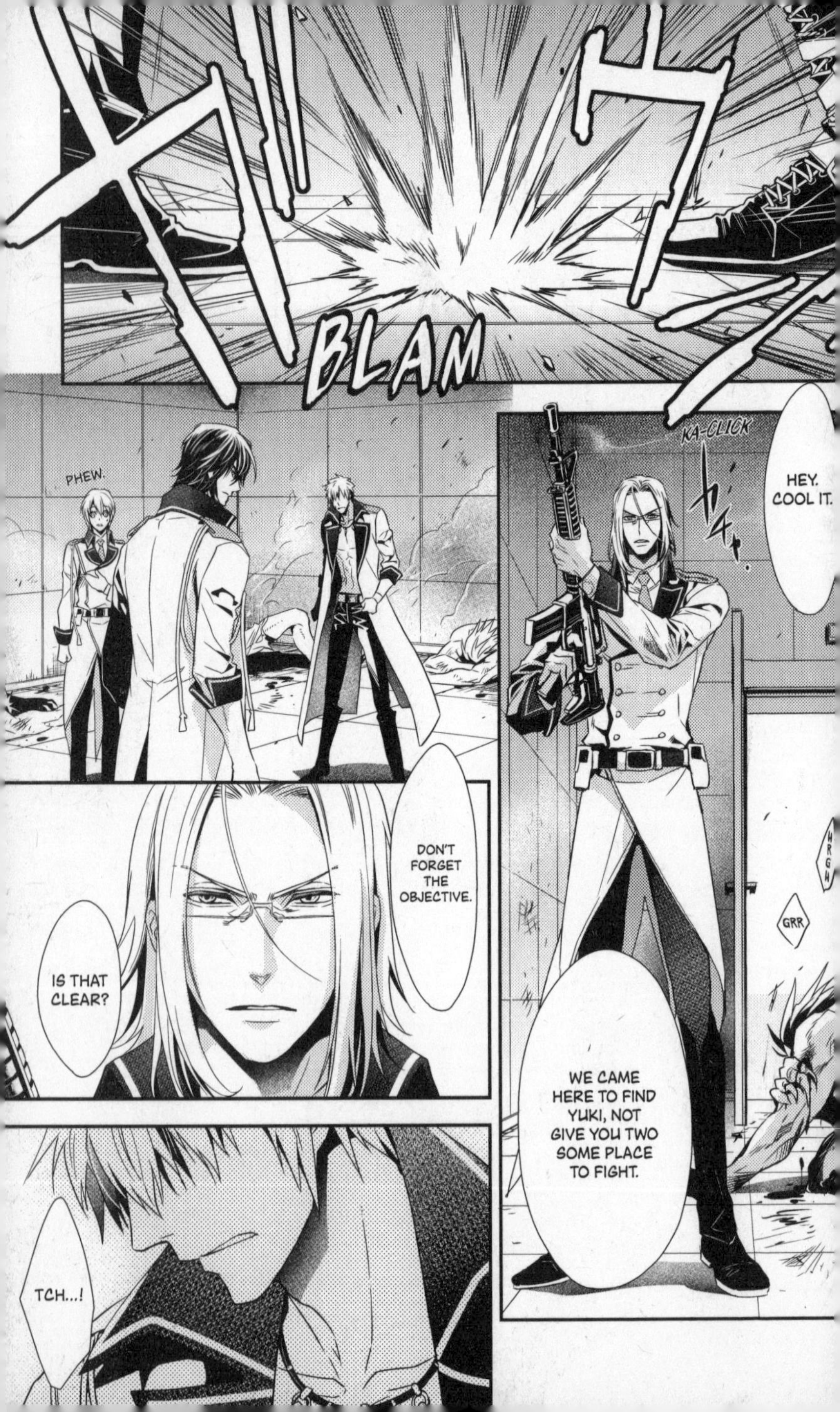
BLAM
KA-CLICK
HEY. COOL IT.
HRGH
GRR
WE CAME HERE TO FIND YUKI, NOT GIVE YOU TWO SOME PLACE TO FIGHT.
PHEW.
DON'T FORGET THE OBJECTIVE.
IS THAT CLEAR?
TCH...!

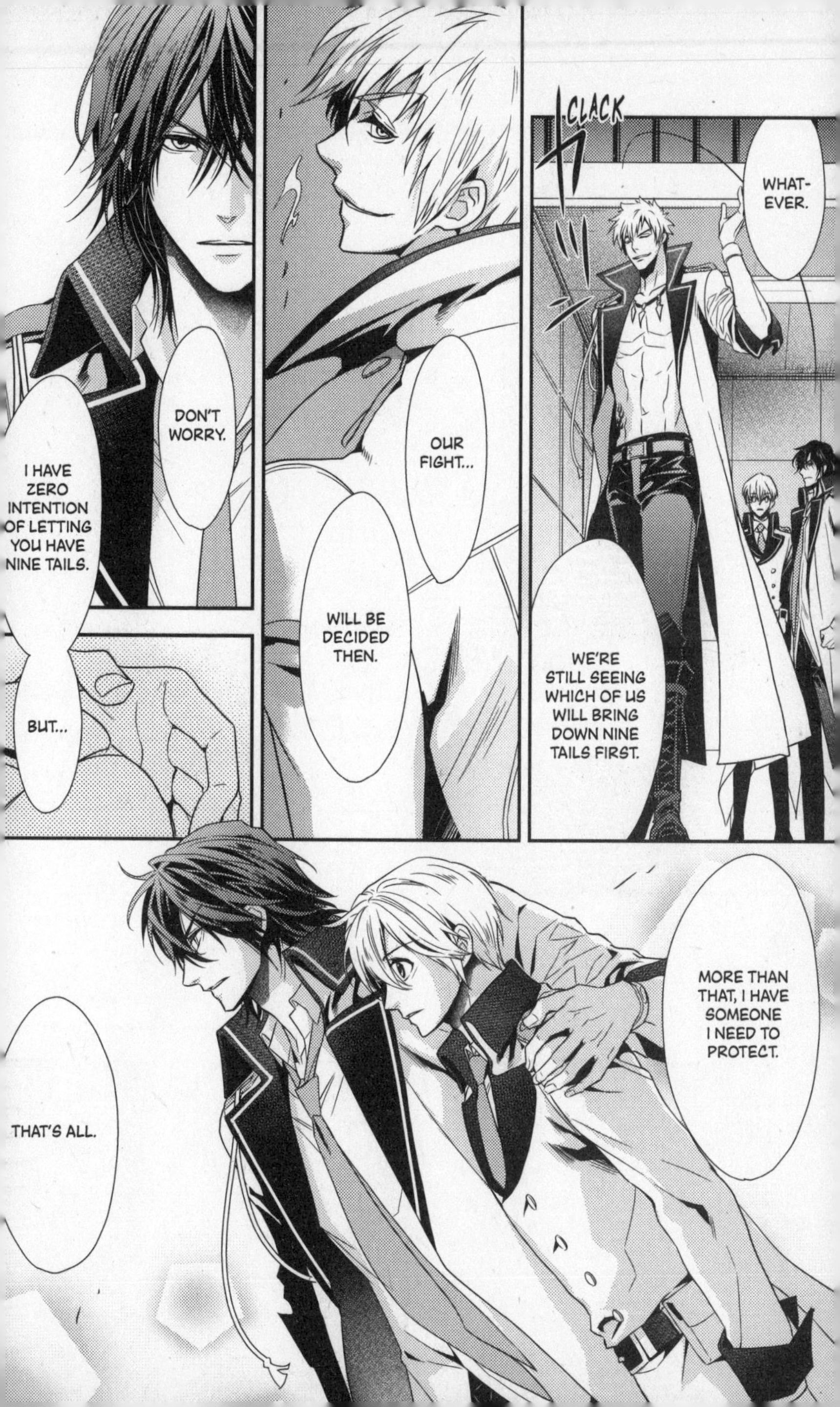
CLACK
WHAT-EVER.
WE'RE STILL SEEING WHICH OF US WILL BRING DOWN NINE TAILS FIRST.
OUR FIGHT...
WILL BE DECIDED THEN.
DON'T WORRY.
I HAVE ZERO INTENTION OF LETTING YOU HAVE NINE TAILS.
BUT...
MORE THAN THAT, I HAVE SOMEONE I NEED TO PROTECT.
THAT'S ALL.

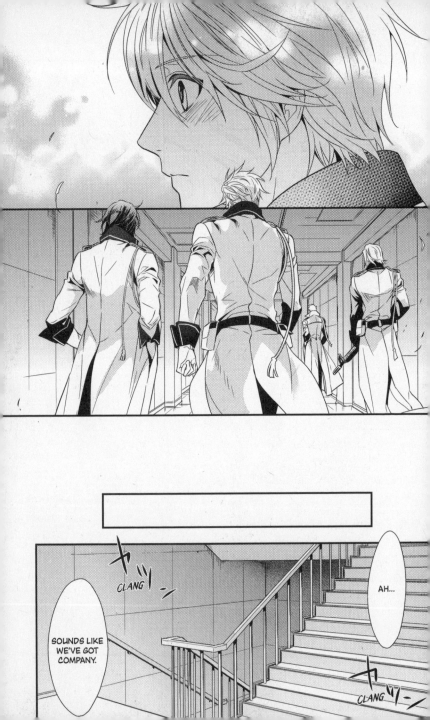

CLANG

AH...

SOUNDS LIKE
WE'VE GOT
COMPANY.

CLANG

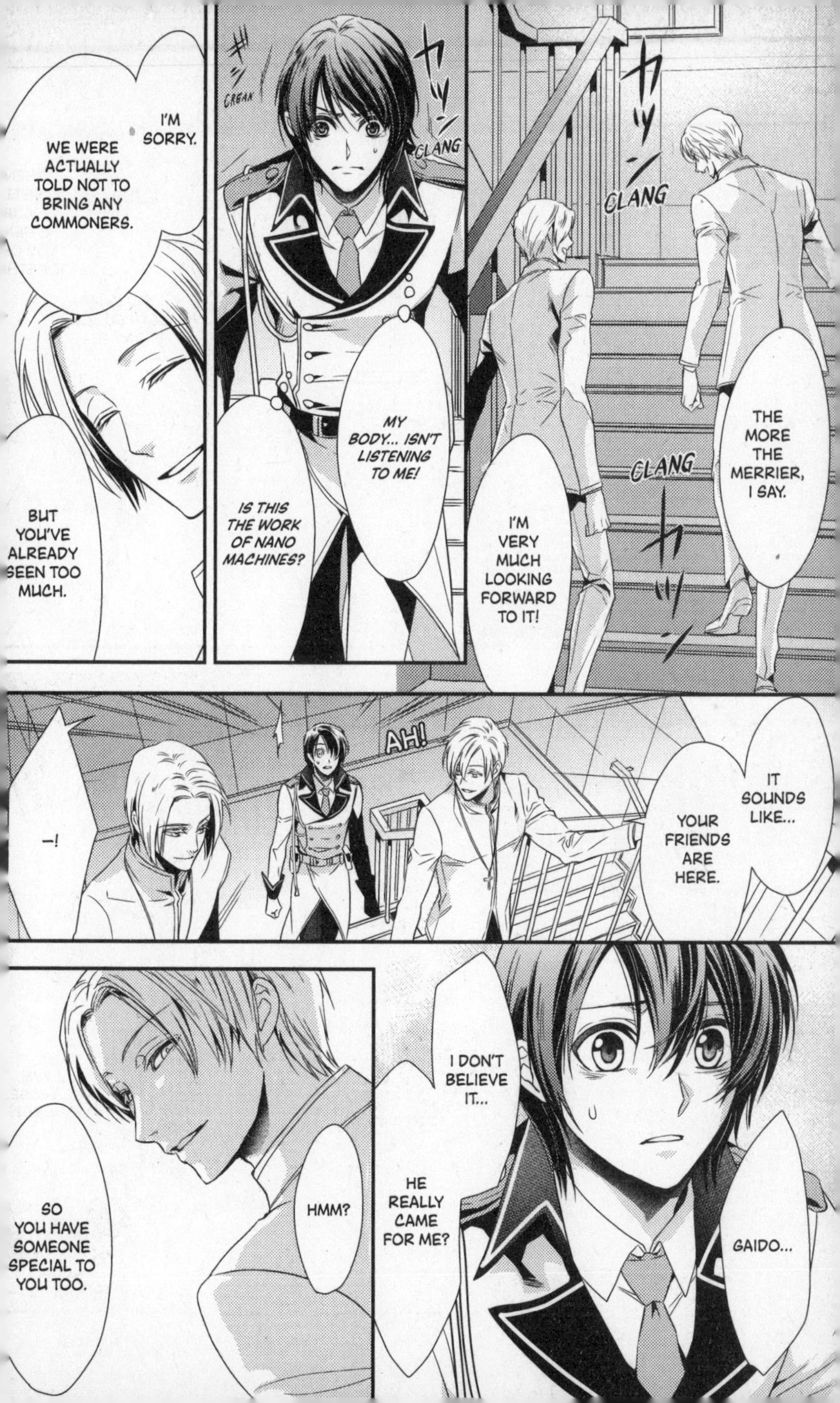
CLANG
CLANG
THE MORE THE MERRIER, I SAY.
I'M VERY MUCH LOOKING FORWARD TO IT!
CREAK
CLANG
MY BODY... ISN'T LISTENING TO ME!
IS THIS THE WORK OF NANO MACHINES?
I'M SORRY.
WE WERE ACTUALLY TOLD NOT TO BRING ANY COMMONERS.
BUT YOU'VE ALREADY SEEN TOO MUCH.
IT SOUNDS LIKE...
YOUR FRIENDS ARE HERE.
AH!
—!
GAIDO...
I DON'T BELIEVE IT...
HE REALLY CAME FOR ME?
HMM?
SO YOU HAVE SOMEONE SPECIAL TO YOU TOO.

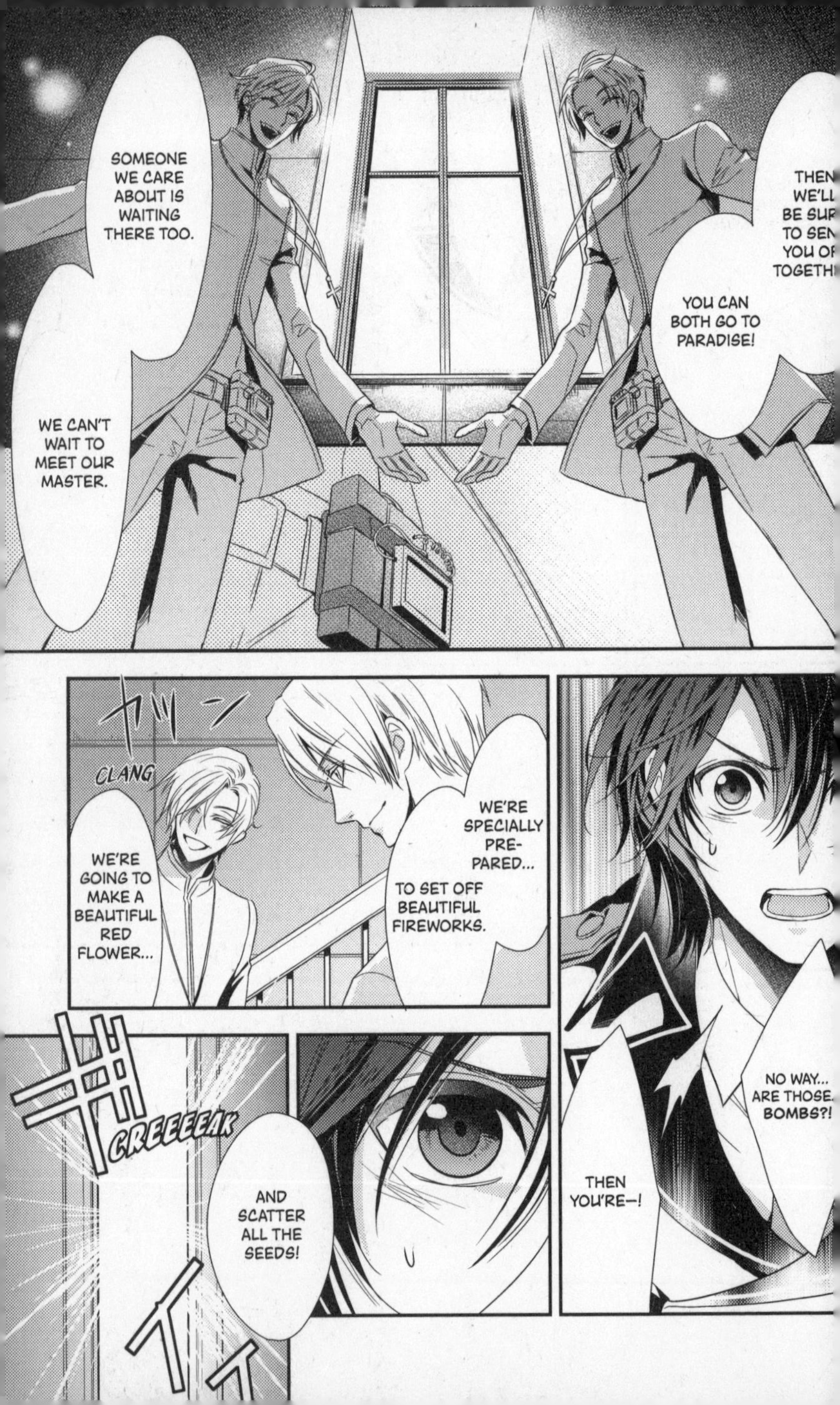
THEN WE'LL BE SUR TO SEN YOU OF TOGETH
YOU CAN BOTH GO TO PARADISE!
SOMEONE WE CARE ABOUT IS WAITING THERE TOO.
WE CAN'T WAIT TO MEET OUR MASTER.
NO WAY... ARE THOSE BOMBS?!
THEN YOU'RE—!
CLANG
WE'RE SPECIALLY PRE-PARED...
TO SET OFF BEAUTIFUL FIREWORKS.
WE'RE GOING TO MAKE A BEAUTIFUL RED FLOWER...
AND SCATTER ALL THE SEEDS!
CREEEEEAK

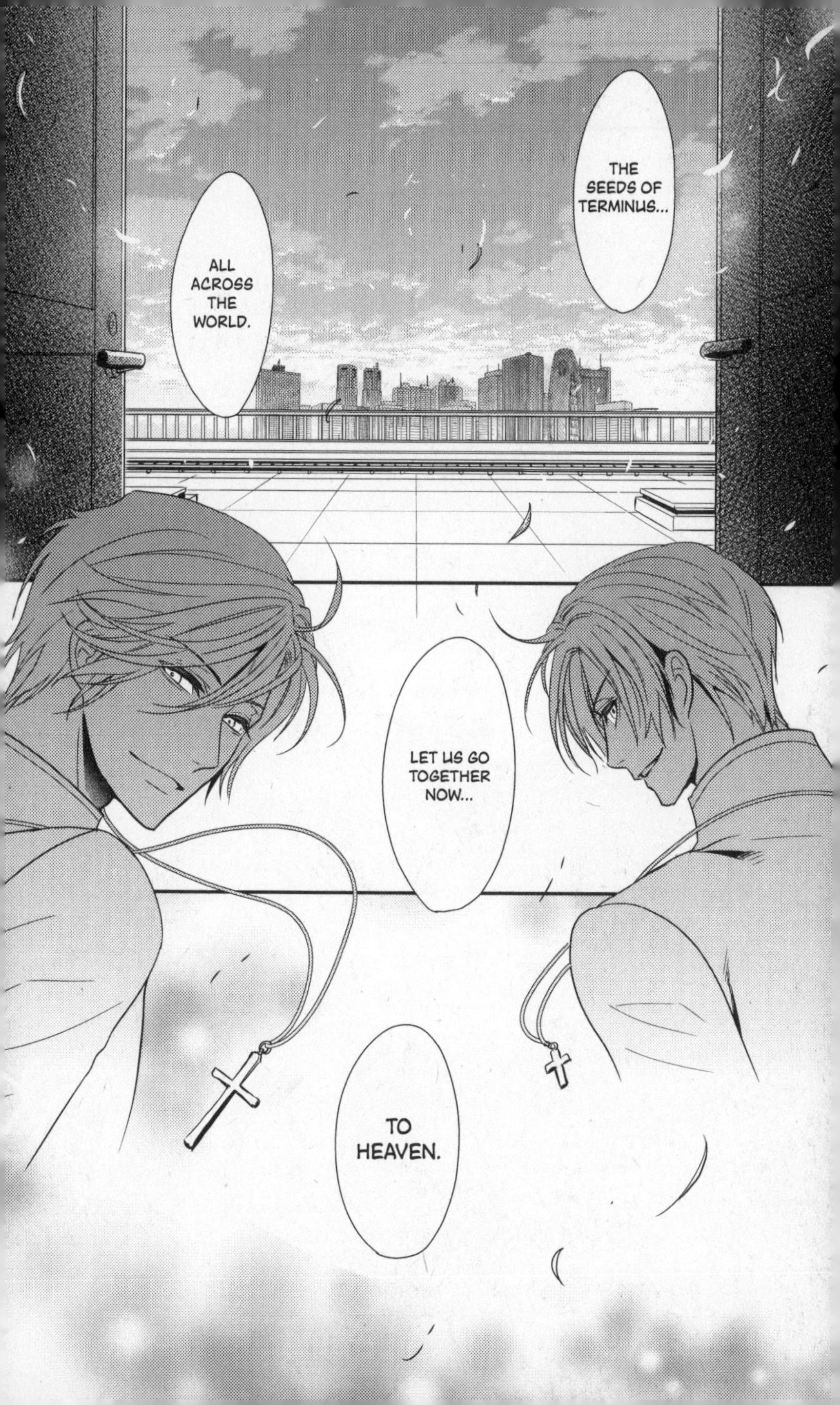
THE SEEDS OF TERMINUS...
ALL ACROSS THE WORLD.
LET US GO TOGETHER NOW...
TO HEAVEN.

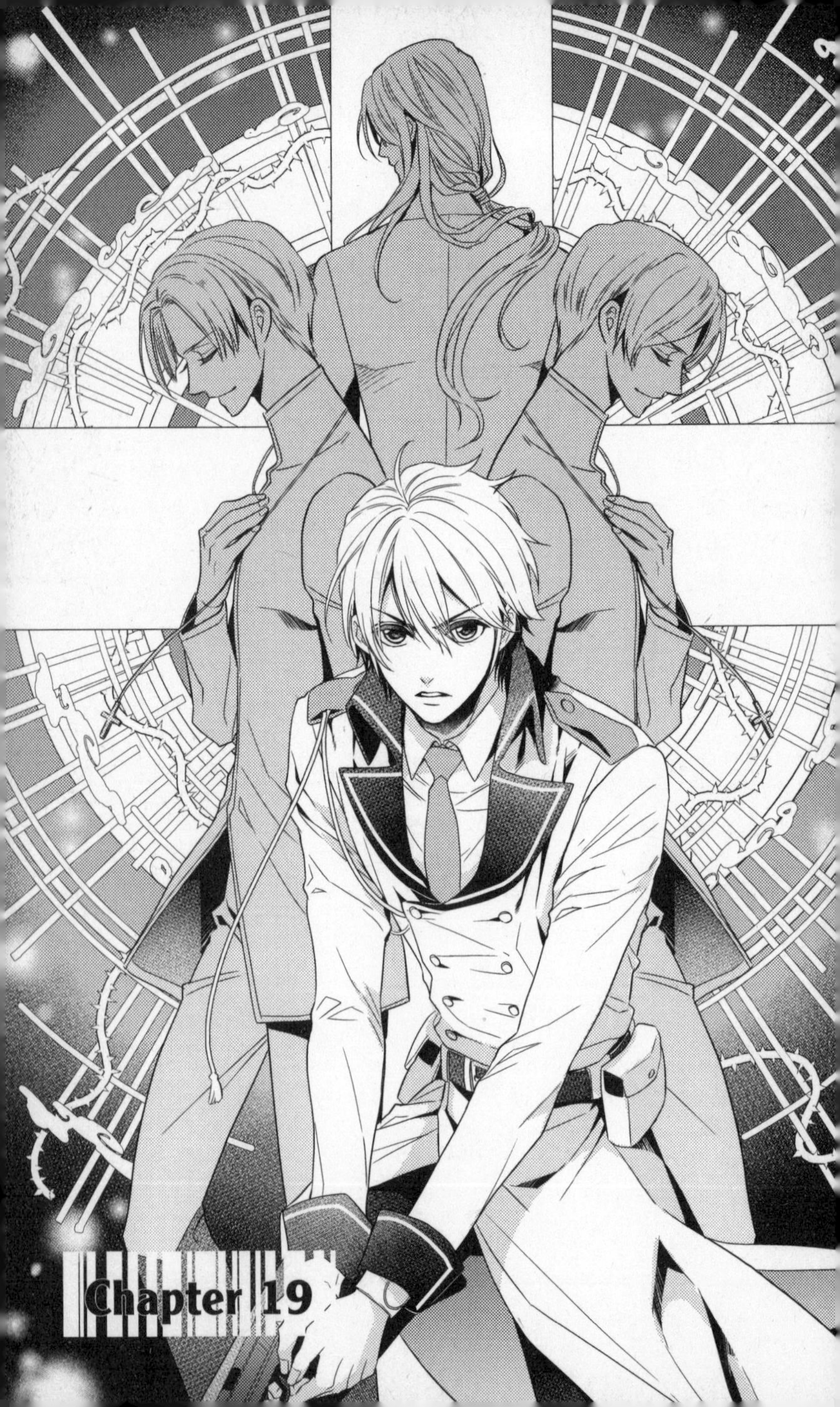
Chapter 19

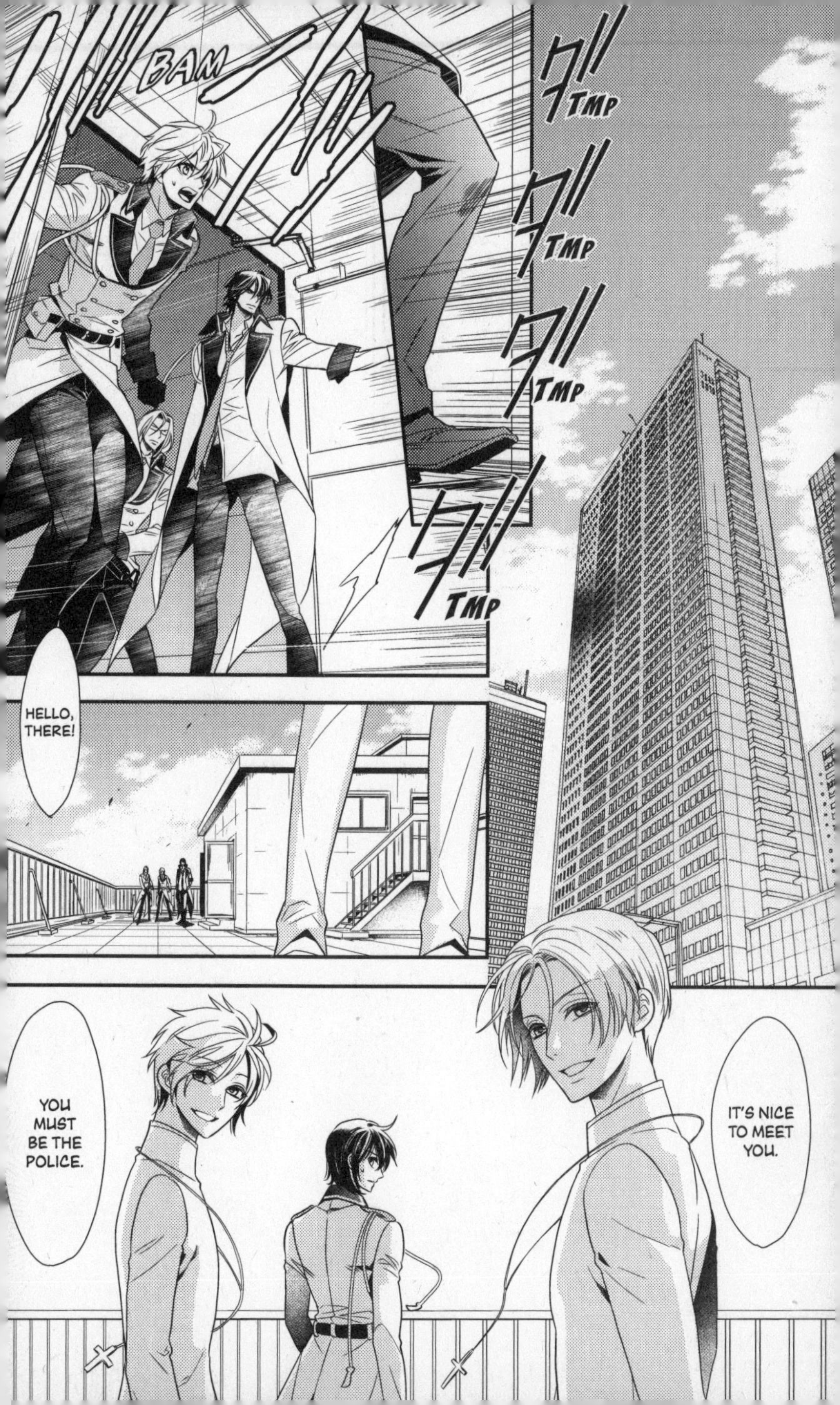
TMP
TMP
TMP
TMP
BAM
HELLO, THERE!
IT'S NICE TO MEET YOU.
YOU MUST BE THE POLICE.

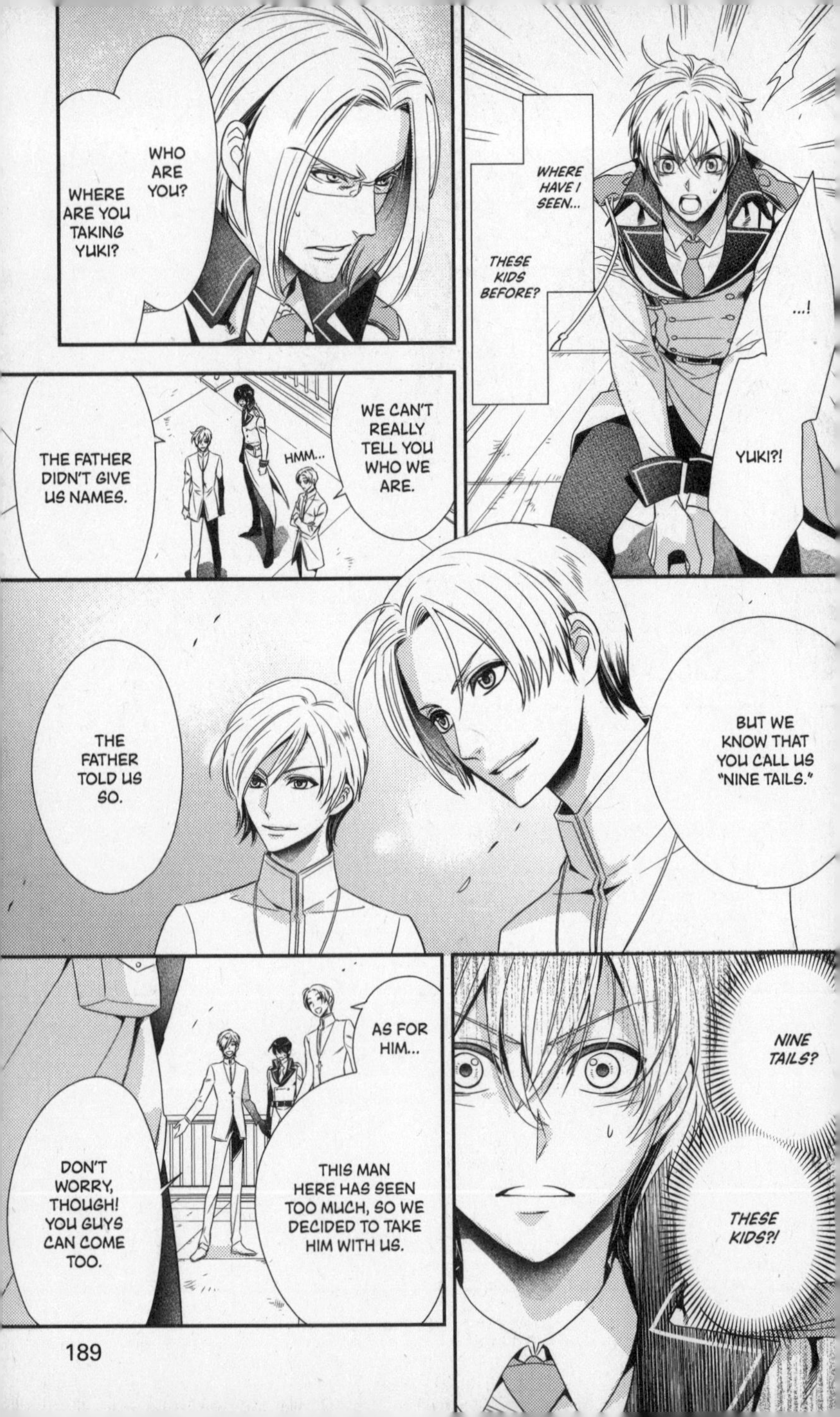
WHERE HAVE I SEEN...
THESE KIDS BEFORE?
...!
YUKI?!
WHO ARE YOU?
WHERE ARE YOU TAKING YUKI?
WE CAN'T REALLY TELL YOU WHO WE ARE.
HMM...
THE FATHER DIDN'T GIVE US NAMES.
BUT WE KNOW THAT YOU CALL US "NINE TAILS."
THE FATHER TOLD US SO.
NINE TAILS?
THESE KIDS?!
AS FOR HIM...
THIS MAN HERE HAS SEEN TOO MUCH, SO WE DECIDED TO TAKE HIM WITH US.
DON'T WORRY, THOUGH! YOU GUYS CAN COME TOO.

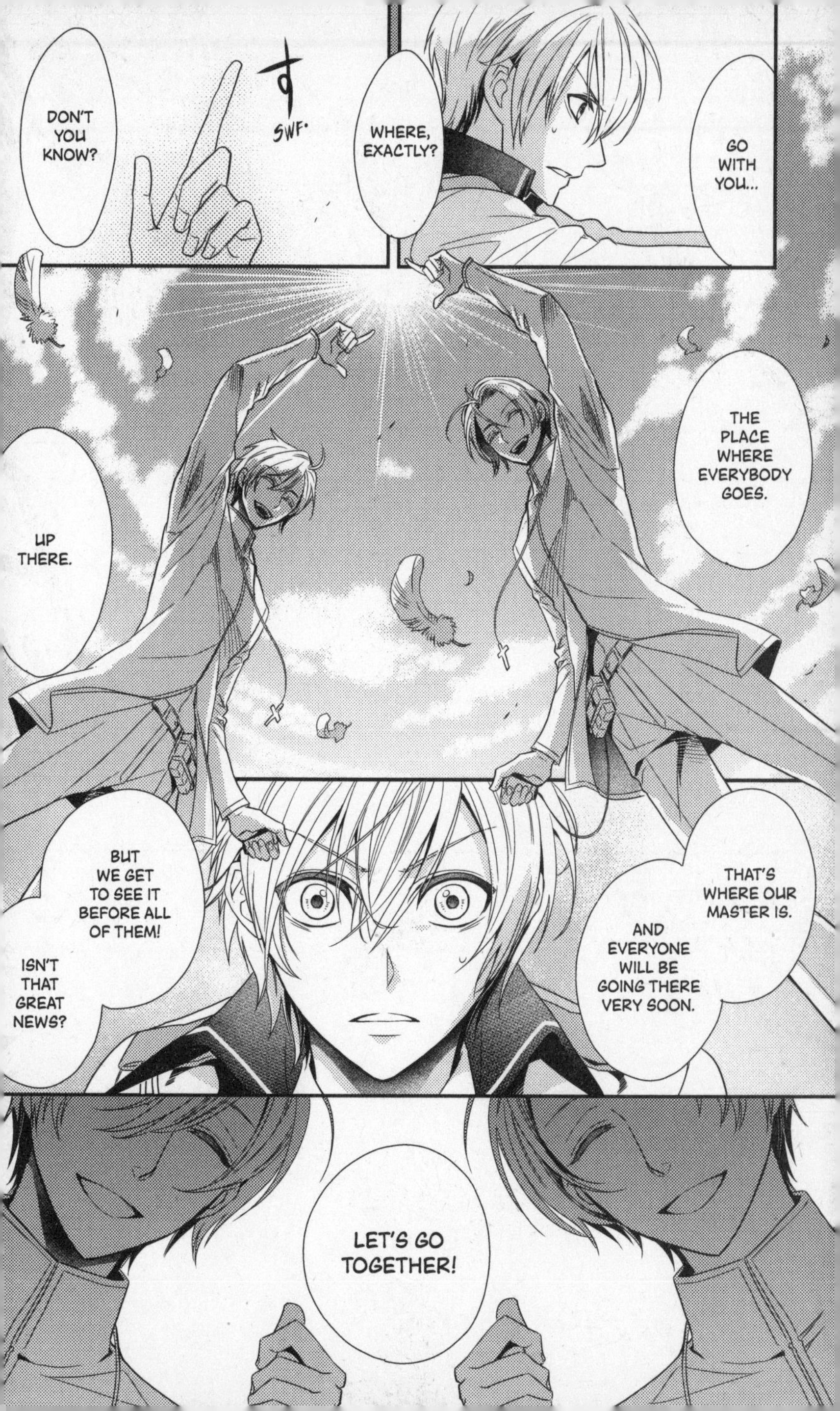
GO WITH YOU...
WHERE, EXACTLY?
す
SWF
DON'T YOU KNOW?
THE PLACE WHERE EVERYBODY GOES.
UP THERE.
THAT'S WHERE OUR MASTER IS.
AND EVERYONE WILL BE GOING THERE VERY SOON.
BUT WE GET TO SEE IT BEFORE ALL OF THEM!
ISN'T THAT GREAT NEWS?
LET'S GO TOGETHER!

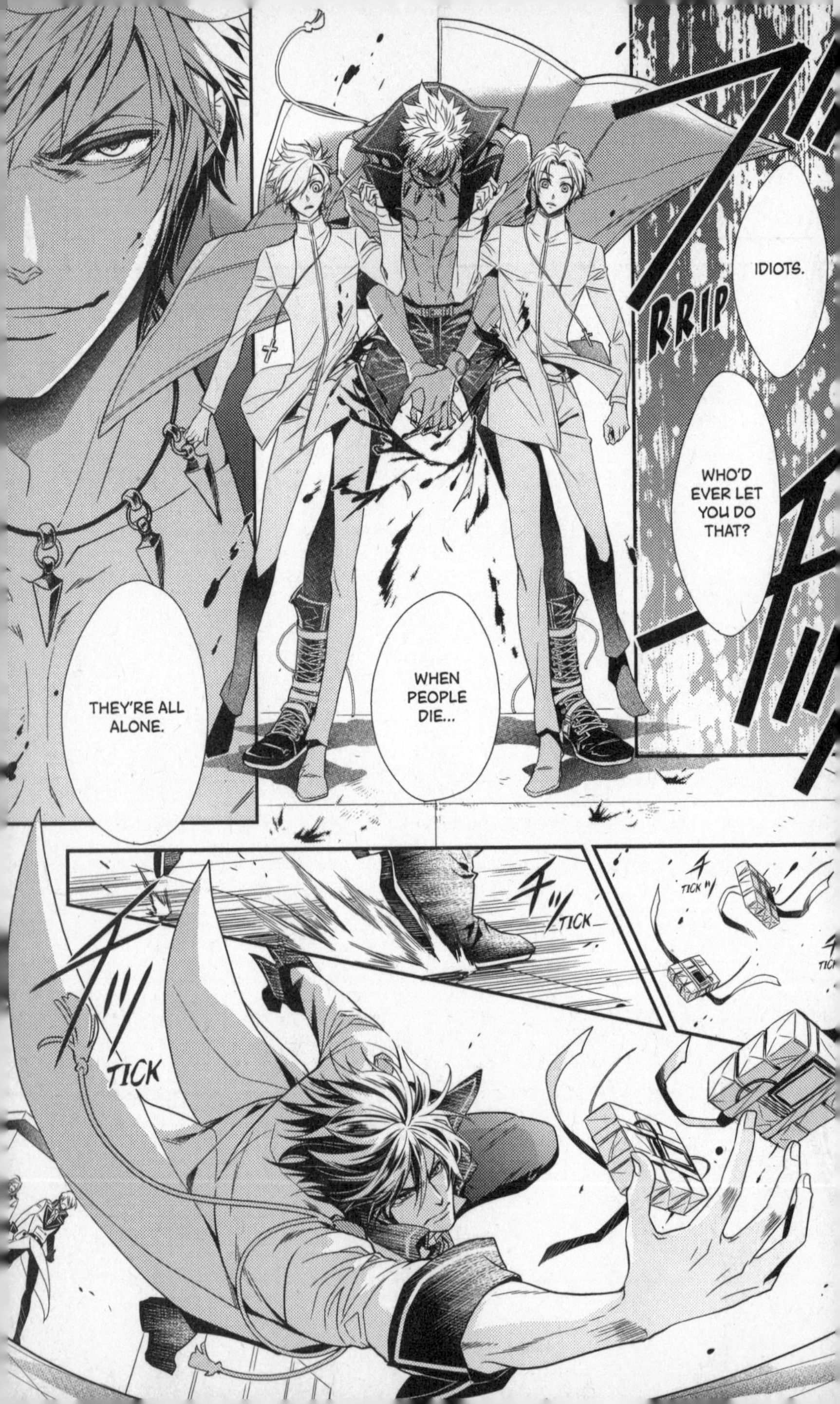

IDIOTS.
RRIP
WHO'D EVER LET YOU DO THAT?
WHEN PEOPLE DIE...
THEY'RE ALL ALONE.
TICK
TICK
TICK
TICK

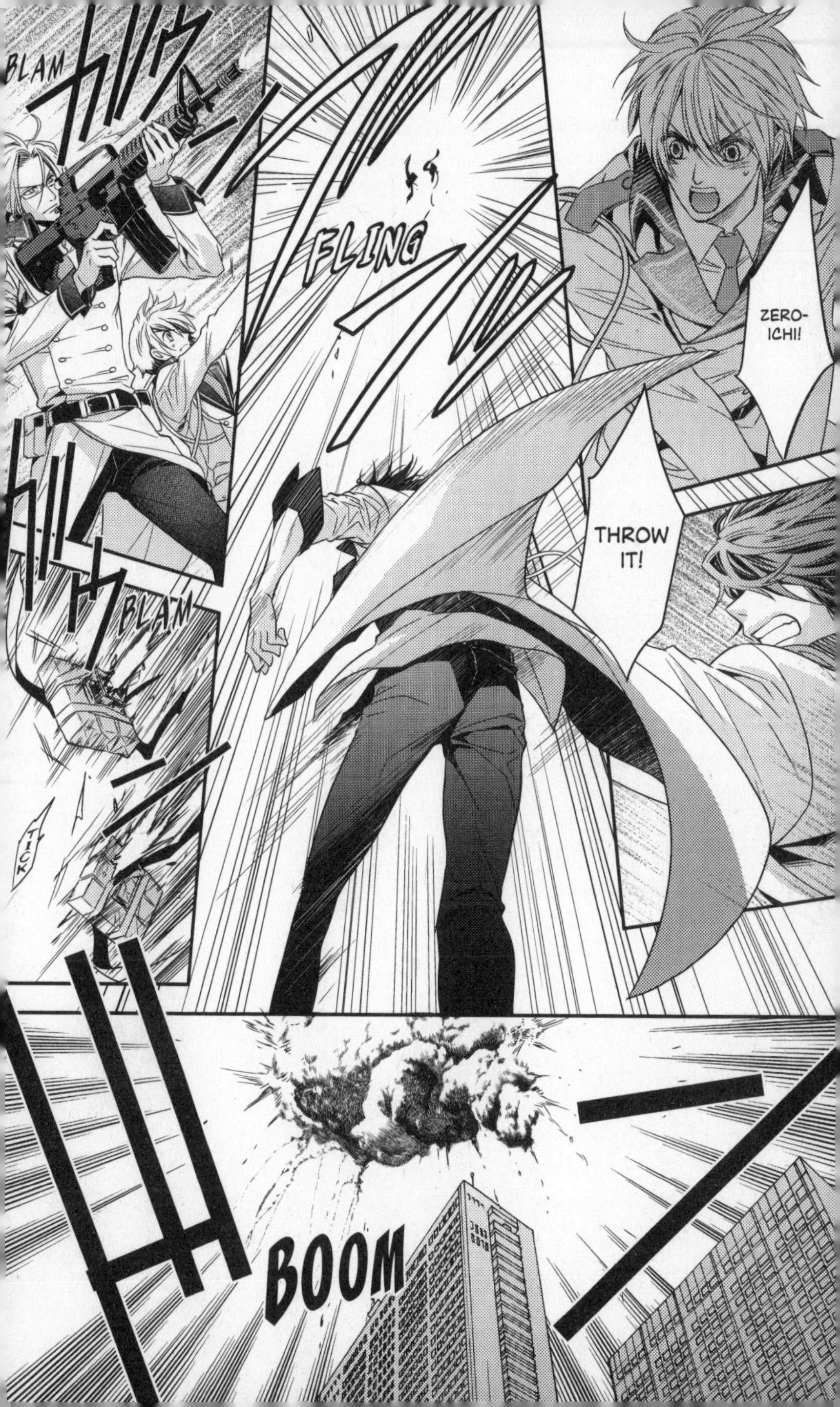
ZERO-ICHI!
THROW IT!
FLING
BLAM
BLAM
TICK
BOOM

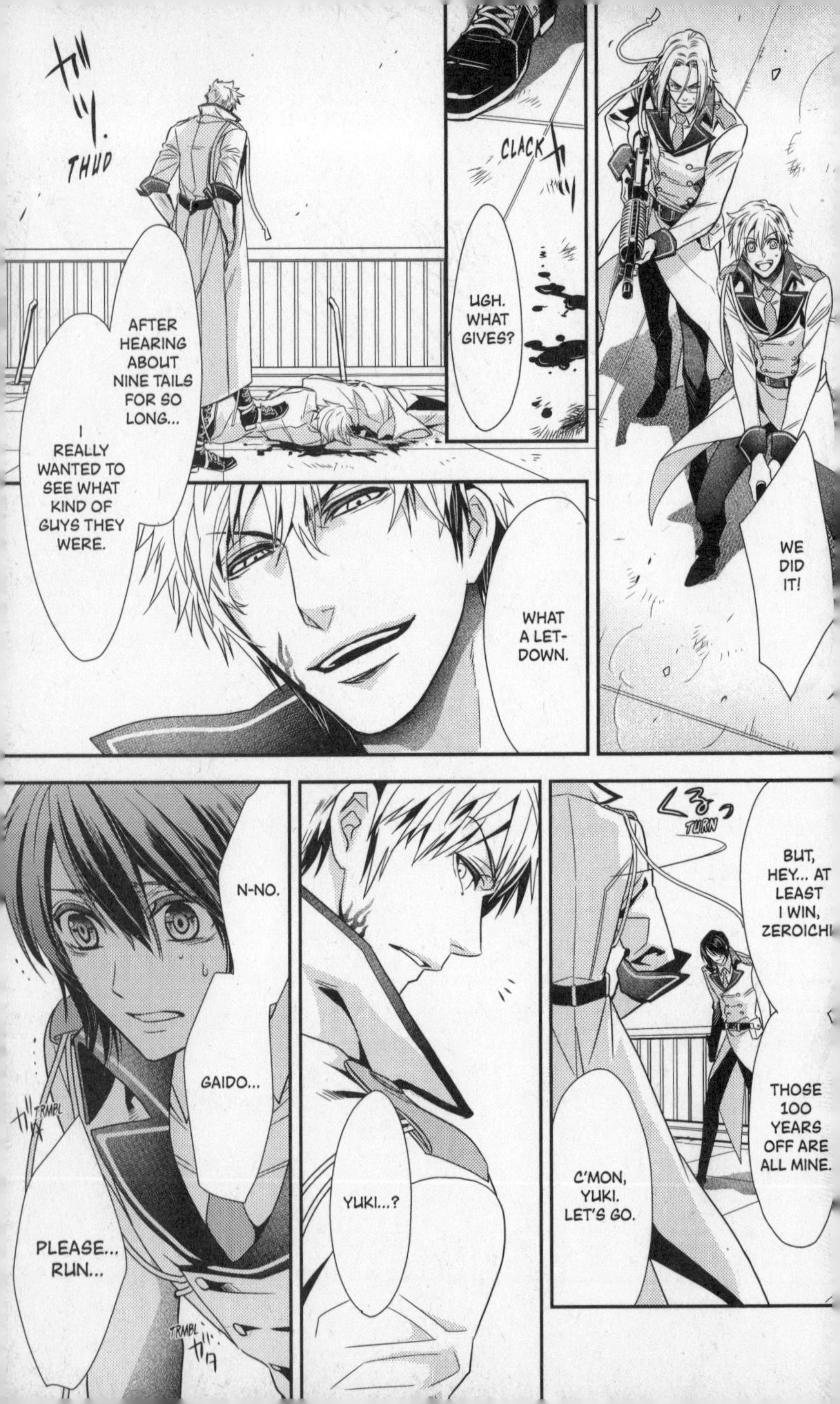
WE DID IT!
CLACK
UGH. WHAT GIVES?
THUD
AFTER HEARING ABOUT NINE TAILS FOR SO LONG...
I REALLY WANTED TO SEE WHAT KIND OF GUYS THEY WERE.
WHAT A LET-DOWN.
TURN
BUT, HEY... AT LEAST I WIN, ZEROICHI
THOSE 100 YEARS OFF ARE ALL MINE.
C'MON, YUKI. LET'S GO.
YUKI...?
N-NO.
GAIDO...
TRMBL
PLEASE... RUN...
TRMBL

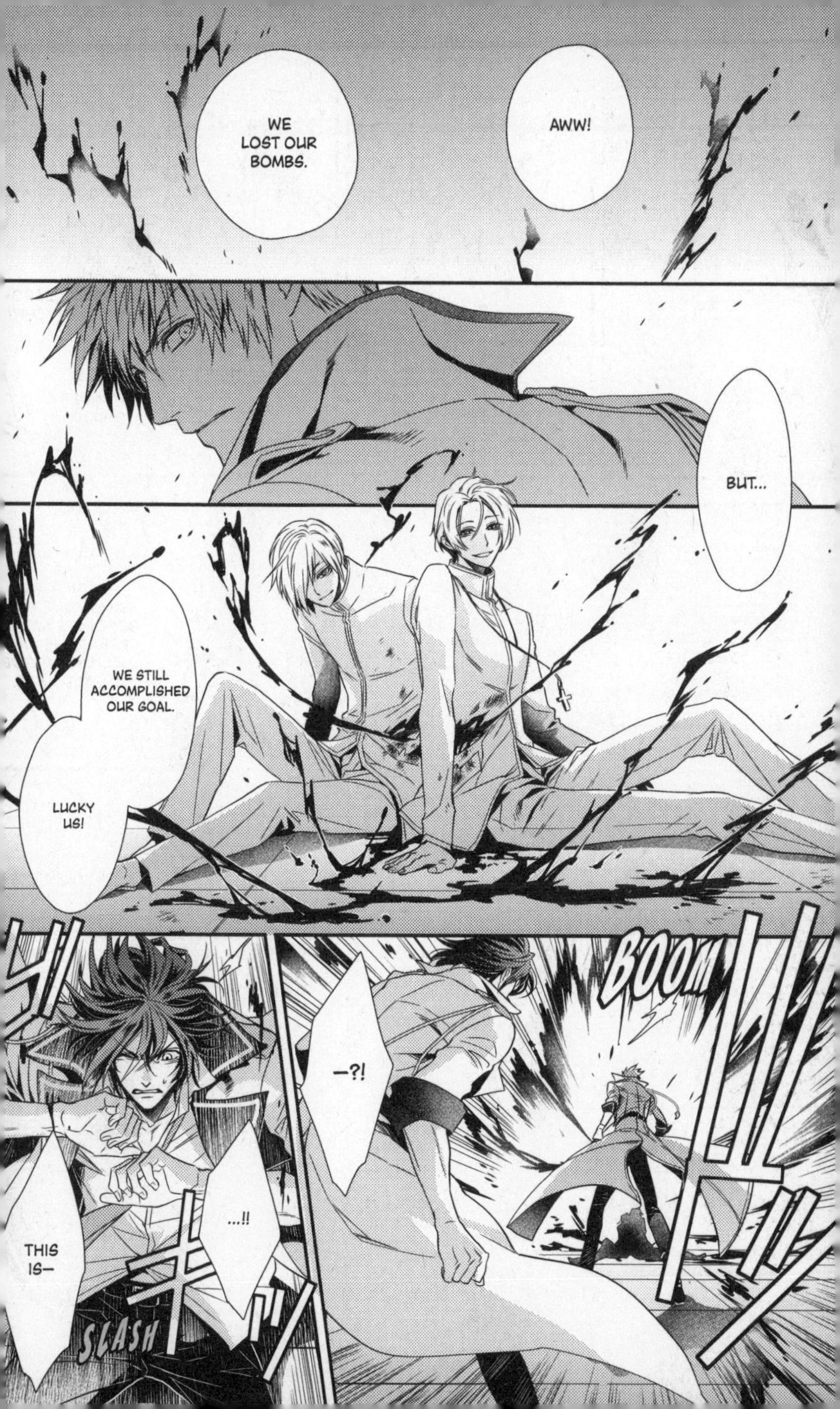

AWW!
WE LOST OUR BOMBS.
BUT...
WE STILL ACCOMPLISHED OUR GOAL.
LUCKY US!
BOOM
—?!
...!!
THIS IS—
SLASH

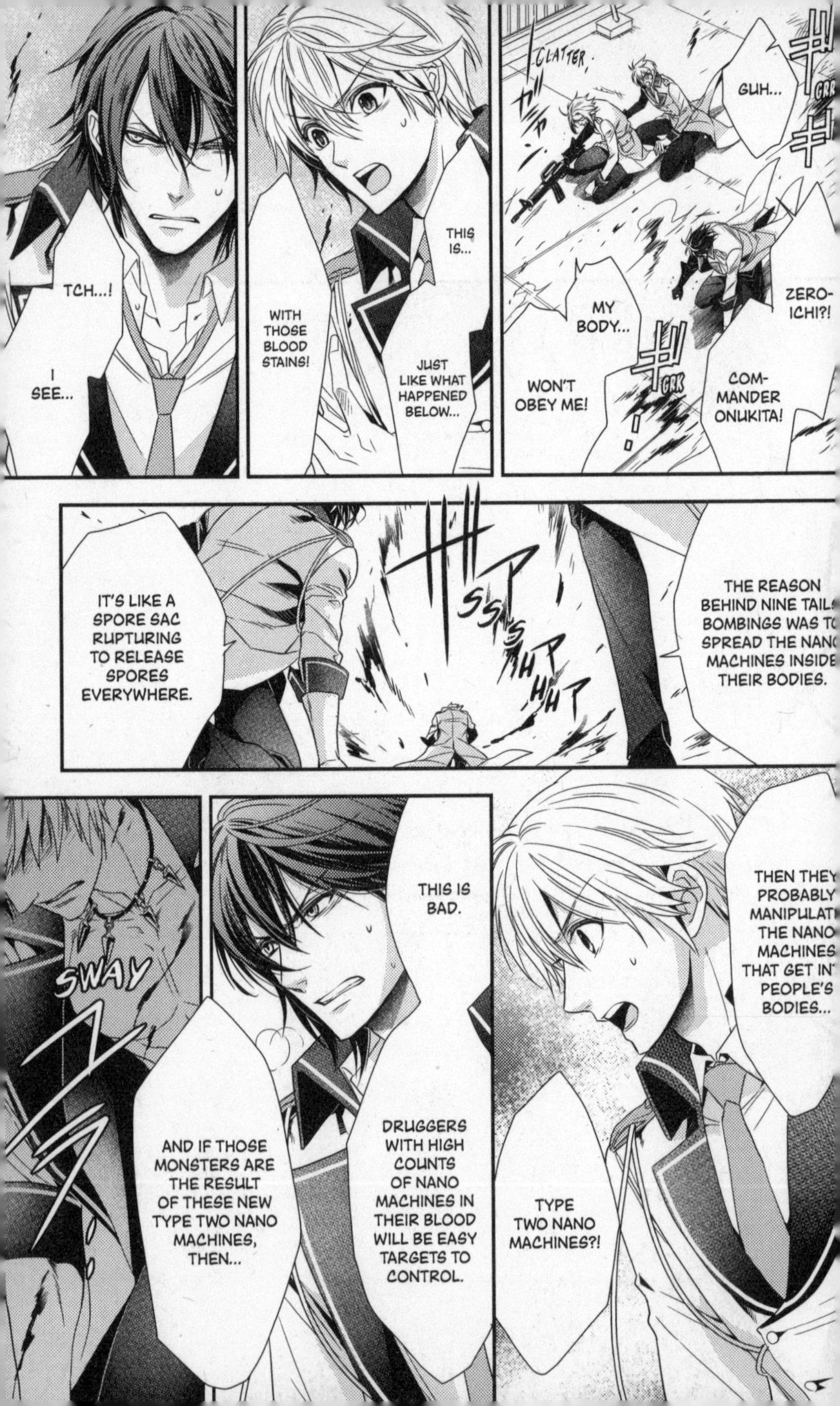
GUH...
GRR
CLATTER
ZERO-ICHI?!
COM-MANDER ONUKITA!
MY BODY...
WON'T OBEY ME!
GRK
THIS IS...
JUST LIKE WHAT HAPPENED BELOW...
WITH THOSE BLOOD STAINS!
TCH...!
I SEE...
THE REASON BEHIND NINE TAIL BOMBINGS WAS T SPREAD THE NAN MACHINES INSID THEIR BODIES.
SSSHHHP
IT'S LIKE A SPORE SAC RUPTURING TO RELEASE SPORES EVERYWHERE.
THEN THE PROBABLY MANIPULAT THE NANO MACHINES THAT GET IN PEOPLE'S BODIES...
TYPE TWO NANO MACHINES?!
THIS IS BAD.
DRUGGERS WITH HIGH COUNTS OF NANO MACHINES IN THEIR BLOOD WILL BE EASY TARGETS TO CONTROL.
AND IF THOSE MONSTERS ARE THE RESULT OF THESE NEW TYPE TWO NANO MACHINES, THEN...
SWAY

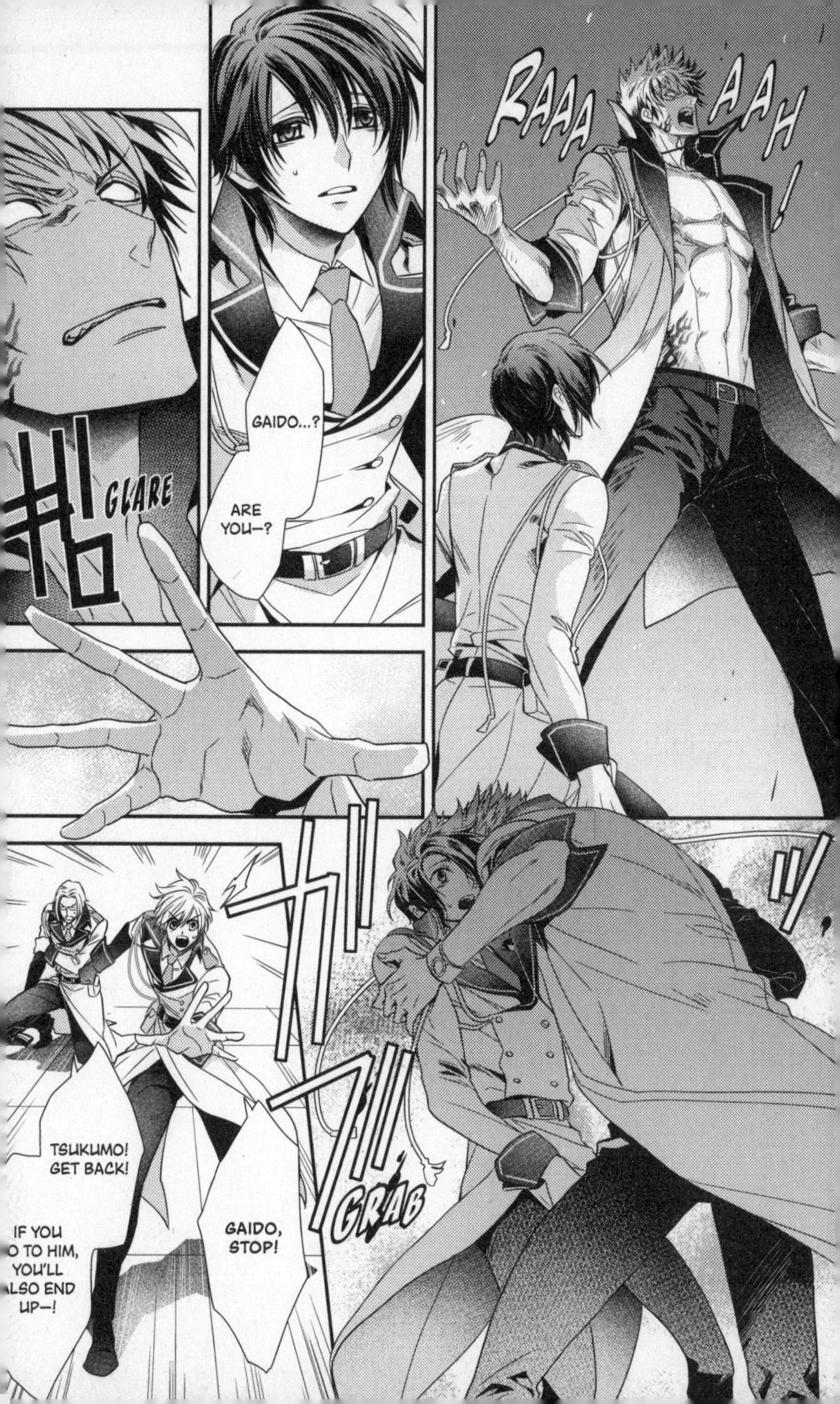
RAAAAAH!
GAIDO...?
ARE YOU—?
GLARE
GRAB
GAIDO, STOP!
TSUKUMO! GET BACK!
IF YOU O TO HIM, YOU'LL LSO END UP—!

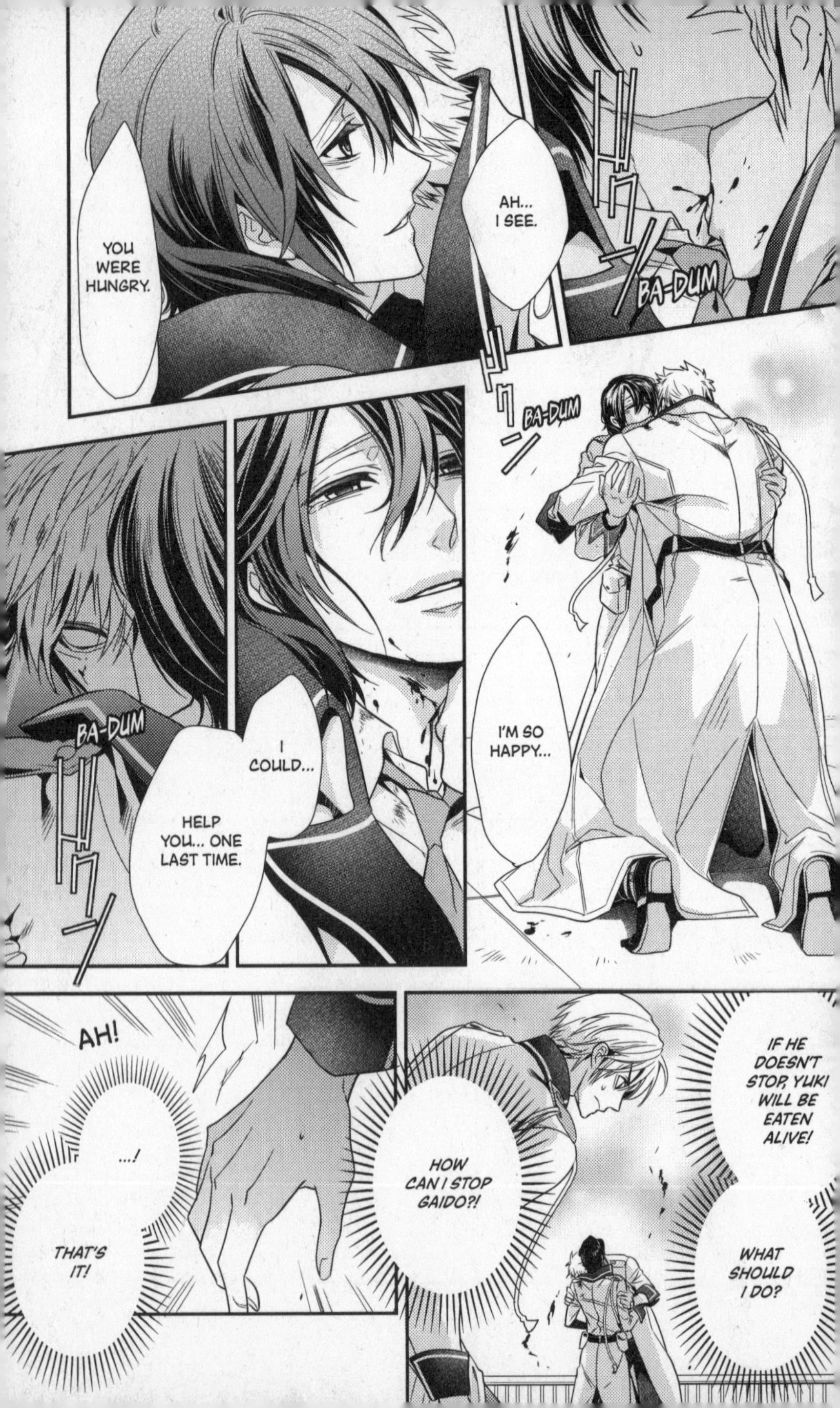
BA-DUM
AH... I SEE.
YOU WERE HUNGRY.
BA-DUM
I'M SO HAPPY...
I COULD...
HELP YOU... ONE LAST TIME.
BA-DUM
IF HE DOESN'T STOP, YUKI WILL BE EATEN ALIVE!
HOW CAN I STOP GAIDO?!
WHAT SHOULD I DO?
AH!
...!
THAT'S IT!

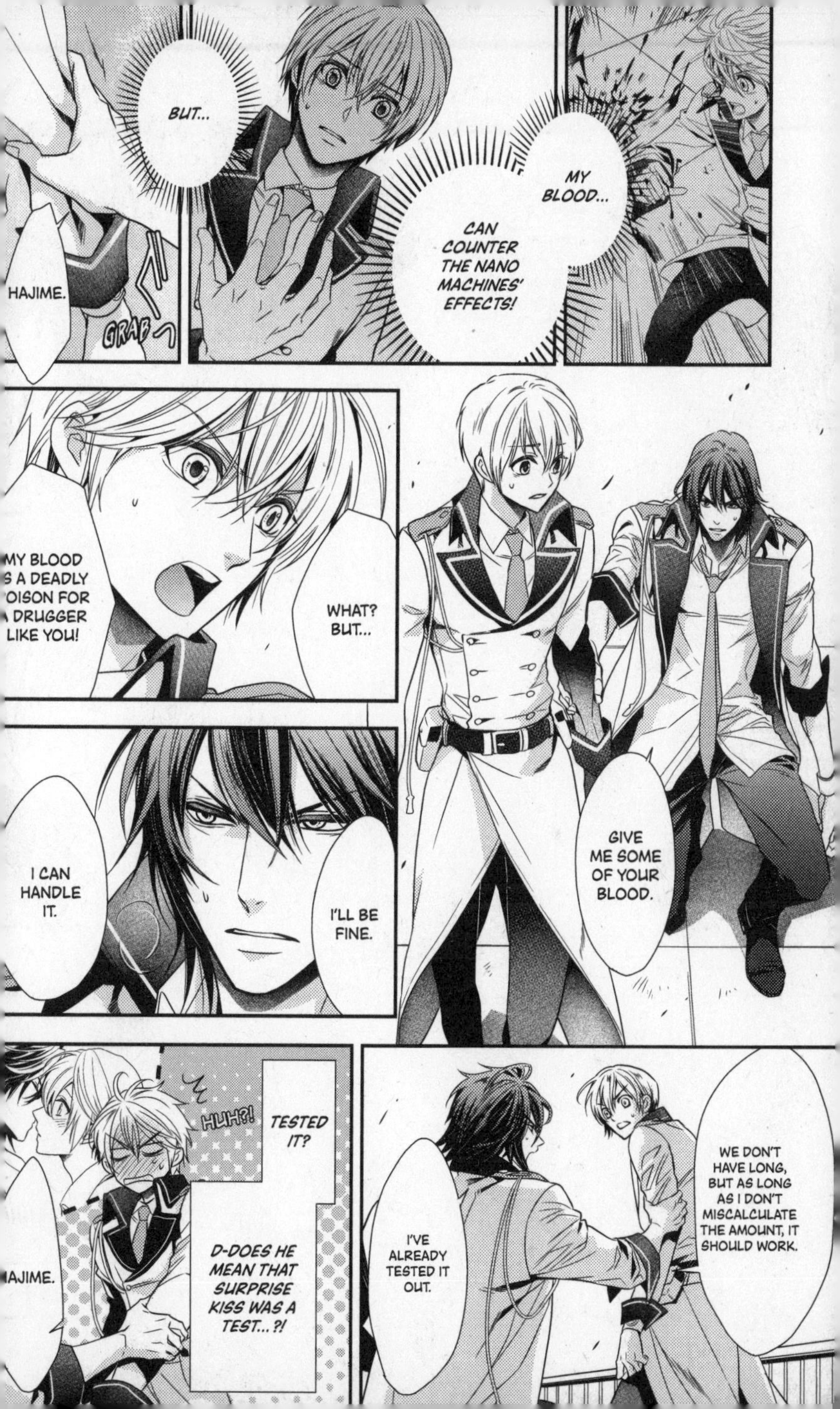

MY BLOOD...
CAN COUNTER THE NANO MACHINES' EFFECTS!
BUT...
HAJIME.
GRAB
GIVE ME SOME OF YOUR BLOOD.
WHAT? BUT...
MY BLOOD S A DEADLY OISON FOR A DRUGGER LIKE YOU!
I'LL BE FINE.
I CAN HANDLE IT.
WE DON'T HAVE LONG, BUT AS LONG AS I DON'T MISCALCULATE THE AMOUNT, IT SHOULD WORK.
I'VE ALREADY TESTED IT OUT.
TESTED IT?
HUH?!
D-DOES HE MEAN THAT SURPRISE KISS WAS A TEST...?!
AJIME.

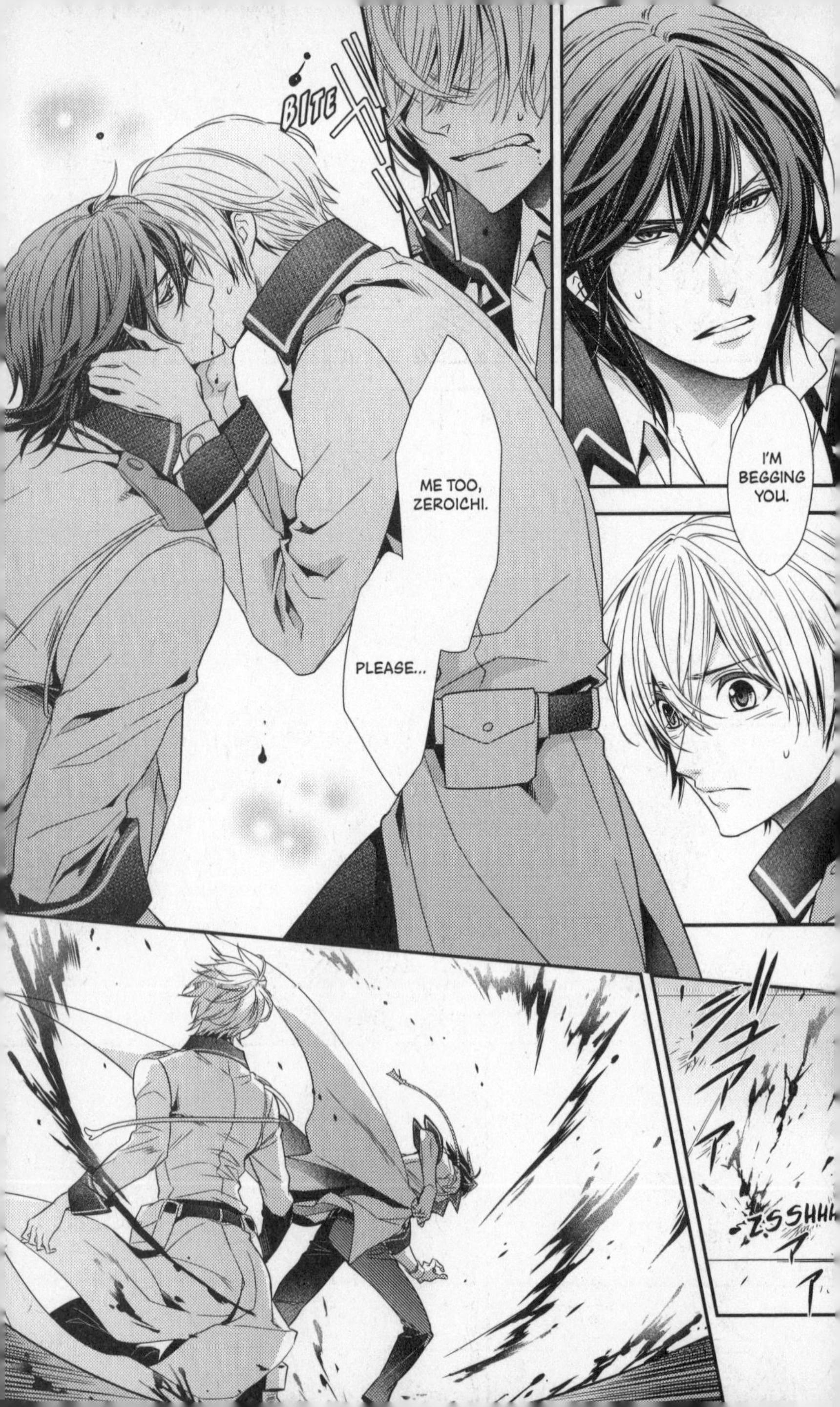

I'M BEGGING YOU.
BITE
ME TOO, ZEROICHI.
PLEASE...
ZSSHHH

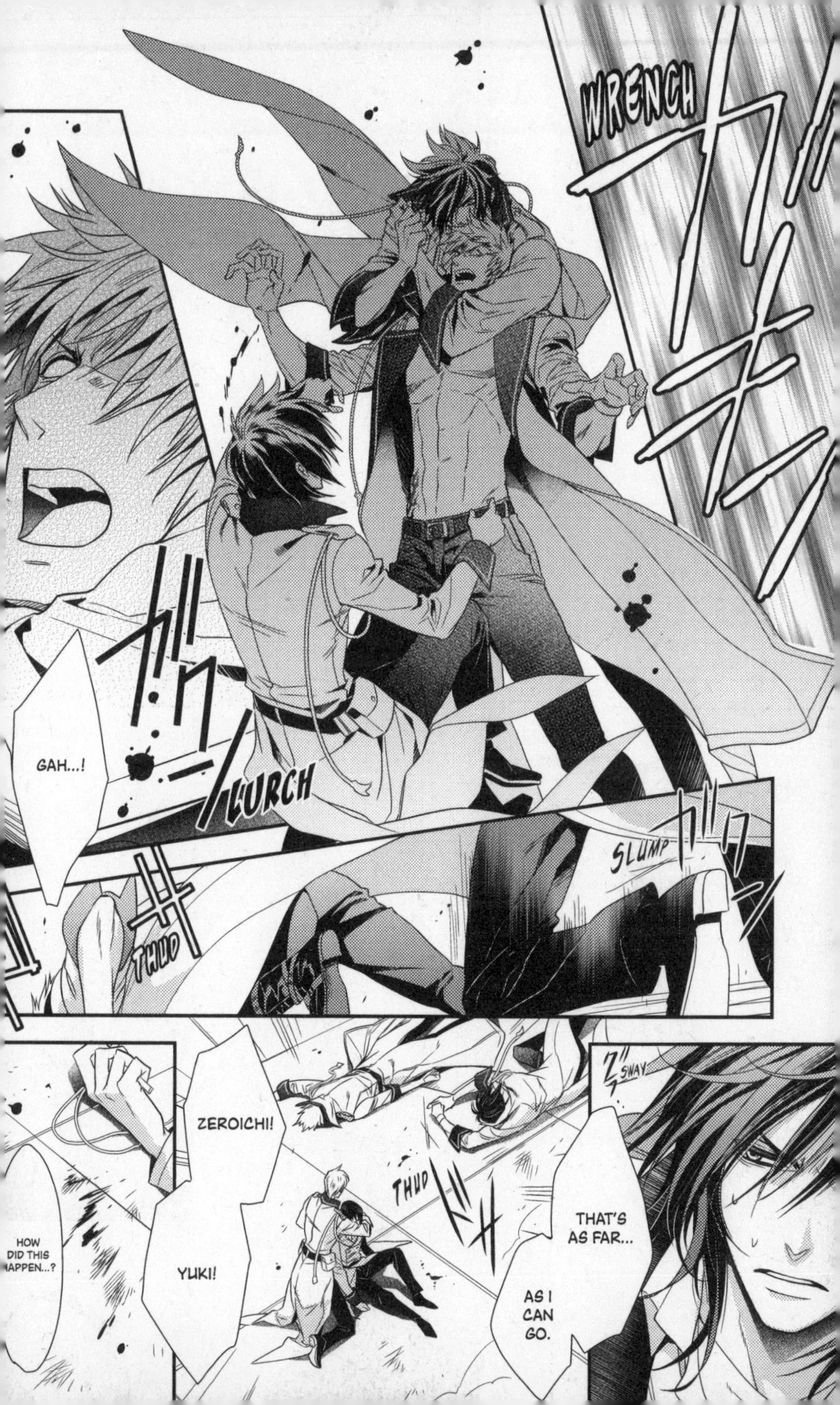
WRENCH
LURCH
GAH...!
SLUMP
THUD
SWAY
THAT'S AS FAR...
AS I CAN GO.
THUD
ZEROICHI!
YUKI!
HOW DID THIS HAPPEN...?

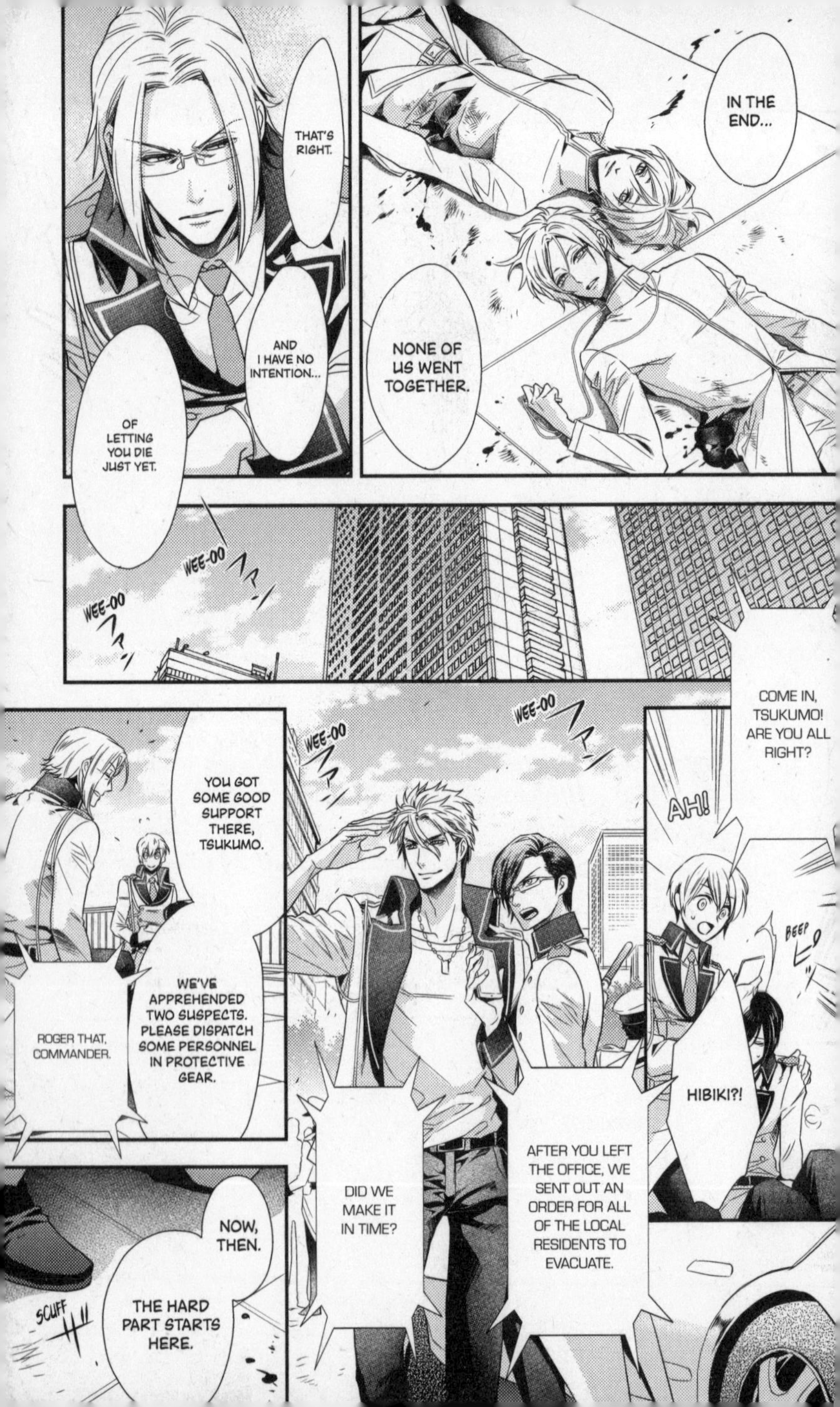
IN THE END...
NONE OF US WENT TOGETHER.
THAT'S RIGHT.
AND I HAVE NO INTENTION...
OF LETTING YOU DIE JUST YET.
WEE-OO
WEE-OO
COME IN, TSUKUMO! ARE YOU ALL RIGHT?
AH!
BEEP
HIBIKI?!
WEE-OO
WEE-OO
AFTER YOU LEFT THE OFFICE, WE SENT OUT AN ORDER FOR ALL OF THE LOCAL RESIDENTS TO EVACUATE.
DID WE MAKE IT IN TIME?
YOU GOT SOME GOOD SUPPORT THERE, TSUKUMO.
WE'VE APPREHENDED TWO SUSPECTS. PLEASE DISPATCH SOME PERSONNEL IN PROTECTIVE GEAR.
ROGER THAT, COMMANDER.
NOW, THEN.
THE HARD PART STARTS HERE.
SCUFF

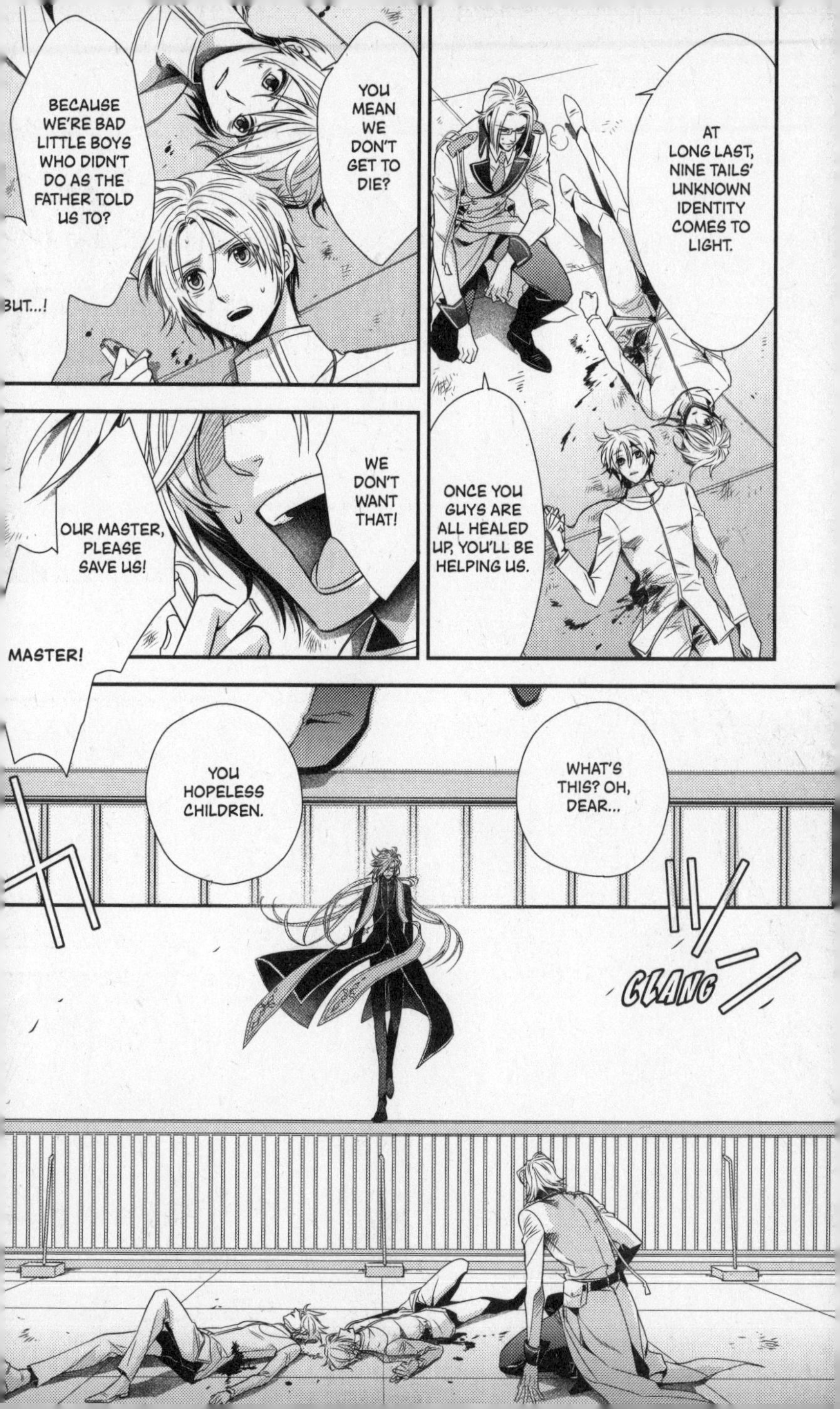
AT LONG LAST, NINE TAILS' UNKNOWN IDENTITY COMES TO LIGHT.
ONCE YOU GUYS ARE ALL HEALED UP, YOU'LL BE HELPING US.
YOU MEAN WE DON'T GET TO DIE?
BECAUSE WE'RE BAD LITTLE BOYS WHO DIDN'T DO AS THE FATHER TOLD US TO?
BUT...!
WE DON'T WANT THAT!
OUR MASTER, PLEASE SAVE US!
MASTER!
WHAT'S THIS? OH, DEAR...
YOU HOPELESS CHILDREN.
CLANG

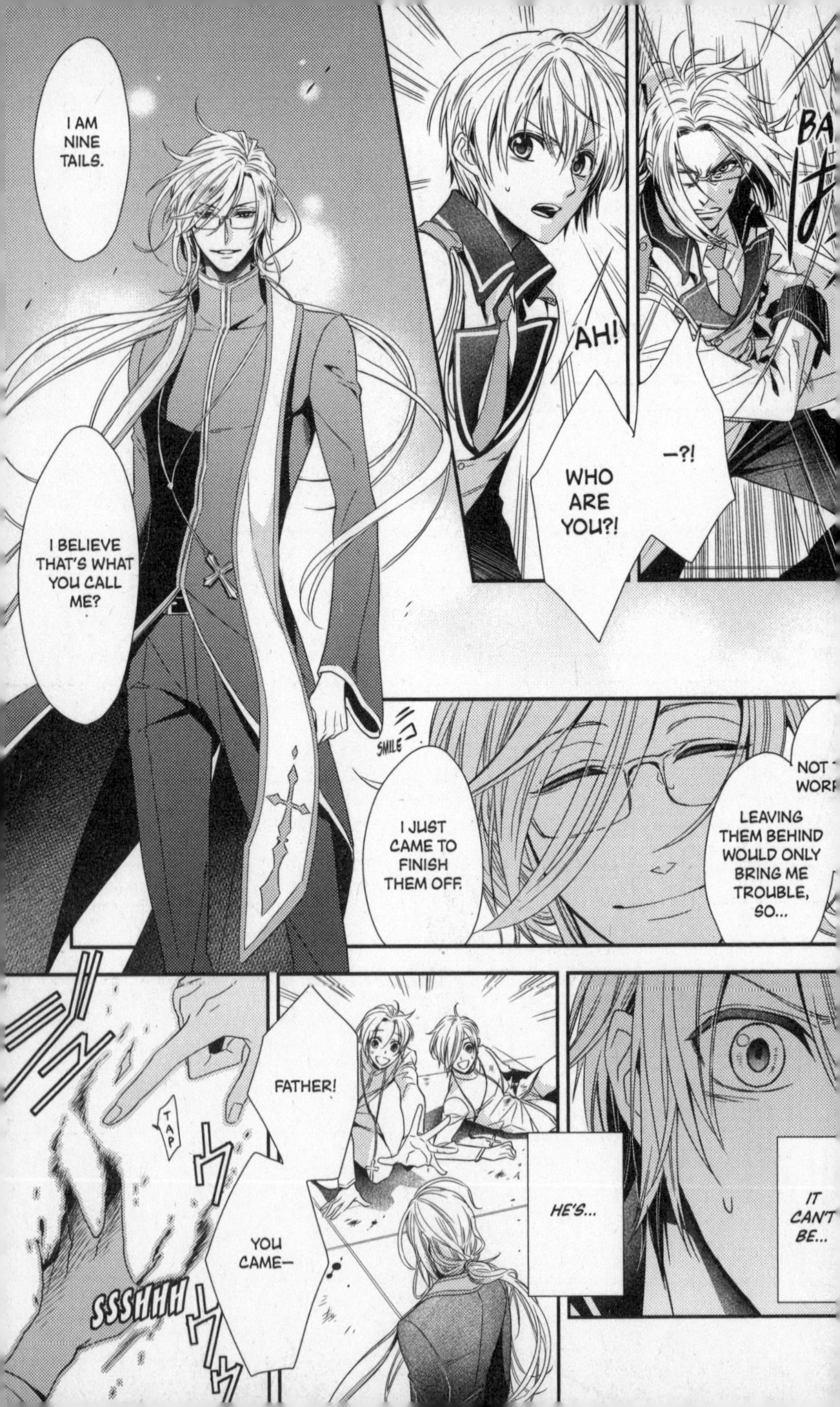

BA
—?!
AH!
WHO ARE YOU?!
NOT
LEAVING THEM BEHIND WOULD ONLY BRING ME TROUBLE, SO...
SMILE
I JUST CAME TO FINISH THEM OFF.
I AM NINE TAILS.
I BELIEVE THAT'S WHAT YOU CALL ME?
IT CAN'T BE...
HE'S...
FATHER!
YOU CAME—
TAP
SSSHHH

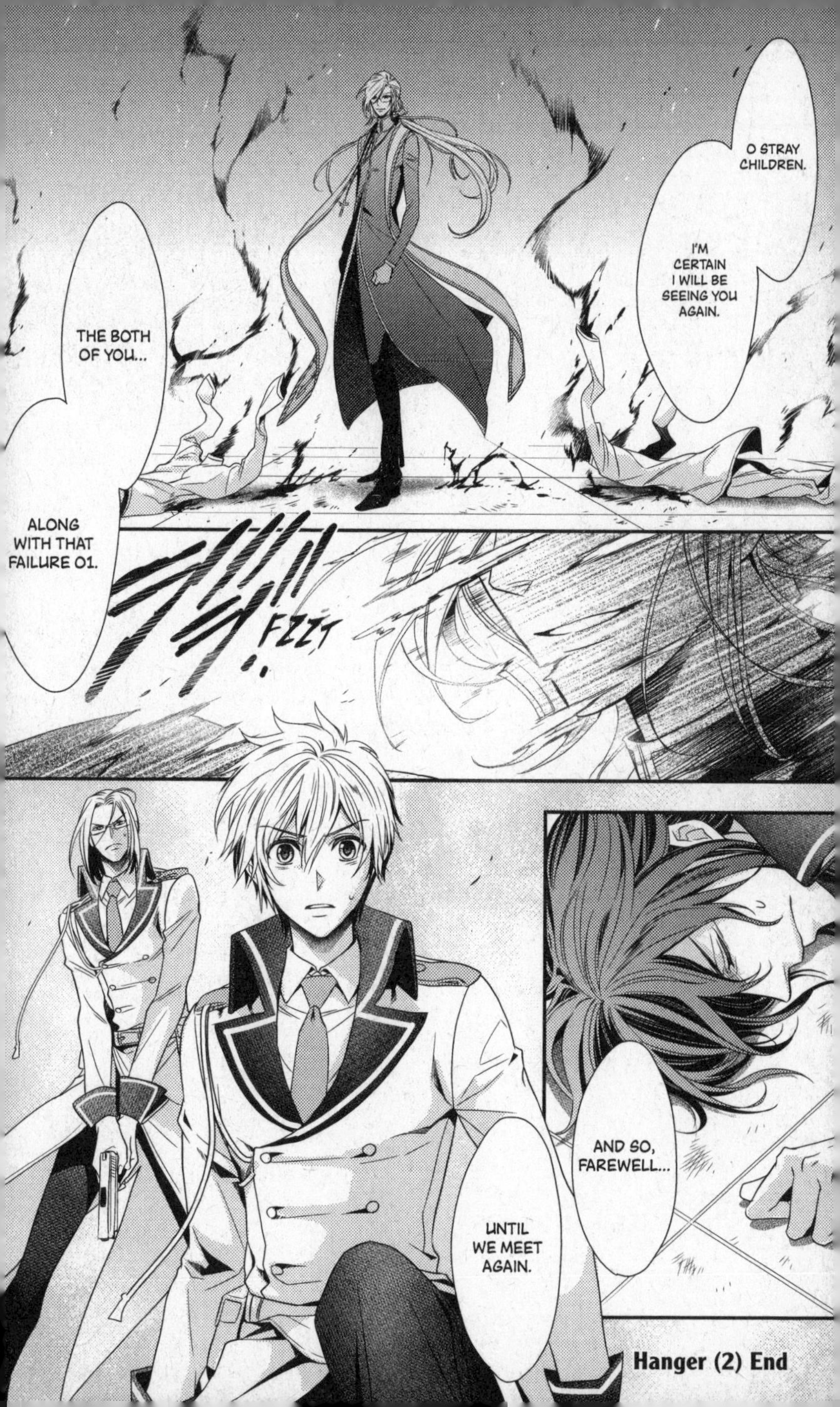
O STRAY CHILDREN.
I'M CERTAIN I WILL BE SEEING YOU AGAIN.
THE BOTH OF YOU...
ALONG WITH THAT FAILURE 01.
FZZT
AND SO, FAREWELL...
UNTIL WE MEET AGAIN.

Hanger (2) End

HANGER

Recent Developments in the Tsukumo Household

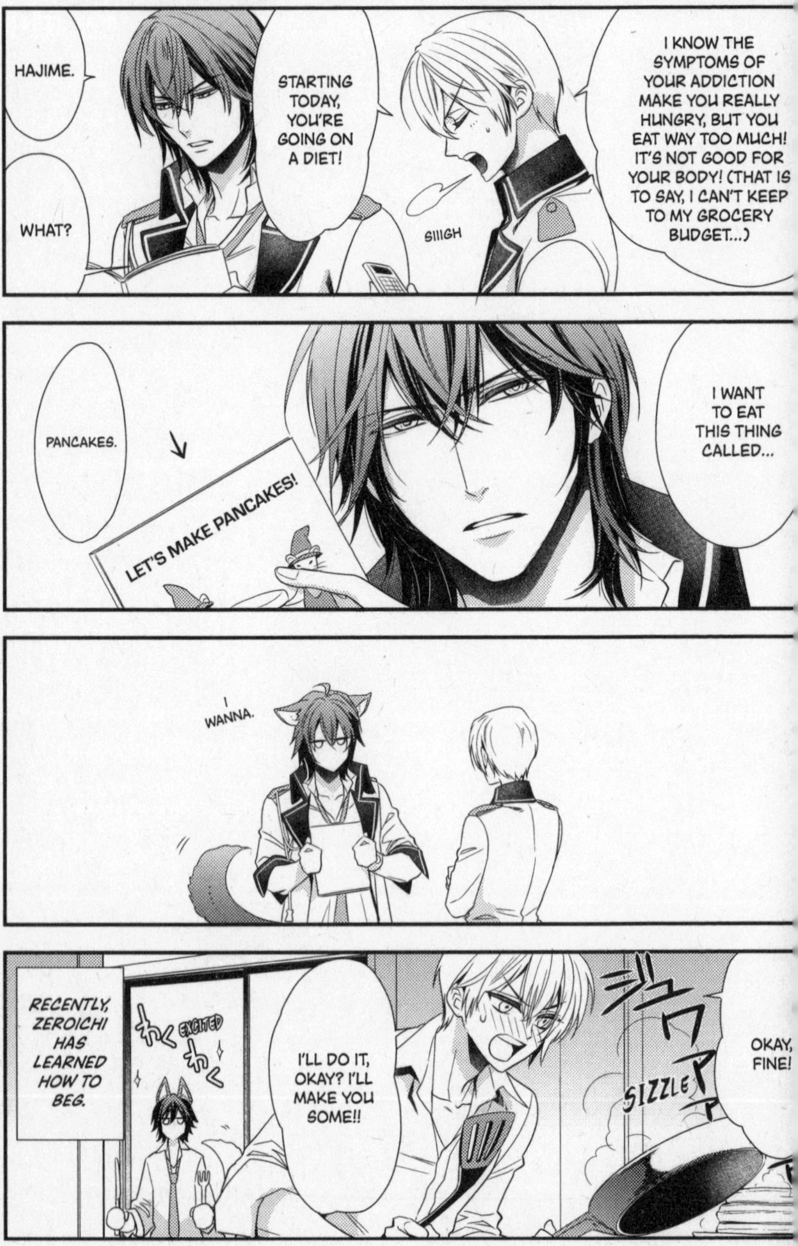
I KNOW THE SYMPTOMS OF YOUR ADDICTION MAKE YOU REALLY HUNGRY, BUT YOU EAT WAY TOO MUCH! IT'S NOT GOOD FOR YOUR BODY! (THAT IS TO SAY, I CAN'T KEEP TO MY GROCERY BUDGET...)
SIIIGH
STARTING TODAY, YOU'RE GOING ON A DIET!
HAJIME.
WHAT?
I WANT TO EAT THIS THING CALLED...
LET'S MAKE PANCAKES!
PANCAKES.
I WANNA.
OKAY, FINE!
ジュワア
SIZZLE
I'LL DO IT, OKAY? I'LL MAKE YOU SOME!!
わくわく
EXCITED
RECENTLY, ZEROICHI HAS LEARNED HOW TO BEG.

An Incident with the Neighbors

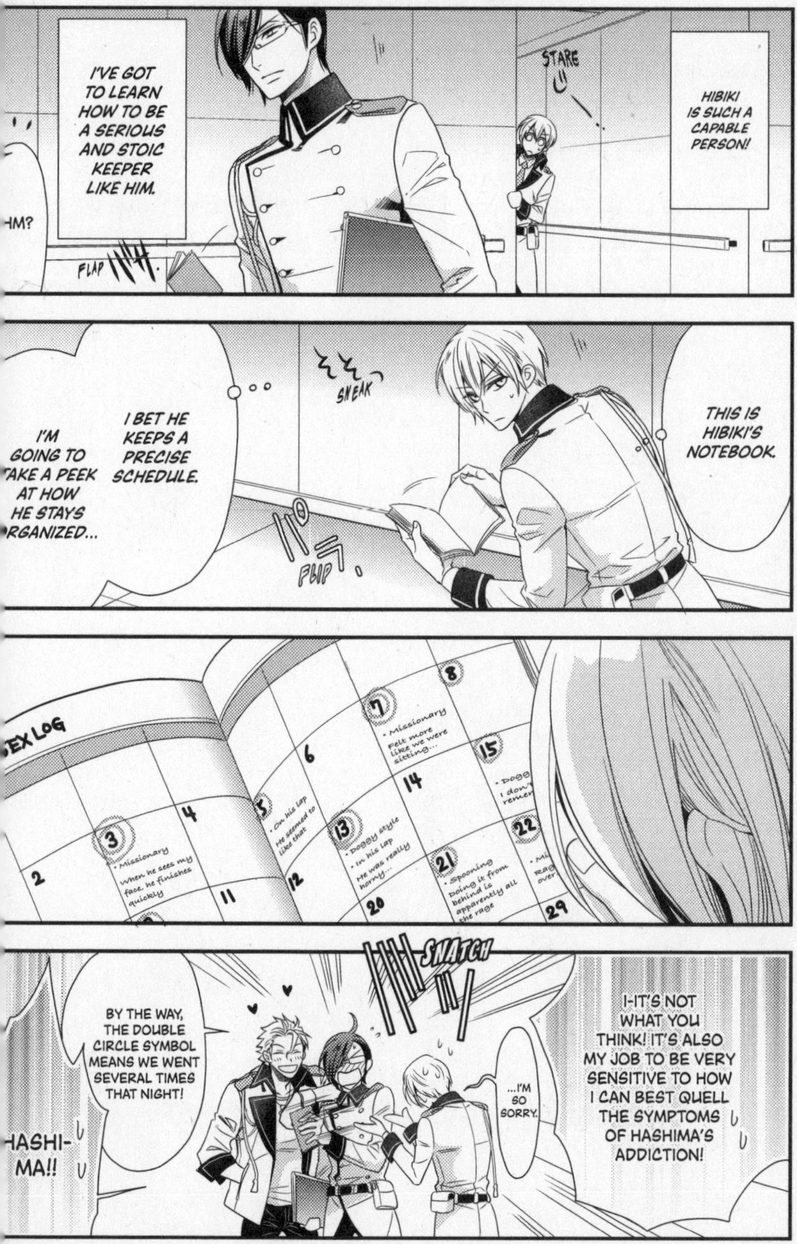
HIBIKI IS SUCH A CAPABLE PERSON!
STARE
I'VE GOT TO LEARN HOW TO BE A SERIOUS AND STOIC KEEPER LIKE HIM.
HM?
FLAP
THIS IS HIBIKI'S NOTEBOOK.
SNEAK
I BET HE KEEPS A PRECISE SCHEDULE.
I'M GOING TO AKE A PEEK AT HOW HE STAYS RGANIZED...
FLIP
EX LOG
8
7 • Missionary Felt more like we were sitting...
6
15
14
5 • On his lap He seemed to like that
4
13 • Doggy style • In his lap He was really horny...
22
3 • Missionary When he sees my face, he finishes quickly
2
12
21 • Spooning Doing it from behind is apparently all the rage
11
20
29
SNATCH
I-IT'S NOT WHAT YOU THINK! IT'S ALSO MY JOB TO BE VERY SENSITIVE TO HOW I CAN BEST QUELL THE SYMPTOMS OF HASHIMA'S ADDICTION!
...I'M SO SORRY.
BY THE WAY, THE DOUBLE CIRCLE SYMBOL MEANS WE WENT SEVERAL TIMES THAT NIGHT!
HASHI- MA!!

Afterword.

■ Hello, this is Hirotaka Kisaragi.

Thank you very much for reading Volume 2 of HANGER. Even though there are actually many different people in Squad 4, it'd be difficult to draw every single one of them, so I just chose to introduce one new pair of Squad 4 members this time. I especially like how Byakuran's looks can change with every appearance she makes.♥ Gaido and Yuki's story will still be continuing, so I hope you look forward to the next volume!

And with that, I'd like to thank everyone from the editorial department who is always taking care of me; everyone involved; and most importantly, all of the readers who read this book. Thank you from the very bottom of my heart!

Hirotaka Kisaragi

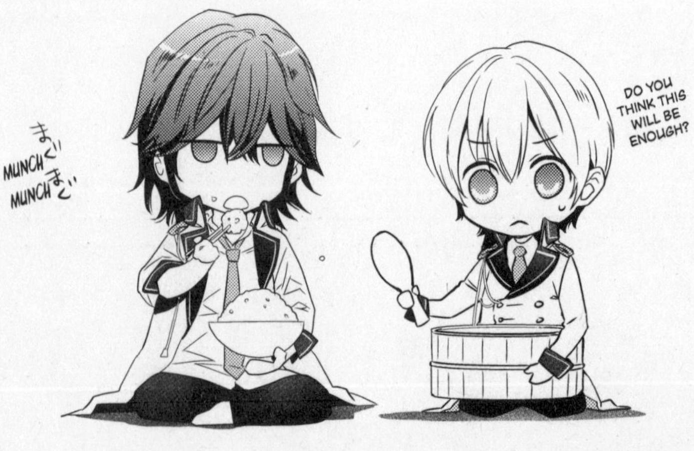
DO YOU THINK THIS WILL BE ENOUGH?
まぐ まぐ
MUNCH MUNCH

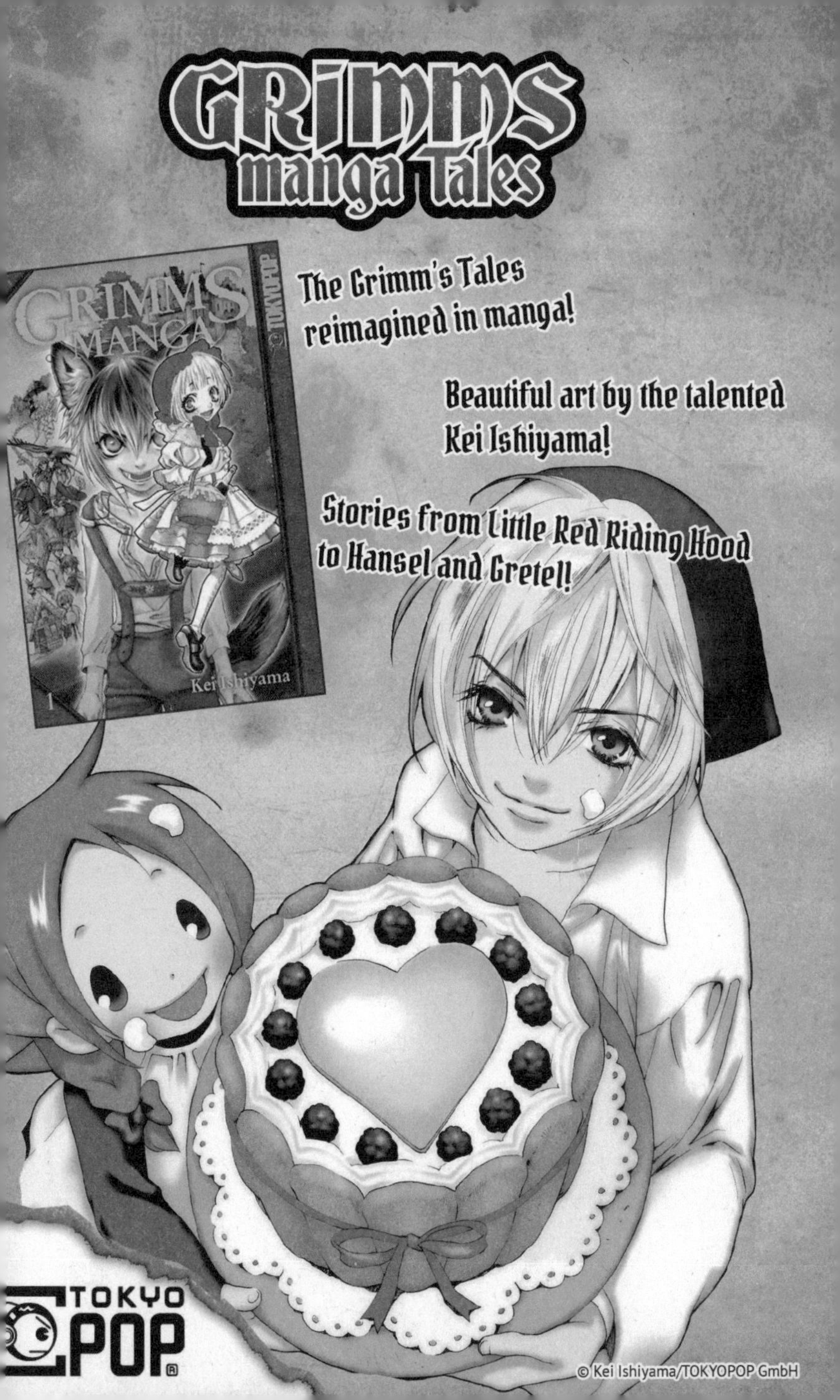

GRIMMS manga Tales
GRIMMS MANGA
TOKYOPOP
Kei Ishiyama
1
The Grimm's Tales reimagined in manga!
Beautiful art by the talented Kei Ishiyama!
Stories from Little Red Riding Hood to Hansel and Gretel!
TOKYO POP
© Kei Ishiyama/TOKYOPOP GmbH

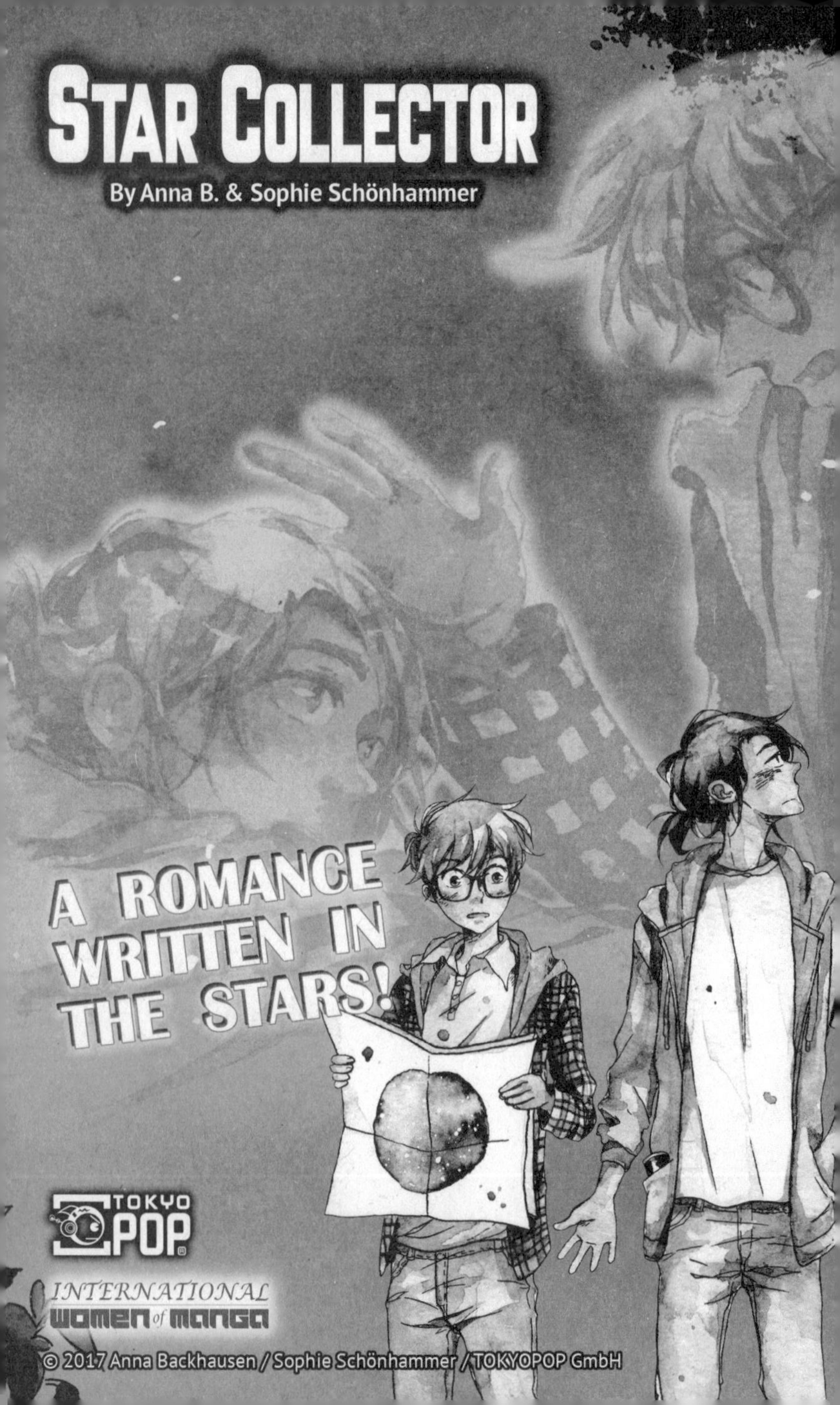
STAR COLLECTOR
By Anna B. & Sophie Schönhammer
A ROMANCE WRITTEN IN THE STARS!
TOKYO POP
INTERNATIONAL women of manga
© 2017 Anna Backhausen / Sophie Schönhammer / TOKYOPOP GmbH

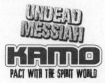

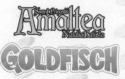

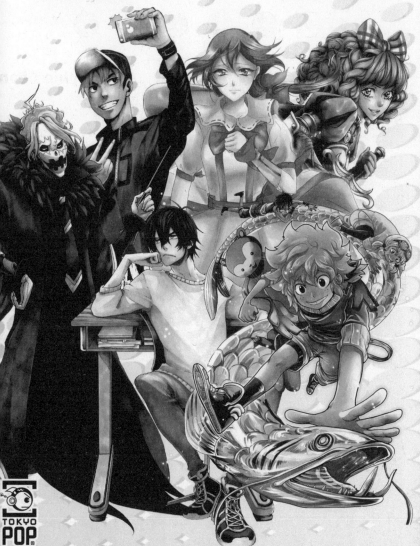

TOKYOPOP GmbH / *Goldfisch* - NANA YAA / *Kamo* - BAN ZARBO / *Undead Messiah* - GIN ZARBO / *Ocean of Secrets* - SOPHIE-CHAN / *Sword Princess Amaltea* - NATALIA BATISTA

TOKYOPOP
•PRESENTS•

INTERNATIONAL WOMEN of MANGA

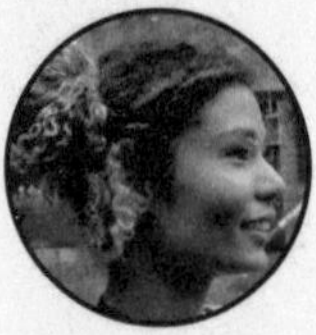

NANA YAA

GOLDFISCH

An award-winning German manga artist with a large following for her free webcomic, ***CRUSHED!!***

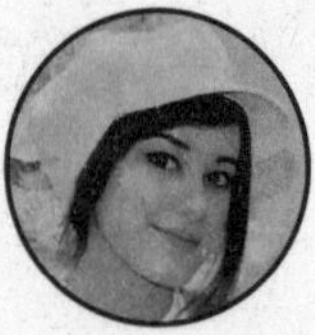

Sophie-Chan

Ocean of Secrets

A self-taught manga artist from th Middle East, with a huge YouTub following!

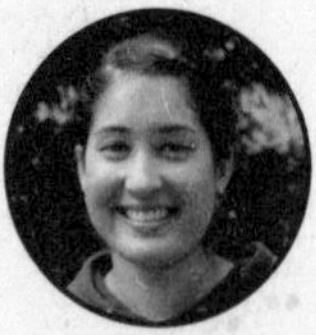

Ban Zarbo

KAMO
PACT WITH THE SPIRIT WORLD

A lifelong manga fan from Switzerland, she and her twin sister take inspiration from their Dominican roots!

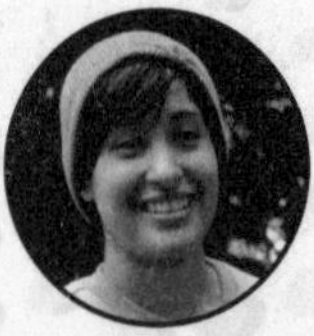

Gin Zarbo

UNDEAD MESSIAH

An aspiring manga artist since she w a child, along with her twin sister sh releasing her debut title!

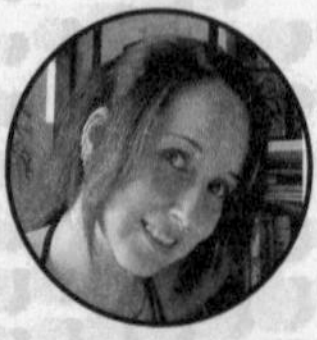

Natalia Batista

Sword Princess Amaltea
Natalia Batista

A Swedish creator whose popular manga has already been published in Sweden, Italy and the Czech Republic!

TO LEARN MORE PLEAS
VISIT OUR WEBSITE

www.TOKYOPOP.com

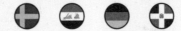

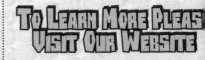

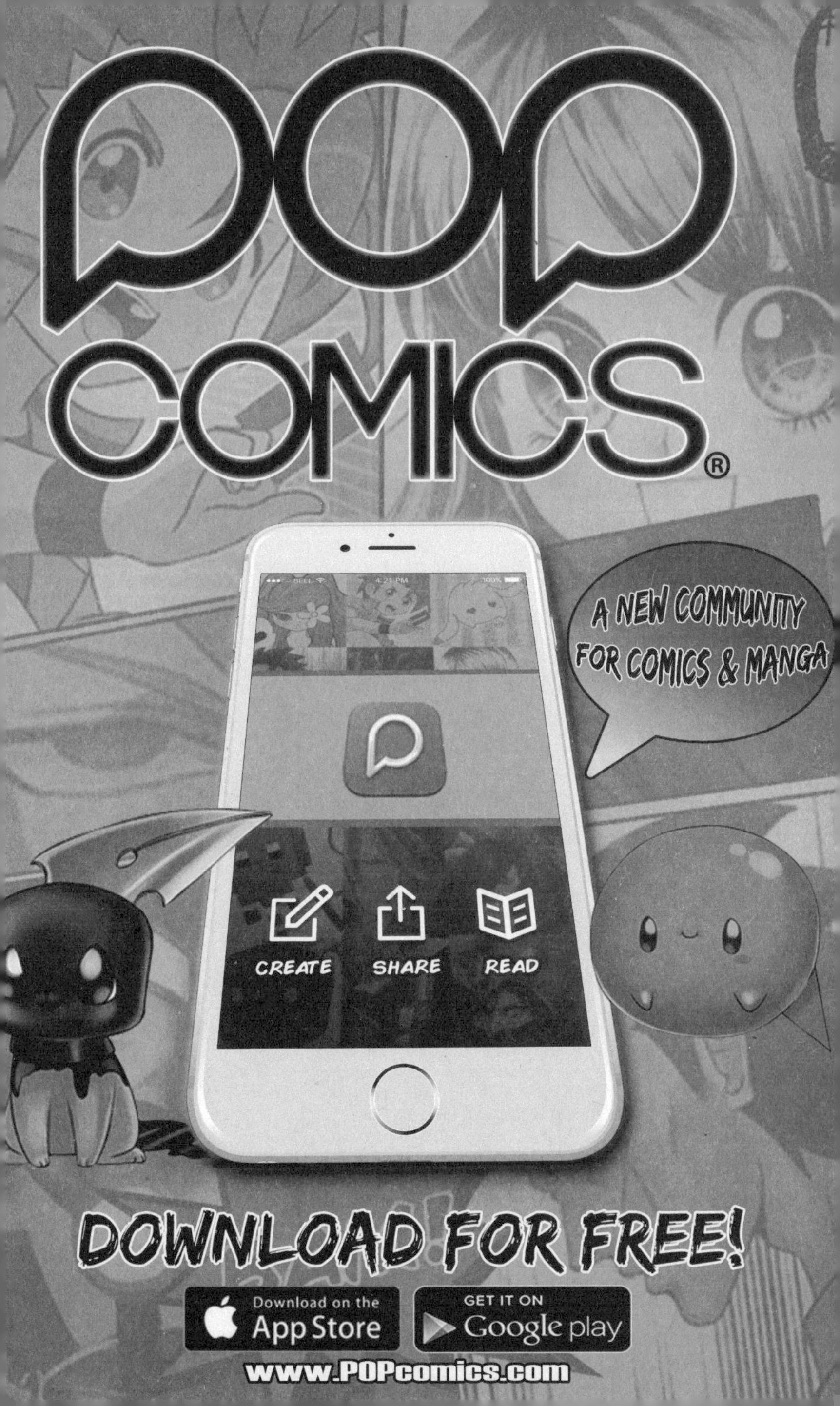
POP COMICS®
A NEW COMMUNITY FOR COMICS & MANGA
CREATE
SHARE
READ
DOWNLOAD FOR FREE!
Download on the App Store
GET IT ON Google play
www.POPcomics.com

Hanger, Volume 2
Hirotaka Kisaragi

Editor - Lena Atanassova
Marketing Associate - Kae Winters
Technology and Digital Media Assistant - Phillip Hong
Translator - Christine Dashiell
Graphic Designer - Phillip Hong
Retouching and Lettering - Vibrraant Publishing Studio
Editor-in-Chief & Publisher - Stu Levy

A 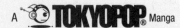 Manga

TOKYOPOP
5200 W Century Blvd
Suite 705
Los Angeles, CA 90045 USA

E-mail: info@TOKYOPOP.com
Come visit us online at www.TOKYOPOP.com

f www.facebook.com/TOKYOPOP
🐦 www.twitter.com/TOKYOPOP
▶ www.youtube.com/TOKYOPOPTV
P www.pinterest.com/TOKYOPOP
📷 www.instagram.com/TOKYOPOP

ISBN: 978-1-4278-5962-4
First TOKYOPOP Printing: July 2018
10 9 8 7 6 5 4 3 2 1
Printed in CANADA

STOP

THIS IS THE BACK OF THE BOOK!

How do you read manga-style? It's simple! To learn,
just start in the top right panel and follow the numbers:

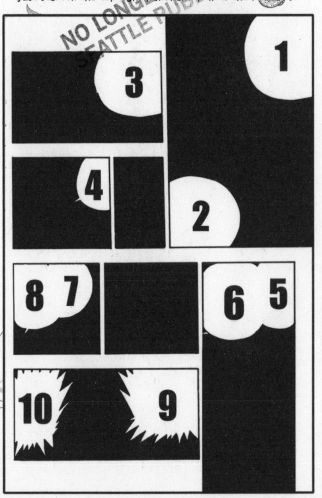